Swimming in the Sea of Talmud

Swimming in the Sea of Talmud

Lessons for Everyday Living

by
Michael Katz
and
Gershon Schwartz

The Jewish Publication Society
Philadelphia
1998/5758

The Jewish Publication Society
2100 Arch Street, 2nd Floor
Philadelphia, PA 19103

Manufactured in the United States of America

Library of Congress Cataloging-in Publication Data
Katz, Michael, Rabbi, date.
Swimming in the sea of Talmud: Lessons for Everyday Living / by Michael Katz and Gershon Schwartz.
p. cm.
Includes indexes.
ISBN 0-8276-0607-9
1. Talmud--Introductions. I. Schwartz, Gershon. II. Title.
BM503.5.K38 1997
296.1'2061--dc21 97-6195
r97

Designed by Shepherd, Inc.

Typeset by Shepherd, Inc.

10 9

To our parents, who gave us life שֶׁהֶחֱיָנוּ
Miriam Katz and Irving Katz ז"ל, and Shirley N. Schwartz and Samuel Schwartz ז"ל

and to our in-laws
Nettie and Morris Bunder, and Gilla P. Rubin ז"ל and Rabbi Mordecai Rubin ז"ל

To our wives, whose love sustains us daily וְקִיְּמָנוּ
Fran Shuly

To our children, whose desire to learn וְהִגִּיעָנוּ
the beauty of the Jewish tradition brought us to write this book
Ariel Moshe
Eliana Tali
Elie
Hadar

The publication of this book was made possible by a gift from
Solomon J. & Edith K. Freedman
in memory of their parents,
Benjamin & Seema Pulier and Louis & Sylvia Freedman.

Contents

Preface

What began as a weekly Talmud study session, a *ḥavruta* of two friends, has become a book. There are numerous people who have helped us along the way, and we are grateful to each and every one of them.

The members of our congregations, Temple Beth Torah of Westbury and Congregation Shaarei Shalom-South Baldwin Jewish Center, have supported us continuously both in pastoral duties and in our studies of traditional Jewish texts. Our officers and board members have been encouraging as we worked on this book. We owe special thanks to our secretaries, Jane Bauman and Barbara Mazzei, for their help on various parts of the manuscript.

Our teachers Dr. Richard Kalmin and Dr. Burton Visotzky have been an ongoing source of guidance and inspiration. They read through drafts of the manuscript and generously gave numerous suggestions. Their teaching has not only helped us avoid errors in translation and interpretation but also has enhanced our appreciation of the Talmud.

Many have offered us advice and counsel in the preparation of the manuscript. Early in the writing process, Elisheva Urbas and Nessa Rapoport gave us guidance concerning publication. Arnie Gordon and Libby Rosenberg read early drafts of the manuscript as interested laypeople, helping us to make the book more understandable and user-friendly. Rabbi Miles Cohen, Dr. Stephen Garfinkel, Dr. Neil Gillman, Dr. David Golomb, Dr. Judith Hauptman and Dr. David Marcus made suggestions which improved the text. Rabbi Sidney Greenberg, Rabbi Jack Riemer, Rabbi Saul Teplitz, Annette M. Botnick, and Danny Siegel helped us track down stories on the Talmud.

The staff of JPS has been a delight to work with. We especially thank Dr. Ellen Frankel, our editor, and Christine Sweeney, our project editor. When we might have veered off course, they steered us in the right direction.

We give thanks to God for having allowed us the privilege of being involved in this endeavor.

Michael Katz Gershon Schwartz

Acknowledgments

The authors express thanks to the following for kind permission to reprint from copyrighted material:

The Rabbinical Assembly for permission to use translations of Kiddush for Shabbat, ("Praised are You . . . who hallows Shabbat"), *Modim* ("We proclaim that You . . . our hope in You."), Meditation before putting on tallit ("I wrap myself in a tallit . . . in every generation") and Meditation before putting on tefillin ("I put on tefillin . . . praised be He.") reprinted from *Siddur Sim Shalom,* edited by Rabbi Jules Harlow. Copyright by the Rabbinical Assembly, 1985. Reprinted by permission of the Rabbinical Assembly.

The Jewish Publication Society for permission to use excerpts from *Tanakh: A New Translation of the Holy Scriptures,* copyright 1985 by the Jewish Publication Society; and from *Ma'aseh Book: Book of Jewish Tales and Legends,* translated by Moses Gaster, copyright 1981 by the Jewish Publication Society.

B'nai B'rith for permission to use excerpts from "What I Have Learned" by Nahum N. Glatzer which appeared in *Jewish Heritage,* summer/fall 1973, published by the Commission on Adult Jewish Education of B'nai B'rith.

PART

Prologue

A story: Many years ago, there was a man who worked very hard at his job. His responsibilities demanded a lot from him—patience, thoughtful planning, constantly being alert for signs of trouble. At times he had to fight to protect those in his charge. All in all, he did quite well in his work.

In his occupation, he often found himself alone with his thoughts during long stretches of boredom. More and more, he began to sense an emptiness within himself. There were other things that he longed to do, opportunities he had dreamed of, but after so many years of doing one thing, he despaired of ever being able to open the door to these new worlds. "I just don't know enough."

Then, two things happened to change the course of his life. First, he met someone special who said to him: "I see your incredible potential. You have the capability of going out in new directions and excelling. Believe in yourself as much as I believe in you, and I'll be there to help you."

He was heartened by these words but still had his doubts. "Maybe if I were younger. . . . It's too late now. . . . I can't start all over again, not at my age, not at this point in my life. There is too much I don't know, too much I don't understand. . . ."

It was then that the second event occurred, another incident that would shape his life. It was not a blinding revelation from Heaven that told him what to do. It was not a close call with death that made him reevaluate who he was and where he was going. It was a very ordinary, mundane experience: He chanced upon a rock that had a deep impression cut into it. He looked closely and saw that what had carved into the solid stone was nothing more than drops of water continuously falling on the same spot, day after day, year after year. He suddenly realized: "If this can happen in nature, then it can happen to me as well. I'm going to begin to learn, a little each day, until I feel comfortable with what I know."

At the end of many generations, there will arise a man, Akiva ben Yosef by name. (Menaḥot *29b*) •

Rabbi Akiva was a shepherd forty years. (Sifrei Devarim *357*) •

What were Akiva's beginnings? It is said: Up to the age of forty, he had not yet studied a thing. (Avot derabbi Natan *6*) •

When Raḥel, Kalba Savua's daughter, saw that even though he was unassuming there was something extraordinary about him, she said, "If I am willing to be betrothed to you, will you attend a house of study?" (Ketubbot *62b-63a*) •

One time, standing by the mouth of a well in Lydda, he inquired, "Who hollowed out this stone?" . . . And he was told, "Akiva . . . it was water falling upon it constantly, day after day." At that, Akiva asked himself: Is my mind harder than this stone? I will go and study at least one section of Torah. •

He went directly to a school, and he and his son began reading from a child's tablet. Akiva took hold of one end of the tablet and his son the other. The teacher wrote down alef *and* bet *for him, and he learned them.* Alef *to* tav *and he learned them. The book of Leviticus and he learned it. He went on studying until he learned the whole Torah.* (Avot derabbi Natan 6) •

He went away and for twelve years sat in a house of study in the presence of Rabbi Eliezer and Rabbi Yehoshua. At the end of twelve years, he arose and returned to his home, bringing with him 12,000 disciples. •

. . . Had not Rabbi Akiva arisen in his time, the Torah might have been forgotten in Israel. (Sifrei Devarim 48) •

With encouragement from a friend and the strength that was within, he decided to take the first step. He felt awkward and out of place, even a bit like a child. Some laughed at him. At first, few people took him seriously. "It's just a phase he's going through," they said. After a while, though, people stopped laughing. They saw his persistence and felt his sincerity. Then they, too, began to see the incredible potential that had been lying dormant within him for all those years. As time passed, the man created a new life for himself, opening many of those doors that he had once dreamed about. He came to touch the lives of countless others, not only with what he had to say, but also with how he had turned around his own life.

As can be seen from the rabbinic texts above, the story we have told is a tale that goes back some nineteen centuries. Yet it is also a contemporary parable, one that speaks to our own modern society. Many of us share Akiva's sense that something is missing in life. We may turn to our religious heritage, seeking help and guidance in facing the very complex and frightening challenges of the world in which we live. We want to know how to maintain our honesty in a business environment that is often ruthless and cutthroat. Parents need to know what to teach about relationships, love and sex, how to convey a positive message to their children in a world that is often scary and negative. We are looking for a way to find happiness and fulfillment in a specialized society where choices made decades ago continue to have an impact on our lives. All of us are searching for a way to understand suffering and the meaning of life and death.

Like Akiva, we feel that we just do not know enough. Our education may have made us experts in specific areas of life, but it also narrowed our focus, leaving so much that we have not explored. As intelligent, successful men and women, we may find ourselves feeling inadequate and uncomfortable when confronting disciplines that are unfamiliar to us, be they science, technology, medicine, finance . . . or religion. We sense that the Bible and the later Jewish tradition that evolved from it may have something to say to us. Some of us have tried on our own to study religious texts like the Talmud, only to be lost and baffled. Even in translation, the traditional Talmud text, with its organic style and complex thoughts, is overwhelming. We may feel inept and incompetent, and respond either by turning to a member of the clergy or a teacher to give us "the answers," or by avoiding the subject of religious matters totally.

We, the authors of this volume, understand all of these frustrations. As rabbis, we have each attempted to make the beauty and wisdom of the Jewish tradition more accessible to our congregants. We have sensed that many of the people we teach are like Akiva: They are bright and competent, but they often despair of being able to enter the world of traditional Jewish learning. This book is an attempt to give them—and you—the encouragement and tools that will unlock the doors of classical Jewish texts.

On a personal level, we can relate to these frustrations because, not so long ago, we were there ourselves. Our own upbringings were not too different from those of many American Jews. While we were children, the treasures of the Jewish learning were largely unknown to us. Our Jewish educations, though good, left many gaps. As teenagers, each of us was encouraged to view our Judaism more seriously; in college, we began in-depth study of Jewish texts. We came to see that, like Akiva, we could start learning later in life, even if we would never come close to his erudition and stature. We became the students of Rabbi Akiva, not only of *what* he taught (his specific teachings in the Talmud and Midrash) but also of *how* he learned. From his example, we saw that it is never too late to start studying and that the effort is well worth the struggle.

Our book, an introduction to the study of the Talmud and the application of its wisdom and values to contemporary life, is divided into three major sections. Part I gives a general introduction to the Talmud—its language, style of writing, mode of thinking and outlook on the world. Part II presents over ninety Talmud texts in a novel format: Each selection, chosen from the Babylonian Talmud, begins with a famous talmudic aphorism or maxim. Next, we present a short selection of Talmud text, within which the aphorism is embedded, in a new, modern translation. We have attempted to reproduce some of the beauty and utility of the standard printing of the Talmud, the "Vilna edition," by employing marginal notes to identify people and terms that relate directly to the text but that are not indispensable to an understanding of the talmudic argument.

Nonetheless, it is not only the language of the Talmud that is enigmatic: The concepts, values and world-view are often difficult for us to understand. The "Context" section is a response to this challenge. Here, we bring in the background to the rabbinic discussions, placing them within

Hebrew language is not gender neutral; there is no neuter in Hebrew, and every word has gender. In addition, the thinking of the Rabbis clearly reflects the male-dominated life and society of that era. With few exceptions, the study houses were the domain of men. Our translation of talmudic texts attempts to capture and retain the actual language and thought of the Rabbis. In our discussions, however, we have attempted, as far as possible, to reflect the contemporary sensitivity to gender-neutral language. We have tried to do the same whenever we speak about God.

Transliterating Hebrew language to English letters is, at best, an imprecise art. We have not followed scholarly conventions but, rather, have attempted to make the text clear and readable for the layperson. In doing so, we have tried to be as logical and consistent as possible in these choices.

In addition, as noted later in this volume, the traditional text of the Talmud has no punctuation or vowels. In order to make our translation comprehensible, we have added punctuation, according to our understanding of the text. At times, we have included italics for emphasis as well as quotation marks and parentheses, though they do not exist in the original Hebrew/Aramaic text, so that the English-language reader can understand the talmudic discussion. •

historical perspective. We elucidate those idioms that may be foreign to us today and also attempt to explain the thought-process of the Rabbis.

Finally, in the "D'rash" section, we have given modern applications of the talmudic teachings. (A "D'rash" is an interpretive treatment of a text.) We believe strongly in a "conceptual approach" to the Talmud, that the Rabbis were dealing with much more than the details of Jewish ritual practice. Their discussions, though often couched in legalistic language, are about much more: There are principles, concepts and, in short, a whole world-view that underlie the legal positions of the Rabbis. By examining these texts, we are able to learn how the Rabbis perceived the world and find for ourselves an approach to our own lives and challenges. Part III contains glossary and indexes to make this book user-friendly as well as guidance for the reader who wishes to continue the study of Talmud on his or her own.

As rabbis, we often hear questions that begin with "What does Judaism say about . . .?" Sometimes there are simple, specific responses that most rabbinic authorities agree upon. More often, however, Jewish concerns and values may lead us to several possible Jewish answers. As we study the Talmud, we begin to realize that it does not contain set answers as much as astute questions. The reader will find that this work, like the Talmud, will not provide simple, quick responses to what are, in fact, complex issues. If one is interested primarily in "What is the tradition?" he or she may turn to a code of Jewish law like the *Shulḥan Arukh* or *Mishneh Torah*. One studies the Talmud in order to learn to ask the right questions and to search for the issues and values that are essential to a thinking, committed, yet struggling Jew. It is our hope and prayer that we have presented an introduction to the Talmud that teaches the reader not only some of what the Talmud says but, more importantly, how the Rabbis of the Talmud think (and we use the present tense deliberately). Our ultimate goal is for our readers to use the very same thinking process in confronting any and all of the critical issues we face in the contemporary world.

In fact, talmudic logic often leads to more questions and further soul-searching and introspection. The Rabbis force us to face serious issues and to ask how traditional values come to play in our lives. When a text gives us a moral lesson, even a moral imperative, there are a dozen new questions arising from that message: Can this lesson be applied to other, similar situations? Is this lesson still applicable today? What would the Rabbis of the Talmud say to our particular situation, which differs slightly from the case they presented? Is the conclusion reached and the lesson derived from the text the most relevant and meaningful message?

The Talmud is compared to a sea (*yam ha-Talmud* in Hebrew, "the sea of Talmud") for many reasons: The Talmud is as massive and as deep as a sea. Like the sea, much of the Talmud is hidden from the eye, beneath the surface. Ironically, the sea is both a source of life and of nourishment *and* a dangerous, forbidding place. One is cleansed, purified and nourished by it, yet one can also easily drown in its deep waters and harsh currents. We have entitled our work *Swimming in the Sea of Talmud* in the prayer that this text will help transform a perplexing, overwhelming experience into an enriching, life-enhancing one. It is our fervent hope that this book will encourage you to take the first steps into the deep waters of the Jewish tradition, enabling you, like Akiva, to navigate *yam ha-Talmud,* the sea of Talmud.

What Is the Talmud?

The Bible and the Talmud

The Bible and the Talmud are the two central works of the Jewish people. While the Bible is the most popular and well-known Jewish text, the Talmud remains a closed book and a mystery to the majority of Jews, not to mention non-Jews. Yet ironically, Judaism as we know it today is derived more from the Talmud than from the Bible.

The Bible is a collection of twenty-four books that begin with the creation of the world and take the reader through fifth century B.C.E. Jewish history. English Bibles divide some of these books into their parts, like I Kings and II Kings, and thus list thirty-nine separate biblical books. The Bible is often printed in one volume of about 1,500 pages; there are literally dozens of versions in various translations. Because Christians view the Hebrew Bible (or the "Old Testament," as they call it) as Holy Scripture, the book has become a pillar of western civilization, and thus is familiar to Jews and non-Jews alike.

Jews often use the term B.C.E., before the common era, in place of B.C., before Christ. Similarly, Jews use C.E., common era, rather than A.D., which stands for Anno Domini, "the year of our Lord." ●

The Talmud (Hebrew for "study") is the record of rabbinic teachings that spans a period of more than six hundred years, beginning in the first century C.E. and continuing through the sixth and seventh centuries C.E. The Talmud is actually made up of two separate works: The Mishnah, primarily a compilation of Jewish laws, written in Hebrew and edited around the year 200 C.E. in Israel; and the Gemara, the rabbinic commentaries and discussions on the Mishnah, written in Hebrew and Aramaic, emanating from both Babylonia and Israel over the next three hundred to five hundred years. In actuality, there are two Talmuds—the Yerushalmi (the "Jerusalem" Talmud, or to be more geographically precise, the Talmud of the Land of Israel), and the Bavli (the "Babylonian" Talmud). The Bavli was edited after the Yerushalmi and is much more widely known, studied, and quoted. The Babylonian Talmud is generally printed in twenty folio (or oversize) volumes. It contains over 5,400 pages, and is composed of more than 2,500,000 words. There are many people who study a page of Talmud every day; it takes them over seven years to complete the entire work.

From Bible to Midrash

In order to understand what the Talmud is, it is crucial to understand how it is related to, yet different from, the Bible. Many people assume that the Bible contains the answers to every question that a person may face in life and that what it says is always crystal clear. Neither assumption is correct. Look at the Ten Commandments, for example. The Fourth Commandment teaches us to keep the Sabbath holy and to refrain from work. This simple notion actually leads a thinking reader to a multitude of questions: What does "holy" really mean? How can a period of time be kept *holy*? What exactly constitutes work? Is it physical exertion, or a job that one is paid for, or perhaps a labor that one would rather not do? Or is it something else entirely?

Or take the Sixth Commandment, "You shall not murder." It sounds perfectly logical and clear. Yet many translations read "You shall not kill." Is there a difference between killing and murdering? Is self-defense allowed? How does this commandment apply to soldiers in war? Or to a police officer chasing a criminal? Is capital punishment considered killing or murder, and is it permitted?

Consider one of the most divisive social issues of our time—abortion. There does not seem to be a single clear reference to abortion in the entire Bible. A person searching the Bible for guidance on this question would come away frustrated and deeply confused. One might ask: Does the Sixth Commandment have anything to add, one way or another, to the debate on abortion? No hint of an answer is forthcoming.

From the very moment that the people of Israel received the written laws (the *Torah she-bikhtav*) there was a need to elucidate just exactly what the laws meant. This process, according to the Torah, began with Moses himself: "On the other side of the Jordan, in the land of Moab, Moses undertook to expound this Teaching" (Deuteronomy 1:5). The result came to be known as the Oral Law *(Torah she-b'al peh)*. These oral teachings, according to tradition, were given to Moses by God. Moses memorized them and passed them on to Joshua, and then each generation learned them and taught them to the next. A more critical view of the Oral Law sees it as the accumulated wisdom of the wise people of each generation, attempting to explain the Torah and apply it to contemporary issues and concerns. These leaders served in various roles, and were called by different titles over the course of history. They pored over the Bible verse by verse, word by word, and often, letter by letter. Every line was scrutinized, analyzed and elucidated. An entire literature of commentaries and interpretations was developed for each book of the Bible. This literature was called Midrash, from the Hebrew root meaning "to search." A person who wanted to know what a particular verse meant went to a particular book of Midrash and looked up the interpretation on it.

From Midrash to Mishnah

Suppose, however, that a person was interested not in a specific verse but in a specific topic. Where would he or she turn? Shabbat, for example, is mentioned in over one hundred different places throughout the Bible. Since the Midrash was organized by book and by verse, a person had to look up every single reference in order to learn all the teachings. The Rabbis needed a more efficient way of collecting traditions by subject. At the beginning of the third century C.E., according to tradition, Rabbi Yehudah ha-Nasi edited such a work that came to be known as the Mishnah ("the teaching"). It was organized into six major sections: *Zeraim* ("seeds"), *Moed* ("holiday"), *Nashim* ("women"), *Nezikin* ("damages"), *Kodashim* ("Holy Things") and *Teharot* ("Clean Things"). Each of these sections was further divided into subsections (sixty-three in all), known as *masekhtot,* or tractates. There were, for example, twelve *masekhtot* in *Moed* covering the various holidays and their observances, including separate ones on Shabbat, Pesaḥ, Rosh Hashanah, Yom Kippur, Sukkot, and Purim. A tractate or *masekhet* was made up of several chapters, and every chapter contained a number of individual teachings, each called a Mishnah.

The Mishnah is written in Hebrew and is very concise. Laws are generally given without the explanations that were so indicative of the Midrash. Alternate traditions are sometimes mentioned, though no justification is given why one tradition is chosen over another. In addition, only the Bible (the "Written Law") was to be committed to writing; this served to fix and close the text. There was a tradition that the Oral Law not be written down. Thus, the Mishnah was so

Thus, the term Mishnah has two meanings: The *Mishnah is the collection of laws attributed by tradition to the editorship of Rabbi Yehudah ha-Nasi, c. 200* C.E. A *Mishnah is any particular law in this collection.* •

concise since brief statements were easier to memorize, and it remained fluid and expandable because it had never been written down. The Rabbis received these oral traditions, added their own insights, and then passed them on to the next generations.

From Mishnah to Gemara

The process of teaching continued in both in Israel and Babylonia. Almost as soon as the Mishnah was completed, the Rabbis found that new situations or cases arose which were not covered by the Mishnah. Just as previous generations had studied the Bible to apply it to their day, subsequent generations of Rabbis sat down and studied the Mishnah, scrutinizing, analyzing, and interpreting it and debating how it should be applied to their own times and situations. They drew on the great storehouse of traditions that they had received, such as the Midrash and the *baraitot* (those first- and second-century teachings that Rabbi Yehudah Ha-Nasi had not included in his edition of the Mishnah). And they used their own insights and logic to try to explain what the Mishnah meant and how it was to be applied. For over three centuries, this giant corpus of material grew. Known as Gemara, it was then edited and ultimately put into writing. The Mishnah and Gemara together came to be called the Talmud. (In fact, the term "Gemara" originally meant a terse statement with little or no explanation. What we now call "Gemara" was at first called simply "Talmud." During the Middle Ages, the word Gemara came to replace Talmud in an attempt to fool Christian censors.)

From Kohen to Rabbi

In order to understand the Talmud, we need to understand the key figures who created Israelite religion and the Judaism that grew from it. Solomon built the Temple in the tenth century B.C.E. While the Temple stood in Jerusalem the essence of Israelite religion, according to the Bible, was its sacrificial cult. For example, the Torah speaks in great detail about the lamb that was to be sacrificed on Pesaḥ. The Torah says that "you shall explain [the exodus from Egypt] to your son on that day" (Exodus 13:8), but there is no mention in the Bible of families getting together for a Seder with the youngest child asking the Four Questions. Similarly, the Bible says nothing about praying all day on Yom Kippur and listening to the cantor chant *Kol Nidrei.* Rather, it explains about the two goats that were brought to the Temple, and how the *Kohen Gadol,* the High Priest, was to offer one as a sacrifice and send the other off into the desert. Consequently, the most important religious figure was the *kohen,* a descendant of Moses' brother Aaron, who was responsible for offering the prescribed sacrifices of the people to God.

By the end of the biblical period, there were other important leaders in addition to the *kohen: shofet* (judge), *melekh* (king), and *navi* (prophet). Their roles varied over time and place (Israel in the north, and Judea in the south) and were often multifaceted. There were tensions between, for example, *kohen* and *navi,* since each served broad social and administrative functions. Few Israelites could aspire to any of these roles, since they were, by and large, nondemocratic. One could not study or work to become a prophet (in the classical sense), and one became a king (with a few exceptions) through heredity.

By the close of the biblical period, with the development of "wisdom literature" (those biblical books like Proverbs and Ecclesiastes that offer the reader wise advice), another model of leadership had become an archetype: the *ḥakham,* or sage. This was a role that any Israelite (that is, any *male* Israelite) could aspire to and grow into. One could become a sage even without lineage, and it did not require a "calling" from God. While there was a degree of personal involvement on the prophet's part, the *ḥakham* developed largely because of his own efforts. Learning wisdom by means of intellect, he could serve as the student of another wise master and grow even more. Over time, the role of sage became that of rabbi.

By the time the final books of the Bible were being canonized (accepted as both sacred and authoritative), the Sages were already playing a key role. The later Rabbis of the Talmud claimed that an institution called *K'nesset ha-Gedolah,* the "Great Assembly," had served as a legislative body during this time (approximately the fifth to the third centuries B.C.E.) and had been responsible for the canonization of several books of the Bible and major parts of the liturgy. While we are unsure if this institution ever existed, it is clear that the later Rabbis of the talmudic age saw the power of knowledge and learning as having begun much earlier.

By the next two centuries (from 200 B.C.E. until approximately 20 C.E.), knowledge and authority were focused in what later generations called the *zugot,* or pairs. Two men in each generation were considered by tradition to be the leaders of the Sanhedrin, the great judicial body. Hillel and Shammai are the last and the most famous of these pairs.

The first century C.E. in Israel was among the most tumultuous and trying times in all of Jewish history. Roman occupation and persecution reached its zenith. The Jewish community was divided into many factions. (The historian Josephus writes of four sects: The Pharisees, who were to become the spiritual progenitors of talmudic Judaism; the Sadducees, a conservative group with strong ties to the Temple cult; the Essenes, a pietistic group that went off to create utopian communities in the desert, and which is associated by many with the Dead Sea Scrolls; and the Zealots, a group of ultranationalists who strove for Jewish independence and who made a famous last stand at Masada. It is likely that these constituted only a small percentage of the Jews in Judea.) In addition, the claim that Jesus was the Messiah attracted some in the Jewish community. And most significantly, in the year 70 C.E., in the course of putting down a revolt of the Jews, the Romans destroyed the Temple. The destruction of the Temple meant the end of the Israelite religion based on the sacrificial cult. The Jewish people faced their single greatest crisis: Their political independence was gone; the center of their religious life lay in ruins; countless Jews were slaughtered; and other religions (such as the nascent Christian church) were there to attract away the survivors.

It was at this critical moment that a new kind of leader stepped into the breach to pick up the pieces and recreate the Jewish religion. This leader was so unique that a new title was created: "Rabbi."

Rabbis

In the text of a play, before the very first scene, a list of players, the *dramatis personae,* is presented. We are thus introduced to the heroes (and villains) who will populate the drama. By scanning this roster of roles, we learn if we are dealing with kings or clowns, and we get a first impression of the world that we are about to enter. The *dramatis personae* of the Talmud are almost entirely rabbis. That might lead us—mistakenly—to the conclusion that we are dealing with clergymen (and women) who are spiritual leaders of synagogues and temples and who "run" Sabbath and holiday services. What the Talmud meant by "Rabbi" is quite different from our contemporary meaning of the term.

The title "Rabbi" (or *rah-**bee*** as it is pronounced in Hebrew) comes from a root word meaning "great." (In Babylonia, a slightly different title with the same meaning evolved; there, the Rabbis were called *Rav.*) During the period of the Talmud, one did not receive the title Rabbi by enrolling in a rabbinical seminary and completing a fixed course of study. It was conveyed upon a man by his teacher after having studied for a significant period of time. Ordination was often accompanied by *semikhah,* a ceremonial "laying on of the hands." A Rabbi could then decide religious questions and, with additional training, could serve as a judge in civil cases.

There was no such thing as a "professional rabbinate" during talmudic times. Rabbis received no salaries; they were not employed by synagogues. The Rabbis were men of great learning but people who had professions in which they worked and earned their livelihood. We find Rabbis who did everything from being a blacksmith to brewing and selling beer.

In this book, the term "the Rabbis" (capitalized) refers to the sages mentioned in the Talmud.

Sometimes, Rabbis gave public sermons or lectures on Shabbat on the most basic issues of Jewish law and ethics. Other times, they debated and argued among themselves, in the study houses, on the most complex and arcane of legal subjects. They were the ones to whom people now turned in trying to understand what God wanted of them.

Rabbi Yoḥanan ben Zakkai is the most significant figure in the generation following the destruction of the Temple. He moved the seat of power from Jerusalem to the town of Yavneh. He attracted other great teachers and together they studied and taught the Torah and then began to build a new religion out of the ashes of the old. The synagogue came to take the place of the Temple; prayer took the place of sacrifice.

The Rabbis of the next five generations (spanning approximately one hundred fifty years) came to be known as the *Tannaim* (from the Aramaic word "repeaters," because they memorized, repeated, and passed on the traditions). It was their work which ultimately culminated in the Mishnah.

Babylonia was already a major center of Jewish life, rivaling Israel. Beginning in the third century, rabbinic study houses began to flourish there. The Rabbis in Babylonia began to study and expand on the Mishnah in the same way that Rabbis in Israel did. These teachers in the post-Mishnaic period, in both Babylonia and Israel, were known as the *Amoraim* (Aramaic for "explainers").

Some time in the early fifth century in Israel, the record of the teachings and discussions of the *Amoraim* based on, but not limited to, the Mishnah were gathered and edited and became known as the Gemara. The same process occurred in Babylonia a century or two later. Some time between the sixth and the seventh centuries, a new work appeared: Made up of the Mishnah and the Gemara, it came to be known as the Talmud.

From the Talmud to Today

In the centuries following the completion of the Talmud, rabbis all over the world continued to build upon it. In various eras, they were known by different names: *Savoraim,* "reasoners," who are actually part of the Talmud and who helped to put the final touches on the text in the sixth and seventh centuries; *Geonim,* "excellent ones," who were the heads of the Babylonian academies from the end of the seventh century through the middle of the eleventh century; *Rishonim,* "early" authorities, until the sixteenth century; and *Aḥaronim,* "latter" authorities, after the sixteenth century (and the publication of the seminal work of Jewish law, the *Shulḥan Arukh*) who helped to shape the halakhic, or legal, decisions on issues raised in the Talmud.

As each generation studied the Talmud, they put their own imprint on it. One can see this very graphically by looking at a page of the Talmud in the traditional Vilna printing and seeing the various commentaries that surround the text of the Mishnah and the Gemara, and help to elucidate them:

Commentary	*Function*	*Time and Place*
Rabbenu Ḥananel	One of the earliest commentaries to the Talmud	10th century, north Africa
Rashi (Rabbi Shlomo Itzḥaki)	Most important commentary to the Talmud	11th century, France
Tosafot	Short essays attempting to reconcile different talmudic traditions; a supercommentary on Rashi	11th-13th century, France, Germany
Torah Or (Rabbi Yehoshua Boaz)	Sources of biblical quotes mentioned in the Talmud	16th century, Italy
Ein Mishpat-Ner Mitzvah (Rabbi Yehoshua Boaz)	References to halakhic codes and how legal issues in Talmud are decided	16th century, Italy
Hagahot ha-Baḥ (Rabbi Yoel Sirkes)	Textual emendations or corrections	16th century, Poland
Mesoret ha-Shas (Rabbi Yeshayahu Berlin)	Cross references to identical passages in the Talmud	18th century, Breslau
Hagahot ha-Gra (Rabbi Eliyahu, the Vilna Gaon)	Textual emendations and corrections	18th century, Vilna
Gilayon ha-Shas (Rabbi Akiva Eger)	Explanatory notes	19th century, Posen

Fifteen hundred years after it was "finished," the Talmud continues to grow through new commentaries, translations and studies that are published each year. It is indeed appropriate to speak of "the sea of Talmud" because it is so immense, so deep, and so full of life.

שנים

שנים *אוחזין בטלית זה אומר אני מצאתיה וזה אומר אני מצאתיה זה אומר כולה שלי וזה אומר כולה שלי זה ישבע שאין לו בה פחות מחציה וזה ישבע שאין לו בה פחות מחציה ויחלוקו °זה אומר כולה שלי וזה אומר חציה שלי האומר כולה שלי ישבע שאין לו בה פחות משלשה חלקים והאומר חציה שלי ישבע שאין לו בה פחות מרביע זה נוטל שלשה חלקים וזה נוטל רביע *היו שנים רוכבין על גבי בהמה או שהיה אחד רוכב ואחד מנהיג זה אומר כולה שלי וזה אומר כולה שלי זה ישבע שאין לו בה פחות מחציה וזה ישבע שאין לו בה פחות מחציה ויחלוקו בזמן שהם מודים או שיש להן עדים חולקין בלא שבועה: **גמ'** למה לי למתנא זה אומר אני מצאתיה וזה אומר אני מצאתיה זה אומר כולה שלי וזה אומר כולה שלי ליתני חדא חדא קתני זה אומר אני מצאתיה וכולה שלי וזה אומר אני מצאתיה וכולה שלי וליתני אני מצאתיה ואנא ידענא דכולה שלי אי תנא אני מצאתיה הוה אמינא מאי מצאתיה ראיתיה אע"ג דלא אתאי לידיה בראיה בעלמא קני תנא כולה שלי דבראיה לא קני ומי מצית אמרת מאי מצאתיה ראיתיה *והא אמר רבנאי °ומצאתה דאתאי לידיה משמע ומיהו תנא לישנא דעלמא נקט ומדחזי ליה אמר אנא אשכחתיה ואע"ג דלא אתאי לידיה בראיה בעלמא קני תני כולה שלי דבראיה בעלמא לא קני וליתני כולה שלי ולא בעי אני מצאתיה אי תני כולה שלי הוה אמינא בעלמא דקתני מצאתיה בראיה קני תנא אני מצאתיה והדר תנא כולה שלי דממשנה יתירה אשמעינן דראיה לא קני ומי מצית אמרת חדא קתני והא זה וזה קתני זה אומר אני מצאתיה וזה אומר כולה שלי וכו' אמר רב פפא ואיתימא רב שימי בר אשי ואמרי לה *כדי *רישא במציאה °וסיפא במקח וממכר וצריכא דאי

רש"י

שנים אוחזין בטלית. דוקא אוחזין דשניהם מוחזקים בה ואין לזה כח בה יותר מזה שאילו היתה ביד אחד לבדו הוי אידך המוציא מחבירו ועליו להביא ראיה בעדים שהיא שלו ואינו נאמן זה ליטול בשבועה: זה אומר כולה שלי. בגמרא מפרש למאי תנא תרתי: זה ישבע. מפרש בגמרא (דף ג.) שבועה זו למה: שאין לו בה פחות מחציה. בגמרא (דף ה:) מפ' אמאי תקין כי האי לישנא בהך שבועה: וזה אומר חציה שלי. מודה הוא שהחצי של חבירו ואין דנין אלא על חציה הלכך זה האומר כולה שלי ישבע כו' כמשפט הראשון מה שהן דנין עליו נשבעין שניהם שאין לכל אחד בו פחות מחציו ונוטל כל אחד חציו: היו שנים רוכבין כו'. לאשמועינן אתא (א) דרוכב ומנהיג שניהם שוין לקנות בהמה מן ההפקר: בזמן שהן מודין. בגמרא (דף ח.) מפרש [דבהאי] אשמעינן דהמגביה מציאה לחבירו קנה חבירו: **גמ'** ראיתיה. קודם *שהגבהת אותה: בראיה קני. מדקתני יחלוקו: תנא כולה שלי. בחזקה גמורה שהגבהתי תחילה ואתה תפסת מידי משזכיתי בה: והאמר רבנאי. בבבא קמא בהגוזל ומאכיל*: ומצאתה דאתא לידיה משמע. ואפי' הכי אחיך ולא עובד כוכבים ולא תימא כי מיעט רחמנא עובד כוכבים היכא דלא אתאי לידיה דישראל לא מיחייב למטרח עלה ולאהדורה אבל אתא לידיה מיחייב להחזירה דאבידתו אסורה: תנא לישנא דעלמא נקט. אי לא הדר תנא כולה שלי הוה אמינא מאי מצאתיה דקתני תנא לשון בני אדם אתו במשנתנו ולא לשון המקרא והרבה בני אדם קורין לה מציאה משעת ראיה: בעלמא דקתני מצאתיה. בכ"מ ששנינו שהמוצא מציאה קנאה הוה אמינא דמציאה קני לה משעת ראיה דלא אשמעינן שום תנא דלא קני לה אלא בהגבהה להכי אשמעינן הכא ממשנה יתירה: והא זה וזה קתני. גבי מצאתיה תנא זה אומר וגבי כולה שלי קתני זה אומר ואי חדא הוא הכי אבעי ליה למתני זה אומר מצאתיה וכולה שלי: במקח וממכר. קניתיה מיד פלוני ודוקא מקח וממכר הוא דאמרינן יחלוקו בשבועה דאיכא למימר שניהם קנאוה ולשניהם נתרצה המוכר אבל זה אומר אני ארגתיה וזה אומר אני ארגתיה לא יחלוקו דודאי חד מינייהו רמאי הוא ותהא מונחת עד שיבא אליהו:

תוספות

שנים אוחזין בטלית. איידי דאיירי בהגוזל בתרא (ב"ק דף קיט.) מחלוקת נסורת נגר ובעל הבית דקתני במעצד הרי אלו שלו ובכשיל הרי אלו של בעל הבית תני הכא נמי דיני חלוקות ואע"ג דבתרי מסכתא אין סדר למשנה* ואיכא מ"ד כולה נזיקין לאו חדא מסכתא הוא ה"מ לענין מחלוקת ואח"כ סתם לפי שרבי לא היה לומד כסדר אלא כמו שהיו שואלים התלמידים אבל כשחברם על הסדר חברם וצריך בכל מסכתא טעם למה נשנית אחר שלפניה כדדייק בריש מסכת שבועות (דף ב.) מכדי תנא ממכות קסליק כו' וכן בסוטה (דף ב.):

ויחלוקו. תימה דמאי שנא מההיא דאיכא דאמר כל דאלים גבר פרק חזקת הבתים (ב"ב דף לד: ושם) וי"ל דאוחזין שאני דחשיב כאילו כל אחד יש לו בה בודאי החצי דאכן סהדי דמאי דתפיס האי דידיה הוא וכן במנה שלישי דמדמי בגמרא לטלית חשיב ההוא שהפקד תופס בחזקת שניהם כאילו הם עצמם מוחזקים בו לכך משני דהתם ודאי דחד מינייהו הוא ואין החלוקה יכולה להיות אמת ולכך יהא מונח אבל טלית דאיכא למימר דתרוייהו הוא יחלוקו וכן שנים אדוקים בשטר דמדמי לקמן (דף ז.) למתני' משום דשניהם אדוקים בו דהחלוקה יכולה להיות אמת דאפשר שפרע לו החצי ובמנה אין דרך שיקנה לו החצי אחרי שהוא ביד חבירו אבל בארבא אע"ג דאפשר שהיא של שניהם כיון דאין מוחזקין בו הוי דינא כל דאלים גבר ולסומכוס אע"ג דאין מוחזקין בו ואין החלוקה יכולה להיות אמת היכא דאיכא דררא דממונא פירוש שבלא טענותיהם יש ספק לבית דין יחלוקו:

וזה נוטל רביע. וא"ת יהא נאמן דחציו שלו מיגו דאי בעי אמר כולה שלי כדאמרי' בגמ' (לקמן דף ח.) האי מיגו גופיה לפטרו משבועה אי לא משום דאיערומי קמערים ומפרש ריב"ם דמיגו להוציא לא אמרי' דבחציו השני מוחזק זה כמו זה והיא דחזקת הבתים (ב"ב דף לג: ושם*) דנחין ולאחיש ליה לרבה אין שטרא זייפא הוא ומיהו שטרא מעליא הוה לי בידי ואבד והימניה רבה להוציא במיגו דאי בעי אמר שטרא מעליא הוא °התם הייט טעמא משום דאפי' הוה שתיק רק שלא היה מודה שהוא מזוייף היה נאמן כי החתימה היתה נכרת לעומדים שם ורב יוסף אית ליה דאפילו מיגו לא הוה כיון שטענה ראשונה שהוא טוען בהאי שטרא הוא שקר ואין לומר מיגו אלא היכא שטענתו ראשונה היא אמת מיגו שהיה טוען אחרת ולכך אינו מיגו אפילו להחזיק כגון בעובדא קמייתא וא"ת וכימא דאין ספק מוציא מידי ודאי דהאומר כולה שלי יש לו בודאי חציה והאומר חציה שלי ספק אם יש לו בה כלום כדאמרינן בפרק החולץ (יבמות דף לח.) ספק ויבם שבאו לחלוק בנכסי סבא ספק אמר אנא בר מתנא אנא ואית לי פלגא ויבם אמר את ברא דידי ולית לך ולא מידי הוה ליה יבם ודאי וספק ספק ואין ספק מוציא מידי ודאי וי"ל דהתם יבם שהוא בנו של סבא הוי ודאי יורשו ולא יוציא הספק מספק ממונו אבל הכא אין סברא מה שהוא ודאי בחציו שיועיל לו לחציו השני: **בראיה** בעלמא קנה. אע"ג דקתני במתני' (לקמן דף ט:) ראה את המציאה ואמר לחבירו תנה לי דלא קנה בראיה וכן ראה את המציאה ונפל עליה (לקמן דף י.) קתני נמי דלא קני מאי למדחי כיון דאמר תנה לי או שנפל עליה גלי דעתיה דלא ניחא ליה למקני עד שיגיע לידו: **דבראיה** בעלמא לא קני. °והא דאמרי' בפרק הבית והעלייה (לקמן דף קיח. ושם) הבטה בהפקר קני הייט שעשה מעשה כל דהו כגון שגדר גדר קטן: **והא** זה וזה קתני. איכא דוכתי דפריך כי האי גוונא ואיכא דוכתי דלא פריך: [ע' תוס' בכורות דף נא: ד"ה א"כ]

א

עין משפט נר מצוה

א א מיי' פ"ט מהלכות טוען ונטען הל' ז סמג עשין לה טוש"ע ח"מ סי' קלח סעיף א: [ב"ק קב.]

ב ב מיי' שם הלכה ח טוש"ע שם סעיף ג:

ג ג מיי' שם הלכה ז טוש"ע שם סעיף א:

ד ד מיי' פי"ז מהלכות גזלה ואבידה הל' א סמג עשין עד טוש"ע ח"מ סי' רסח סעיף א:

ה ה מיי' פ"כ מהלכות מכירה הל' ד ועיין בהשגות ובמ"מ סמג עשין פב טוש"ע ח"מ סי' רכב סעיף א:

רבינו חננאל

שנים אוחזין בטלית זה אומר אני מצאתיה וכו'. ואקשי' עלה למה לי למתנא תרי זה אומר כולה שלי הלא באומרו אני מצאתיה משמע דכולה שלי היא. ופרקי' הא אתא לאשמועי' דבראיה בעלמא לא קני לה למציאה. הא לא מיבעיא דהא אמר רבינא ומצאתה דאתאי לידיה משמע. דברי רבינא בהגוזל בתרא הל' אין פורטין מתיבת המוכסין ופשוטה היא. ואוקימנא למתני' רישא במציאה וסיפא דקתני זה אומר כולה שלי בקנייתא בשטוען אני קניתיה ונתתי דמיה לבעליה

[ד"ה אמאי]

גליון הש"ס

תוס' ד"ה וזה כו' התם כו' ע"ש וכו'. עיין לקמן דף קטו ע"א תוס' ד"ה והא:

מסורת הש"ס / הגהות הב"ח

ב"ק קי. | שהגבהתי רש"א | [לקמן ח.] | [דף קיג:] | לקמן ח. ב"ק קיג: רבינא רש"ל | [עיין רש"ל] | [לקמן ח.] | [ד"ה אמאי] | דברים כב | תורה אור

הגהות הב"ח (א) רש"י ד"ה היו וכו' אתא דרוכב ומנהיג:

Before the Bookshelf

From far away, I am inexplicably drawn to it. It catches my eye and mysteriously pulls me towards it.

The volumes sit (no, stand *is the appropriate word) majestically on the shelf—tall and at attention. A more careful look reveals that a few of the books on the end are leaning to the side, as if on the broad shoulders of their companions. It is not that they are asleep; rather, they seem to be at rest for a moment, exhausted after some numbingly difficult work.*

One can't help but sense that these are not just another set of books. Though still and quiet, they are in some profound sense alive.

I come closer. The shelf is chest-high, and because of the height of the books, they seem even taller than I am. Standing before them, I have to look up to them. But they don't seem to be looking down at me; instead, they gaze straight out, just over my head.

From up close, I notice the details of the beautiful leather covers. They are cracked from age. The gold imprinting on the edges tells me more than just the titles of the individual volumes: It informs me that I stand before something royal and majestic. That some of the gold is faded and rubbed away hints at the use that they have received.

I count the volumes in the set. Twenty in all. They take up almost a yard of space on the shelf.

What could possibly be in these books? What wisdom do they hold? What secrets do they keep? What treasures do they hide?

I let my fingers touch the books, running flesh across leather. I hear the sound this makes: This road is not smooth; it is a bumpy one.

My fingers stop somewhere in the middle of the set. I randomly select a volume and try to pull it from the others towards me. It resists my first meager effort. Perhaps it is the weight of the other books that holds it back. Or maybe it just will not surrender so easily to a stranger.

But I won't give up so quickly. I put my other hand on the adjacent volumes to use them as an anchor. I push away with my left hand and pull with my right. The book begins to give. But I hear the creaking sound of ancient leather. It is almost like a ripping noise. I wonder if the book is resisting me, crying out as it is torn from its companions.

I quickly sense that the volume is much heavier than I thought it would be. I can't hold it with a meager three-fingered grip as I could any other book. I squeeze tightly to keep it from escaping from my grasp. My left hand quickly comes around to catch it before it falls to the floor.

I now notice something that was hidden from my eye as the books stood on the shelf. The edges of the pages on the three exposed sides, hidden while they were on the shelf, are decorated with an unusual and magnificent splattering design of red and blue. This is but the first of the countless hidden treasures that the Gemara will reveal to me.

The red could easily be the color of blood. Is it to remind me of the blood of those, like Akiva, who were willing to risk their lives and even die because of their devotion to what is found in these pages? Or is it the blood that the book demands from anyone who would study this difficult, yet sublime work?

I look at the blue splotches and try to interpret them the same way a lover or a child does the clouds in the sky. I see the outlines of countries on a map. Perhaps these are every place on the globe where Jews have studied the Talmud.

My nostrils pick up a trace of a scent that was not there a moment before. I bring the heavy text close to my face and try to learn this book through another of my senses. My nose detects leather and old paper and age. But it also picks up the smell of dampness. Is it from lying too long on a dirty shelf in a musty room? Or is it the dampness born of tears, from those who pored over the pages as tears poured from their eyes? And were those the tears of persecution and poverty, or the tears of joy—of studying a book that had the effect of bringing human beings and God together on a page?

I bring the book over to the desk. I gently and reverently open the cover. On the title page I see a picture of an entranceway built upon four magnificent pillars, topped off with a roof. Two lions sit, one on each side. Are they there to threaten me, to drive me away, to tear me to pieces? Or are they there to greet me, guard me, and accompany me?

I open the book to some place in the middle.

My eyes are bombarded by thousands of points of black and white. The blacks are the letters, in various sizes and shapes. The whites are the spaces, between letters, words, and sections. My eyes try to focus, but in scanning back and forth, the page seems to be alive, moving this way and that.

I pick out a rectangular shape in the very center of the page. Surrounding this rectangle are two bracket-like shapes, one to the left, one to the right. The Hebrew letters that make up these brackets are smaller, and are of a subtly different typeface.

I check the adjacent pages and notice that the shapes of sections are always different: Here the center piece is a small square, there it is like a large, fat letter L. On many pages, the bracketed section appears to be a periscope, spying from below on the mysteries up above.

To the sides of the bracketed sections are smaller units, deployed here and there along the periphery of the page like an army, surrounding and guarding the inner settlements. It is as if the page has been designed to make it very difficult to break in and conquer this material. And once inside, it will be equally difficult to get out.

My hand touches the page. I try to read it as if it were braille and I were blind. But here I feel no bumps. I find that I am blinder than the blind.

I look carefully at the text. I discover that there is no punctuation: no periods, no commas, no question marks. The volume appears to be one enormously long sentence that goes on and on for two hundred pages. But a closer examination reveals that there are breaks. Each volume is divided up into a few tractates, each tractate into chapters, and each chapter into a Mishnah and its Gemara. But there are still pages upon pages of material. Where do I begin?

I am overwhelmed by the quantity of text. I bring the book closer and closer to my face until my eyes can no longer focus on any individual word or letter. It all begins to blur into a vast sea of black that pulses and moves. For a moment I fear that I will drown in it.

In frustration I pull back. I slam the book shut. I bring it back to the shelf. With my left hand I dig in among the other volumes and clear a space. With my right hand I swing the heavy book back into its spot. I quickly try to walk away, to turn my back on the books before me. But my right hand is not yet free of the books. They have closed in on my fingers and hold me. They seem not to want to let me go so quickly. It is as if they—these books on the shelf—have pushed me away with one hand and drawn me back with the other.

I turn back and free my hand. I take a long look at the Talmud. The volumes look silently back, this time, it seems, not over and above my head but right into my eyes.

Something compels me to try again. I pull the first volume off the shelf. It comes easier this time. I know what it will weigh, so this time it does not almost fall to the ground. I take the book to my chest and hold it tightly. With my free right hand, I pull another volume from the shelf: A talmudic dictionary. And then another: An English translation. And a third: A modern commentary. I bring all four books back to the desk. I spread them all out before me. I am ready to try again. I take a deep breath. And I open the Talmud to the first page and dive in . . .

Beneath the Surface

A casual glance at the sea from the shore or even from the deck of a boat reveals very little about the incredible secrets below; the variety of life, the riches, the beauty and wonder are all hidden. The novice who takes a first glance at the Talmud is faced with a similar problem: One has to plunge into the depths of the text in order to see it properly and to truly appreciate what it is really about.

But just descending beneath the surface of the water does not guarantee that the explorer will *understand* the mysterious world down below. You can easily be overwhelmed by what is seen, not having a clue of what you're looking at, why it is there and how it functions.

The same is true of the sea of Talmud. Many people assume that as long as they can translate the words, there should be no problem in understanding the text. They plunge, unprepared, into the Talmud and are quickly overwhelmed by it. They forget, or do not realize, that it comes from a different time and place, and has a radically different way of looking at the *word,* and the *world.*

Come with us as we go beneath the surface of the Talmud to see some of the secrets that lie below. We will serve as your guides on this voyage, explaining some of the most typical—and puzzling—features of the Talmud.

Language

The Talmud is written in two different languages, Hebrew and Aramaic. These two tongues are related and have many affinities. They are both written with the same alphabet, but each has its own vocabulary, grammar, and linguistic peculiarities. The Mishnah is in Hebrew, while the Gemara uses some Hebrew but mostly Aramaic. (The Babylonian Talmud uses an *eastern* Aramaic dialect; the Talmud of the land of

Israel a somewhat different *western* dialect.) Aramaic served as the "vernacular," the common, everyday spoken language of the Jews in Israel and Babylonia during the talmudic age. (American Jews are not the first to turn to translations in order to understand our sacred texts!) Paying careful attention to the language being used gives us important clues as to who is talking and when and where they lived.

Punctuation

The Talmud, in its traditional form, lacks vowels and punctuation. (In this, it is similar to the text of the Five Books of Moses as it is traditionally written in a Torah scroll.) Try to decipher the following translation of the opening Mishnah of the Talmud:

FRM WHN DS N RD TH SHM N TH VNNG

It can take some time to figure out that it asks "From when does one read the *Sh'ma* in the evening?"

Vowels in Hebrew and Aramaic are very different from the consonants. They consist of dots and dashes beneath, above or in the middle of the normal letters of the alphabet. Hebrew is based on three-letter roots; by changing the vowels, or adding prefixes or suffixes, an almost infinite variety of nuances and meanings is given to a finite number of roots. While in modern Hebrew, vowels are added whenever there is some confusion about the proper pronunciation and meaning, this was not done by ancient and medieval copiers and publishers of the Talmud. We are often left to try to figure out which vowels to assign which letters in order to decipher what a particular word may mean.

Here's one example of the difficulty: The Hebrew word אֵין, *ain* (*alef-yud-nun,* with a two-dot vowel), means "no." But the Aramaic word אִין, *een* (also *alef-yud-nun,* with a one-dot vowel), means "yes." We may have figured out the issue that the Rabbis are debating, but until we determine which language they are speaking and which vowels they use, we do not know whether they decided "Yes" or "No"!

The lack of punctuation means that we aren't always sure where one sentence ends and the next one begins. Once we do figure that out, we have to determine if it requires a question mark, an explanation point, or just a period.

To study Talmud, it often helps to have the skills of a cryptographer trying to break a secret code. We learn early in the endeavor the habit of considering all the possibilities, trying them out, and testing each one to see which makes the best sense.

The Elliptical Nature of the Discourse

The Talmud was originally an "oral law:" it was for a long time memorized and passed on, without being written down. This necessitated a terse, sparse style that could be committed to memory and easily recalled. Thus, more was left unsaid in a discussion than was actually expressed. The Rabbis who taught and transmitted these statements knew their own intent; they could elucidate their brief teachings with precise explanations and extensive commentaries. However, once the Oral Torah was written down and the original teachers passed from the scene, there could never be total certainty as to what the text actually meant. In some ways, studying Talmud is like playing a 2,000-year-old game of "Telephone," where one person whispers a message to a second, who whispers it to a third: We try to make sense of a communication that sometimes seems incomprehensible.

A common difficulty is found in an extended debate or conversation. Two Rabbis argue back and forth, sometimes in multiple exchanges. But instead of identifying the speaker at each stage, the Gemara simply notes "He said . . ." and "he said . . .". It requires the concentration of a chess-master to follow each move, and to keep track of *who* is saying *what.*

The Logic of the Talmud

Western civilization is much beholden to Greek values, philosophy, and thought. The Greek approach to logic, exemplified by the "outline form"—

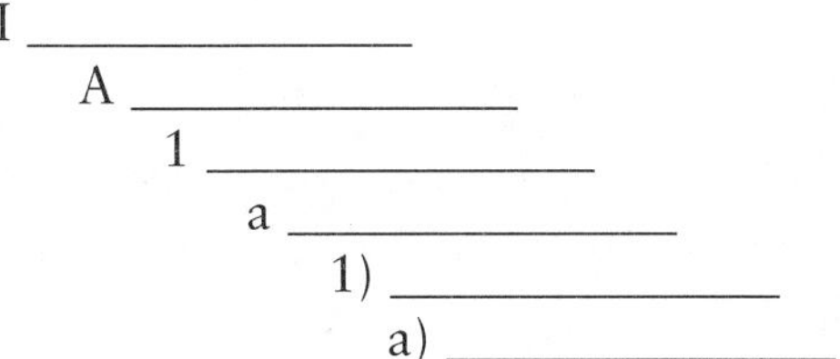

—is the one we have been inculcated with in all of our educational endeavors. We move from the general to the specific, from the simple to the complex, starting at the "beginning," moving to the "middle," and finishing up at the "end." At any given point we know where we are, where we've been, and where we are headed.

Rabbinic logic is of a totally different nature. It does not function on the same horizontal (beginning to end) or vertical (bottom to top) planes. A circle is a more appropriate model: Without beginning or end, going on eternally. (Consider the Jewish custom of finishing the yearly reading of the Torah and then *immediately* beginning the cycle all over again.) You can start learning Talmud with any text. You break into the circle at any point and then move on from there.

While western logic assumes you know only what you have been taught previously, rabbinic logic works under the assumption that you are already familiar with everything the Rabbis are discussing. This requires the learner to stop frequently along the way, to pause, and "catch up" by looking up and learning another source or concept before being able to continue. In some sense, it is like learning to swim by being thrown into the deep end of the pool. At first it's a struggle to even stay afloat. But after a while, you find yourself navigating quite freely and capably in even the most difficult conditions. This means, however, that you can't go very quickly. The Talmud cannot be "read"; it is *learned,* slowly, methodically, and thoroughly, step by step.

The Rabbis operated on the "logic of association." One idea brings to mind a second, and that leads us to a third. For example, early in *Masekhet Shabbat,* there is a discussion about candle lighting at the onset of the Sabbath. That leads the Rabbis to consider candle lighting for the festival of Hanukkah. Once involved in the laws of lighting the candles, the Rabbis move on to discuss the origin and meaning of Hanukkah. When the topic of Hanukkah is completed, the Gemara returns to its original subject, Shabbat, as if saying, "Oh yes, where were we?" Going off on tangents is typical of the Talmud. We are thus taught: No topic is off-limits. Everything in the Talmud—and in life—is interrelated and interdependent. Every text is "relevant" and personal because any text can and does lead us into any and every subject.

Intergenerational Discourse

Just as the Talmud can jump from one topic to another, so too it jumps from one time and place to another. Imagine the following conversation being recorded in a history book:

> *Thomas Jefferson told Abraham Lincoln: "I do not think that the framers of the Constitution had it in mind to prohibit slavery." To which Lincoln answered: "I cannot conceive that they did not!" John Kennedy interrupted: "Mr. Jefferson, you are correct in theory. And Mr. Lincoln, you are correct in practice!"*

We understand immediately that such a conversation never took place. Yet in the Talmud, such exchanges are found on every page. The editors of the Talmud "cut and pasted" together snippets of teachings from a five-hundred-year period. Sometimes they were conversations that actually took place; other times they created the *appearance* of a conversation by putting together the sayings of two teachers (from two eras) on a single topic. Very often the Gemara goes a step further: It puts an argument into the mouth of a particular Rabbi, implying: "Here's what so-and-so might have said about this had he been there. . . . "

From this approach, we learn that the Talmud is a vibrant, dynamic, organic work. It is not restricted by time or space. It brings us back into the past and enables us to question and address people long since gone about how they dealt with the critical issues in their lives. It also enables us to bring those from the past into the present, so that we can see how they would apply the lessons of the past to the problems of today.

The Conceptual Approach of the Rabbis

When we first open the pages of the Talmud, we might expect to read deep, philosophical debates on the most critical issues of human existence. We look forward to learning sublime words of wisdom that answer life's most difficult questions. We wait in anticipation for sparks of genius that will help to illuminate the dark world that we live in.

But we are in for a shock. Our first impressions of the subject matter of the Talmud might leave us confused, perplexed, even disappointed. Much of the Gemara is concerned with details of the most mundane and pedestrian topics: What objects can be carried in and out of a house on the Sabbath; who is responsible for damage done by an ox that gores another animal; how long must a woman wait after her monthly period before resuming marital relations? These and a thousand other such questions occupy the pages of the Talmud. Many people peruse these discussions and ask: "Is that all there is?"

We who have been brought up on western literature expect deep philosophical issues to be dealt with through serious essays and monographs. The Rabbis of the Talmud use a very different method to deal with the very same issues: Instead of addressing the macrocosm, they concentrate on the microcosm, focusing on the minute details of everyday life. We do them—and ourselves—a terrible disservice if we think that they were interested only in minute and trivial matters. The Rabbis found God in the details of the mundane and the everyday. We must learn to read their discussions *conceptually.* We must search beneath the surface, reading between the lines in order to truly understand what the Talmud is teaching us. For example, the question about carrying on the Sabbath is in reality about the significance of time and how one makes ordinary occasions into special ones. The discussion of the goring ox is actually about the extent of an individual's responsibility towards others in a community. And the debates about the menstrual cycle are in essence about the nature of sexuality and the role it plays in a marriage. It's easy to see what the Rabbis are saying. The challenge, however, is to understand their deeper meanings and ultimate concerns.

P'shat and D'rash

One of the most puzzling aspects of the Talmud is the way the Rabbis read, quote, and use the Bible. Take, as an example, what they do with this sensual verse from the Song of Songs:

> "Your breasts are like two fawns, twins of a gazelle, browsing among the lilies." *(4:5) These are Moses and Aaron. For just as a woman's breasts are filled with milk, so too Moses and Aaron sustained Israel through the Torah.* (Midrash Song of Songs Rabbah 4:5)

What are we to make of this strange interpretation? Did the Rabbis believe that this erotic description of a woman's body was really talking about two old men who taught the people Torah? If they did, how are we to take them seriously? Or did they merely twist and manipulate the sacred words of the Bible to suit their own purposes? If they did *that,* how can we have respect for them?

The Rabbis believed that the Bible was to be read in two very different ways, P'shat and D'rash. P'shat referred to the simple, contextual meaning of the passage. In the above example, the P'shat would be a man poetically describing the physical attributes of his beloved. However, read this way, the meaning of the Bible was limited and finite. In order for the Bible to serve as a source of inspiration, future generations would need to be able to turn to it and find in it answers to their own particular questions. The method that gave the Bible this elasticity was Midrash. The belief was that

God had sown the seeds of future interpretations into the written text. It was the task of the Rabbis to cultivate the text so that it would flourish and produce a bountiful harvest of spiritual nourishment throughout history. (Some saw the Rabbis as merely uncovering what God had put there; others understood that the creative genius of the Rabbis played a large part in the process.) A D'rash, or creative reading and application of a sacred text (from the same Hebrew root as Midrash), is at the very heart of what the Talmud is about: Breathing life into our tradition so that it speaks to each and every generation.

Halakhah and Aggadah

After studying the Talmud for even a brief time, one quickly discovers that there are two very different kinds of discourse. The first (and that which constitutes the greater portion) is called halakhah. It comes from the root meaning "to go" or "to walk." Halakhah, often translated as "law," deals with the questions "What are we obligated to do and how are we to do it?" Halakhah is serious, detailed, and often dry and legalistic.

The second type of material is known as aggadah, often translated, imprecisely, as "legend." The word is based on the same root as haggadah, and actually means "the telling." It is often exciting and engaging material, and includes stories as well as Midrashic expositions of the Bible. If halakhah is the answer to the questions "What?" and "How?," aggadah may be characterized as the response to the question "Why?"

Many people make the mistake of seeing halakhah and aggadah as two separate and distinct realms. Depending on their interests and dispositions, they tend to favor one to the exclusion of the other. The "serious" student, interested in law and its practical applications, views aggadah as frivolous and too easy, something appropriate for children or the beginner. Others find the halakhah too legalistic and trivial and spend their time exploring the *soul* of the Jewish tradition in the aggadah.

In actuality, halakhah and aggadah are two sides of the same coin. They cannot and should not be separated. One can get a true sense of the Talmud only when these two realms are allowed to interact and stand next to each other. They need to function the same way that the heart and the mind do in a human being. The person who acts solely on the intellect is a robot; one who responds only from his emotions is a fool. The two must be in harmony and must work together in balance. The same is true of the Jewish tradition. A Judaism that is concerned only with ritual without understanding *why* those observances are to be followed is a perversion of our religion. In a similar vein, those who reject or ignore ritual and law, claiming that they are Jews "in their hearts," are creating a very hollow hybrid of our rich heritage. Ultimately, the same is true of the Talmud.

Technical Terms

Every discipline develops its own particular "language," a unique way that its practitioners express themselves and communicate with one another. Sometimes it involves using specific words that no one else uses (as when the police speak about "perpetrators"). Other times, it entails giving ordinary words a unique meaning. (When a diplomat says "The talks were constructive," he or she really means that things are going poorly, everyone is yelling at each other, but there is still hope.)

The same is true of the Rabbis in the Talmud. There are literally hundreds of technical terms that they use in the Mishnah and the Gemara. Many are concepts that are specific to the Jewish religion; tefillin, *lulav, yibum, muad, treif,* and *niddah* to name a few. (In this book, we explain these terms as they appear and define them again in the Glossary.) But there is another kind of technical term that is found in almost every line of the Talmud. Translated into English, it may seem obvious and ordinary, but in actuality, there may be a very specific meaning that the Rabbis are attempting to convey. The novice may be unaware of these coded phrases and thus may miss out on what is being taught.

For example, three phrases which are very similar in the Aramaic, and might be rendered into English in the same way, actually have specific meanings:

t'nan ("we are taught") introduces a teaching from another Mishnah;
tanna ("he taught") brings a brief tradition from the Tosefta;
tanya ("it was taught") quotes a passage from a *baraita.*

Sometimes, even a minor change in word order can have real significance:

Amar Rabbi Ploni ("Said Rabbi so and so . . .") —when the word *amar* ("said") *precedes* the name of the Rabbi, the statement will be undisputed.

Rabbi Ploni Amar ("Rabbi so and so said . . .") —when the Rabbi's name comes first, the statement will usually be followed by the views of another Rabbi who disagrees.

Another example: In the give-and-take of a discussion, one view may be introduced with the word *leima,* translated as "let us say." But the use of this particular word is a clue that the opinion stated will ultimately be rejected.

How is the beginner to know any of this? Sometimes we are able to figure these things out by ourselves as we study more and more and notice recurring patterns and forms. It is more likely, however, that we will need to turn to an expert for help. Here we begin to understand the important role a teacher plays in the enterprise of learning Talmud. In addition, it is important to have the proper tools as we begin to swim in this sea. There are dictionaries, encyclopedias, and guides (mentioned in the back of this book) which are indispensable to the study of Talmud.

We're coming back to the surface now, after having taken a brief glimpse of what lies below. Our intent has not been to overwhelm the reader or frighten you away. Rather, it is to make the point that the Talmud is a very complex literature. Having said that, we hasten to add: There is nothing to match its power, its beauty, and its wisdom. Anyone who seriously undertakes to study Talmud will be rewarded immensely by the experience. At times it will be quite difficult. If you stick with it, and if you reach out for help, you will find your way. You will also find that swimming in this sea will change your life.

How to Use this Book: A Sample Entry

זִיל גְּמוֹר **Go and learn!**

Each of the entries in this book is headlined by a *pitgam*, or maxim. The rabbinic saying is found as part of the Talmud passage that is studied in the "Text" section. Since talmudic times, many of these sayings have found their way into the collective Jewish consciousness and are often repeated in both secular and religious contexts. The Hebrew edition of *Sefer ha-Aggadah,* translated into English as *The Book of Legends,* edited by H.N. Bialik and Y.N. Ravnitzky, lists over two thousand such proverbs.

TEXT

Shabbat 31a

In citing a text from the Babylonian Talmud, the *masekhet,* or tractate (defined above as one of the sixty-three topical subsections of the Talmud) is listed, followed by a page number. The two-sided leaf of a folio page (one of the 5,400+ oversized pages of the traditional Vilna printing of the Babylonian Talmud) is numbered only on the front, which is called side "a." The second side of the page is referred to as side "b." For example, *Shabbat* 31a refers to the tractate *Shabbat,* the first side of the oversized folio page numbered 31.

Another story of a non-Jew who came before Shammai. He said to him: "Convert me on the condition that you teach me the entire Torah while I stand on one foot." He [Shammai] pushed him away with the builder's measuring rod that was in his hand. He [the non-Jew] came before Hillel who converted him. He [Hillel] said to him: "What you hate, do not do to your friend. That is the whole Torah. The rest is commentary. Go and learn!"

Earlier in the Gemara, we read: Our Rabbis taught: "A person should always be as humble as Hillel and not as strict as Shammai." (Shabbat *30b*) *Later, the Gemara adds: Shammai's strictness could drive us out of the world; Hillel's humility brought us under the wings of the Divine Presence.* (Shabbat *31a*) •

We have chosen short, self-contained texts that the reader can, with some effort, comprehend and even master. It should be understood, however, that in the Talmud these units are found as part of longer *sugyot,* or sections. Many modern scholars believe that the editors of the Talmud often joined together several independent and separate units, creating the appearance of long, complex discussions and debates.

The reader is cautioned that a first, casual reading of a talmudic text may leave you puzzled and confused. Talmudic style is extremely terse and elliptical. It is often difficult even to figure out who exactly is speaking. We have attempted to translate the text as genuinely as possible so as to capture the authentic words and thoughts of the Talmud, cryptic as they sometimes may be. Occasionally, for the sake of clarity, we have added a word or phrase in brackets.

CONTEXT

Hillel and Shammai were the two great leaders of the Jewish people in Israel in the first century B.C.E. They were known for their very different personalities and philosophies. Our section is one of a series of stories that accentuate these differences.

Shammai seems to have taken the non-Jew's challenge as impertinence, having no patience for those who exhibited disrespect for him or for his tradition. Hillel, on the other hand, saw the challenge as an opportunity. He interpreted the non-Jew's question as a sincere request to learn about the essence of Judaism in "twenty-five words or less," as we might say today.

Hillel's answer is a variation of the "Golden Rule" found in the Christian Bible. We should remember that Hillel lived some fifty years before Jesus. Both men probably based their saying on a verse in the Bible: "Love your fellow as yourself" (Leviticus 19:18).

In the Context section, we attempt to explain the Gemara, providing background information about the individuals and the issues that are mentioned. We show how the particular text we have chosen fits into the overall discussion of the tractate. We offer elucidation of the texts so that the reader can fill in the gaps and better understand not only what the Rabbis said, but also what it was that they meant.

In the Marginal Notes, there is additional material that helps to explain and bring a focus to the Gemara. These notes are often quotations from the Bible or from sections of rabbinic literature other than the one being studied. This approach follows that of Rashi (Rabbi Shlomo Itzḥaki, 1040-1105) whose brief explanations are printed in the margins of the traditional Talmud text and are indispensable to understanding the Gemara.

D'RASH

A young girl is reading a book and comes across a big word she has never seen before. She runs over to her father and asks, "What does this mean?" Her dad looks at the word and smiles, but instead of giving her the answer, he pulls a dictionary off the shelf and tells her, "Go look it up!" "Come on, Dad, I know you know it. Just tell me what it means!" He sticks to his guns and insists that she look up the word herself. After she finds the definition, the father tells his daughter: "I want you to get into the habit of learning things for yourself. When you do that, you'll really remember. If I always gave you the answers so easily, they just wouldn't stay with you. And besides, I won't always be here to give you the answer. You've got to learn to rely on yourself."

Hillel taught much the same lesson to the non-Jew: I can give you the short answer, but if you really want to understand the Torah, you have to go out and learn it yourself.

The same holds true for those who want to learn Talmud. This book will give the short answer—a brief introduction. The real path to "swimming in the sea of Talmud" comes when the reader takes to heart Hillel's key words: "The rest is commentary." Once you have learned the maxim and the text, you must make your own commentary, connecting Talmud texts to your own life.

In the Context section, we endeavor to explain what the Gemara meant to the Rabbis who are mentioned in our texts. In the D'rash section, we try to apply *the Gemara to our* own *world and the issues that confront us today. We believe very much in taking a conceptual approach to the Talmud: Even though it appears that the Rabbis were dealing with arcane ritual matters, in truth their debates were really about issues that are relevant to all people at all times.*

In trying to have the Rabbis of the Talmud speak to us, we often use stories and questions that resonate to the modern ear. We give our own interpretations to the words of the Rabbis as we try to apply their wisdom to our lives.

We recognize that these applications are subjective understandings; they are by no means the only *interpretations. The reader may come up with his or her own ways of connecting the teachings of the Rabbis to the contemporary world. This is exactly what should happen. The study of Talmud has been one of the most authentically Jewish activities* precisely *because it demands that we connect the past to the present. When we make this connection, we all become students of Hillel.*

Go and learn!

PART

"The Six Orders" and "The Encampments by the Water"

You have come to the heart of this book, the individual chapter entries. In arranging these selections, we have followed the organizing principle of the Talmud, setting the texts in the order that they are found in the traditional division known as the "Six Orders." You may recall the next to the last song in the Passover Haggadah, *"Eḥad Mi Yode'a,"* or "Who Knows One?" Halfway through the riddle-song, the question is asked, "Who knows [the significance of the number] six?" The answer is: "Six are the Orders of the Mishnah!" This refers to the fact that Rabbi Yehudah ha-Nasi divided the Mishnah into six major "Orders," each section (*seder* in Hebrew) dealing with a specific topic:

Zeraim ("Seeds")—agricultural laws;
Moed ("Holiday")—Shabbat and festivals;
Nashim ("Women")—marriage and divorce;
Nezikin ("Damages")—civil & criminal law;
Kodashim ("Holy Things")—sacrifices;
Teharot ("Clean Things")—ritual purity.

While the Mishnah is arranged according to these six broad topics, the Gemara does not restrict or limit itself at all to these particular subjects. By its very nature, the Talmud is organic; its commentaries move from topic to tangent, encompassing every conceivable issue. The reader of this book will quickly discover that our texts and D'rashot (plural of D'rash), while arranged in the order of the tractates of the Mishnah, are as wide-ranging as is the Gemara.

At the beginning of each Order, we will give a brief introduction to that section of the Mishnah and to the tractates that it contains. The individual entries, found in that Order, will then follow. At the conclusion of each section, we bring a short piece called "Rest Stop." The study of the Talmud is like a journey (at times, a very difficult one). Just as one needs to stop and rest along the way on a journey, so, too, one needs to pause and reflect after studying challenging texts. We offer some brief stories—talmudic, hasidic, and modern—that enable the reader to stop and think, and to put the learning into the broader perspective. We hope these tales serve to refresh you, so that you may continue the journey, stronger and wiser. To highlight the rest stops, we have placed them in the context of the journeys of the Israelites: From Egypt (slavery) to Sinai (and the receiving of the Torah) to Israel (the ultimate destination, and the Promised Land). Significantly, these rest stops, or encampments, were at places near bodies of water. The Rabbis saw water as a metaphor for Torah and learning; it is for the very same reason that the Talmud was often called a sea.

Seder Zeraim

Introduction to Seder Zeraim

The first Order of the Mishnah is called *Zeraim,* or "Seeds." It deals with agricultural laws, especially those that applied to the land of Israel. For this reason, the Rabbis in Babylonia did not spend a large amount of time discussing these laws, and to ten of the eleven tractates in this Order in the Babylonian Talmud there is no Gemara. However, the Order begins with a tractate called *Berakhot* ("Blessings") that discusses prayer. This tractate does not technically belong to a discussion of agricultural laws; the Rabbis placed it here because blessings were required before eating the fruits and produce grown from the land. *Berakhot* is one of the favorite talmudic tractates for study specifically because it deals with familiar, practical issues like the order of the daily prayers and the proper time and order of blessings.

אֵין הַקֹּמֶץ מַשְׂבִּיעַ אֶת הָאֲרִי A handful cannot satisfy the lion.

TEXT

Berakhot 3b

> *Rav Aḥa bar Bizna said in the name of Rabbi Shimon Ḥasida: "A harp was hung over the bed of David. At midnight, a north wind came and blew upon it, making it play music all by itself. David immediately stood up and engaged in the study of Torah until dawn. At dawn, the wise men of Israel entered and said to him: 'Our lord the king—your people Israel require sustenance!' He said to them: 'Go, and let them support one another!' They said to him: 'A handful cannot satisfy the lion, and a pit cannot be filled up with its own earth.' He said to them: 'Send out the troops to fight.'"*

The Talmud continues its story: Rav Yitzḥak bar Ada, and some say Rav Yitzḥak, son of Rav Idi, said: "What is the verse [that shows that a harp was hanging over his bed to wake him up]? 'Awake, O my soul! Awake, O harp and lyre! I will wake the dawn' [Psalms 57:9]." Rashi explains: "With other kings, the dawn awakens them; I [David], on the other hand, awaken the dawn." •

CONTEXT

In this section of the Gemara, the Rabbis tell a story about David, one that is not found in the Bible itself. When the advisors of King David inform him that the Israelites are suffering food shortages, he tells them to take from those who have and to give to those who need. The wise men respond with two proverbs: The meaning of the first—"A handful cannot satisfy the lion"—is that the needs of the people are greater than the meager resources available. The second piece of wisdom is a little more obscure. Two different interpretations are offered for "A pit cannot be filled up with its own earth." Rashi explains that when you dig a pit and then shovel the dirt back into the hole, the pit seems to remain unfilled, probably because of the shifting ground. While in mathematics, the *whole* is always equal to the sum of its parts, in life, sometimes the *hole* is greater than the sum of its parts. The sages are thus telling the king that it is impossible for the people to be self-sufficient; they need to find some outside resource in order to "fill up the pit." The Tosafot, on the other hand, take a different tack, holding that Rashi's metaphor does not precisely fit the circumstances. The king, after all, did not expect that the poor should help to feed the poor. He wanted the resources taken from the rich and then given to the needy. (Thus the pit was not to be filled with its own earth.) Rabbenu Tam explains that a well will never be filled simply by collecting the rain that falls into it; pipes and canals are required to bring more water from another, outside source.

David accepts the advice of the wise men and orders that the people should be organized into troops and sent into battle. The king proposes that the spoils of war will serve as the outside resource that the people so desperately need.

D'RASH

It was pitch dark outside when the alarm went off in what seemed like the middle of the night. Sweet, soothing music came over the clock-radio. He dragged himself out of bed, threw some water on his face, and headed downstairs. He turned on the small desk lamp, pulled a book off the shelf and, with a yawn, began to study.

Dave had been following this routine for some time. It had started with a New Year's resolution—"I'm going to set aside some regular time to learn"—that had been broken three years in a row. The desire was there, but there just wasn't enough time in the day. Things had been so hectic at the office that he had been putting in more and more hours just to keep up with the workload. Spending time with his family, which should have been first priority, was always relegated to second place, after work. Spiritual concerns like prayer, study, and *tzedakah* didn't seem to get any time whatsoever.

"If I'd let it, work would gobble up sixteen hours of my day, seven days a week. For a while, I let it. I was missing out on my kids' growing up. I wasn't there to help them with their homework, or watch their Little League games. I didn't even know who their friends were. Then my wife laid it on the line for me. 'David,' she said, 'when people are on their deathbeds, they never say with regret: "I should have spent more time at *work!*"' She was right. So I cut back at the office and decided to spend more time at home. But there was still no time for *me,* for my growth as a person. I decided that the only time that was available was before dawn. It was quiet and peaceful, and it was a wonderful way to start my day on the right note. I could always catch up on my sleep on the train to work."

After twenty minutes of study, the phone rang. He looked at the clock on his desk. 7:05. He picked up the receiver. Another emergency at the office. He had come to think of work as a hungry lion, constantly roaring for more and more food. "I'll give it as much as I can, but I won't let it consume me. I'll fight for time with my family, and I'll fight for time for myself. If I don't grow and renew myself, I'll be no good for anyone else."

He smiled as he put a bookmark in the book. It would be a reminder where to pick up his studying when he came back to it later in the day. He turned to go upstairs, but then he stopped for a moment and picked up the book. "Maybe I can learn a little over lunch," he thought. With book in hand, David went to fix breakfast for his family before heading out to work.

אֵין חָבוּשׁ מַתִּיר עַצְמוֹ מִבֵּית הָאֲסוּרִים **The prisoner cannot free himself from prison.**

TEXT

Berakhot 5b

Rabbi Ḥiyya bar Abba fell ill. Rabbi Yoḥanan went to visit him. He [Yoḥanan] said to him: "Are your sufferings dear to you?" He [Ḥiyya] answered: "Not them, not their rewards." He [Yoḥanan] said to him: "Give me your hand." He [Ḥiyya] gave him his hand, and he [Yoḥanan] raised him.

Rabbi Yoḥanan fell ill. Rabbi Ḥanina went to visit him. He [Ḥanina] said to him: "Are your sufferings dear to you?" He [Yoḥanan] answered: "Not them, not their rewards." He [Ḥanina] said to him: "Give me your hand." He [Yoḥanan] gave him his hand, and he [Ḥanina] raised him. Why could Rabbi Yoḥanan [not] raise himself? It is said: "The prisoner cannot free himself from prison."

CONTEXT

Among the most critical questions that religion tries to answer is why good people suffer. A standard explanation is that suffering comes as a punishment for sins. But what if the afflicted person is righteous or the suffering is more severe than the sins seem to warrant? In response to this problem, the Rabbis developed a concept known as *yissurin shel ahavah,* "afflictions of love." Suffering may have been sent by God as a sign of divine love. The afflictions could help the righteous person to become more humble or cause her to examine her actions or induce her to further prayer, study, and good deeds. Afflictions in this life could lead to even greater rewards in the World-to-Come by purifying people of their sins now, instead of later.

This is the background of the question asked of the sick people in our story: "Are your sufferings dear to you?" The implication is that since the sick man is a righteous rabbi, the sufferings he is enduring cannot be punishment for his sins; they must, rather, be *yissurin shel ahavah,* afflictions of love sent by God for some other purpose. The question then means: "Have you been able to use this suffering to some higher end? Has it made you a better person?" In both cases, the answer is no. The pain has been so great that it has been impossible to move beyond the suffering. The visiting rabbi,

The Talmud goes on to tell us another touching story about Rabbi Yoḥanan in which we learn that he was wealthy, very handsome, and scarred by many personal tragedies:

Rabbi Eliezer fell ill. Rabbi Yoḥanan went to visit him. Rabbi Yoḥanan saw that he was lying in a dark house. Rabbi Yoḥanan uncovered his arm and light radiated from it. He saw that Rabbi Eliezer was crying. He [Rabbi Yoḥanan] said: "Why are you crying? Is it because of the Torah you never studied? We learned that one who does much and the one who does little are equal, so long as they direct their hearts to heaven. Is it because of [a lack of] food? Not everyone is fortunate to have two tables [of Torah and *of food]. Is it because of [not having] children? Here is a bone of my tenth son [all ten of my children died]." He [Rabbi Eliezer] said to him: "I cry for your beauty which one day will disintegrate in the dust."* •

seeing that the pain is serving no worthwhile purpose, seeks to relieve the suffering. The miraculous ability of a rabbi to heal by the touch of his hand speaks of the talmudic assumption that Torah, and those who embody it, have the power of life and healing.

Our section ends with a logical question: If Rabbi Yoḥanan had the power to heal his student Rabbi Ḥiyya bar Abba, why couldn't he heal himself? The answer is that just as a prisoner cannot free himself from jail, so too, a sick person cannot effect self-healing.

D'RASH

A student has become a serious behavior problem in school. The principal asks the parents, both of whom are psychologists, to come in for a conference. The mother acknowledges that there have been problems at home as well, and the father assures the principal that they are "on top of the situation" and are dealing with it. The principal suggests that they turn to an outside psychologist to deal with the problem. The parents are taken aback.

"Are you implying that we're not professionally competent to deal with this situation?" the father angrily asks. "We both have Ph.D.s in clinical psychology; we have been in private practice for over twenty years; and we have outstanding reputations in the community! And how do you think our sending our child to someone else would look? People would say, 'They can't even handle their own problems; how in the world can they help me with mine?' If you meant to insult us, you've certainly succeeded!"

The principal tries to reassure the parents. "The last thing in the world I want to do is question your competence. I have the utmost respect for you, personally and professionally. The issue here is not competence but *closeness*. Sometimes we're just too close to a situation to be able to be as effective as we'd like to be. I think I'm a pretty good educator, but my wife and I felt that it would be in everyone's best interest if our daughter went to a different high school from mine. My sister is a pediatrician, but when her kids get sick, she takes them to another doctor. She feels too close to the situation, too emotionally involved to be able to give them the best treatment. The truth is that I wouldn't hesitate for a minute to send my kids to you for help; I *know* how good you are. But I think you ought to consider sending your child to someone else for help. Sometimes, what we can do for others, we can't do for ourselves. That's unfortunate, but it's true."

Often in life, we are imprisoned by our own egos. The harder we struggle to free ourselves, the more trapped we become. Sometimes, all that we need is to let someone else give us a hand.

לוּחוֹת וְשִׁבְרֵי לוּחוֹת
מֻנָּחוֹת בָּאָרוֹן

The tablets and the broken tablets were placed in the Ark.

TEXT

Berakhot 8a-b

Rav Huna bar Yehudah said in the name of Rabbi Ammi: "One should always complete one's portions with the community, twice Scripture and once translation, even 'Ataroth, Dibon . . .' [Numbers 32:3], for anyone who completes the portion with the community has days and years lengthened." Rav Bivi bar Abaye thought of finishing his portions of the entire year on the eve of Yom Kippur. Ḥiyya bar Rav from Difti taught him: "It is written: 'You shall practice self-denial, on the ninth day of the month at evening' [Leviticus 23:32]. Do we fast on the ninth? Don't we fast on the tenth?! This teaches us that whoever eats and drinks on the ninth is regarded by Scripture as if he fasted both on the ninth and on the tenth." He [Rav Bivi bar Abaye] thought of finishing earlier, but some elder said to him: "It is taught: 'As long as he does not go ahead or fall behind.'" Just as Rabbi Yehoshua ben Levi said to his son: "Finish your portions with the community, and be careful of the veins according to [the opinion of] Rabbi Yehudah, and it is taught: Rabbi Yehudah says: 'Until he slaughters the veins, and be careful with an old man who forgot his learning because of circumstances, as it is said: "The tablets and the broken tablets were placed in the Ark."'"

The Lord spoke to Moses, saying: Mark, the tenth day of this seventh month is the Day of Atonement. It shall be a sacred occasion for you: you shall practice self-denial, and you shall bring an offering by fire to the Lord; you shall do no work throughout that day. For it is a Day of Atonement, on which expiation is made on your behalf before the Lord your God. (Leviticus 23:26–28) •

As soon as Moses came near the camp and saw the calf and the dancing, he became enraged; and he hurled the tablets from his hands and shattered them at the foot of the mountain. He took the calf that they had made and burned it; he ground it to powder and strewed it upon the water and so made the Israelites drink it. (Exodus 32:19–20) •

CONTEXT

"One should always complete one's portions with the community" refers to study of the weekly public reading of the Torah. All of the Rabbis agree that one should constantly study Torah. Rav Huna has a special understanding of this rule: One should study the same section or portion as is being read in the synagogue that Shabbat, completing it during the same week.

A story is told about Rav Bivi bar Abaye who fell behind in the weekly study of the Torah portions and hoped to catch up right before Yom Kippur, when he would have some free time. However, he was reminded by Ḥiyya that the day before Yom Kippur is—according to the well-known Midrash on the verse from Leviticus—a day for eating and drinking. The Midrash is based on the fact that the verse says to fast from the *ninth* day of the seventh month, rather than from the tenth day. The contextual meaning of the verse is simply that the fast of Yom Kippur starts the night before; even though Jewish days start at dark (and, thus, technically at the beginning of the tenth day of the month), people think of Yom Kippur eve as part of the ninth day of the month. When Rav Bivi wanted to finish studying the weekly Torah portions before Yom Kippur, he was reminded that one should neither go ahead nor fall behind, that is, one should follow the weekly cycle at the right time and study along with it.

The teaching of Rabbi Yehudah adds two pieces of advice. First, when one slaughters a fowl, the cut should be made so that the veins are entirely severed. Even though this is not technically required by law, it is nonetheless good advice. Second, one should honor a person who used to have great knowledge but has since forgotten it. This is analogous to the holiness given to the broken tablets of the Law. When Moses saw the Golden Calf, he became angry and shattered the first tablets that God had given him. These broken tablets of the Law were later carried by Moses in the Ark, along with the second set that God gave to Moses. The first set retained its holiness and was not discarded, even though it was no longer usable. Similarly, one should revere a teacher who had previously been venerated for knowledge, even if this person is now "broken," that is, forgetful because of old age.

D'RASH

We live in a disposable society. Everything from pens to soda bottles, from diapers to "plastic silverware" (an oxymoron of the modern age) is throw-away. We hold on to so little, especially after items have fulfilled their short-lived purposes. Objects that were once used over and over again are now used once and discarded, even if they have some use left to them. Things that we refilled or recycled (like the old-fashioned glass milk bottle) have been replaced by disposable counterparts.

These examples are quite obvious, yet there are dozens of others on a more subtle level. Decades ago, the standard rotary telephone was made to withstand years of use and abuse. It was rare that one had to be replaced. Many tell stories of growing up and using the same phone (and there was only one style) for thirty or forty years. Today, technology has given us telephones that outperform these early models in almost every way but one. These new phones come with speed dialing, automatic redial, and one-button memory of commonly used numbers. Today's phones can be programmed to do a host of chores that were inconceivable a generation ago. Yet, the old black rotary phone excelled in one way: it seemed to last forever. Many of us consider ourselves lucky if our telephones outlast the warranty.

Today, we are used to throwing out so many things that break. Even if we follow the environmentalists' rule of Reduce-Reuse-Recycle, we find ourselves using more and more items that are made to be used for shorter periods of time and then discarded. Some call this "planned obsolescence." Among the problems this lifestyle creates is a garbage glut.

If Rabbi Yehudah were alive today, he would probably tell us (perhaps by e-mail or fax) that we should not be so hasty in throwing old things out. Sometimes they still have a usefulness, even if it is not their original function. "The tablets and the broken tablets were placed in the Ark" means that what once had life and purpose can often be used to instruct us and inspire us.

Yet, Rabbi Yehudah is talking not only about objects, but also about experiences. We learn from our experiences—both good and bad—and we should not discard any of them. Despite the fact that Oscar Wilde quipped "Experience is the name everyone gives to their mistakes," our past errors *can* be helpful to us. Thomas Edison patented 1,093 inventions in his lifetime, describing his work as "1 percent inspiration and 99 percent perspiration." He worked for over two years just on the incandescent light bulb, trying to find the ideal filament to conduct electricity. Edison knew that he would eventually find an element that would give off sufficient light when electricity flowed through it, but would not burn out in the process. Each of his failures led him to try a different substance. Without dogged persistence, including his countless failures, Edison would not have succeeded in discovering carbonized thread as the successful filament material.

In *The Evolution of Useful Things,* Henry Petroski, a professor at Duke University, describes how everyday useful items are often the result of decades and even centuries of development. Few, if any, of the gadgets of everyday life—from the fork and the straight pin to the zipper and the can opener—were invented in perfect form. Most, if not all, inventions come as improvements of earlier designs or failed models:

> *Clever people in the past, whom we today might call inventors, designers, or engineers, observed the failure of existing things to function as well as might be imagined.*

By focusing on the shortcomings of things, innovators altered these items to remove the imperfections, thus producing new, improved objects.

Few of us like to recall our mistakes, yet without them, we cannot develop as human beings. Unless we carry our "broken tablets," the negative experiences, we cannot understand how to avoid repeating them and move on to positive experiences. If we do not keep a record of where we have failed, we will be unable to narrow down the likely circumstances for success. We would prefer not having others pointing out our faults and foibles, but we do need to carry our own personal record of failure—not as a depressing reminder of where we have fallen short, but as an inspiring chronicle of the roads to success.

מִצְוֹת צְרִיכוֹת כַּוָּנָה **Mitzvot require proper intention.**

TEXT

Berakhot 13a

> Mishnah *(2:1): If he was reading in the Torah and it was time to recite [the Sh'ma], if he had proper intention, he fulfilled his responsibility.*
> Gemara: *We learn from this: Mitzvot require proper intention. What if his intention was to read? To read? But he is reading! He is reading to correct.*

CONTEXT

A Jew is required to recite the *Sh'ma* ("Hear, O Israel . . ."; Deuteronomy 6:4–9) twice a day, based on the rabbinic reading of those verses, to "recite them when you stay at home and when you are away, when you lie down and when you get up." This recitation is a mitzvah, a religious obligation (plural: mitzvot). But is the requirement simply to mutter the words, or does the person have to think about what is being said? If one read the words without focusing on them, has the obligation been fulfilled? In other words, do mitzvot require proper intention?

The Mishnah deals with the situation where one is reading the words of the *Sh'ma* from a Torah scroll at the time when one should be reciting the *Sh'ma.* Does this perfunctory reading fulfill the responsibility to recite the *Sh'ma?* The Mishnah simply states that if the reader had proper intention (in Hebrew: "directed his heart," i.e., was attentive; the heart is seen as the seat of thought) then the obligation has indeed been fulfilled.

The Gemara asks what exactly this man was doing when he was reading from a Torah scroll. Rashi assumes that the man was reading a Torah scroll without paying attention to the words, simply reciting word after word to detect mistakes in the Torah scroll. The Tosafot say that one who reads to correct *always* pays attention. How else can one correct mistakes in a Torah scroll? However, say the Tosafot, the man was not reading the words with proper pronunciation, but was reading them in such a way to check out the spelling and letters in the Torah scroll.

The question still remains: Is it enough simply to read the words of *Sh'ma,* or does one have to realize that one is fulfilling a religious responsibility? The Gemara never comes to a clear conclusion. Later Jewish law codifies a split decision: rabbinic enactments do not require intent, but laws from the Torah, like reciting the *Sh'ma,* do. (Even though the law of reading the *Sh'ma* twice daily is derived by *rabbinic* interpretation, the Rabbis considered it to be a law *d'oraita,* from the Torah.)

In some Jewish communities, the spirit of this law was incorporated into *Kavvanot,* prayers of intention that were often added to the worship service, for example, to announce that "Behold I am inviting my mouth to thank, praise, and extol my Creator." While these prayers themselves eventually became rote, their purpose remained a noble one—to focus the attention and intention of the worshiper on the act.

D'RASH

Some of the things that people do are almost mechanical in nature. When the salesperson in the store says: "Thanks, and have a nice day" or "How are you doing today?" we assume that they are giving a conventional greeting. We do not really expect that person to hear the story of our day. We do not foresee a merchant who hardly knows us to take a sincere interest in our lives. The greeting is perfunctory at best.

Yet, when we receive a greeting card for a birthday or anniversary, we do expect that it was given with "every good intention." That is, we assume that the sender truly hoped that we have a happy birthday or anniversary. None of us would want to receive a card that was sent without proper intention, even if we received only a standard greeting card with a simple signature and no personal greeting added. Thus, it appears that even in our lives, some things can be done mechanically, requiring little thought or purpose, while other actions need our focus and attention.

The Rabbis, in discussing the recitation of the *Sh'ma,* were also talking about the problem of Jewish worship. Does every prayer require our specific intention? Must we totally concentrate on what we are doing? Clearly, by saying that some mitzvot do not require proper intention, the Rabbis were allowing for the fact that not every action, every minute of the day, can be so focused. By saying that the *Sh'ma* requires specific intention, the Rabbis were also saying that those things which are the most important to us should be the object of our attention.

A mitzvah like *niḥum aveilim,* comforting mourners, is the type of important experience that needs our attention.

The Kavvanah for putting on the tallit:

I wrap myself in a tallit with fringes to fulfill the mitzvah of my Creator, as written in the Torah: "They shall put fringes on the corners of their garments in every generation."

The Kavvanah for putting on tefillin:

I put on tefillin to fulfill the mitzvah of my Creator, as written in the Torah: "Bind them as a sign upon your hand, and set them as a symbol above your eyes" [Deuteronomy 6:8]. The tefillin contain four passages from the Torah. They teach us the unity and uniqueness of God, recall the miracle of the Exodus, declare God's dominion over all that is in the heavens and on earth, and affirm our duty to serve God with all our being. We place the tefillah [singular of tefillin] on the arm, pointed toward the heart, that we may recall God's outstretched arm and be reminded to direct our impulses and desires to His service. We place the tefillah on the head to remind us to devote all of the power of our mind to the service of God, praised be He. (*Translation,* Siddur Sim Shalom) •

We may say a ritualized formula that is provided by our tradition—"May God comfort you among the mourners of Zion and Jerusalem"—but we need not say it in a mechanical or cursory way. Even a ritual can be done with feeling.

Every so often, we read the story of a famous actor, powerful politician or world-renowned scientist who, despite little or no parental attention or direction, became a successful, qualified, distinguished adult. We know this to be possible but it is the exception, rather than the rule. In general, good outcomes require our concentration and attention along the way. As parents, we know that our actions require intent. It is possible, but not likely, that our children will learn the values we want them to learn without our focus and efforts. It is more likely that they will become the type of adults we envision if we have the proper intention.

Some mitzvot can be performed accidentally, while others require specific and formal intention. What seems clear and unambiguous is the message of the Gemara: As an ideal, before the fact, we should pay proper attention to our actions.

לְעוֹלָם אַל יִפְתַּח אָדָם פִּיו לְשָׂטָן **A person should never give Satan an opening.**

TEXT

Berakhot 17b, 19a

Mishnah *(3:1): One whose dead relative has not yet been buried is exempt from reciting the* Sh'ma, *from the* Tefillah *[Amidah] and from tefillin, and from all the mitzvot stated in the Torah. The pallbearers and all those who take over for them—whether in front of or behind the bier: those who are in front of the bier, are exempt; those who are behind the bier, if they are needed, they are obligated; and both are exempt from the* Tefillah.

Gemara: *The Rabbis taught: "Those who are involved with the eulogy when the dead has not yet been buried slip away one by one and recite* [*the* Sh'ma]. *If the body is not in their presence, they sit and recite it, and he [the mourner] sits silent. They stand up and pray* [*the* Amidah] *and he stands up and accepts the judgment and says: 'Lord of the Universe! I have greatly sinned before You, and You did not punish me one-thousandth part. May it be Your will, Lord our God, that You repair our breaches and the breaches of all Your people, the house of Israel, with mercy.'" Abaye said: "A person must not talk this way, since Rabbi Shimon ben Lakish said, and so it was taught in the name of Rabbi Yosé: 'A person should never give Satan an opening [open one's mouth to Satan].'" And Rabbi Yosef said: "Where in the text do we get this from? As it says: 'We should be like Sodom' [Isaiah 1:9]. What did the prophet answer them? 'Hear the word of the Lord, you chieftains of Sodom' [Isaiah 1:10]."*

Tefillin are often called phylacteries. This term is based on the Greek translation of tefillin, meaning "a protection" or "amulet," and is found in the Christian Bible, Matthew 23:5. The Rabbis sometimes refer to the tefillin as an amulet of sorts as well. The Torah prescribes tefillin not as a preventative but "as a sign on your hand . . . as a symbol on your forehead" (Deuteronomy 6:8). In reality, the Torah talks of "sign" and "symbol" (or "frontlet") but does not specify what kind. *The Rabbis were well aware that the exact nature of this mitzvah is not given in the Torah, and they justify the tefillin as an enactment "of the Scribes," that is, a rabbinic law based on oral tradition. Apparently, many Jews did not wear tefillin during the time of the Talmud, and this mitzvah was not widely observed in medieval France and Spain. Moses of Coucy reprimanded the Jews of Spain in 1296, and—according to his account—thousands accepted the duty of putting on tefillin. While tefillin has been largely a male ritual throughout the ages, some women today have accepted this mitzvah. There is reference in the*

CONTEXT

The original discussion in the Mishnah and Gemara is on exemptions from reciting the *Sh'ma* while occupied in the burial of the dead. *Sh'ma* is a central prayer in Jewish worship. It consists of three paragraphs from the Torah and is recited twice daily, morning and night. The word *Tefillah* is used in modern Hebrew for prayer or worship. In the Talmud, it refers to *the* prayer par excellence, the *Amidah*, literally "the standing" prayer. Tefillin are boxes with leather straps, worn during weekday morning prayer and containing four sections of the Torah on parchment.

This topic leads to the question of what the mourners should say while involved in the burial of the dead and which

Talmud to a woman, Michal, daughter of Saul, putting on tefillin. (Eruvin *96a*) •

of the usual prayers they are exempt from reciting. The text presents an anonymous source that holds that the mourner should accept God's judgment, admitting that God has given better than was deserved. But this approach presents a problem to Rabbi Shimon ben Lakish and Rabbi Yosé. In their eyes, the mourner's admission of being spared from even a small part of the punishment is "giving Satan an opening," an invitation to Satan to speak, in other words, asking for trouble. Why tell God that you deserve more punishment than you have received?

In Jewish sources, Satan sometimes appears as an actual personality, the chief devil who opposes God. Satan (in Hebrew, the accent on the second syllable and the definite article is used: *ha-Satan, the* Satan) means "the adversary," that which obstructs, and has come to symbolize the sum total of the evil forces in the world.

Rabbi Yosé agrees that one is exempt from reciting *Sh'ma* while occupied with the dead. (The reason for this exemption is partly based on the rule that "one who is doing one mitzvah is freed from doing another mitzvah.") At the same time, he feels that you should never say or do anything that would be the cause of your own calamity.

"The breaches" refers to the destruction of the Temple. Rabbi Yosef expands on Rabbi Yosé's idea by finding a prooftext from Isaiah. In actuality, Rabbi Yosef takes Isaiah slightly out of context. Isaiah's exact words (translated) are: "Had not the Lord of Hosts left us some survivors, we should be like Sodom, another Gomorrah. Hear the word of the Lord, you chieftains of Sodom; give ear to our destruction, you folk of Gomorrah!"

Rabbi Yosef attempts to show that the Israelites gave Satan an opening and brought their own fate upon themselves. The Israelites said: "We should be *like* Sodom." By comparing themselves to Sodom and giving Satan an opening—says Rabbi Yosef—they created a self-fulfilling prophecy, for Isaiah then calls them "You chieftains of Sodom" (without the word "like"). Their own words are thrown back in their faces; their own image becomes their fate!

D'RASH

Rabbi Yosé's words, "Don't give Satan an opening," are often used in modern speech to mean "Don't tempt fate," that is, if you say something bad, it might just happen. We do not believe in Satan, but we do know the evil that surrounds us, all the bad things Satan symbolizes. Speaking of bad things may just make them happen! Several years ago, an editorial cartoon pictured a public school principal speaking to a group of parents. He told them, "Teen pregnancy could be reduced if society wasn't too embarrassed to talk about you know what with you know who before they end up you know how."

If we believe that just speaking about a bad thing can make it happen, isn't the converse true, that saying something good can help to bring it about? Aren't there also self-fulfilling prophecies for good? A famous study in the 1960s proved that when we expect good from people, we often find just that. Psychologists gave students in an elementary school an "intelligence test," later informing teachers that five students in each class had done exceptionally well and were likely to excel in school that year. In actuality, the students had been chosen at random. Nonetheless, by the end of that school year, those students had done significantly better. Based on the study's name, psychologists dubbed this "the Pygmalion effect." Teachers saw students who were labeled as "likely to succeed" and helped them—unconsciously and subtly—achieve these gains.

In our day and age, we see self-fulfilling prophecies at work all the time. We know that it is not because of Satan or fate, but because of the Pygmalion effect: what we see in others is what we get from them. A youngster labeled "problem child" will likely become one, fulfilling the prophecy, whether or not the child has the ability to change and become a better person. Does that student fail because of fate, character—or because of living up to the label we have given the youngster?

Conversely, when we see potential good in people, we may find these qualities. How often has it happened that we have achieved more because a parent, teacher, or friend saw the good (or potential good) in us and said "You have the ability to do more"? We may not have believed it at the time, but that person helped us believe in ourselves and thus achieve more. The Rabbis of the Talmud were not so much superstitious as psychologically astute: More often than not, what we expect *is* what we get.

לֹא נִתְּנָה תוֹרָה לְמַלְאֲכֵי הַשָּׁרֵת

The Torah was not given to the ministering angels.

TEXT

Berakhot 25b

The Rabbis taught: "In clear water, he sits in it up to his neck and recites [the Sh'ma*]." Some say: "He stirs it with his foot." According to the first teacher, his heart sees his nakedness! He [the first teacher] thinks: "His heart seeing his nakedness is permitted." But his heel sees his nakedness! He thinks: "His heel seeing his nakedness is permitted." It is taught: "His heel seeing his nakedness is permitted." Touching—Abaye said it is prohibited, while Rava said it is permitted. This is how Rav Zevid taught it. But Rav Ḥin'na son of Rav Ikka taught it this way: "Touching—everyone agrees that it is forbidden. Seeing—Abaye said it is forbidden, while Rava said it is permitted: The Torah was not given to the ministering angels." And the law is: Touching is forbidden, seeing is permitted.*

Hear, O Israel! The Lord is our God, the Lord alone. You shall love the Lord your God with all your heart and with all your soul and with all your might. Take to heart these instructions with which I charge you this day. Impress them upon your children. Recite them when you stay at home and when you are away, when you lie down and when you get up. Bind them as a sign on your hand and let them serve as a symbol on your forehead; inscribe them on the doorposts of your house and on your gates. (Deuteronomy 6:4–9) •

CONTEXT

The Talmud's teaching about the *Sh'ma* is based on people's experiences. Those who recite the *Sh'ma* religiously, morning and evening, every day of the year, will eventually be in a situation where the time for *Sh'ma* arrives and they are unprepared or unfit for it. This is the case being discussed in this Gemara: It is early morning and a man, taking a pre-dawn bath, has not yet recited the morning *Sh'ma* which, according to one opinion, must be recited before sunrise. Normally, a person would recite the *Sh'ma* fully dressed, as a sign of respect. However, in our case, he will not have time to get out of the water and get dressed before the time for reciting the *Sh'ma* has passed. What should this man do?

The Rabbis teach that he covers himself with water up to his neck, using the water as a "garment," and recites the *Sh'ma*. There is another opinion, though: ("Some say") that the man should muddy the waters with his foot so that he does not see his own nudity while reciting the *Sh'ma*. But, asks the Gemara, as long as he is still nude, isn't this still disrespectful ("his heart sees his nakedness")? The *Tanna Kamma,* or unnamed first teacher, holds that being naked is permitted (and is preferable to allowing the time for the *Sh'ma* to elapse). The Gemara then says: "But his heel sees his nakedness," that is, his own body, crouched down in the water, is touching skin to skin and is aware of his nudity. Certainly this is improper, disrespectful, and distracting. No, answers the Gemara; the *Tanna Kamma* holds that "his heel seeing his nakedness," that is, his body crouched in the water and close to itself, is permitted.

Yet, this is only *seeing* his nakedness, that is, being nude without touching skin to skin. With regard to touching one body part to another while covered with water, Abaye holds that this is not allowed, while Rava says it is allowed. However, Rav Ḥin'na has a different tradition. He learned that everyone believes that touching body part to body part while under water is forbidden. The questionable action is *seeing* his own nudity (and, presumably, being distracted while reciting the *Sh'ma*). According to Rav Ḥin'na, there is no argument that touching is prohibited. Abaye and Rava argue over a man *seeing* himself in the water while reciting the *Sh'ma,* Abaye holding that it is not allowed, Rava that it is.

Rava's reasoning is that "the Torah was not given to the ministering angels"; in other words, only angels would be able to live under the stringencies that Abaye expects of a person reciting the *Sh'ma* in water. In Rava's mind, it is enough to expect a man quickly to cover himself up to his neck with water and recite the *Sh'ma* before the time has passed. In so doing, he should not touch his heel to his genitals. Expecting this man not to be able to see himself in the water is virtuous and exemplary but practically impossible for human beings.

D'RASH

The disagreement of Abaye and Rava works on two levels. In one sense, it is about the recitation of the *Sh'ma.* How can we make sure that a person recites the *Sh'ma* regularly, at the right time, in the right state of mind and the proper dress?

Yet, Abaye and Rava are also talking about human expectations, about the excuses that all of us give at one time or another. They are asking: How much can realistically be expected from a Jew? Both sages speak out of love for God, Torah, and the Jewish people, yet each with a particular emphasis. According to Rav Ḥin'na, the son of Rav Ikka, Abaye seems much more concerned with the legal implications. Even if it creates a hardship and involves great personal sacrifice, the law nonetheless must be upheld, lest the man recite the *Sh'ma* in an improper condition. Rava, however, tilts the scale more towards the human dimension. The Torah does not expect the impossible, and reciting the *Sh'ma,* at the last possible moment, while immersed in water up to one's neck, is as much as Rava can demand from a person. Any prohibition beyond that is too much for him. After all, the Torah was not given to angels, but to human beings!

Every one of us, at one time or another, has said: "This is impossible, and I can't do it!" More than one has quoted the Yiddish proverb "*Shver tzu zayn a Yid*—It's hard being a Jew." We may think: "What does God want from me? I'm only human!" When we feel overwhelmed, we tell the world: "I can't do any more than this. Your demands on me are too much." Milton Steinberg, a well-known rabbi and preacher, collected a series of his sermons in a work called *Only Human—The Eternal Alibi*. . . . His point was that we use this excuse to excess; we plead humanity when we really mean laziness, forgetfulness, or indifference.

Rava's words, "The Torah was not given to the ministering angels," can be a great comfort to us today. They remind us that anything demanded of us by Judaism must, by its very nature, be possible, for the Torah was not given to *angels,* but to *humans.* Nevertheless, Rava's words are a two-edged sword. Our sense of comfort is limited by the realization that we cannot run away from these demands or beg off with the words: "It's not humanly possible!"

Just as Rava comforts us, he also challenges us: If it seems impossible, it is not, for the Torah was not given to the angels. Therefore, everything in it is achievable, although sometimes with tremendous effort. To see that life's demands, which may seem overwhelming, can in reality be attained is both a great relief and a tremendous challenge.

אֵין תּוֹכוֹ כְּבָרוֹ His inside is not like his outside.

TEXT

Berakhot 28a

It was taught: On that day, they dismissed the doorkeeper and gave permission for the students to enter. For Rabban Gamliel used to announce: "Any student whose inside is not like his outside should not enter the study house." That day, they added seats. Rabbi Yoḥanan said: "There is a disagreement between Abba Yosef ben Dostai and the Rabbis. One said: 'They added four hundred seats.' The other said: 'Seven hundred seats.' Rabban Gamliel became upset and said: 'Perhaps, God forbid, I have withheld Torah from Israel.' He was seized by a dream in which he saw white jugs filled with ashes. But it was not so; that was only to appease him."

CONTEXT

"That day" refers to the day on which Rabban Gamliel was overthrown as head of the study house in Yavneh and replaced by Rabbi Elazar ben Azariah. On "that day," the students rebelled against Rabban Gamliel's authority, installing this younger and apparently kinder teacher, Rabbi Elazar ben Azariah, in his stead. On "that day" there was a change not only of administration but also of attitude. Previously, admission to the study house had been highly selective. Rabban Gamliel had ruled that anyone whose qualities and attributes on the inside—his heart and soul—did not equal what was visible on the outside—his deeds and learning—should not enter the study house. A doorkeeper was posted to prevent undesirable students from entering. Rabbi Elazar changed that and allowed anyone who wanted to enter his school. On "that day," hundreds of students took up his offer.

There is disagreement over the exact number of students, but it is clear that many new students came to the study house after Rabbi Elazar ben Azariah took over. Rabban Gamliel is saddened that his actions may have caused a decrease in Torah knowledge. His distress is lessened when he dreams of jugs filled with ashes. In talmudic times, dreams were often seen as signs or portents, and the image of ash-filled casks is taken by Rabban Gamliel to symbolize the new students. While their number may be great, they are not worthy students but hollow containers. However, the Gemara itself disagrees. Rabban Gamliel may feel better about his

Rabbi Elazar ben Azariah is known to many as one of the rabbis mentioned in the traditional haggadah used at the Pesaḥ Seder. The Talmud, in the section immediately before our text above, relates what happened on "that day," that is, the day he took over authority of the study house: Though Rabbi Elazar confessed to being "like a man of seventy years," he was actually only eighteen years old at the time! Upon becoming head of the study house, he quickly learned about the awesome burdens of public office; his hair immediately turned gray and he remarked that he felt "like *a man of seventy years." Here is a case where, in a different sense, his inside was not like his outside: Rabbi Elazar was still quite young but looked (and apparently felt) quite old. Such is the price paid by many for leadership.* •

dream, but its meaning is not what he thinks. The purpose of the dream was only to appease Rabban Gamliel; the fact stands that he caused a diminution of Torah.

D'RASH

Rabban Gamliel and Rabbi Elazar offer two radically different approaches to life and to many of the situations we face. On the one hand, we have Rabban Gamliel who holds up a very high standard for scholars. Their insides *should* equal their outsides. Today, those who enter seminaries for religious study and ordination are often carefully scrutinized so that not only their intelligence—the outside—but also their personalities, moral qualities, and attributes like compassion and understanding—the inside—meet the highest standards.

On the other hand, we find those following the approach of Rabbi Elazar, who believes that anyone who wants to study should be welcome, at whatever level. Academies of learning—college, universities, adult education programs—cannot be only for those who are *already* knowledgeable. Part of the purpose of schooling is to help perfect the student who is, by definition, imperfect. How much poorer our Judaism would be today without the innumerable contributions of teachers like Rabbi Akiva whose learning, piety, and love of the Jewish people did not blossom until later in life!

Many of us have faced a similar dilemma when we have been forced to make a decision about health care: Which doctor should we choose? What standard should we use in making this choice? One option may be a physician who is proven by years of experience to be an expert diagnostician. Her knowledge and expertise are renowned, though she is a bit aloof and scholarly at times and lacks bedside manners. The other choice is a doctor who is known for her kindness and warmth rather than for being "the best in the field." We know that we will find personal attention and kindness in this doctor, as well as competence, if not excellence. How can we make a proper decision?

The answer may lie in an interesting historical note: Some time after the rebellion, Rabban Gamliel was apparently reinstated as head of the study house, with Rabbi Elazar ben Azariah serving either under him or as a second dean. Perhaps the scholars of that era had come to some accommodation, realizing that not only was the standard of Rabban Gamliel too high, but that of Rabbi Elazar was too lenient; having both men in charge was an attempt to find the perfect balance.

When facing an important decision, we, much like the Rabbis in the study house, can try to find the same balance between the two extremes. The story of Rabban Gamliel and Rabbi Elazar ben Azariah shows us not only how these approaches play themselves out in real life, but also how we can use the positive standards of each position to make our own sound decisions.

שַׁעֲרֵי דִמְעָה לֹא נִנְעֲלוּ׃ **The gates of tears are not closed.**

TEXT

Berakhot 32b

Rabbi Elazar said: "From the day the Temple was destroyed, the gates of prayer have been closed, as it says: 'And when I shout and plead, He shuts out my prayer' [Lamentations 3:8, author's translation]. But even though the gates of prayer are closed, the gates of tears are open, as it says: 'Hear my prayer, O Lord, give ear to my appeal; do not disregard my tears' [Psalms 39:13, author's translation].

Rabbi Elazar's comment—"From the day the Temple was destroyed, the gates of prayer have been closed"—might be puzzling to the modern mind. We would expect just the opposite from the Rabbis, that the destruction of the Temple with its elaborate sacrificial system led to the development *of prayer rather than its* demise*! In our minds, Jews who were no longer able to offer animal sacrifices on the altar turned to the gates of prayer, what the Rabbis called "service [worship] of the heart," as opposed to worship by sacrifices (the same Hebrew word,* avodah *is used for both types of worship). The Rabbis, however, saw the Temple as a central focus of Jewish worship and its destruction as a diminution of the power of prayer.* •

CONTEXT

Rabbi Elazar is commenting on the efficacy of prayer. He sees that many prayers go unanswered by God and presents as proof a verse from Lamentations, one of the saddest books of the Bible. After the destruction of the Temple, it appears that God does not listen to prayers. How else could the author cry and plead before God with no answer? However, when tears are added, as proved by the verse from Psalms, God cannot disregard prayer. Rashi and Tosafot, medieval commentators on the Talmud, note that Rabbi Elazar's interpretation of the verse seems to be: God will *automatically* hear the prayer of one who prays with tears. Tears alone are enough for acceptance by God.

This is not to say that Rabbi Elazar would necessarily devalue all ritual and rote prayer. He simply adds that we cannot expect the prayers to have an impact on God if they are routine formulas that do not have personal involvement. Rabbi Elazar knows that tears symbolize the sincerity, emotions, and involvement of the worshiper. The gates of heaven are open to the person who not only says the right words, but also has the emotions to back up these words. Prayer is ultimately effective when accompanied by tears.

D'RASH

A parent says to a child: "Maybe you didn't see that lady's toes when you drove the shopping cart over them. I think that she deserves an apology." More often than not, the child mumbles "Sorry." Is that enough? To a certain degree, it depends on the emotions used in the apology. The child's "Sorry" may or may not reflect sincere regret. The words themselves are only an opportunity to express true feelings. Most of us would agree that saying "I'm sorry" is insufficient without the genuine emotions and sentiments that go with the words.

Every "Sorry" and "I love you" is a formula, an opportunity for expressing what we truly feel. We need not delete such expressions from our language simply because some are perfunctory. On the contrary: They are the opportunity to express our sincerest sentiments. The words which reflect our innermost feelings will touch not only others but ourselves as well.

This means not only that we have to offer our prayers with tears. We also have to be moved by the tears of others, as they cry, appeal to us, seek understanding and compassion from us. Only if *we* respond to *others'* tears can we expect God to be touched by *ours*.

The great medieval Hebrew poet Moshe ibn Ezra said: "Words that come from the heart enter another heart." If we expect others to be moved, we must be moved, beyond words to our very heart and soul. If we want others to listen, we must first listen, in the fullest sense of the word. If we ask God not to disregard our appeal but to answer our prayers, then we have to respond to them ourselves by being moved by them, even moved to tears.

פוק חֲזִי מַאי עַמָּא דָּבַר

Go and see what the people are doing.

TEXT

Berakhot 44a, 45a

Mishnah *(6:8): One who drinks water to quench his thirst recites the blessing ". . . by whose word all things come into being." Rabbi Tarfon says: ". . . Who creates many beings and their needs."*
Gemara: *"Rabbi Tarfon says: '. . . Who creates many beings and their needs.'" Rava bar Rav Ḥanan said to Abaye—but some say to Rav Yosef: "What is the law?" He said to him: "Go and see what the people are doing."*

Today, the laws regarding which berakhah *to say over which food are well established. The first opinion, that of the anonymous teacher, is now the accepted practice: Before drinks like water and fruit juices, one recites* shehakol nihyeh bidvaro, *"by whose word all things come into being." However, Rabbi Tarfon's formula has been incorporated into the tradition, even if his opinion of* when *to recite it was rejected. Rather than being recited before drinks, it is recited* after *eating or drinking anything that requires the* berakhah shehakol nihyeh bidvaro, *"by whose word all things come into being."*

> *Over most fruits, vegetables, and all other things which are not grown in the ground, the concluding berakhah is ". . . borei nefashot rabbot (Who creates many beings and their needs)."* (Shulḥan Arukh, Oraḥ Ḥayyim 207) •

CONTEXT

In the Mishnah, there is a disagreement over which *berakhah,* or blessing, is recited by a person before drinking water. The first opinion is to recite ". . . *shehakol nihyeh bidvaro,*" or "[Praised are You, Lord our God, King of the universe] by whose word all things come into being." The view of Rabbi Tarfon is that a different *berakhah,* ". . . *borei nefashot,*" or "[Praised are You, Lord our God, King of the universe] Who creates many beings and their needs," is recited.

In the time of the Mishnah and Gemara, these rules were still quite fluid (even when dealing with water!). Here, we see the process of debating what the law should actually be. A century after the Mishnah, the law had not yet been fixed, and Rava was still attempting to understand which opinion of the Mishnah to follow. The answer of Abaye is: Either opinion could be legitimate. We follow what people are doing. One genuine way of knowing which of the two legitimate positions has become the law is to go and see how people actually observe.

D'RASH

Every religion has laws and ritual procedures. People need to know the *right* way of doing these *rites.* For Jewish practice, a rabbi can usually answer this question. The rabbi will know the law or will consult books that teach the correct way of doing things. But there are times when even a rabbi does not know the law, because there is no one right way and because the accepted practice is "what the people are doing."

Local customs develop; these become the practice of the people, the actual law, passed down from one generation to the next. The beauty of Abaye's answer is that it shows that he and his colleagues are not deciding the matter at hand from an ivory tower. Rather, they are in touch with the masses of people, for their ruling will be legitimate and binding only in so far as it reflects reality and is accepted. To determine this, they say: "Go and see what the people are doing."

A simple contemporary example of "Go and see what the people are doing" from the Pesaḥ Seder tables may help explain this concept, especially since Rabbi Tarfon is well known from the haggadah. During the Seder, we praise God with the psalms of Hallel. As we do, we remember the Egyptians at whose expense our victory came about, and we remove some wine from our cups, as if to say: Our joy is not complete because the victory came at someone else's expense. Therefore, our cup cannot be full.

Now the question arises: *How* should this ritual be performed? How should the drops of wine for the Ten Plagues be removed from the cup? Should they be spilled, taken out with a spoon, or dipped out with a finger? And if the last, with which finger? There is no exact law on this, only custom, and the best a person can do is "go and see" the practice of others. Most Jews spill the ten drops of wine from the cup at their Seder table not based on a theoretical legal ruling, but based on what they have seen practiced at other Seders.

At times, there is one law, very clear and very specific, based on theoretical rationales or philosophical justifications, clearly codified in the traditional literature. At other times, though, law is determined by the practice of Jews—not just any Jews but, as Robert Gordis delineated, "the body of men and women in the Jewish people who accept the authority of Jewish law and are concerned with Jewish observance as a genuine issue." In many cases, a rabbi can say, "*The* halakhah (*the* law) is . . ." However, there are times when, like Abaye, the rabbi will say: "In order to know what Jewish law is, we need to go and see what the people are doing."

Some may feel that the realm of Jewish law is owned by rabbis and, therefore, is a closed book. Abaye is showing that the practice of the people is important, and what Jews do plays a central role in the development of the law. Rabbis need to be aware of and to consult with "the people" as one of the important elements in the creation of halakhah. The wise arbiter will have a finger on the pulse of the people and will make not only a truly authentic ruling but also one that is acceptable and accepted.

מִצְוָה הַבָּאָה בַּעֲבֵרָה **A mitzvah performed by means of a transgression.**

TEXT

Berakhot 47b

> *"Women, slaves and minors may not be counted in the* zimmun.*" Rabbi Yosé said: "A minor lying in a cradle is counted in the* zimmun.*" But is it not taught: "Women, slaves and minors may not be counted in the* zimmun*"? What he said follows the opinion of Rabbi Yehoshua ben Levi, for Rabbi Yehoshua ben Levi said: "Even though they said: 'A minor in a cradle may not be counted in the* zimmun,*' we make him a 'wedge' for the ten." And Rabbi Yehoshua ben Levi said: "Nine and a slave are counted together." They objected: It once happened that Rabbi Eliezer entered the synagogue and did not find ten; he freed his servant and completed the ten. If he freed him, yes [he is counted]; if he did not free him, no. Two were needed; he freed one and added one. How could he do this? Did not Rav Yehudah say: "Whoever frees his slave violates a positive mitzvah, as it says: 'They shall serve you forever' [Leviticus 25:46, author's translation]!" It is different for a mitzvah. But it is a mitzvah performed by means of a transgression! A mitzvah affecting many is different.*

CONTEXT

The Gemara is discussing who may be counted for a minyan and who for a *zimmun*. A minyan is the ten worshipers needed to recite certain prayers and to read from the Torah. A *zimmun* is the introduction in the *birkat ha-mazon*, the blessings after a meal, recited when three or more eat bread together. Both minyan and *zimmun* are desirable: we would want to have a minyan for prayer and a *zimmun* for *birkat ha-mazon* since, in each case, we add words of praise of God that can be recited only with a required number of people. The Gemara tells us that "women, slaves and minors" are exempt and not included. However, a minor may be used as a "wedge," the final piece that is added to make up the whole. Thus, the minor is counted as the tenth in a minyan.

Next, a story about Rabbi Eliezer is brought in to add a point of case-law. Even though slaves were not counted in the minyan, may a *freed* slave be added to the minyan as the tenth? The case here deals with a non-Jewish servant owned by a Jew. In rabbinic times, many non-Jewish slaves were educated household managers and were circumcised. Thus,

The expression "counted for a minyan" is redundant, since minyan means "counting" or "numbering" and refers to the ten adult males who the Rabbis said are needed for certain public rituals like Torah reading and Kaddish. (In many congregations today, women are also counted in the minyan.) The Talmud traces the number ten, by verbal analogy, to the ten spies who brought back the negative report on the land of Israel (Numbers 14). There are many other references to minyan in the Talmud, with several different biblical sources cited as proof. It is likely, therefore, that the requirement of a minyan predated the Talmud's reasoning. Today, we require a minyan for repetition of the Amidah *with* Kedushah, *for recitation of certain prayers like* Kaddish *and* Bar'khu, *for reading the Torah in public, as well as for several other ceremonies and parts of the liturgy. The practice of adding a minor as a "wedge" is still used today; a minor who knows how to answer "Amen" and knows that he (or, in some communities, she) is praying to God may be counted as the tenth for a minyan where no adult may be found. Often, the minor is given a* Bible *to hold.*

The problem of finding ten worshipers for a minyan is not unique to our times. There are several references in the Gemara to batlanim, *idle or unemployed men who would always be available for the minyan. In fact, the Mishnah* (Megillah *1:3) defines a "big city" as one with ten* batlanim, *that is, ten men always ready and available for a minyan.* •

on a minute's notice, the master of the house could free a servant, making him Jewish (according to the standard of that day)—and theoretically solving the minyan problem. However, there is a disagreement as to whether this is allowed, since the text in Leviticus may actually prohibit this practice. The verse—"They shall serve you forever"—can be understood in two different ways: If the Torah means that they *may* serve you in perpetuity, then one may free such a slave. However, if the intention of the text is that they *must* serve you in perpetuity, then we are not allowed to free such a slave.

An answer is suggested: Even if the text means "they *must* serve you," we are allowed to transgress this rule in order to fulfill a mitzvah, having a minyan. But then, the Gemara answers, we are performing a mitzvah via a transgression, which is clearly prohibited! No, respond the Rabbis, if it is for the communal good, it is not a true transgression of the Torah's rule.

D'RASH

There is much to be said against any mitzvah performed by means of a transgression, of doing a good deed in a way that breaks the law. Robin Hood stole from the rich and gave to the poor. While aiding the needy is a laudable act, accomplishing this act by defrauding others is less than praiseworthy. After all, we still express our moral disapproval by saying that Robin Hood "*stole*" from the rich—not "borrowed," "recovered," or even "took."

Thus, we are aware that we must be careful not only *that* we do mitzvot, but also *how* we perform them. The power of this rule is attested to by the fact that all of us know of those who perform mitzvot through a transgression and thus bring shame to God, the Torah, and the Jewish people. The slumlord who keeps his tenants living in squalor, who denies them heat in the winter and running water all year long, yet gives generously to many worthy causes has performed a mitzvah by means of a transgression.

Surprisingly, the Gemara does not come down unequivocally against the mitzvah performed by a transgression. It seems that if the transgression is insignificant (freeing a slave) or the need is great (a minyan to fulfill the prayer obligation), then the general rule is waived, and the mitzvah is allowed even though a minor transgression is involved.

But what is a minor transgression? What constitutes the "public good" or a "great need?" The answers to these questions are surely debatable and subjective. Perhaps this is the point of the Gemara. There are no hard-and-fast rules for conduct that will cover every possible case. This text, like much of the Gemara, forces us to think without thinking for us.

Every one of us will undoubtedly face issues where we see good happening via corruption. We can then recall this Gemara and ask ourselves: Is the need that great that we can allow the transgression? And is the sin so awful that we have to speak out against the good that will be done? Some would prefer a legal system that gives us every answer and covers each conceivable situation. Halakhah, Jewish law, does not do this, not only for practical reasons (it's impossible), but also for philosophical reasons (it's unhealthy). Though we are made uncomfortable by the situation, and by our need to work out a suitable answer, we are reassured by our texts which limit the choices and bring the values into focus, while not totally limiting our free will and personal involvement.

תָּדִיר וְשֶׁאֵינוֹ תָּדִיר—
תָּדִיר קוֹדֵם

The frequent and the infrequent
—the frequent takes precedence.

TEXT

Berakhot 51b

Our Rabbis taught: "The differences between Bet Shammai and Bet Hillel regarding a meal—Bet Shammai says: 'The blessing is first said over the day and then over the wine, because it is on account of the day that the wine is used; and the day already was sanctified before the wine was brought.' Bet Hillel says: 'The blessing is first said over the wine and then over the day, because the wine provides the opportunity for the prayer of sanctification to be said.' Another explanation: 'The blessing over the wine is said frequently, while the blessing over the day is said only infrequently, and [in a case of] the frequent and the infrequent—the frequent takes precedence.'"

CONTEXT

At the beginning of Shabbat and festivals, a special prayer, *kiddush* ("sanctification"), is recited over a cup of wine at the evening meal. *Kiddush* is composed of two parts: A one-line blessing for the wine, and a longer blessing praising God for having created the special day. The question that Bet Shammai and Bet Hillel are discussing is which of the two blessings is recited first. Bet Shammai holds that Shabbat begins Friday at sunset; only afterwards do we sit down to a meal and recite the *kiddush* over the wine. Therefore, the blessing over the day ("Praised are You, O Lord, Who hallows Shabbat") is recited first. It is then followed by the blessing over the wine ("Praised are You, O Lord . . . Who creates fruit of the vine").

Bet Hillel takes the opposite position: The prayer praising God for having created the special day is recited only by virtue of our drinking wine in celebration of the day. Therefore, the blessing over the wine should come first. Another reason is offered by the Gemara for this position: We drink wine quite often, and the blessing over wine is recited each time we do so. But the blessing "over the day" is recited only at the onset of that special occasion. Bet Hillel follows the principle that things which comes frequently take precedence over things which come infrequently.

The text of kiddush *recited Friday evening:*

Praised are You, Lord our God, King of the universe who creates fruit of the vine. Praised are You, Lord our God, King of the Universe whose mitzvot add holiness to our lives, cherishing us through the gift of His holy Shabbat granted lovingly, gladly, a reminder of Creation. It is the first among our days of sacred assembly which recall the Exodus from Egypt. Thus You have chosen us, endowing us with holiness, from among all peoples by granting us Your holy Shabbat lovingly and gladly. Praised are You, Lord who hallows Shabbat. (*Translation,* Siddur Sim Shalom) •

The halakhah today follows the opinion of Bet Hillel: We begin with the blessing over the wine and follow with the blessing over the day.

D'RASH

Two scenes from a marriage: The first—the couple on their wedding day. The bride is absolutely breathtaking, the groom incredibly handsome. They are surrounded and attended by loving family and dearest friends. At the end of the ceremony, when the groom breaks the glass, they kiss with such passion and feeling that some of the guests actually cry. The orchestra plays romantic music while the caterer serves the most delicious feast. The photographer mentions that he has rarely seen two young people so much in love: They cannot take their eyes off each other. When they dance, they hold each other tightly and gaze into each other's eyes.

The second scene—same couple, seven years later, an ordinary day. The living room is cluttered with baby toys strewn all over the floor. The sink is filled with dirty dishes. The wife is wearing a T-shirt covered with an infant's spit-up. The baby is crying, chewing on a teething ring. The husband is sitting at the dining room table, desperately trying to finish the report that is due on the boss's desk at 9 A.M. the next day. He is also trying to figure out how he is going to pay this month's mortgage, the electric bill, the oil bill, the car loan, *and* fix the leaky roof. Amid the stress, the tumult, and the chaos, the wife comes over and puts her hand on her husband's shoulder; he kisses her hand. They look into one another's eyes and smile.

There are those, like Bet Shammai, who hold that "we live for the moments," that what is most important are the infrequent, special occasions which mark our lives—the birth of a baby, a Bar/Bat Mitzvah, a college graduation, a wedding, a fiftieth anniversary. We look forward to them and when they come, we celebrate with all our heart and soul. The same is true of holidays that come along once a year, or even of Shabbat, which stands out as the unique day in seven. When these special times come, we put aside all else because they are so very important and meaningful to us.

Other people, like Bet Hillel, acknowledge the importance of unique occasions, but they hold that what counts more in life is not the special, but the everyday. You can tell more about a couple's marriage from how they are doing on that mundane, ordinary day seven years after that romantic wedding day. Life is made up mostly of the regular, frequent moments and what we make of them. Special occasions come and go. Bet Hillel, by placing the blessing over the wine *first,* is teaching us that what remains primary is the blessing over the *wine* that was probably said every single day. We should anticipate the blessings that come to us in the special, infrequent moments, but we must also look forward to the blessings that are found every single day, all around us.

חַיָּב אָדָם לְבָרֵךְ עַל הָרָעָה
כְּשֵׁם שֶׁמְּבָרֵךְ עַל הַטּוֹבָה

A person must bless God for the bad just as one must bless God for the good.

TEXT

Berakhot 54a, 60b

Mishnah *(9:5): A person must bless God for the bad just as one must bless God for the good, as it says: "You shall love the Lord your God with all your heart" [Deuteronomy 6:5]. "With all your heart"—with both inclinations, with the good inclination and with the evil inclination. "With all your soul"—even if He takes your soul. "And with all your might"—with all your money. Another interpretation: "With all your might"* (me'odekha)*—with each and every measure* (midah) *that He gives* (moded) *you, you are to acknowledge* (modeh) *Him.*

Gemara: *What is meant by "A person must bless God for the bad just as one must bless God for the good"? If you say that just as we recite the blessing "[Blessed are You, Lord,] Who is good and Who does good" for good things, so too we recite the blessing "Who is good and Who does good" for bad things. Has it not been taught: "Over good news, one says 'Who is good and Who does good'; over bad news, one says 'Blessed are You the Judge of truth'?" Rava said: "We require this to teach us to accept it with joy."*

To "bless" does not mean the same thing as "to thank." Despite Rava's comment at the end of the Gemara, it is too much to expect most people to actually thank God for the bad things that happen to them. Barukh, *the Hebrew word for "bless," comes from the same root as the word for knee,* berekh. *Many scholars see a connection: To bless God is to kneel or bow before the Divine (either literally or symbolically), acknowledging God as greater and more powerful, and the Source of all—both good and bad—that happens.* •

CONTEXT

The Mishnah teaches that we must recite a *berakhah,* or blessing, for the bad things that occur, just as we are obligated to recite one for the good things. The biblical source for this notion is found in the *Sh'ma.* The Rabbis first note the unusual spelling of the expression "your heart" (*l'vavvkha,* with a double *vet,* instead of the less poetic word *lib'kha*). They interpret this spelling to allude to our dual impulses, one toward good, one toward bad. The *yetzer hara* or "the evil inclination" is the rabbinic name for the selfish, darker side of human nature. The Rabbis often counsel that we should channel these impulses for good. Sexuality, for instance, is not repressed or denied but is channeled positively within marriage.

The second phrase ("with all your soul") teaches that we are to love God even to the point of sacrificing our lives. Finally, the third phrase ("with all your might") is interpreted by means of a word play *(me'od, midah, modeh)* that makes the point that we are to acknowledge God for *all* that God gives us. The Gemara asks the specific halakhic question: Which *berakhah* is actually to be in response to misfortune or bad news? The answer is the formula *barukh Dayan ha-emet,* "Blessed are You the Judge of truth." This is, by the way, the same blessing that is recited by a mourner when he or she tears clothing (or a ribbon pinned onto the clothing) just prior to the funeral or burial of an immediate relative.

D'RASH

A man sits in front of the television, his lottery ticket in hand. He listens attentively as the state lottery spokeswoman greets the viewers, and then begins to pick the winning numbers. 4. 17. 33. 38. 46 . . . and 61. The man watches and listens, staring in disbelief at the numbers on his ticket. They are identical! He cannot believe this has happened! He looks at the screen one more time as the numbers are listed. He checks his ticket a second, and then a third time. "Yes!" He has won the lottery. He gets down on his knees, on the floor, and looks up to the ceiling. "Thank you, God! Thank you! Thank you! Thank you!"

A year goes by, but the money he won turns out not to have been such a blessing. His marriage has broken up, and most of his old friends no longer talk to him. Much of the money is gone, squandered on silly extravagances and poor investments. What originally looked to be a great blessing turned out to be a real curse.

A child sits by the front window, looking out at the pouring rain. There is an unmistakable expression of disappointment on her face. Today was the day of her birthday party picnic, which had to be postponed because of the weather. Her mother tries to explain that friends and family will all get together next weekend and try again, but those words bring no comfort. Today is her actual birthday, and she had her hopes set on *this* day for a marvelous celebration. She looks up at the heavens and angrily asks God: "What did I ever do to You to deserve Your doing this to me?"

The next morning the family reads in the newspaper about a helicopter crash. The accident took place at the same site where the party was to be held and during the exact time that the family would have been gathered. What seemed yesterday like a curse today seems like a blessing in disguise.

Perhaps this is the reason we are taught to bless God for the bad as well as the good: We never really know how things will ultimately turn out. Events, sometimes, are not what they first appear to be. It may be that it is quite short-sighted and quite self-centered for us to thank God for what seems good and to blame or ignore God for what appears to be bad. Perhaps the Rabbis were being more realistic when they advised us that we need to be careful with the good, for it can turn on us and become a curse. And we need to be patient with what seems to be bad: It may turn out to be a real blessing in the long run.

Everything comes from God; that is what reciting a blessing reminds us. Everything, both good and bad, is just another opportunity. We cannot make much of opportunities until we are open enough to see them.

אוֹרֵחַ טוֹב מַהוּ אוֹמֵר — What does a good guest say?

כַּמָּה טְרָחוֹת טָרַח בַּעַל הַבַּיִת בִּשְׁבִילִי — How much trouble has my host gone to just for me!

Blessings (in Hebrew, berakhot) *are an important part of the Jewish tradition. The better known blessings are those for foods like wine and bread, but there are also blessings for various occasions like studying a traditional text, seeing a rainbow, and hearing good news or bad news. Judaism sees each of these occasions as an opportunity for us to witness God's presence in the world. Thus, we acknowledge God as the giver of Torah, the One who remembers God's covenant with Noah, and who is either good and beneficent, or the true Judge.* •

TEXT

Berakhot 58a

The Rabbis taught: "One who sees a crowd of Israelites says: 'Blessed is He who understands secrets.' For each one's mind is different, and each one's face is different." Ben Zoma once saw a crowd on the steps of the Temple Mount. He said: "Blessed is He who understands secrets, and blessed is He who created all these just to serve me!" He used to say: "How much trouble Adam had to go to just to get some bread to eat! He plowed, sowed, reaped, bound sheaves, threshed them, winnowed, selected, ground, sifted, kneaded and baked—and then he ate. And I simply get up and find all of these done for me. How much trouble did Adam go to in order to find clothes to wear! He sheared, cleaned the wool, beat it, spun it, weaved it—and then he had clothing to wear. And I simply get up and find all these done for me. All kinds of craftsmen anxiously come to my door, and I simply get up and find these done for me." He used to say: "What does a good guest say? 'How much trouble has my host gone to just for me! How much meat has he brought for me! How much wine has he brought for me! How much cake has he brought for me! All his trouble, he has done just for me!' But what does a bad guest say? 'How much trouble has my host gone to? I ate one slice of bread, I ate one piece of meat, I drank one cup of wine. All his trouble, he has done just for his wife and his children.'"

CONTEXT

This section of Gemara lists the proper blessings to be recited for certain foods and upon seeing specific people (like a king) or places (for example, where a miracle occurred). Ben Zoma feels that one should thank God not only for the individuality of each person ("Blessed is He Who understands secrets") but also for each person's labors on his behalf. Since these blessings are, in part, an attempt to formalize a sense of thankfulness, Ben Zoma believes that one should be thankful for the simple fact that one's life is so easy. To prove this, Ben Zoma compares his life with that of Adam in the Garden of Eden. Adam had to work so much harder to produce food or clothing. "And I simply get up and find all of these done for me!"

As a continuation of Ben Zoma's thoughts on gratitude, a famous quote of his ("He used to say . . . ") is introduced. Just as we should be grateful and thank God for the food and clothing we have, we should also be grateful guests and thank our host for what he has done for us. Thus, a person should not think: "My host was making dinner anyway. He just added some water to the soup and a place setting at the table." Rather, one should think: "My host went out of his way to provide for me. How privileged I am to have such a wonderful host."

D'RASH

Imagine that you are a hospital patient. A friend pays you a visit, and you thank him for visiting. Which response would you rather hear—"It's no big deal; I was driving by anyway," or "I really wanted to see you, and I'm glad that you and I had this time together"? Most of us would prefer the latter, showing that our friends pay special attention to us, notice us, even go out of their way for us. These are the sentiments that Ben Zoma expresses. None of us wants to think that what has been done for us required no effort. On the contrary: We enjoy being pampered and having someone pay special attention to us.

This is especially true because we live in a huge, impersonal world. Much of the time, no one goes out of their way just for us. When we spend hours trying to get a question answered in a huge bureaucracy, we may feel as if we are simply numbers in a computer. If we do our banking at an automated teller machine, months may go by without our seeing a human teller. To the employee at the drive-through fast food place, we are one of hundreds of anonymous patrons who will pick up dinner in a bag that night.

In this nameless, cold world of impersonal machines and detached people, any sign of personal attention is most welcome. It deserves not only our notice but also our gratitude. Thus, Ben Zoma reminds us of two things: First, we must appreciate the good things that people do for us and express our thanks to them. When we do not notice, we only contribute to the increased impersonality of society. Second, we should, whenever possible, give that extra special personal attention to others. We become better hosts—as well as employers, employees, friends, and relatives—by catering to the needs of others. By appreciating the kindness that is shown to us both by God and by people, and by showing kindness to others, we make a cold world a much warmer place.

Rest Stop

Tell the Israelites to turn back and encamp before Pi-hahiroth, between Migdol and the sea, before Baal-zephon; you shall encamp facing it, by the sea. (Exodus 14:2)

Words of Torah are compared to water . . . as it says: "Ho, all who are thirsty, come for water" [Isaiah 55:1]. . . . Just as water restores the soul, as it says: "So God split open the hollow which is at Lehi, and the water gushed out of it; he drank, regained his strength, and revived" [Judges 15:19], so too with Torah, as it says: "The teaching of the Lord is perfect, renewing life" [Psalms 19:8]. (*Song of Songs Rabbah* 1, 3)

They asked Rabbi Levi Yitzḥak: "Why is the *first* page number missing in all the tractates of the Babylonian Talmud? Why does each begin with the *second?*" He replied: "However much a man may learn, he should always remember that he has not even gotten to the first page." (Martin Buber. *Tales of the Hasidim, Early Masters.* New York: Schocken Books, 1970, p. 232)

Seder Moed

Introduction to Seder Moed

The second Order of the Mishnah is called *Moed,* or "Holiday." It is comprised of twelve tractates that discuss the laws of the various festivals of the Jewish year. The Order begins with two tractates concerning Shabbat. They are followed by sections that cover Pesaḥ, Yom Kippur, Sukkot, Rosh Hashanah, Purim, and fast days, as well as the laws of what is permitted and prohibited during a holiday and the intermediate days of the festivals.

הַנּוֹתֵן מַתָּנָה לַחֲבֵרוֹ צָרִיךְ לְהוֹדִיעוֹ

One who gives a gift to a friend must inform him.

TEXT

Shabbat 10b

Rava bar Meḥasya said in the name of Rav Ḥama bar Gurya in the name of Rav: "One who gives a gift to a friend must inform him, as it says: 'That you may know that I the Lord have consecrated you' [Exodus 31:13]." It is also taught: "That you may know that I the Lord have consecrated you" [Ibid.]. The Holy One said to Moses: "I have a great gift in my treasury, and its name is Shabbat. I want to give it to Israel; go inform them!"

Based on this, Rabban Shimon ben Gamliel said: "One who gives bread to a child must inform his mother." What should be done to him? Abaye said: "Rub him with oil and paint his eyes." But now that we are concerned with witchcraft, what should be done? Rav Papa said: "Rub him with what he gave him." . . . Rav Ḥisda held two gift oxen in his hands. He said: "Whoever can tell me a new teaching of Rav, I will give these to him." Rava bar Meḥasya said to him: "This is what Rav said: 'One who gives a gift to his friend must inform him, as it says: "That you may know that I the Lord have consecrated you."'" He gave them to him. He said to him: "Are Rav's teachings so precious to you?" He said: "Yes." He said: "A thing is precious to its wearer."

CONTEXT

These stories all teach the same lesson, based on the saying of Rava bar Meḥasya, that one must announce a gift before giving it. Rava bar Meḥasya uses as proof a verse from Exodus: "That you may know that I the Lord have consecrated you." The verse appears in a section where God appoints Bezalel to build the *mishkan,* or portable tabernacle that the Israelites used in the wilderness. (The verse is repeated—"It is also taught"—because first Rava uses it for his explanation, and then the verse is brought in to prove the point about God.) Rava comments on the strange language of the verse, that God wants the Israelites to *know* that God has consecrated them. In other words, God doesn't just give the great gift of Shabbat but announces it first. The connection with the *mishkan* is, apparently, that God expects the Shabbat to be observed even by the builders of the Sanctuary. The Shabbat may be one of the great treasures in God's storehouse, but the

The Lord spoke to Moses: See, I have singled out by name Bezalel son of Uri son of Hur, of the tribe of Judah. I have endowed him with a divine spirit of skill, ability, and knowledge in every kind of craft; to make designs for work in gold, silver, and copper, to cut stones for setting and to carve wood—to work in every kind of craft. . . . And the Lord said to Moses: Speak to the

recipients, Israel, must be willing to accept it. If it is not seen as a treasure, it will be a wasted gift.

Since a child will probably not remember to tell his mother, Rabban Shimon ben Gamliel teaches that we must inform the child's mother when we give the youngster bread. Yet, there must be a child-proof means of informing her. Abaye recommends putting on oil and paint (probably a blue eye makeup that was commonly used). The mother will surely notice these, ask the child, and find out that he has recently eaten bread. However, these cosmetics were used in forms of witchcraft, and therefore fell into disuse by the Jews. In this case, Rav Papa recommends that we take some of the food itself and rub it onto the child. A youngster who returns home with bread crumbs all over will undoubtedly be asked about it.

In the first section of the Gemara, Rava records the teaching of Rav, with a biblical verse as the proof. In the second and parallel account, the proof is in a clever story about the giving of a gift. (It is possible that these two stories originated in the same incident.) Rav Ḥisda announces that he will give a gift (two oxen fit for presentation to the *kohanim* in the Temple) to anyone who can teach him a saying by his mentor, Rav, that he had never heard before. The answer is ironic, for Rava responds by quoting a teaching of Rav on *giving gifts:* One must announce a gift in public before giving it. This humor was not lost on the editors of the Talmud. Rava uses Rav Ḥisda's challenge, and Rav's teaching about gifts, not only to instruct others but also to receive a gift for himself! Rava, however, is a bit puzzled that Rav Ḥisda would give away two oxen for an original saying by Rav. Rav Ḥisda's answer, "A thing is precious to its wearer," seems to mean that only one who "wears" the words of his teacher truly cherishes them. Rav Ḥisda is one such person. In directing his words to Rava, Rav Ḥisda is also complimenting his colleague Rava who finds Rav's words equally precious.

Israelite people and say: Nevertheless, you must keep My sabbaths, for this is a sign between Me and you throughout the ages, that you may know that I the Lord have consecrated you. (Exodus 31:1-5, 12-13) •

D'RASH

Most of us want gifts. We enjoy receiving them—for birthdays, graduations, and other special occasions. Yet, we know that some gifts are simply unneeded or unwanted. Each of us likely has one such item stored in a closet or sitting on a shelf—unopened, unused, and collecting dust. Officers of nonprofit organizations tell stories of receiving countless unusable donations. For example, people frequently drop off old school textbooks at libraries. These volumes are not only unusable; they are also a disposal problem. In the end, such "gifts" end up costing the recipient much time and expense. Often, the donor expects a letter attesting that the contribution was worth a great deal of money.

At the same time, we have received—and given—enough gifts to know that we cannot possibly inform the recipient of *every* present beforehand. Nonetheless, as a general principle, the words of Rava bar Meḥasya, that a gift should be wanted by the recipient, are sound. Rava's words can apply equally to other "gifts" that we give. Notification in advance is advisable. When we "dish out" advice to a friend, we think of it as helpful, but advice, like a gift, should be wanted. Doesn't the advice we receive from others go farther when they first say to us: "Would you like my comments about your dress?" "Can I share with you a thought about your report?" "Would you mind my being frank about this plan?"

Whether we are giving another a birthday gift or words of wisdom, we should strive to make sure that we inform the recipient. Doing less may leave our gift or favor unusable and unwanted. Informing another means that the gift can be both given and received in the same welcome spirit.

מַעֲלִין בַּקֹּדֶשׁ וְאֵין מוֹרִידִין

We raise up in matters of holiness, not bring down.

TEXT

Shabbat 21b

Our Rabbis taught: "The mitzvah of Hanukkah—a light for a man and his household. Those who are particular—a light for each and every person. Those who are extremely particular—Bet Shammai says: 'On the first day light eight; from then on, continue to decrease.' Bet Hillel says: 'On the first day light one; from then on continue to add.'" Ulla said: "Two Amoraim in the West, Rabbi Yosé bar Avin and Rabbi Yosé bar Zavida, disagreed. One said: 'The reason of Bet Shammai is that it corresponds to the days that are left, and the reason of Bet Hillel is that it corresponds to the days that are past.' The other said: 'The reason of Bet Shammai is that it corresponds to the bulls [offered] on the festival [of Sukkot], and the reason of Bet Hillel is that we raise up in matters of holiness, not bring down.'"

CONTEXT

Though the lighting of the Hanukkah menorah is such a well-known ritual, we read in the Gemara that there were four different traditions of how it was to be done. The basic method was to kindle one light each night of the festival: the first night, one light; then on the second night, again only one light was kindled. The second method was a variation of the first, but each *individual* kindled one light, every night. The last two methods are those of Bet Hillel and Bet Shammai. Bet Hillel set the custom that we follow to this day. Bet Shammai practiced that custom, but in reverse.

Two explanations are brought for the different practices of the two schools. Bet Shammai's lighting eight candles the first day and gradually decreasing the lights reminds us of how many days are left in the holiday; Bet Hillel's starting with one and then increasing highlights which day we are on. Additionally, the decreasing candles parallel the decreasing number of bulls sacrificed during Sukkot. (The connection between Hanukkah and Sukkot is interesting: Both are observed for eight days. In addition, after the Maccabees liberated and rededicated the Temple, they celebrated the Sukkot festival, because they had been unable to celebrate it while in the wilderness, fighting.) Bet Hillel had a philosophical basis for its custom: In matters of holiness, in other

On the fifteenth day of the seventh month [the festival of Sukkot], you shall observe a sacred occasion. . . . You shall present a burnt offering, an offering by fire of pleasing odor to the Lord: Thirteen bulls of the herd. . . . Second day: Twelve bulls of the herd. . . . Third day: Eleven bulls. . . . Fourth day: Ten bulls. . . . Fifth day: Nine bulls. . . . Sixth day: Eight bulls. . . . Seventh day: Seven bulls. . . . On the eighth day you shall hold a solemn gathering. . . . You shall present a burnt offering, an offering by fire of pleasing odor to the Lord; one bull. . . . (Numbers 29:12-36) •

words, in things relating to God and religion, it was important to "raise up," rather than bring down. Bet Shammai's practice makes us feel that the ritual is dwindling and disappearing; Bet Hillel's custom leaves us with a sense of growth and strength.

D'RASH

It is human nature to be excited and enthusiastic at the outset about something new. Kids get a new toy and cannot tear themselves away from it for a second. Adults make New Year's resolutions to lose weight or to stop smoking and are "gung-ho" about sticking to the program. A new president takes office and the people and the press are caught-up in the good feelings of the "honeymoon period."

Yet, it is also human nature to quickly grow bored, complacent, or forgetful of the intense feelings that we had not too long ago. The child leaves the favorite toy in the closet and moves on to something else. The temptation to eat a rich dessert or to smoke that one cigarette are just too much for us. We soon take out our frustrations and disappointments on our leaders and mercilessly criticize and complain. The enthusiasm we once had is gone, and we fall back into our old patterns and behaviors.

The Rabbis understood human behavior and our propensity to get bored rather easily. They knew that we would be more excited about Hanukkah on the first night than we would be on the last. This may be why Bet Hillel, in designing the menorah ritual, came up with the brilliant suggestion of increasing the number of lights each night. They recognized that as our natural enthusiasm would begin to wane, our excitement and interest could be piqued by having us look forward to a menorah filled with brilliantly burning wicks at the end of the holiday week. Interestingly (and not coincidentally), the word Hanukkah means "rededication"; it signifies when the Maccabees came back to restore the desecrated Temple and to recommit themselves to all that it stood for. The message of "We raise up in matters of holiness . . ." is that we must rededicate ourselves to the things in our lives that are of ultimate importance.

Bet Hillel anticipated where and when the let-downs would come, and it planned ahead to compensate for them. Instead of allowing a toy to collect dust in a chest, a child can be taught the lessons of sharing and giving by being encouraged to present it to another child. Turning to a support group for assistance can be a source of great strength for someone tempted by things that can hurt them. A president can plan new initiatives at different milestones that can bring new excitement and enthusiasm to the nation.

The Rabbis counseled us to go against our nature and to strive to ascend in matters of holiness: Fight the complacency, struggle with the boredom, wrestle with the waning commitment. Make every effort to do better, not worse. Don't be satisfied to stay at the status quo. Try whenever possible to go up in matters of holiness.

אֵין מִקְרָא יוֹצֵא מִידֵי פְּשׁוּטוֹ

A verse never loses its contextual meaning.

TEXT

Shabbat 63a

Mishnah *(6:4): A man should not go out with a sword, a bow, a shield, a lance, or a spear, and if he did go out, he is liable a sin-offering. Rabbi Eliezer says: "These are his ornaments." But the Sages say: "They are harmful, as it is written: 'And they shall beat their swords into ploughshares and their spears into pruning hooks; nation shall not take up sword against nation; they shall never again know war' [Isaiah 2:4]."*
Gemara: *Abaye said to Rav Dimi—some say to Rav Avya—and some say Rav Yosef to Rav Dimi—and some say to Rav Avya—and some say Abaye to Rav Yosef: "What is the prooftext that Rabbi Eliezer said that they are ornaments? As it is written: 'Gird your sword upon your thigh, O hero, in your splendor and glory' [Psalms 45:4]." Rav Kahana said to Mar son of Rav Huna: "This is speaking about words of Torah!" He said to him: "A verse never loses its contextual meaning."*

CONTEXT

The previous Mishnah listed objects (like certain jewelry) that a woman would likely wear and which may not be carried outside on Shabbat. This would be a violation of one of the traditional Shabbat prohibitions, carrying from domain to domain. This Mishnah continues the theme, listing objects that a man would likely wear. The Sages argue that these are weapons and, thus, prohibited. Rabbi Eliezer, however, sees them as ornaments. Just as a woman is allowed to wear her jewelry on Shabbat, so too a man may wear his ornaments—a sword, a bow, a shield, a lance, or a spear—in the public domain on Shabbat.

One of the objects of jewelry mentioned in the previous Mishnah is a "golden city," perhaps a golden pendant with a picture of Jerusalem etched into it. (Recent research shows this to be a golden tiara.) There is a famous story in the Talmud (Nedarim *50a) about Rabbi Akiva and a "golden city" tiara. Before he was a famous scholar and teacher, Akiva was a poor shepherd working for Kalba Savua (also called Bar Kalba Savua), one of the richest men in Jerusalem. The daughter of Kalba Savua,*

The discussion in the Gemara asks for proof from a verse, for a rabbinic argument is stronger with biblical substantiation. Thus, the verse from Psalms is cited. However, this verse was already known for its metaphoric, homiletical meaning. According to Rav Kahana, the "hero" is really a scholar, and his weapon, the "sword," is Torah. He is answered by Mar who, while not denying the possibility of this metaphoric reading of the verse, asserts that "sword" means not only "Torah," its assigned meaning in the Midrash, but also a weapon, its simple, contextual meaning in the psalm. Thus, Mar can answer Rav Kahana: A verse, even when used for a sermonic purpose, still retains its obvious meaning in the context.

D'RASH

The midrashic process of interpreting biblical verses, a traditional rabbinic approach to Scripture, often assigns specific symbolic meaning to certain words. For example, nourishment words (water, milk) are frequently taken as referring to Torah, since it sustains us. The love poetry of Song of Songs is seen not simply as the yearning of a man for a woman, but as a metaphor for the love of God for the Jewish people.

The traditional midrashic form of interpretation takes many of these terms and ideas and assigns them meaning on a purely symbolic level. Mar's reminder is that we should not lose sight of the original verse. Freud expressed a similar idea when (in a story which is likely apocryphal) he was asked if the cigar in his mouth was not a phallic symbol. To this query, Freud supposedly quipped: "Sometimes a cigar is just a cigar." That is, despite the fact that he had expounded that there is usually a deeper meaning to things, sometimes there is *no* deeper meaning, and a cigar is not a phallic symbol but only a cigar.

A youngster is caught defacing property by spray-painting swastikas. When arrested by the police, he denies any hatred or anti-Jewish prejudice in his actions. The teen claims: "I'm not an anti-Semite. I'm not a neo-Nazi. I disagree with what the Nazis did to the Jews. I just like the shape of the swastika, and I like painting it on walls." To this young man, we can respond that symbols never really lose their meaning, that the message is wrapped up in the medium. The swastika, like German uniforms and flags, will always represent Nazi values. Even when one claims that the symbol is unimportant, we know that it still carries its message.

Today, we often hear criticism of the music that people, especially teenagers, listen to. The lyrics are filled with hate and bigotry. The songs express ideas and values contrary to those of our religious system, our community, or family. Yet, when asked about these songs, the teen may answer: "I don't

Raḥel, found something appealing in Akiva and promised to marry him if he dedicated his life to the study house. Akiva agreed, but Kalba Savua disapproved of this ignorant shepherd named Akiva. Kalba Savua cut off his daughter from her family money. She and Akiva lived in poverty, so much so that in the winter they slept on straw to keep warm. One time, as Akiva picked straw from Raḥel's hair, he told her: "If I could, I would buy you a Jerusalem of gold!" Of course, Akiva went on to become one of the greatest sages of the Talmudic era.

In the days of the Talmud, love of Jerusalem was shown by wearing an image of the city on one's jewelry. Today, we are more likely to sing about the city, and "Jerusalem of Gold" refers not to the tiara but to the city itself. This is largely because of the Naomi Shemer song "Yerushalayim shel Zahav," or "Jerusalem of Gold," written in 1967 only days before the Six-Day War. Naomi Shemer used the talmudic image as the basis for her lyrics. ●

listen to the lyrics. I just like the music." To this, we can respond that just as a verse never loses its contextual meaning, so too a song cannot be taken out of the context of its words. The music may be exciting and vibrant, but if the song is malicious or amoral, it is dangerous.

כָּל מָקוֹם שֶׁאָסְרוּ חֲכָמִים	Wherever the Sages prohibited
מִפְּנֵי מַרְאִית עַיִן	something because of
אֲפִלּוּ בְּחַדְרֵי חֲדָרִים	appearance's sake,
אָסוּר	it is also prohibited in private.

TEXT

Shabbat 64b-65a

Rav Yehudah said in the name of Rav: "Wherever the Sages prohibited something because of appearance's sake, it is also prohibited in private." It is taught: ". . . nor with a bell, even if it is plugged up." But in another place it was taught: "The bell around its neck can be plugged up, and he can walk it in the courtyard." This is a difference of opinion among the Tannaim, as it is taught: "They are spread out in the sun, but not where everyone can see them. Rabbi Eliezer and Rabbi Shimon forbid it."

A donkey may not go out [on Shabbat] with a blanket that is not tied on [before Shabbat], nor with a bell, even if it is plugged up, nor with a yoke fashioned like a ladder around its neck, nor with a thong around its foot. (Mishnah Shabbat *5:4*) •

But an animal can go out [on Shabbat] with a bandage on a wound, or with splints on a fracture, or with the after-birth hanging down, and the bell around its neck can be plugged up and he can walk it in the courtyard. (Shabbat *53a*) •

One whose clothes slipped into the water on the road can walk in them and need not fear. When he reaches the outer courtyard, he spreads them out in the sun, but not where everyone can see. (Mishnah Shabbat *22:4*) •

CONTEXT

Much of *Masekhet Shabbat* deals with what is permitted and prohibited on the Sabbath. Some activities were forbidden because they were violations of the prohibition against working on the seventh day. Other things which were not actual violations were also prohibited because they *appeared* to be violations. This is known in Hebrew as *mar'it ayin,* "what the eye sees." The Rabbis were afraid that someone not well-versed in the law might draw the wrong conclusions from what was seen. Watching a person do an act that appeared to be a prohibited activity, one might assume that either, a) the forbidden act was actually permitted (and the observer would go out and do that prohibited act); or b) the person doing that act (who is actually committing no breach of law) is a flagrant sinner. To prevent these incorrect conclusions, the Rabbis established a category of law whereby certain otherwise permitted acts were prohibited because of "appearance's sake."

The first example presented by the Talmud is the prohibition on Shabbat to walk a donkey with a bell tied around its neck. It is prohibited to ring a bell on Shabbat. The Rabbis extended the prohibition so that even if the bell was plugged up and produced no sound, it was still prohibited to put it on a donkey and take the animal for a walk on Shabbat. People might assume the person was taking the donkey to market to sell it—a clear violation of the laws of Shabbat. (It was the custom to "dress up" an animal before selling it by placing a bell around its neck.)

This led the Rabbis to the principle that whatever the Sages prohibited because of appearance's sake was also prohibited in private. But the principle is challenged by another teaching that specifically allowed the plugged-up bell on the donkey, as long as the donkey was kept within one's own courtyard (where no one would see it).

These two conflicting traditions are apparently unreconcilable. They go back to an early disagreement among the *Tannaim,* the Rabbis of the mishnaic period (the first and second centuries). One viewpoint held that clothing that fell into water on Shabbat could be spread out in the sun, but only in an area where people would not see it. The Rabbis were afraid that people seeing clothes left out to dry on Shabbat would wrongly conclude that it was permitted to wash clothing on Shabbat. Rabbi Eliezer and Rabbi Shimon prohibit even that, following the principle that what the Sages prohibited for appearance's sake was forbidden even in private.

D'RASH

A married man is seen at a romantic little restaurant having a candlelit dinner with a woman who is not his wife. Within days, the community is all abuzz about the "affair." Only later is it discovered that the other woman was actually his sister, in for a visit from out of town.

A woman buys an expensive new luxury car just one month after becoming the treasurer of the elementary school PTA. People begin to ask jokingly if the two facts are somehow related, but the kidding becomes serious when someone claims to have heard that significant funds are missing from the bank account. Only after the treasurer is accused of embezzling does it come out that the rumors were false and that the woman had recently received a modest inheritance upon the death of her mother.

Congregants spot the local rabbi walking into a fast-food restaurant during the afternoon break on Yom Kippur. By the time services conclude that evening, many of the members have already heard a story of how the rabbi ate nonkosher food on the holiest day of the year, a fast day. At the next synagogue board meeting, the embarrassed rabbi has to admit to indeed entering the restaurant, but to relieve a weak bladder.

The concern about *mar'it ayin* is a troubling one: Why should someone who is doing the right thing have to be worried about what someone else mistakingly thinks? Yet as we see in the above examples, "what the eye sees" can lead to a wrecked marriage, to criminal charges, and to a ruined reputation. In warning us to be sensitive to such things, the Rabbis teach us about the world—not as it should be, but as it is. We are reminded that no matter where we are, someone may well be watching us. The Rabbis would also teach us that no matter where we are, Someone *is* always watching us.

פְּסִיק רֵישָׁא וְלֹא יָמוּת

Can you cut off its head without it dying?

TEXT

Shabbat 75a

Our Rabbis taught: "One who catches a snail and crushes it is liable for one [sin-offering]." Rabbi Yehudah says: "Crushing falls into the category of threshing." They said to him: "Crushing does not *fall into the category of threshing."*

Rava said: "What is the reason of the Rabbis? They hold that threshing applies only to things grown in the ground." Maybe he is also liable for taking a life! Rabbi Yoḥanan said: "When he crushed it, it was already dead." Rava said: "Even if you say that it was alive when he crushed it, he was intent on something else when its life was taken." But did not Abaye and Rava both say that Rabbi Shimon admits "Can you cut off its head without it dying?" Here the case is different—it is better for him while it [the snail] is alive, because the dye is clearer.

"Hillazon in rabbinical literature is a land or sea snail (Sanhedrin 91a). Among the latter there are species in whose bodies is a gland containing a clear liquid, which when it comes into contact with the air becomes greenish: this is tekhelet which, after the addition of various chemicals, receives its purple color, the "royal purple" of literature." (Encyclopaedia Judaica, *volume 15, p. 914*) *The dye of the* ḥillazon *was used, among other things, for the "thread of blue" in the tzitzit or fringes attached to four-cornered garments like the tallit. (Numbers 15:38)* •

CONTEXT

The Mishnah lists thirty-nine major categories of labor that are forbidden on Shabbat. Among them is hunting a deer (and by extension, all forms of hunting and trapping). The Rabbis here are debating the violations involved in catching a particular species of snail that was the source of much sought-after dye. The shell of the snail first had to be crushed and broken so that the dye could be squeezed from the snail. The Rabbis teach that doing this on Shabbat violated one prohibition, and thus a single sin-offering had to be brought to the Temple. Rabbi Yehudah holds that a second violation was involved: The crushing of the shell would fall into the classification of "threshing," another of the thirty-nine categories of forbidden labor. (Both threshing and crushing required force to break and remove an outer shell in order to get the sought-after inner product.) The Rabbis disagree, saying that "threshing" applies only to things like wheat that grow from the ground.

A question is posed: If crushing the snail is not the same as threshing, is it not the same as "slaughtering," which *is* among the thirty-nine labors? Rabbi Yoḥanan answers that in this case, the snail was already dead; the only violation is hunting. Rava holds that even if the snail *was* killed, the person who crushed it is not liable, because he never intended to kill it, only to extract the dye. This seems to contradict a principle that Rava himself, along with Abaye, stated on another occasion: A person cannot say "I wanted only to cut off the animal's head; I never intended that the animal should die!" Rabbi Shimon is the authority who held that a labor was permitted, even if it resulted in a forbidden action, so long as that forbidden action was unintentional. (For example, walking on the grass on Shabbat is permitted, even though the act of walking may cause the grass to be uprooted, so long as it was *not* the intent of the person to uproot the grass.) But even Rabbi Shimon admits that if the forbidden result was *inevitable,* then the labor *is* forbidden. Cutting off the animal's head *always* leads to death, regardless of the intention, and is therefore forbidden.

The contradiction between Rava's two statements is resolved by saying that not only is the death of the snail unintentional, it is counter-productive. The quality of the dye is much better when it comes from a living snail.

D'RASH

A teenager boils a pot of water to make hot chocolate. After the water is ready and the drink is made, the youngster puts the kettle back on the flame and leaves the house. The water eventually boils off, the pot burns, and the kitchen catches fire. When the parents question the teen on the lack of responsibility, the reply is: "What did I do wrong? All I did was put water on the stove. Is that a crime?" By itself, of course not. But an unwatched pot of water will *always* boil off and then burn.

A laborer from the Department of Public Works digs a three-foot hole in the sidewalk, trying to get to some gas lines. At the end of the day, he leaves the pit uncovered, without warning signs or barricades. After dark, an elderly woman falls into the pit and is severely injured. The worker asks: "What did I do wrong? I just dug a pit! That's what I'm paid to do." Combine the innocent digging of a pit with the lack of protection and the coming of darkness, and there is a real disaster in the making.

Physicists in Germany during World War II are engaged by the government to experiment with rocket science. They turn over their research, which is used by Germany to build missiles that deliver payloads of death and destruction hundreds of miles away. After Germany's defeat, these scientists are tried for war crimes. They plead not guilty. "We were only involved in theoretical scientific issues. What the government and the army did with it is not our fault and not our responsibility."

The Rabbis take a tougher stance. One cannot avoid responsibility by saying: "It's not my fault! What *I* did was okay. I'm not to blame if something else happened. I never intended *that*. I never in a million years thought . . ." It's ludicrous to say, "I cut off its head, but I never meant it to die!" Just as ludicrous is the way that so many people refuse to see the consequences of their actions.

אֵין מְבִיאִין רְאָיָה מִן הַשּׁוֹטִים

We do not bring proof from fools!

TEXT

Shabbat 104b

Mishnah *(12:4): One who writes in one act of forgetfulness is liable. If he wrote with ink, paint, red paint, gum, vitriol, or anything else that leaves a mark, on two corner walls or on two pages of a tablet which are read together, he is liable. He who writes on his flesh is liable. He who scratches on his flesh—Rabbi Eliezer makes him liable for a sin offering, while the Sages exempt him.*

Gemara: *"He who scratches on his flesh." It was taught: Rabbi Eliezer said to the Sages: "Didn't Ben S'tada bring witchcraft from Egypt using scratches on his flesh?" They said to him: "He was a fool, and we do not bring proof from fools!"*

CONTEXT

The Mishnah teaches who is liable to bring a sin offering, a type of sacrifice given for an accidental transgression, in this case, of the Shabbat. For example, what if one *forgot* that it was Shabbat and wrote something, in violation of a Shabbat prohibition? Is that person liable to bring a sin offering? First, it must be "one act of forgetfulness," that is, writing at least two letters at once. (Two letters are the equivalent of the shortest possible Hebrew word and, thus, the minimal requirement for breaking the law of Shabbat.) The next Mishnah will teach that the Rabbis exempt from bringing a sin offering one who forgot that it was Shabbat early in the day and wrote a letter, and then later in the day forgot again and wrote another letter.

Second, one is liable for a Shabbat violation only for writing that is permanent. Thus, all of the writing materials—"ink, paint, red paint, gum, vitriol, or anything else that leaves a mark"—are mentioned. Each leaves a specific type of permanent mark.

What if someone wrote on two adjoining walls, one letter on each wall? (Rashi says, for example, one on the eastern and one on the northern.) In such a case, that person is "liable" and must bring a sin offering. The same is true in the case of two leaves of a tablet (like a sales ledger).

This leads to the disagreement between Rabbi Eliezer and the Rabbis over writing on one's flesh (as opposed to writing

Ben S'tada is an obscure figure mentioned several times in the Talmud. In Sanhedrin *67a, we are told that he was taken out from Lydda on Pesaḥ eve and hanged. His mother is identified as Miriam. Given these two facts, some have speculated that Ben S'tada is another name for Jesus, though this seems impossible based on the chronology: Ben S'tada lived a century after Jesus. Apparently, he was a figure known in rabbinic circles for having stolen some of the secrets of Egyptian sorcery and witchcraft on an ancient version of a "crib sheet." He was also not very well respected; the Gemara in* Sanhedrin *describes his lineage in particularly crude terms. These few particulars leave more unknown than known about Ben S'tada—except for the fact that the Rabbis were sure that he was a fool!* ●

on paper or parchment with a type of ink). Is such scratching considered permanent writing? Rabbi Eliezer says that it is, bringing proof from Ben S'tada, a man who (supposedly) smuggled the secrets of Egyptian witchcraft out of that country by scratching the words onto his skin. The Rabbis respond to Rabbi Eliezer that Ben S'tada's actions are no proof, for it was known that Ben S'tada was a fool.

D'RASH

Many of us have had the experience of seeing an incredible newspaper headline: "12 U.S. Senators Are Aliens!" "Woman Murdered by Fur Coat!" or "UFO Lands in Middle of Wedding Ceremony!" Studies have shown that while some people actually believe the headlines or the stories behind them, most know that these tabloids are sources of entertainment, rather than of factual news. Because the origin of such stories is a disreputable newspaper, the veracity of the story is automatically suspect.

The Rabbis are reminding us to be a bit skeptical when reading, to consider not only *what* is being said but also *who* is saying it. Ben S'tada was unacceptable on both counts. Not only was he a well-known fool, but he also taught witchcraft. The combination of person (Ben S'tada) and topic (sorcery) dooms the evidence that Rabbi Eliezer attempts to introduce. The Rabbis, thus, approach this topic, as many, with a dose of healthy skepticism.

In recent years, books have been written asserting that the Holocaust never took place or that it was a minor case of prejudice, not the genocide that has been accounted and documented for a generation. Most knowledgeable people approach this "historic revisionism" with similar healthy skepticism. What is the "truth" that is being presented? Haven't hundreds, if not thousands, of books already been written documenting not only the atrocities of the Holocaust but also its extent? Don't the "sources" and "documents" the revisionists bring in as proof contradict what is common knowledge? Furthermore, *who* is writing these materials? Are they world-renowned scholars, historians at prestigious universities? Most of the time, these diatribes are penned by second-class teachers without reputable credentials. Unfortunately, these works are often popular, but they are not credible by either standard.

Similarly, books have appeared "proving" that Jews were central to the American slave trade in the eighteenth and nineteenth centuries. The authors seek to show that Jews continue to enslave blacks through economic means. A similar skepticism towards such books is healthy. Who are these authors? What are their "facts"? Why is it that most respected scholars have disavowed such works as political ax-grinding? What is the political agenda of such authors?

When both the message and the messenger are suspect, we can refer to our Gemara and reject such "proof." The Rabbis set a precedent centuries ago, one which we would do well to follow today.

כְּחָתָן בֵּין אֲבֵלִים . . .	Like a groom among mourners . . .
כְּאָבֵל בֵּין חֲתָנִים	Like a mourner among grooms.

TEXT

Shabbat 114a

Rabbi Shimon ben Lakish said: "These garments are clothes [olaryin] that come from overseas." Does this mean to say that they are white? Did not Rabbi Yannai say to his sons: "My sons, do not bury me in white garments, nor in black garments. White—in case I lack merit, and I will be like a groom among mourners. Black—in case I do merit, and I will be like a mourner among grooms. But bury me in clothes [olaryin] that come from overseas."

Olaryin (*read by some as* olarin *or* ulirin) *is a word of questionable origin, perhaps from the Greek. It has been described by some as cloaks worn in the bathhouse, by others as royal cloaks or robes, perhaps used at the bathhouse. What is clear is that these clothes would be suitable for shrouds as well.* •

CONTEXT

The previous Mishnah speaks of folding clothes on Shabbat, teaching that items for use on Shabbat may be folded on Shabbat, but not items for use after Shabbat, in preparation for a weekday. This Mishnah leads the Gemara to a discussion of clothing in general and the rules of dress for scholars in specific. The text next brings in a number of traditions about scholars, who they are and how the community must respect them. Each section is an extension of the previous idea, though farther away from the original question of folding on Shabbat. Thus, the progression of thought is 1) folding clothes on Shabbat, 2) clothing, 3) a scholar's clothes, 4) definition of a scholar, 5) respect due a scholar.

One of the terms that the Gemara uses for some scholars is *banaim,* "builders." These are defined as people who "engage in improving the world all their lives," that is, *builders* of a better world. Since the Gemara has defined the people who are *banaim* and the deference due them, it also attempts to define the clothing of *banaim.* Thus, Rabbi Shimon ben Lakish (known as Resh Lakish) states that among the clothing of *banaim* are garments called *olaryin.* What are *olaryin?* Based on the story of Rabbi Yannai, it appears that these are garments that are imported and are neither black nor white. Rabbi Yannai asks to be buried in these so that he may feel comfortable and not be out of place.

Rabbi Shimon ben Lakish is often known as Resh Lakish, Resh being an acronym for Rabbi Shimon. Resh Lakish was a third-century Palestinian Amora and was the brother-in-law of Rabbi Yoḥanan, head of the famous study house in Tiberias. While he sometimes disagreed with his

Rabbi Yannai may be using "sons" less in the sense of biological children and more as those who would bear the responsibility for burial, the sage's pupils. Rabbi Yannai, though a great scholar and generous teacher, is worried about his own fate after his death. He does not want to be out of place. If he "merits," that is, is rewarded after death with Heaven, where all are dressed in white, then he would not want to be the only one in black. If, however, he does not merit and is sent to Gehinnom or hell, then Rabbi Yannai would certainly not want to be the only one in white! Note that white is seen as pure and heavenly, black as evil and hellish.

D'RASH

Who among us hasn't, like Rabbi Yannai, feared being out of place? While each of us wants to be an individual, none of us wants to stick out like a sore thumb. Rabbi Yannai's words aptly reflect this anxiety. Rabbi Yannai is talking about planning for important events in life, and by asking to be buried neither in white nor in black in preparation for two possible eventualities is thinking ahead to save himself embarrassment, in this case, after death. Wearing *olaryin* will allow him to be neither like a groom among mourners nor like a mourner among grooms.

Many of us have had the experience, at one time or another, of walking into a room and feeling inappropriately dressed. A friend says, "Let's go out for a casual dinner," but her definition of casual and ours do not mesh. Because of the way we are dressed, we end up fidgeting in our seat all night long, like a mourner among grooms. We may remember the one man who, for whatever reason, came to a black-tie reception wearing a light-colored suit. Perhaps he could not afford a tuxedo; maybe he misread the invitation. Whatever the reason, he stood out like a groom among mourners.

We can avoid embarrassment by planning ahead, not only in how we dress but in other kinds of preparations. In order to enjoy the opera and not feel out of place, you read the libretto to understand the plot and story-line. Similarly, if you are invited to a life-cycle ritual in a different religious tradition, or even in your own tradition, you might benefit and feel more comfortable by finding out the customs of manners and dress beforehand.

Suppose you are invited to a *simḥat bat,* the new ritual that has developed over past decades as a special way of welcoming a baby girl into the Jewish community. If this is the first *simḥat bat* you are attending, you may feel apprehensive about feeling out of place. A little research, however, will

brother-in-law and teacher, he was also venerated by him. Tractate Bava Metzia *84a tells the story of how Resh Lakish studied with Rabbi Yoḥanan, only to be insulted by him when he disagreed with his teacher in a matter of law. Rabbi Yoḥanan said of Resh Lakish: "A thief knows his thievery!" Some see this as a reference to Resh Lakish's life prior to his studying Torah. According to several sources, he had spent his early years outside the sphere of rabbinic Judaism, apparently as a circus entertainer or gladiator in the Roman theater, a common way for poor young men to earn a livelihood. It is not certain, however, if this biographical fact is true. Nonetheless, the Gemara relates that Rabbi Yoḥanan regretted this insult and, in refusing to be comforted over the death of Rabbi Shimon ben Lakish, cried out on his own deathbed: "Where are you, son of Lakisha? Where are you, son of Lakisha?"* •

help increase the comfort level. "How long does a *simḥat bat* last? How formal is it? Will I need any preparation? Are there others with whom I can share my anxieties?"

We can never be 100 percent sure that we'll feel comfortable where we are. Life is just too complicated for that. Still, we want to feel as much at ease as possible, wherever we are. By properly thinking and planning ahead, we can make sure that we fit in and that we do not feel like either a groom among mourners or a mourner among grooms.

אֵלוּ וָאֵלוּ דִּבְרֵי אֱלֹהִים חַיִּים

Both are the words of the living God.

TEXT

Eruvin 13b

Rabbi Abba said in the name of Shmuel: "For three years there was a dispute between Bet Shammai and Bet Hillel, the former saying: 'The law follows our *views, and the latter saying: 'The law follows* our *views.' A voice from heaven proclaimed: 'Both are the words of the living God but the law follows Bet Hillel.'" Since both are the words of the living God, why did Bet Hillel merit having the law follow their views? Because they were kind and modest; they used to teach their views and the views of Bet Shammai; moreover, they used to mention Bet Shammai's views before their own.*

CONTEXT

Hillel and Shammai were the two great rabbinic leaders at the end of the first century, B.C.E. The disciples of these two men over the next century were known, respectively, as Bet ("The House of") Hillel and Bet Shammai. These two groups shaped much of Judaism as we know it today during the critical years just prior to, and immediately after, the destruction of the Temple in the year 70 C.E. Over three hundred of their halakhic disputes are recorded throughout the Talmud. Many scholars used to see a philosophical or sociological basis for the legal disagreements. Bet Hillel is often more lenient and may have represented the lower classes. Bet Shammai usually takes a stricter position, and its members may have come from the wealthier upper classes. However, this approach is disputed today.

In our section, Bet Hillel and Bet Shammai have been arguing for a considerable amount of time over whose views best reflected God's will. The answer comes from a *bat kol,* a "small voice," which is understood to be a message from God in heaven. This message could come as an actual voice, or it could be revealed in a dream. Once prophecy came to an end, a *bat kol* was the sole means of receiving direct communication from God.

Both Bet Hillel and Bet Shammai believed that in their opinions and legal rulings, they were uncovering and transmitting the will of God. The Written Law, the Torah given by God to Moses on Mount Sinai, was often imprecise or even

Another of the discussions and disagreements of Bet Hillel and Bet Shammai found on the very same page in the Talmud:

> *For two and a half years, Bet Shammai and Bet Hillel disagreed: One said: "It would have been better if humans had not been created." The other said: "It is better that humans have been created." They voted and concluded: "It would have been better if humans had not been created. But now that humans have been created, let them search their [past] actions." Others say: "Let them look into their [future] deeds."* •

silent about many details and issues. What the Rabbis attempted to do in the Oral Law (the Midrash and the Talmud) was to try to discover what God had in mind. They struggled to understand the Torah and to apply its teachings to their own times. They often came up with very different interpretations. But, as we see here, they deeply believed that each interpretation reflected God's truth. Nevertheless, the law—what was to be normative, accepted behavior—had to be fixed; otherwise the unity of the people would be destroyed by numerous practices. More often than not, Bet Hillel's views were chosen not because Bet Hillel was right and Bet Shammai was wrong. Rather, Bet Hillel's views became law, according to the Talmud, as a reward for the way they treated those they disagreed with.

D'RASH

We live in a world that is very complex. In order to try to make sense of it, we often fall into the trap of simplifying things. Issues are black or white, people are good or bad, countries are allies or enemies, statements are true or false. But experience teaches us that life is not so simple. Truth is to be found in many places, in many shades.

There is a well-known tale called "The Blind Men and the Elephant." Four men, unable to see, are led to an animal they know nothing about. One touches the trunk and concludes that the elephant is like a hose. Another feels the tusks and assumes that the animal is as hard as a rock. The third pats the body, and thinks the beast is like a mountain. The fourth blind man holds the tail and conjures in his mind the image of a rope. Which of the four was right? They all were correct. There was truth in what each thought, but alone, each had only part of the truth. The total story could be discovered if they accounted for their own limitations and sought to share what they knew with their fellows.

There was truth in what Bet Hillel thought and truth in what Bet Shammai thought. Both of their teachings contained the words of the living God. The secret of Bet Hillel's success was that it understood that arrogance and self-righteousness only blind us to discovering the whole truth. By admitting that other people have much to teach us, we open our eyes and see things that were hidden from us before. By recognizing that *our* answers are not the *only* answers, we open ourselves up to learning and understanding. Modesty and humility are the keys that enable us to search for, and find, the subtleties of truth in all places.

מִתּוֹךְ שֶׁלֹּא לִשְׁמָהּ
בָּא לִשְׁמָהּ

Even if for the wrong reason, eventually it will be for the right reason.

TEXT

Pesaḥim 50b

Rava contrasted two verses: "It is written: 'For Your faithfulness is as high as heaven' [Psalms 57:11], but it is also written 'For Your faithfulness is higher than the heavens' [Psalms 108:5]. How is this possible? In the latter case, it refers to those who do [a mitzvah] for the right reason; in the former case, to those who do it for the wrong reason. This follows Rav Yehudah, for Rav Yehudah said in the name of Rav: "A person should always occupy himself with Torah and mitzvot, even if for the wrong reason, for eventually it will be for the right reason."

I will praise You among
the peoples, O Lord;
I will sing a hymn to You
among the nations;
for Your faithfulness is as
high as heaven;
Your steadfastness
reaches to the sky.
Exalt Yourself over the
heavens, O God,
let Your glory be over
all the earth! (Psalms
57:10–12)
I will praise You among
the peoples, O Lord,
sing a hymn to You
among the nations;
for Your faithfulness is
higher than the heavens;
Your steadfastness
reaches to the sky.
Exalt Yourself over the
heavens, O God;
let Your glory be over
all the earth! (Psalms
108:4–5) •

CONTEXT

Rava notices two biblical verses which are identical except for one word. This seeming discrepancy in the book of Psalms allows Rava to ask: Is God's faithfulness *as high as* the heavens (as Psalms 57 attests) or *higher than* the heavens (as Psalms 108 claims)? (The translation uses "Heaven/the heavens," but the verses use the same Hebrew word, *shamayim*, for both. This word can be translated either way.) This inconsistency allows Rava to expound on the verses and make a point.

If one does a mitzvah for the wrong reason, then God's faithfulness to that person is as high as heaven. However, when one performs a mitzvah for the *right* reason and with the correct motivation, then God's faithfulness extends higher than the heavens.

Rav Yehudah explains that it is best that one live a life of Torah and perform mitzvot with the right intentions; but it is better to do a mitzvah even with the wrong intentions than not to do one at all, for "even if for the wrong reason, eventually it will be for the right reason." That is, even if one performs a mitzvah without the proper intent or with totally wrong intent, that person may, by virtue of having done a mitzvah, eventually learn to do the mitzvah for the right reason.

D'RASH

Often, we complain that people who help others do so for the wrong reasons. They act out of self-interest, for publicity, or to be like their neighbors. A man donates $10 million to a hospital less because of a concern for health care and more because he wants to see a new building named after him. A couple spends the afternoon working as volunteers in a local soup kitchen not because they care about feeding the poor or ending hunger, but simply because they have nothing to do one afternoon a week. The charity work fills up their empty time. A high school student works as a "candy striper" in the local hospital not out of any interest in healing the sick or relieving those in pain, but simply because it will look good on her college résumé. Rav Yehudah is reminding us not to be so critical of such people. At least they're *doing* something good—albeit for empty, silly, or selfish reasons. Perhaps next time, their motivation will be purer. At least now, the deed is in place. They can then move on to raise the level of the act, to make it "higher than the heavens."

A woman joins a health club not for the exercise benefits, but because it is the "in" place to go, where the trend-setters are seen. The last thing on her mind is her own physical fitness and health benefits. However, because she is at a place where people are involved with regular exercise, she begins to participate more and more in aerobic activities. While she initially came "to see and be seen," and she still enjoys the company of the trend-setters, she now is benefitting greatly from and enjoying the physical fitness, even if this originally was an incidental reason for her being there.

Jewish tradition has taken a similar approach to the giving of the Law at Sinai. The Israelites are highly praised not only for accepting the Torah, but also for *how* they accepted it. "And they said: 'All that the Lord has spoken we will faithfully do.'(Exodus 24:7)" "We will faithfully do" is actually two Hebrew verbs: *na'aseh,* "we will do," and *v'nishmah,* "we will listen." Together, the meaning is "we will faithfully do," but the Rabbis saw in these verbs a lesson. The Israelites first agreed to do and to practice. Only later would they listen and find out the rationales. Even if they obeyed without knowing why, even if they observed for reasons that would later prove illogical or inexact, the Israelites were first *doing.* The Rabbis saw a great value in their response.

There are few things that we do in our lives for pure reasons. At work or at play, at home or even in the synagogue, much of what we do has some ulterior motive. Rav Yehudah, in the name of Rav, informs us that this is natural. He is reminding us that positive motivations often follow positive actions. We should do these good things, even if for the wrong reasons, because this will train us to do them for the right reasons.

לָא סָמְכִינַן אַנִּיסָּא

We do not rely on a miracle.

TEXT

Pesaḥim 64a-b

Mishnah *(5:5): The Passover offering is slaughtered by three groups, as it says: "And all the assembled congregation of the Israelites shall slaughter it" [Exodus 12:6] —"assembled," "congregation" and "Israelites." When the first group entered, the courtyard was filled, and the doors of the courtyard were closed, and they blew a long note, short notes, and a long note.*

Gemara: *"When the first group entered." It has been said: Abaye said: "We have learned: 'They [the doors] are closed.'" Rava said: "We have learned: 'We close them.'" What's the difference? Here is the difference: Relying on a miracle. Abaye said: "We have learned: 'They are closed,' and whoever got in is in, and we rely on a miracle." But Rava said: "'We close them,' and we do not rely on a miracle."*

The discussion about the sacrificial system of the Temple may seem foreign to us, more like a philosophical argument than a relevant matter of practical Jewish law. In fact, the rules and regulations of the Temple period were no longer relevant to Abaye and Rava, living two to three hundred years after the destruction of the second Temple! Why, then, the concern with how the doors were closed?

First, the Rabbis prayed for and hoped for the rebuilding of the Temple. Their discussions could have practical implications as preparation for the time when the sacrifices would be restored "as in olden days."

In addition, this discussion, like many arguments of the Talmud, is a theoretical one, a practice in reading and interpretation of text. The Rabbis found intellectual challenge in arguing their points back and forth. Furthermore, as we have seen, every disagreement even about a theoretical issue like the closing of the doors reflects differing world views. The Rabbis teach their general attitudes towards important questions from such specific discussions. •

CONTEXT

The Pesaḥ sacrifice that was originally offered as the Israelites left Egypt was later transferred to the Temple ritual. This Mishnah and Gemara are discussing the order for the sacrifice. According to the Mishnah, those offering the sacrifice are divided into three groups, based on the verse from Exodus. To the rabbinic mind, the Hebrew verse seems redundant, and any of the three words—*kahal* (assemblage/assembled), *eidah* (congregation), or *Yisrael* (Israelites)—would have sufficed. According to this reading of the verse, the redundancy is there to prove that three shifts should participate in the sacrifice of the paschal offering, one after the other, while the shofar is sounded.

The disagreement between Abaye and Rava starts with a minute point of Hebrew grammar in the Mishnah's wording. The Mishnah uses a phrase which, because of the nature of Hebrew, is unclear in its intent. The words *na'alu daltot ha-azarah,* "the doors of the courtyard are closed," is as ambiguous in the Hebrew as in the English translation. How do the doors of the courtyard get closed, especially when there will be so many pilgrims in the Temple court on the Pesaḥ holiday? The Hebrew verb, *na'alu,* supports two possible readings. Abaye understands it as *nina'lu,* a passive verb meaning "they are closed." From this inactive verb, Abaye learns that we ourselves do not push the doors shut but let whoever wants to enter the courtyard do so, even if this may be too many people. We rely on a miracle, that is, divine intervention, to insure that the courtyard will not be overcrowded at this time. Rava, however, has a different reading of the Mishnah. He says that the word is to be understood as *no'alin,* an active verb, implying "we close." It is *our* responsibility to close the gates to the Temple courtyard so that only a certain number of people enter. We do not expect divine intervention, nor do we wait for a miracle.

D'RASH

Abaye and Rava bring two different perspectives on the problems we face in life. Abaye presages the modern idiom "God will provide." In a difficult situation, we assume that there will be divine intervention. When the biblical figure Mordecai was confronted by the possible destruction of the Jews of Shushan by Haman, he turned to Esther for help. When she seemed unwilling to assist him, Mordecai sent her the message that she, too, would be destroyed by the wicked Haman, and that if she did not help, "relief and deliverance will come to the Jews from another quarter" (Esther 4:14). Mordecai asks for Esther's help; lacking that, he foresees assistance from some "other quarter." As Ivan Turgenev wrote: "Whatever a man prays for, he prays for a miracle."

Rava offers a different approach. Facing a potential problem, Rava proposes that we act. We do not wait for or expect God's help. If the doors must be closed and overcrowding might be a problem, then it is our responsibility to do something. Rava might say: "The meaning of 'God will provide' is that God provides us with the motivation and the means to get us out of difficult situations."

We see different approaches as we deal with health and medical issues in our lives. Some take a passive approach to medical crises: "A cure will be found. Help will be provided." Mary Baker Eddy founded the Church of Christ, Scientist, home of the Christian Scientists, based on a philosophy that when humans wake to the reality of God as wholly good and all-powerful, healing will follow. Many would see this as a passive approach to medicine. "God will heal."

Most of us, however, assume a more aggressive, active role in health maintenance and the healing of disease. "*We* will find a cure." "I'll do whatever I can to make myself healthy again." We see ourselves as agents of God, not waiting for *God* to send healing, but actively going out and providing it ourselves. In so doing, we are not committing a sacrilege but performing a service, making of ourselves instruments of divine will.

Today, it remains unclear as to how doors in the Temple courtyard were to be closed. It seems unambiguous, however, that the doors to good health and full healing must be opened through conscious activity on our part.

כַּמָּה חֲבִיבָה מִצְוָה בִּשְׁעָתָהּ

How precious is a mitzvah in its proper time.

TEXT

Pesaḥim 65b, 68b

> Mishnah *(6:1): These are the things of the Passover [offering] that override [the laws of] Shabbat: The slaughtering, the sprinkling of the blood, the cleansing of the entrails and the burning of the fat, but the roasting and the rinsing of the entrails do not override [the laws of] Shabbat.*
> Gemara: *It was taught: Rabbi Shimon said: "Come and see how precious is a mitzvah in its proper time, for the burning of the fat and the limbs and the fat-pieces is acceptable all night long, yet we do not wait until dark."*

CONTEXT

When the Temple was in existence in Jerusalem, the festival of Pesaḥ was celebrated by the sacrifice of a paschal lamb. The Mishnah here deals with the question of how that sacrifice was to be performed if Passover began on a Saturday evening. The problem was that so many things had to be done on the day before the holiday to prepare for the festival; yet the day before Passover was Shabbat, when many activities and labors were prohibited. How was this conflict to be dealt with?

The slaughtering of the lamb and the ritual of sprinkling its blood on the altar were to take place, according to the Torah, on the fourteenth of Nisan (the day prior to Passover; in this particular case, the fourteenth is Shabbat). Because the Torah specified the fourteenth, the sacrifice could not be advanced a day to Friday (the thirteenth of Nisan) or delayed a day to Sunday (the fifteenth, the first day of the festival). Once the sacrifice was offered, the cleansing of the entrails had to be done on the same day; postponement until after Shabbat would have resulted in the putrification of the animal's carcass. Consequently, these activities were all done on Saturday, the mitzvah to do them taking precedence over the normal Shabbat prohibitions. Finally, the Rabbis raise the question: What about burning of the animal's body on the altar—can *it* be delayed until after dark (when Shabbat is over) or should it take place, along with the other activities, on Saturday? Technically, this part of the sacrifice *could* have waited until Saturday night: The burning of the fat of a sacrifice could take place anytime during the night following its

Let the Israelite people offer the passover sacrifice at its set time: you shall offer it on the fourteenth day of this month, at twilight, at its set time; you shall offer it in accordance with all its rules and rites. (Numbers 9:2–3) •

offering. The Rabbis, however, choose to have it done on Shabbat, following the principle: "How precious is a mitzvah in its proper time." Just as the slaughter of the lamb overrides Shabbat, so too, the burning of the fat will also override Shabbat and take place during Saturday, the fourteenth of Nisan.

D'RASH

A couple has been planning a vacation for months. The day of the departure finally arrives. They finish packing their suitcases, hail a cab, and head for the airport. But upon checking in, they notice a flashing message next to their flight number on the departure screen: "Delayed."

A woman has been scheduled for surgery to determine if the lump in her breast is benign or malignant. She has had two weeks to prepare herself mentally and physically for this traumatic moment. And then, an hour before checking into the hospital, the surgeon's office phones: The doctor has been called away on a family emergency. The procedure has been postponed until the end of the week.

The family of a murder victim has been waiting for their day in court when they can, at last, confront the men who killed their daughter. They have gotten themselves emotionally ready for reliving all the pain and anguish of a year ago. And then, the night before the trial is to begin, they receive a call from the district attorney that the judge has granted the defense motion to delay the trial for another month.

We have all learned how important timing can be. It is not just that we are disappointed when things do not happen when we want them to. Many things in life require a great deal of preparation, either of a physical kind or of an emotional nature. We need to "psyche" ourselves up for certain events and experiences. An unexpected delay can be devastating, throwing our bodies and minds completely out of kilter.

Often, these matters are simply out of our control. Outside forces and events dictate where and when things will occur, and we are powerless to do anything but react—after the fact. On other occasions, things seem to come together at precisely the perfect moment. How wonderful it is when the timing is just right, when there are no delays, when things we have waited for and planned for take place at exactly the right moment.

But sometimes, it is more than just luck that determines when things take place. The Gemara shows us that the *calendar* dictated that Pesaḥ would begin on Saturday evening, right after Shabbat; the *Torah* determined when particular things had to be done; but it was the *Rabbis* who decided that certain mitzvot could be performed sooner, rather than later.

So it is in our lives: When it comes to timing, much is out of our hands. But there is also a great deal that we *can* determine. We do not have to remain totally passive. By being sensitive to time, by understanding the possibilities, and by stepping forward to make critical choices, we are able to shape many of the moments of our lives. And then we, too, with Rabbi Shimon, can say: "How precious it is!"

יוֹתֵר מִמַּה שֶׁהָעֵגֶל רוֹצֶה לִינֹק פָּרָה רוֹצָה לְהָנִיק

The cow wants to nurse more than the calf wants to suckle.

TEXT

Pesaḥim 112a

Rabbi Akiva taught Rabbi Shimon bar Yoḥai five things while he was being held in prison. He [Shimon] had said to him: "Master, teach me Torah!" He [Akiva] said: "I will not teach you." He said: "If you do not teach me, I will tell my father, Yoḥai, and you will be handed over to the government." He said to him: "My son, the cow wants to nurse more than the calf wants to suckle." He said to him: "And who is in danger? Is not the calf in danger?"

Once the evil government decreed that the Jews should not learn Torah. Papus ben Yehudah came and found Rabbi Akiva gathering groups in public and teaching them Torah. He said to him: "Akiva, are you not afraid of the government?" He said to him: "I will give you a parable to show you what this is similar to: A fox was walking by the river; he saw schools of fish going from one place to another. He said to them: 'What are you fleeing from?' They said: 'From the nets that humans throw.' He said to them: 'Why don't you come up here on the dry land, and we'll live together.' They said: 'Are you the one they call the wisest of the animals? You are stupid! If in our own element we are afraid, how much more so will we be in a place of death?' So too with us. If, when we sit and study Torah, of which it is written 'For thereby shall you have life' (Deuteronomy 30:20) it is thus: when we go and neglect it, how much worse off will we be?" They said: It was not long after that Rabbi Akiva was captured and thrown in prison. (Berakhot 61*b*) •

CONTEXT

Shimon bar Yoḥai was one of Rabbi Akiva's most zealous students. He was so committed to learning the Torah that he visited his teacher in prison and asked Akiva to teach him right there! Akiva at first refused to do so, knowing that it would place his student at great risk: Should the Romans discover them, Shimon, as well, would surely be thrown into prison. Shimon bar Yoḥai's zeal for Torah is seen in the threat he hurls at his teacher: Either teach me, or I will see to it that the Romans get you in even more trouble! (It is hard for us to take this threat seriously. Shimon's hatred for the Romans was as great as his love for Torah and for his teacher.) Akiva explains his reluctance: He would love nothing more than to teach Torah to Shimon, but he is trying to protect his beloved student. Akiva tells him: I want to teach you even more than you want to learn from me. The metaphor is a touching one: The teacher is like the mother cow, whose udder is filled with milk. The calf (Shimon) may be hungry for milk (Torah), but the cow (Akiva) has an even stronger desire to nurse the young one. The udder is heavy, and only by feeding her young can she find relief. More importantly, as a mother, the cow has an instinct to feed and nourish her precious calf.

Shimon answers: I am the calf, and it is the calf, not the cow who is at risk. I am willing to take my chances. Akiva relented and taught five lessons to his pupil.

D'RASH

A youth group is asked by the social worker of a children's hospital to come and spend a few hours with the patients. The teenagers at first seem hesitant; a few are even worried that being around sick kids will put them in danger. But the youth leader convinces them that it will be a safe and worthwhile experience.

The date arrives, and the teens are driven to the hospital. They get a tour of the facilities and then meet with some of the children on the ward, serving them refreshments. The time comes for the "show": The youth group sings some songs, puts on a skit, and even presents a few magic tricks. During the performance, the youth leader looks around and is very concerned: The patients don't seem to be enjoying themselves. A few of the kids have fallen asleep; one cries during the entire show. A certain youngster has to be escorted to the bathroom every fifteen minutes; one little girl "gets sick" all over herself and has to be changed. A disturbed child screams out at a teenager who touches him: "I'm going to kill you!" The applause at the end of the program is sparse. The leader expects his teenagers to be very upset and depressed.

To everyone's surprise, the teenagers have an incredible experience. They are deeply moved by what they have seen. These adolescents, who are so blessed materially and so sheltered emotionally, have gotten a glimpse of a side of life that they barely knew existed. They walk away having learned so much about sickness and health. They appreciate, perhaps for the first time, how fortunate and lucky they really are. Most importantly, they feel wonderful about themselves and how much they have been able to do for others. When they return home, they immediately beg their youth leader to set up another visit for some time soon.

To the children in the hospital ward, it was merely an hour's diversion that didn't make much of an impression. To the teenagers, it was a day that they would remember for many years to come. As it turns out, the teenagers wanted to help even more than the children wanted to be entertained. It is often that way: The ones who give get more out of the experience than those who receive. Cynics often think of human beings as needy and selfish. Deep down, it seems, we have a real need to share, to help, and to nourish others.

מַתְחִיל בִּגְנוּת וּמְסַיֵּם בְּשֶׁבַח

Begin with disgrace and end with praise.

TEXT

Pesaḥim 116a

Mishnah *(10:4): According to the ability of the son should the father teach. Begin with disgrace and end with praise, explaining from "My father was a fugitive Aramean" [Deuteronomy 26:5] until finishing the entire section.*
Gemara: *What does "disgrace" mean? Rav said: "In the beginning, our ancestors were idol worshipers." Shmuel said: "We were slaves." Rav Naḥman said to Daru his servant: "What should a servant, whose master has freed him and given him silver and gold, say to him?" He said to him: "He should thank him and praise him!" He [Rav Naḥman] said: "You have exempted us from saying 'How is this night different . . .'" He began by saying "We were slaves."*

My father was a fugitive Aramean. He went down to Egypt with meager numbers and sojourned there; but there he became a great and very populous nation. The Egyptians dealt harshly with us and oppressed us; they imposed heavy labor upon us. We cried to the Lord, the God of our fathers, and the Lord heard our plea and saw our plight, our misery, and our oppression. The Lord freed us from Egypt by a mighty hand, by an outstretched arm and awesome power, and by signs and portents. (Deuteronomy 26:5-8) •

In the beginning our ancestors served idols, but then God brought us close to Him that we might serve Him, as it is written, "Then Joshua said to all the people, 'Thus said the Lord, the God of Israel: In olden times, your forefathers—Terah, father of Abraham and father of Nahor—lived beyond the Euphrates and worshipped other gods' (Joshua 24:2-3)." (Passover Haggadah) •

We were slaves to Pharaoh in Egypt, and the Lord our God brought us forth from there with a mighty hand and an outstretched arm.

CONTEXT

The tenth chapter of *Pesaḥim* discusses in great detail the Seder meal and the rituals of the festival of Passover. Today, people follow the Haggadah which includes stories, biblical and rabbinic texts, and songs, to guide them through these rituals. But in the first and second centuries, there was not yet a fixed, formal book. Instead, there was a series of guidelines that each family used as a basis for its Seder meal. Our Mishnah gives three of these guidelines. First, the father (or leader of the Seder) should "tailor" the ceremony to the age and abilities of the children and other participants sitting around the table. The second direction is that we should begin the story by recounting the sad events of our past, and then end on the positive note of God's liberation. Finally, the Mishnah instructs that the core text to be discussed at the Seder is Deuteronomy 26:5-8, which summarizes what befell our ancestors in Egypt.

The Gemara, picking up on the second issue, asks what exactly is meant by "disgrace." Two views are offered. Rav understands disgrace to mean shameful things that our people did long ago in our past: they worshipped idols. Shmuel, on the other hand, sees disgrace in what was done *to* our ancestors by the Egyptians: They persecuted and enslaved them.

The Gemara ends with a story of Rav Naḥman asking his own servant how he would respond to being set free. Daru's reply, that he would thank and praise his master, enables Rav Naḥman to understand and even feel the joy that the Israelite slaves must have felt.

And if the Holy One, blessed be He, had not brought forth our ancestors from Egypt, then we and our children and our children's children would still be slaves to Pharaoh in Egypt. (Passover Haggadah) •

D'RASH

The football team has had a terrible first half. They are down by three touchdowns. The coach is embarrassed, and he is angry. The players have made many mistakes, and they are not playing on the level or in the way that he has taught them. The critical moment of the game may be right now, as he prepares to speak to them and tries to get them ready for the second half.

"That was really terrible . . . Our game so far has been a disgrace!" He then proceeds to review the botched plays and mistakes that the players have made. But then he is at a fork in the road, and he can go in two very different directions:

"I'm ashamed of you! You played like a bunch of old ladies. I don't know who you are any more! I'm embarrassed to say I'm your coach! If that was the best you could do, you might as well get dressed and go home right now! All right, let's go out there and make sure you don't humiliate yourselves like that again!"

Or he could end like this: "I know you guys. You can do much better. You *have* done much better, time and time again. Remember the upset we pulled off last month? You all made me so proud. Well, if you've done it before, I know you can do it again. Let's reach down and find the guts and the determination to win this thing. You guys are the best! *Show me!!* Let's go out and do it!!"

Too often, when we are angered, troubled, or disappointed by someone's performance, we either say nothing, afraid to hurt their feelings and precipitate an angry confrontation, or we "unload" on them, critically telling them of their failings. Unfortunately, neither approach is very helpful or constructive.

The Rabbis hint at the perfect middle road: Begin with "disgrace," with the negative, but conclude with praise, with the positive. Ignoring a problem does not mean that it will go away. We need honestly to confront the difficult issues that exist. But we must also leave the person with his or her dignity intact, motivated to go on, improve and do better. The last words we say are what a person is left with; it is from those last words that they begin to grow and rebuild.

Reading our history, we learn that our people were once slaves and idol worshipers. Yet they were able to rise above that past and become, in the words of the Torah, "a kingdom of priests and a holy nation" (Exodus 19:6). Perhaps that is due, in part, to the way God spoke to us, always leaving us with a message of what we could aspire to do and to become.

הַזְרִיזִין מַקְדִּימִין לְמִצְוֹות

The diligent do the mitzvot as early as possible.

TEXT

Yoma 28b

Rav Safra said: "The prayer of Abraham [is recited] from the time that the walls turn dark." Rav Yosef said: "Do we learn from and decide according to Abraham?" Rava said: "A tanna learned from Abraham, shouldn't we as well? As it is taught 'On the eighth day the flesh of his foreskin shall be circumcised' [Leviticus 12:3]. This teaches that the entire day is proper for circumcision, but the diligent do the mitzvot as early as possible, as it says: 'So early next morning, Abraham saddled his ass' [Genesis 22:3]."

CONTEXT

The prayer of Abraham is *Minḥah,* the afternoon service. Rav Safra wants to know the earliest time this prayer may be said. The answer given is that it may be recited after mid-day, when the sun will no longer shine directly on walls facing east. Rav Yosef questions whether halakhah can be learned from Abraham (who according to tradition, fixed the time for this prayer service). The implication of the question is that since Abraham predates Moses and the giving of the Torah (and hence the obligation of the Jews to observe the mitzvot), it makes no logical sense to base the mitzvot on what Abraham did.

Rava responds that Abraham is indeed a source for later Jewish law. The example brought is about *b'rit milah,* ritual circumcision. The Torah commands that it be done on the eighth day, and since no specific time is mentioned, any time during that day would be appropriate. But the prevailing custom has become to perform a *b'rit milah* not only in the morning, but as early in the day as possible. The basis of this is the behavior of Abraham (who, coincidentally, was the first person to perform the mitzvah). God had commanded Abraham to take his son Isaac and offer him as a sacrifice. Abraham, we are told, awoke *early* next morning and took Isaac right away to fulfill the command of God.

It was taught in accordance with Rabbi Yosé son of Rabbi Ḥanina: Abraham instituted the morning service, as it says: "Next morning, Abraham hurried to the place where he had stood before the Lord" [Genesis 19:27]. And "stood" can mean only in prayer, as it says "Phinehas stood and prayed" [Psalms 106:30, author's translation].

Isaac instituted the afternoon prayer, as it says: "And Isaac went out to meditate in the field toward evening" [Genesis 24:63]. And "meditate" can mean only in prayer, as it says: "A prayer of the lowly man when he is faint and pours forth his meditation before the Lord" [Psalms 102:1, author's translation].

Jacob instituted the evening prayer, as it says: "He approached a certain place and stopped there for the night" [Genesis 28:11, author's translation]. And "approached" can mean only in prayer, as it says: "As for you, do not pray for this people, do not raise a cry of prayer on their behalf, do not approach Me" [Jeremiah 7:16, author's translation]. (Berakhot 26*b*) •

D'RASH

Abraham is commanded by God to bring his beloved son to Mount Moriah and there to take a knife to him and offer him up as a sacrifice. Abraham had a number of options in

Tradition says that Abraham instituted the Shaḥarit morning service and Isaac the Minḥah afternoon service. Yet the Gemara

indicates that Minḥah is known as "the prayer of Abraham." The Tosafot were bothered by this contradiction and offered the following reconciliation:

"Isaac instituted the afternoon prayer." Even though it says: "The prayer of Abraham [is recited] from the time that the walls turn dark," one can respond that Abraham fixed the time after Isaac instituted it. (Tosafot, Berakhot *26b)* •

response to this difficult command: he could have argued; he could have refused; he could have fled; he could have agonized and delayed. Yet he chose to carry out God's instruction, and he did so, according to our understanding of the Torah, at the earliest possible opportunity.

Jewish parents are commanded by God to circumcise their beloved sons. This is usually accomplished by bringing the baby to a *mohel,* who will take a knife and enter the boy into the covenant of circumcision. Many mothers and fathers probably contemplate their options as the prescribed time for the *bris* of their tiny, precious child draws near. Yet Jews have chosen, for over 3,700 years, to carry out God's instruction, and they have traditionally done so on the eighth day at the earliest possible opportunity.

What does one do when faced with a terribly difficult decision? It is human nature to struggle with the options and to put off a course of action until we are 100 percent certain that we are making the right choice. But life rarely provides us with the luxury of time for such deliberations. All too often, "the one who hesitates is lost."

While making rash decisions is never to be encouraged, the Gemara nevertheless praises those who carry out instructions and mitzvot as quickly as possible. Rashi, in his commentary to the Talmud (*Ḥullin* 107b) teaches: "Diligence (or alacrity) is preferable to caution." A cautious person will be very careful not to make a mistake or to commit a transgression; the diligent person, on the other hand, will plan ahead and be prepared for all contingencies, so that when the critical moment comes for a decision, the correct choices can be made on the spot.

Blind obedience to authority can lead to the infamous response: "I was only following orders." Civilized societies can accept no such excuses. The Rabbis were quite strict in their expectations of moral responsibility on the part of the individual. How then does one find the perfect balance between making ethical decisions, on the one hand, and making quick decisions, on the other? In the case of Abraham, there was a complete and total faith in the One issuing the commands—God. With a *bris,* Jews have the experience of almost four thousand years of our people following this practice to rely upon. In other situations, we try to follow the teaching of Rashi who urges us to look into the future and to be ready for the critical moments, so that we can be diligent to do the mitzvot as early as possible.

הַתּוֹרָה חָסָה עַל מָמוֹנָן שֶׁל יִשְׂרָאֵל

The Torah worries about Israel's money.

TEXT

Yoma 43b, 44b

> Mishnah *(4:3): He slaughtered it and received its blood in a silver bowl, and gave it to the one who stirred it while standing on the fourth terrace in the sanctuary, so that it would not congeal. He took the fire pan and went to the top of the altar. He cleared the coals on both sides, and he took a panful of coals from below. He came down and placed it [the fire pan] on the fourth terrace in the courtyard. Every other day, he would clear the coals with a silver fire pan, but today he cleared it with one of gold.*
> Gemara: *"Every other day, he would clear the coals with a silver fire pan, etc." What is the reason? The Torah worries about Israel's money.*

CONTEXT

Masekhet Yoma deals with the laws and rituals of *yoma,* Aramaic for *the* day, that is Yom Kippur, the Day of Atonement. Large sections of this tractate deal with the Yom Kippur ceremonies for the *Kohen Gadol,* or High Priest, at the Temple in Jerusalem. The specifics of the ritual are interesting though not applicable to our lives today. In fact, the workings of the Temple were not applicable even to many of the Rabbis of the Talmud who lived after the destruction of the second Temple in 70 C.E. Nonetheless, they are listed in the Torah, taught in the Mishnah, and expounded on in the Gemara. The Torah teaches about the Tabernacle which the Israelites used in the Sinai wilderness. Aaron and his sons were the participants in the Yom Kippur ritual. These rituals were transferred to the Temple which later replaced the portable Tabernacle as the central shrine.

Part of the Yom Kippur ritual involved scooping up burning coals with a special fire pan. The Torah says that Aaron, the *Kohen Gadol,* should place two handfuls of incense on these coals. The Mishnah teaches that on Yom Kippur, the *Kohen Gadol* used a gold fire pan to pick up the coals, but every other day, he used a silver one. We can understand why a gold one would be used on Yom Kippur: It is a special day, perhaps *the* most holy day on the Jewish calendar. But why not use a gold fire pan every day of the year? The Gemara answers: The Torah worries about Israel's money. We may

Aaron is to offer his own bull of sin offering, to make expiation for himself and his household. Aaron shall take the two he-goats and let them stand before the Lord at the entrance of the Tent of Meeting; and he shall place lots upon the two goats, one marked for the Lord and the other marked for Azazel. Aaron shall bring forward the goat designated by lot for the Lord, which he is to offer as a sin offering; while the goat designated by lot for Azazel shall be left standing alive before the Lord, to make expiation with it and to send it off to the wilderness before Azazel. Aaron shall then offer his bull of sin offering . . . and he shall take a panful of glowing coals scooped from the altar before the Lord, and two handfuls of finely ground aromatic incense, and bring this behind the curtain. . . . And this shall be to you a law for all time: In the seventh month, on the tenth day of the month, you shall practice self-denial; and you shall do no manner of work, neither the citizen nor the alien who resides among you. For on this day atonement shall be made for you to cleanse you of all your sins; you shall be clean before the Lord. (Leviticus 16:6-12, 29-30) •

ask: If the *Kohen Gadol* used a silver pan the rest of the year and a gold pan on Yom Kippur, where would there be a savings? Wouldn't there be the same expense of making a gold pan? The commentators note that these pans wore out from wear and tear. If a gold pan were used every day, it would mean the expense of replacing it more often, and the Torah worries about the material possessions of the Jewish people.

D'RASH

Most of us have received mailings from organizations that ask us for money to support a worthy cause. Sometimes, the request is fairly straightforward and the cause seems worthy (even if these examples are fictitious):

> ***Anti-Semitism Is on the Rise!*** *Support the Museum for Jewish Self-Respect, a new center for the education for non-Jews and the re-establishment of positive feelings among Jews.*

At times, the cause seems worthy but we may wonder about the need for another organization and an additional acronym:

> ***Jews Delegitimize Other Jews.*** *The fragmentation of the Jewish community cannot continue unabated. We must put an end to the tension between one Jew and another. Join MAFTIR, the **M**ovement **A**gainst **F**ragmented **T**endencies **I**n **R**eligion.*

And then, there are groups that seem to be part of the very problem they are fighting:

> ***Too Many Jewish Organizations & Not Enough Money!*** *Are you sick and tired of a new organization for every cause? Then it's time for you to support GAINOJG (Yiddish for "enough"): The **G**roup **A**gainst the **I**ncreasing **N**umber **O**f **J**ewish **G**roups.*

While these examples are either apocryphal or humorous, the phenomenon is actual and serious.

Often, these requests come from organizations that seem worthy and that promise to accomplish much for the community. Often, there is a need for such groups. At times, though, they are repetitive of other institutions, duplicating what already has a structure and what similar organizations have done.

Perhaps most disturbing is that established groups that have been working within the community for years go wanting for funds. More than one institution has had to close its doors because of lack of financial support. This is not to say that every established group serves a worthy purpose or that each new association is unnecessary and repetitive. It is a reminder, though, of our limited resources.

Some say "Money is tight." It is likely that, except for some brief periods in history, money has always been tight. The Gemara, in positing that "the Torah worries about Israel's money," is reminding us that Judaism cares about our scarce resources. We have to use them wisely. Had God required the Israelites to use gold fire pans throughout the year, they would have. Yet God—and the Rabbis who interpreted God's laws—were concerned that Israel not spend too much of its funds on gold pans, leaving less for other worthy causes. If the Torah worries about Israel's money, then the implication is that we, too, must worry about money, seeing to it that our limited resources are spent wisely.

Rest Stop

They set out from Marah and came to Elim. There were twelve springs in Elim and seventy palm trees, so they encamped there. (Numbers 33:9)

Words of Torah are compared to water . . . as it says: "Ho, all who are thirsty, come for water" [Isaiah 55:1]. . . . Just as water purifies a person of uncleanliness, as it says: "I will sprinkle clean water upon you, and you shall be clean" [Ezekiel 36:25], so too, Torah cleanses the impure from impurity, as it says: "The words of the Lord are pure words" [Psalms 12:7]. (*Song of Songs Rabbah* 1, 3)

There is a story of a learned man who came to visit a rebbe. The scholar was no longer a young man—he was close to thirty—but he had never before visited a rebbe.

"What have you done all your life?" the master asked him.

"I have gone through the whole of the Talmud three times," answered the learned man.

"Yes, but how much of the Talmud has gone through you?" the rebbe inquired.

(Abraham Joshua Heschel. *The Earth is the Lord's*. New York: Harper & Row, 1966, p. 83)

SEDER MOED, Continued

A Further Introduction to Seder Moed

The tractates of a *seder,* or Order, are arranged according to their size. Thus, the tractates, or *masekhtot,* of *Moed* do not follow the Jewish calendar and the order of the year, as we might expect. Rather, the tractate with the largest number of chapters of Mishnah is first. Hence, the tractate *Shabbat,* with twenty-four chapters of Mishnah, is the first *masekhet* of *Moed,* followed by *Eruvin* and *Pesaḥim,* with ten chapters each, and *Yoma* with eight. We have divided our study of *Seder Moed* into two because of its eighty-eight total chapters and therefore large number of entries in this book. This allowed for the preceding Rest Stop in *Seder Moed.* The entries from the remaining seven tractates of *Moed* follow.

הָעוֹסֵק בְּמִצְוָה
פָּטוּר מִן הַמִּצְוָה

One who is doing one mitzvah
is freed from doing another mitzvah.

TEXT

Sukkah 25a-b

> Mishnah (2:4): *Those who are sent to do a mitzvah are exempt from the Sukkah.*
> Gemara: *Where are these words from? As our Rabbis have taught: "[Recite them] when you stay at home" [Deuteronomy 6:7]. This excludes one who is doing a mitzvah. . . . Does the principle "One who is doing one mitzvah is freed from doing another mitzvah" come from* here? *It comes from* there, *as it has been taught: "But there were some men who were unclean by reason of a corpse" [Numbers 9:6]. Who were those men? Those who carried the coffin of Joseph, according to Rabbi Yosé ha-G'lili. Rabbi Akiva says: "They were Mishael and Elzaphan who were busy with [the bodies of] Nadav and Avihu."*

You shall live in booths seven days; all citizens in Israel shall live in booths, in order that future generations may know that I made the Israelite people live in booths when I brought them out of the land of Egypt, I the Lord your God. (Leviticus 23:42–43) •

Moses instructed the Israelites to offer the passover sacrifice; and they offered the passover sacrifice in the first month, on the fourteenth day of the month, at twilight, in the wilderness of Sinai. Just as the Lord had commanded Moses, so the Israelites did. But there were some men who were unclean by reason of a corpse and could not offer the passover sacrifice on that day. Appearing that same day before Moses and Aaron, those men said to them, "Unclean though we be by reason of a corpse, why must we be debarred from presenting the Lord's offering at its set time with the rest of the Israelites?" (Numbers 9:4–7) •

CONTEXT

The Mishnah begins by telling us that someone engaged in a mitzvah (such as going to free hostages held in captivity) during the festival of Sukkot is exempt from the commandment of building and dwelling in a Sukkah. The Gemara looks for the basis of this exemption in the Torah. Two possibilities are offered. First, the words of the *Sh'ma* (Deuteronomy 6:4–9) are to be recited "when you stay at home." That implies that if a person was away from home engaged in another mitzvah, then he is exempt from this mitzvah. The second prooftext comes from the story of the men who wanted to celebrate Pesaḥ by offering the sacrifice, but were unable to because they had been in physical contact with a dead body. Sacrifices could be offered only by those who were ritually clean; contact with a corpse rendered a person ritually unclean. The Rabbis assume that because these men were engaged in a mitzvah (burying the dead), they therefore are exempt from the performance of another mitzvah (offering the Passover sacrifice at the proper time).

It is interesting to note that the Torah itself does not state explicitly which body the men were dealing with. Trying to identify the anonymous individuals mentioned, and thus turning an ambiguous situation into a specific one, is a common rabbinic way of reading the Bible. Rabbi Yosé believes the men were those carrying the body of Joseph from Egypt on its way to burial in Israel. Rabbi Akiva identifies them as

Mishael and Elzaphan, cousins of Aaron, who are called upon to remove the bodies of Aaron's sons Nadav and Avihu after their sudden death in the sanctuary (Leviticus 10:4).

D'RASH

The letter carrier delivers the mail and among the letters and bills is a summons to come down to city hall; you have been picked for jury duty. Few people enjoy such a duty. For many it is a real burden, economic and otherwise. Yet we all understand that it is one of the obligations of citizenship. Without it, our justice system simply could not function. Despite the hardships, most people go and do their civic duty. Some people try to get out of serving, but the judges are often unsympathetic. Nevertheless, government recognizes that there are instances when an individual has other pressing obligations that would make serving on a jury an unbearable hardship. A parent with an infant is given an exemption; so is a spouse who serves as caretaker for a disabled husband or wife. It is as if the city is saying: "One who is doing one mitzvah is freed from doing another mitzvah."

The Rabbis, however, did *not* teach: "One who has something else to do is freed from doing a mitzvah." It is important to recognize that the word "mitzvah" comes on *both* sides of the equation. We are not freed from our obligations to do a mitzvah or to perform a duty simply because we'd rather be doing something else.

The SAT exams are administered to high school students on Saturdays. A special Sunday sitting of the test is offered, but only to those who can produce a letter from a clergyperson attesting that as Sabbath observers they cannot take the test on Saturday. The Sunday date is not available for those who simply find it more convenient.

Many airlines levy a special fee for passengers who cancel or change their flight reservations. The penalty can be waived, but only if the individual sends an official note, for example from a physician, that explains that there were extenuating circumstances for the change. Illness or a death in the family are seen as acceptable excuses; a preference for another date or flight is not.

It is only a mitzvah—observing Shabbat, caring for the sick, mourning the death of a relative—that exempts one from obligations and commitments. Too often, we confuse convenience for obligation. The Rabbis force us to confront the nature of the excuses we frequently give. The Talmud reminds us that exemptions are given only when we are involved in doing another mitzvah.

אֵין שְׁעַת הַדְּחָק רְאָיָה

An emergency situation does not constitute proof.

TEXT

Sukkah 31a-b

> *If he did not find an* etrog, *he may not bring a quince or a pomegranate or anything else. Withered ones are kosher; dried-up ones are invalid. Rabbi Yehudah says: "Even the dried-up [are kosher]." Rabbi Yehudah said: "There is the case of city-people who would bequeath their* lulavs *to their grandchildren." They said to him: "You bring proof from that? An emergency situation does not constitute proof."*

CONTEXT

To celebrate the festival of Sukkot (the Feast of Tabernacles), the Torah commands: "On the first day you shall take the product of *hadar* trees, branches of palm trees, boughs of leafy trees, and willows of the brook, and you shall rejoice before the Lord your God seven days" (Leviticus 23:40). These "four species" are identified as the *etrog* (a citron), the *lulav* (a palm branch), a myrtle, and willow branches. These species are held and shaken during certain parts of the morning services on Sukkot.

Here, the Rabbis are discussing how the quality of the four species determines whether they are *kasher* (kosher, fit or valid for use in the ritual) or *pasul* (invalid). One should always strive to find the best and most beautiful item that is available for use in worship of God. At times, such quality items may not be available, or they may be beyond the worshiper's means. The question is raised about lesser quality and imperfect items, and if they are acceptable for use.

The notion of serving God in an aesthetically pleasing manner is called hidur mitzvah, *beautifying the commandments. It is based on a rabbinic interpretation of a verse in the Torah:*

> *This is my God and I will glorify Him,*
> *The God of my father, and I will exalt Him.*
> *(Exodus 15:2, author's translation)*

"And I will glorify Him"—Beautify yourself before Him with mitzvot. Make a beautiful Sukkah, a beautiful lulav, *beautiful fringes [for a tallit], a beautiful Torah scroll. (Shabbat 133b)* •

Rabbi Yehudah bases the view that even a dried-up *etrog* or *lulav* is kosher on precedent: He recounts that urban dwellers who did not have access to orchards and fresh palm branches used to hand down their *lulavs* to their grandchildren. Over the course of the years, these palms not only withered, they dried out completely. Yet they were still used, generation after generation. This seems to prove that the use of inferior branches and fruits was deemed acceptable. The Rabbis, however, do not agree. While conceding that this practice was common among some urban dwellers, it was an unusual situation. These were people who had no other choice. To *them,* the use of the dried-out *lulav* or *etrog* was an emergency. But the law, and general practice, cannot be based upon what is permitted in an extreme and unusual situation.

D'RASH

It is policy in a suburban synagogue to celebrate Bar and Bat Mitzvahs only during regular Shabbat services. Each youngster chants a haftarah, reads from the Torah, and leads parts of the service. One year, a family comes before the ritual committee with a special request: They would like their son to be allowed to have his service on the Thursday morning of Thanksgiving. They explain that this date is more convenient for members of the family who are flying in for the holiday but who are unable to remain over the weekend when the Bar Mitzvah was originally scheduled. They point out that the Torah is also read on Monday and Thursday morning, and their child will still be able to lead the service and read from the Five Books of Moses.

The cantor notes that the Torah reading on Thursday is much shorter than the one on Shabbat, that the tunes for the weekday service differ significantly from those on Saturday (which the students have learned), and that there is no haftarah chanted on weekday mornings. The ritual committee, weighing the family's request against the synagogue's policies, votes not to make an exception. The Bar Mitzvah must take place on Saturday.

The family is very upset and goes to the next board meeting to complain. In addition to the arguments presented before the ritual committee, they add one more point: The synagogue is being unfair because it allowed other families in the past to celebrate a Bar Mitzvah on a day other than Saturday. They believe that precedent has been set for a weekday Bar Mitzvah and, therefore, the synagogue is morally bound to allow them to depart from the norm as well.

The rabbi answers that it is true that there was an exception made several years before, but the circumstances were unique. The child was severely developmentally handicapped. He had worked very hard to learn the blessings for an *aliyah,* which was all that he was able to do. But the young boy had a fear of appearing in the synagogue before the large crowd of Shabbat worshipers. The family felt that the only way their son would be able to celebrate becoming a Bar Mitzvah was at a low-keyed service, attended only by the immediate family and a few close friends. The ritual committee at that time, knowing the difficulties this family had in raising their son, and sensing how important this Bar

Mitzvah would be to both the parents and the child, allowed an exception to the rules and set the service for a Monday morning. In his answer to the current request, the rabbi concluded that the former instance was so exceptional that it should not serve as a precedent for any other cases.

The family appearing before the ritual committee, like Rabbi Yehudah, believed very strongly in the power of precedent. If something was allowed before, it should be allowed again. Once an exception has been made, once a precedent has been established, you cannot deny others the same opportunity.

The Rabbis in our Gemara and the rabbi of the synagogue strongly disagree. They fear that following Rabbi Yehudah's principle, almost all standards would fall away and practically anything could be allowed. The Rabbis believe that the law serves to provide parameters and limits of what is acceptable and what is not. They know that the law must be flexible to allow for special cases and unusual circumstances, but exceptions for extraordinary circumstances do not set precedents for ordinary occasions. Knowing when and where to allow for exceptions is one of the great burdens of leadership.

מוּטָב שֶׁיִּהְיוּ שׁוֹגְגִין
וְאַל יִהְיוּ מְזִידִין

Better that they be uninformed transgressors than deliberate transgressors.

TEXT

Betzah 30a

> *Rava bar Rabbi Ḥanin said to Abaye: "It is taught: 'One does not clap hands, slap sides or dance' yet today people do this and we say nothing to them about it!" He said to him: "According to your reasoning, that which Rabbah said, that a man should not sit right near a stick-marker, lest an object roll away and he will carry it four cubits in a public place, but these women carry their jugs to the entrance of an alley and we say nothing to them about it!" Let Israel be: Better that they be uninformed transgressors than deliberate transgressors. Here, too, let Israel be: Better that they be uninformed transgressors than deliberate transgressors.*

CONTEXT

This section deals with the laws of the festivals and Shabbat, specifically which objects may be carried on a holiday. Rava says: There is a specific prohibition against certain other activities on Shabbat and Festivals—hand-clapping and dancing, for example—yet people ignore this law and the Rabbis, in turn, ignore their transgression. There is disagreement among the commentators as to why these activities are prohibited, but it appears that they are preventive measures. This was done so that one will not engage in an activity (like fixing a musical instrument) that is fully prohibited on Shabbat and holidays.

The "stick-marker" that a person sits near delineates where one domain ends and another begins. Thus, carrying from the private domain, on this side of the marker, to the public domain, on the other side, is prohibited. Why is it, Abaye asks Rava, that we are concerned with a man sitting in one spot, troubled that he may transgress, but we do not care about women carrying their water jugs to the alley's entrance on Shabbat? In other words, why are we scrupulous in one case, observing not only the law but also a preventive measure to avert accidental transgression, but in the other case, we see a potential problem and totally ignore it?

The answer is simple: "Let Israel be" means roughly "Leave the Jews alone." If the Jews—in this case, the women

Today, people clap their hands and dance on Shabbat, "and we say nothing to them about it!" There are three interesting historical notes about this law. First, while we think of clapping hands and dancing as part of festivities, hand-clapping was also used in the ancient world as part of mourning rituals. Second, Jewish law largely ignored this rule or legislated it out of existence. Authors of legal codes wrote that Jews by and large no longer fix musical instruments regularly, as they once did. This protection for the law is unnecessary. Third, and perhaps most important, is the fact that hand-clapping became a part of recognized, acceptable Jewish practice on Shabbat and holidays. In certain communities, there is a custom (based on Maimonides' reading of this law) to clap hands with a variation, for example, the back of one hand into the palm of another rather than palms together. This would remind the person that it is Shabbat or a holiday. Thus, the people's practice determines, to a large degree, what the law is and how (or even if!) it will be enforced. •

with water jugs on Shabbat—are going to carry in any case, even if we tell them that it is prohibited, then it is preferable that they do it ignorant of the law than in intentional and flagrant violation of the law. The Rabbis were concerned with law, yet the interest here is less for this *specific law* than for the entire *legal system.* The only way the system works is if people follow rabbinic enactments. If people disobey the law and flaunt this fact, then the entire institution of law suffers. Soon, people will begin to ignore more laws, and the totality of Jewish law suffers. The Rabbis wanted Jews to keep *the laws,* the specific and proper observances of Jewish life. More important, though, they wanted Jews to observe *the law,* the entire system. When it became clear that a law would not be followed, the Rabbis might, in some cases, simply come to the conclusion that it is better not to tell the people that they were in violation. Better that they be uninformed transgressors than deliberate transgressors.

D'RASH

It goes without saying that we should not overlook severe wrongdoings that we see others committing. Even more minor personality faults were subsumed under the biblical injunction to "reprove your kinsman" (Leviticus 19:17). The Rabbis of the Talmud interpreted this to mean that we must correct the faults we see in others, the human imperfections that we cannot see in ourselves. Often, only an outsider can point out these shortcomings.

Yet, we may carry this ideal to an extreme. It is often difficult for us to look the other way when someone we know and care for does something wrong. In addition, our sense of justice and right may compel us to correct others even for the most minor of misdemeanors, or if their wrongs cannot be changed, or for people we do not know. Most of us have witnessed someone telling a stranger: "You shouldn't bite your fingernails" or "Those chips that you're buying really aren't healthy; you should stick to fruits and vegetables." The Rabbis were aware of this tendency in others as well as in themselves. They knew that some more minor actions cannot be legislated or changed and thus should be allowed to exist, even if unlawful. They would not allow Jews to be deliberate transgressors of major Shabbat, theft, or sexual prohibitions, but they had no problem saying, from time to time: "We cannot change everything. In this case, they're going to do it anyway, so let it be."

The Christian theologian Reinhold Niebuhr once penned a "Serenity Prayer." His words sound like a modern reworking of this idea:

> God, give us grace to accept with serenity the things that cannot be changed, courage to change the things which should be changed, and the wisdom to distinguish the one from the other.

We have all met people who have not yet learned this credo. At a testimonial dinner or organizational banquet, an acquaintance will harp on the poor service or the quality of the food. We are not in charge, and once the meal has begun, there is little we can do to change things. Better to accept the inadequacies than to ruin the evening by deliberate, repeated critiques of transgressions which cannot be corrected.

As our children grow up, we see imperfections in their personalities. We try our hardest as parents to help them change, to grow, to improve. And then one day, we realize that our criticisms will not make them any better than they now are. They will continue to mature on their own, making of themselves better people. Time will help them lose some of these bad habits; others may, admittedly, remain. Is it right to constantly harp on these shortcomings? The Rabbis would likely whisper in our ears: Better that we not inform our children of all their minor imperfections than constantly reminding them of that which they cannot, or will not, change. It is better for them, and it is certainly better for us.

מוֹסִיפִין מֵחֹל עַל קֹדֶשׁ

We add from the ordinary onto the sacred.

TEXT

Rosh Hashanah 9a

From where do we learn that we add from the ordinary onto the sacred? As it is taught: "You shall cease from labor even at plowing time and harvest time" [Exodus 34:21]. Rabbi Akiva says: "This text could not be referring to the [prohibition of] plowing and harvesting during the Sabbatical year, for it already says: 'You shall not sow your field' [Leviticus 25:4]. Therefore it must refer to plowing on the eve of the Sabbatical year that leads into the Sabbatical year, and to harvesting in the Sabbatical year which leads into the year following *the Sabbatical year." Rabbi Yishmael says: "Just as plowing is optional, so too harvesting is optional, except for harvesting the Omer, which is a mitzvah." From where does Rabbi Yishmael derive the principle that we add from the ordinary onto the sacred? He learns it from that which is taught: "And you shall practice self-denial; on the ninth day" [Leviticus 23:32]. One might think it is on the ninth; therefore the text says "at evening." If at evening, one might think after it gets dark. Therefore the text says "on the* ninth.*" How can this be? We begin to afflict ourselves while it is still day. This teaches that we add from the ordinary onto the sacred.*

Six days you shall work, but on the seventh day you shall cease from labor; you shall cease from labor even at plowing time and harvest time. (Exodus 34:21) •

When you enter the land that I assign to you, the land shall observe a sabbath of the Lord. Six years you may sow your field and six years you may prune your vineyard and gather in the yield. But in the seventh year the land shall have a sabbath of complete rest, a sabbath of the Lord: you shall not sow your field or prune your vineyard. (Leviticus 25:2–4) •

And should you ask, "What are we to eat in the seventh year, if we may neither sow nor gather in our crops?" I will ordain My blessing for you in the sixth year, so that it shall yield a crop sufficient for three years. When you sow in the eighth year, you will still be eating old grain of that crop; you will be eating the old until the ninth year, until its crops come in." (Leviticus 25:20–22) •

Mark, the tenth day of this seventh month is the Day of Atonement. It shall be a sacred occasion for you: you shall practice self-denial, and you shall bring an offering by fire to the Lord. . . . It

CONTEXT

One of the hallmarks of the Jewish religion is the sacred times, or holy days, that mark the calendar. By definition, a holiday is a twenty-four-hour period. But the Rabbis ordered that these holidays began just a little earlier and end just a little bit later. We are to "borrow" time from the ordinary days that precede and follow the holy day, and add it onto the holy day itself. Shabbat, for example, technically should begin Friday at sunset and end Saturday at sunset. Instead, we begin Shabbat earlier, lighting candles at least eighteen minutes before the sun goes down, and end it later, no earlier than when three stars appear in the sky. Shabbat lasts closer to twenty-five, not twenty-four, hours.

Rabbi Akiva and Rabbi Yishmael attempt to find a basis for this practice in the Torah. Rabbi Akiva does it by turning to the laws about the Sabbatical year. Since it is in Leviticus 25 that the law itself is taught, the reference in Exodus 34:21 must come to teach some other law or principle. (Rabbi

Akiva believes that laws are not just repeated; each time something is mentioned again, it must be to teach a specific, new lesson.) He interprets Exodus 34:21 as teaching that the Sabbatical year actually begins a few months earlier, with a prohibition of plowing in the last weeks of the sixth year, and it ends a few months late, with the prohibition of harvesting in the first weeks of the eighth year.

Rabbi Yishmael disagrees with Rabbi Akiva on the meaning of this particular verse. Whereas Akiva connected the verse with the Sabbatical year, Yishmael connects it to Shabbat, learning that the Omer offering of grain brought beginning on the second day of Passover may be cut and harvested even on Shabbat. Rabbi Yishmael derives the basis of the principle "We add from the ordinary onto the sacred" from the laws concerning Yom Kippur (which falls on the tenth day of Tishrei). The Torah mentions that the fast is supposed to begin on the ninth of Tishrei, late in the afternoon, earlier than we would have expected.

shall be a sabbath of complete rest for you, and you shall practice self-denial; on the ninth day of the month at evening, from evening to evening, you shall observe this your sabbath. (Leviticus 23:27, 32) •

D'RASH

A wedding ceremony can take less than thirty minutes, the reception lasts a few hours. But people sense that this moment is *so* important, and *so* wonderful, that they want it to last as long as possible. Traditional Judaism, in its reluctance to let the wedding day slip away too quickly, "adds from the ordinary onto the sacred." There is the *aufruf,* when the groom (and nowadays, sometimes the bride) is called to the Torah and the couple are given the community's blessing, often on the Shabbat before the wedding. The day of the marriage begins with the *tenaim,* the signing of a formal engagement contract by the two families, accompanied by the breaking of a plate. Then there is the *ḥusan's tish,* "the groom's table," where the men gather to sing, study, and celebrate with their friends. As part of the *Bedeken,* or veiling ceremony, the women attend the bride with songs of joy and praise, and then lead her in dance to the wedding canopy. Following the reception, the husband and wife traditionally remain in the community for the week. Each night, they attend another dinner in their honor, sponsored by different friends or family members. At the conclusion of these meals, a special prayer, the *Sheva Berakhot,* "the seven blessings," is added to the routine grace after meals. In secular wedding culture, the bachelor parties, rehearsal dinners, and cocktail hours serve a similar function before the wedding, while the post-wedding breakfasts and "after-parties" all have the same intention of making this wonderful celebration last a little bit longer.

There are two kinds of moments in life: The ordinary and the special. The former far outnumber the latter. But it is the *latter,* those unique, sacred events and times that give meaning and joy to our lives. The challenge we face is how to savor them when they do come. The Rabbis tried to *protect* these moments and to *prolong* them. By starting Shabbat before sunset and ending it only *after* the stars had come out, two things were accomplished: A "fence" was erected around the day, that made sure ordinary weekday work, like lighting candles, was not done, by accident or by neglect, during the actual sacred time. And another hour was added on to the seventh day. One additional hour on top of the regular twenty-four may not amount to all that much. Yet, the Rabbis were teaching us to cherish each of our special moments, to hold on to them while we have them, and to let them last, even if for only a little while longer. It is one of the great secrets of life—to add from the ordinary on to the sacred.

יִפְתָּח בְּדוֹרוֹ
כִּשְׁמוּאֵל בְּדוֹרוֹ

Jephthah in his generation is like Samuel in his generation.

TEXT

Rosh Hashanah 25a-b

Our Rabbis taught: "Why were the names of the elders not mentioned explicitly? So that people would not say: 'Is so-and-so like Moses and Aaron? Is so-and-so like Nadav and Abihu? Is so-and-so like Eldad and Medad?' It says 'Samuel said to the people: "The Lord, . . . He who appointed Moses and Aaron" [I Sam. 12:6]' and it says 'And the Lord sent Jerubbaal and Bedan and Jephthah and Samuel' [I Sam. 12:11]. Jerubbaal is Gideon. Why is he called Jerubbaal? Because he fought with Baal. Bedan is Samson. Why is he called Bedan? Because he came from Dan. Jephthah is Jephthah.

It says: 'Moses and Aaron among His priests, Samuel, among those who call on His name' [Psalms 99:6]. The text has equated three of the most important men of the world, to tell you that Jerubbaal in his generation is like Moses in his generation; Bedan in his generation is like Aaron in his generation; Jephthah in his generation is like Samuel in his generation—to teach you that even the least important man in the world, once he has been appointed a leader of the community is considered as among the greatest of the great."

Then He said to Moses, "Come up to the Lord, with Aaron, Nadab and Abihu, and seventy elders of Israel, and bow low from afar." (Exodus 24:1) •

[Moses] gathered seventy of the people's elders and stationed them around the tent. Then the Lord came down in a cloud and spoke to him; He drew upon the spirit that was on him and put it upon the seventy elders. And when the spirit rested upon them, they spoke in ecstasy, but did not continue. Two men, one named Eldad and the other Medad, had remained in the camp; yet the spirit rested upon them—they were among those recorded, but they had not gone out to the tent—and they spoke in ecstasy in the camp. (Numbers 11:24–26) •

CONTEXT

The Gemara brings together three verses (two from the book of Samuel, one from Psalms) that mention Israelite leaders. First, the lesser-known names are identified. Jerubbaal is Gideon (Judges 6–8); Bedan is Samson (Judges 14–16). Together with Jephthah (Judges 11–12), they were three of the *shoftim* or judges who led the Israelites in the period between Joshua and King Saul. Each is known, among other things, for his weaknesses: Gideon lacked courage and required constant assurance from God. Samson showed bad judgement in the choice of women he pursued. Jephthah ended up sacrificing his own daughter as a consequence of a rash vow he made to God.

Then, the Gemara notes the incongruity of mentioning these three inferior leaders together with three of the greatest ones: Moses, Aaron, and Samuel. (Samuel was the prophet and judge who led Israel and anointed Saul and David as kings.) Rabbinic methodology is interesting: All three verses contain the name of Samuel. The Rabbis deduce that all the names mentioned in the three verses are somehow similar or equal. Indeed, the verses explicitly state that *God* appointed or sent the leaders, and thus whether great or mediocre, they have the authority of God behind them.

D'RASH

In 1973, the Vice President of the United States resigned his position after pleading *nolo contendre* to charges of financial impropriety. The President of the United States, Richard Nixon, selected Congressman Gerald R. Ford to fill the vacant post. Ford was a popular leader in Congress, but was never known for his brilliance or eloquence. After taking the oath of office, the new vice-president humbly described himself: "I'm a Ford, not a Lincoln." Less than a year later, with the resignation of Nixon, Ford became the thirty-eighth president of the United States. One commentator, recalling Ford's modest self-description, yet impressed by the basic decency of the man, said: "A Ford may be just what our nation needs at this difficult moment."

We live at a time when it is fashionable to "take apart" our leaders and show their every flaw and shortcoming. We lament "how the mighty have fallen" and pine for the good old days of strong, moral, wise leaders. We sigh and wonder why our generation could not be blessed with the likes of a Roosevelt, a Lincoln, a Jefferson, or a Washington.

To be fair, we have to remember that history can be very fickle in its judgements. Lincoln in his own day was vilified and mocked by the media as well as by many in the population. Today, he is considered our greatest president, and his personal status approaches that of a saint. Later revelations about Kennedy as a womanizer and Jefferson as a slaveholder served to tarnish the once pristine reputations of these two leaders.

Yet even when we are justified in belittling our current crop of leaders, we would do well to remember that "Jephthah in his generation is like Samuel in his generation." Even someone as inadequate and as flawed as Jephthah was nevertheless the vehicle for leading the Israelites to victory over their enemies. Looking at the chaos that afflicts so many nations on other continents, we need to remember that even a mediocre leader is superior to a tyrant or the absence of any effective leadership.

Jephthah is a reminder that our leaders may be sent by God, but they do not come from heaven; they rise up out of the people. They are, in the truest sense, a reflection of who we are. We often blame our leaders for failing us. Perhaps we need to keep in mind that a people get the leaders they deserve. Occasionally we merit a Moses, Aaron, or Samuel; other times we get Jerubbaal, Bedan, or Jephthah. The Talmud teaches that even a Jephthah can serve an important function. If we are displeased with our leaders, we need to look inwardly for the answers why.

אֵין הַבְּרָכָה מְצוּיָה
אֶלָּא בְּדָבָר הַסָּמוּי מִן הָעַיִן

Blessing is found only in that which is hidden from the eye.

TEXT

Ta'anit 8b

> *Rabbi Yitzḥak said: "Blessing is found only in that which is hidden from the eye, as it says: 'The Lord will ordain blessings for you upon your barns' [Deuteronomy 28:8]." It was taught in the school of Rabbi Yishmael: "Blessing is found only in that which the eye has no power over, as it says, 'The Lord will ordain blessings for you upon your barns' [Deuteronomy 28:8]." Our sages taught: "One who enters to measure his granary says: 'May it be Your will, Lord our God, that you send blessing on the works of our hands.' If he has started to measure he says: 'Blessed is He who sends blessing to this pile.' If he measured and then blessed, this is a vain prayer, since blessing is not found in something weighed, or something measured, or in something counted, but in that which is hidden from the eye."*

CONTEXT

This section deals with the need for rain and the appropriate prayers that ask for rain, specifically when they are to be said. To an ancient agricultural society, rain was essential. Plentiful rain meant a bountiful harvest, a sign of God's blessing. This is where our Gemara comes in.

Rabbi Yitzḥak's explanation of the verse from Deuteronomy, based on the teaching of the school of Rabbi Yishmael, takes the quotation a bit out of context. In Deuteronomy, God promises blessings for those who obey and curses for those who disobey. Rabbi Yitzḥak reads the verse in its narrowest sense, not that God will grant various blessings to those who follow the right way, but that God will bless you "in your barn." Why *there,* wonders Rabbi Yitzḥak, and not somewhere else? He understands the word *ba-asamekha,* "in your barns," literally, that God's blessings will be found *in* the barn, somewhere enclosed and not clearly visible to the outside.

The Lord will put to rout before you the enemies who attack you; they will march out against you by a single road, but flee from you by many roads. The Lord will ordain blessings for you upon your barns and upon all your undertakings: He will bless you in the land that the Lord your God is giving you. The Lord will establish you as His holy people, as He swore to you, if you keep the commandments of the Lord your God and walk in His ways. (Deuteronomy 28:7–9) •

This narrow reading is a common homiletical approach. Rabbi Yitzḥak's purpose is not to be faithful to the meaning of the Deuteronomic chapter but, rather, to teach a practical lesson based on the verse. It is possible, as well, that Rabbi Yitzḥak is making a pun. The Hebrew words for "hidden" and "your barns"—*samui* and *asamekha*—sound alike.

Perhaps he is making a word play based on the similar sounds: What is truly worthwhile in *asamekha,* your barns, is *samui,* hidden.

D'RASH

A parent is videotaping her daughter's activities. She thinks: "I am so blessed to have such a wonderful child! By capturing her on film, I am recording how intelligent, beautiful, and cute she is. I have a permanent record of my blessings." Perhaps, but Rabbi Yitzḥak would doubt it, for he has a different definition of blessing. Only that which we *cannot* see with the eye—or the videocamera—is our blessing. There is no real way to count, enumerate, or reckon our blessings.

Imagine that this same parent suddenly sees something in her child that overwhelms her, so much so that she puts down the camera while her jaw drops open in awe and she utters: "Wow! That's unbelievable!" *This* moment, to Rabbi Yitzḥak, is when she really finds blessing. Rabbi Yitzḥak holds that we cannot catalog and record blessings; we can only experience them as sudden bursts of realization and awe. Thus, we feel blessed *not* when we are videotaping the child, but when we are suddenly so overwhelmed by what we see in that child.

Rabbi Yitzḥak's notion presages the thinking of Abraham Joshua Heschel who spoke of "wonder" and "radical amazement." Dr. Heschel posited that religious doubt ends where wonder and amazement begin. We are amazed at "the unexpectedness of being," that we and the world and everything in it exist at all! Despite our ability to rationalize and despite our deep knowledge, there comes a point where intellect ends and experience begins. This is when we truly feel blessed. Most of us learn through our minds. We are intelligent, thinking, savvy human beings, as our Jewish tradition wants us to be. Nonetheless, our blessings are seen not with our minds—or our eyes, our intellects or videocameras—but with our hearts.

When we think that the blessings we have can be counted and catalogued, we are often missing the mark. Our blessings are not so neatly packaged and enumerated. We have to train ourselves to see the wonder and beauty in the world, to *experience* life rather than *record* it. When we *think* that we know how many blessings we have, we are—in the eyes of Rabbi Yitzḥak—often deceiving ourselves. The greatest sources of blessing are hidden from our eyes, in serendipitous moments of radical amazement.

אֵין מַטְרִיחִין אֶת הַצִּבּוּר יוֹתֵר מִדַּאי

We do not overburden the community.

TEXT

Ta'anit 14a-b

In the time of Rabbi Yehudah Nesiah there was trouble. He enacted thirteen fasts but was not answered. He thought of enacting more. Rabbi Ammi said to him: "Has it not been taught that we do not overburden the community?" Rabbi Abba son of Rabbi Ḥiyya bar Abba said: "What Rabbi Ammi did, he did for himself." This is what Rabbi Ḥiyya bar Abba said in the name of Rabbi Yoḥanan: "This was taught only for rain, but for other disasters, they continue fasting until they are answered from Heaven!" It has been taught in support of this: "When they said three and seven, this was only for rain, but for other disasters, they continue fasting until they are answered." But this contradicts Rabbi Ammi! Rabbi Ammi could say to you: "We do not enact more than thirteen fasts on the community, because we do not overburden the community, this according to Rabbi." Rabbi Shimon ben Gamliel says: "This is not the reason, rather that the time of rain has passed."

*The best known fast days are Yom Kippur and Tisha b'Av (the ninth of Av, commemorating the destruction of the Temples in Jerusalem). However, there are other fast days commemorating disastrous events in Jewish history. In addition, there seem to have been many other fast days, both personal and communal, in early talmudic times. This trend led the Rabbis to try to limit the number of fasts. Shmuel goes so far as to say: "Whoever fasts is called a sinner" (*Ta'anit *11a). While Shmuel's statement is an exaggeration of sorts, it does reflect the rabbinic tendency to restrict fasting.* •

CONTEXT

The Tractate *Ta'anit,* from which this text is taken, teaches about fast days and the prayers associated with them. The Mishnah just prior to this section of Gemara teaches us that if, during a time of drought, individual fasting and petition were not effective, then the community would impose a fast upon itself. A community fast was more severe and restrictive, and thus seen as potentially more effective than a personal one, though a community fast was still only a sunrise to sunset fast (as opposed to Yom Kippur which is sunset to sunset).

The "three" and "seven" of the Gemara ("When they said three and seven . . .") refers to the number of days of fasting. Three and seven, plus the original three, would bring the community to the maximum of thirteen (nonconsecutive) days of fasting. In the case of the last seven days, shops would be closed as well. If no rain fell as a result of this period of self-deprivation, then other measures were instituted, including restricting construction, planting, and weddings. Any additional fasting would not only be ineffective—for thirteen fast days had gone unanswered—but would also be a burden on the community.

D'RASH

There are at least two different ways of looking at natural disasters. Some people may see them as the direct result of God's decree, but most people today would likely have a different view of God's control over nature, not seeing natural disasters as the specific work of the Creator. Such people, in a drought, would seed the clouds, dam the rivers, and desalinate ocean water. They would not call for a day of national fasting and prayer for rain.

Nonetheless, the principle annunciated by Rabbi Ammi, that we do not overburden the community, does apply to our lives today, regardless of our theology of God and nature. In the synagogue, this ideal is seen in the way Torah scrolls are used. Rolling the *Sefer Torah,* the Torah scroll, to the correct place can take quite a bit of time. Doing so while the congregation sits and waits for the reading is considered a burden on the community. Thus, the *Sefer Torah* is rolled to the correct place for that day's reading *before* the congregation arrives. Similarly, we often use two or even three Torah scrolls on special occasions so that the congregation does not have to wait while one Torah scroll is rolled from one reading to another.

The principle that we should not overburden the community is also relevant in secular life. In Congress, the entire bill being voted on is supposed to be formally read. However, after the first few sentences, some member of Congress will usually make a motion that since everyone agrees on the bill as it was printed and distributed, the formal reading can be dispensed with. The members of Congress assent so that their precious time not be wasted.

Just as we do not want to be overburdened *by* others, we must be careful not to cause the overburdening *of* others. In our jobs and in organizational work, we may create unnecessary paperwork and endless bureaucracy. Does the form really have to be filled out in *triplicate?* Would one sign, posted at the entrance, save overburdening workers with countless memoranda? With a little more trust in those who work under us, we could eliminate a large percentage of the countless repetitive exercises and drills that we require.

There are times when even *we* overextend ourselves, causing or exacerbating our own burdens. With every good intention, we sign up for several different committees, even though we cannot possibly do the work involved, and do it well. Rather than being seen as helpful volunteers and good workers, we become "dead weight" or "the albatross." As we try to establish, or to expand, our businesses and families, we may take on too many debts and burdens. In the end, these serve to thwart our very efforts and bring us less security, rather than more. The Rabbis' injunction not to overburden the community is a reminder to be sensitive to the needs both of others and of ourselves, for the burdens we carry can often be eased.

טוֹבֵל . . . וְשֶׁרֶץ בְּיָדוֹ **He immerses . . . with a reptile in his hand.**

TEXT

Ta'anit 16a

> *Rav Ada bar Ahava said: "A person who committed a sin and then confesses it, but who does not stop sinning, to what can he be compared? To a person who holds a reptile in his hand, for even if he were to immerse in all the waters in the world, the immersion would not be effective. If he lets go, once he immerses in forty* seahs, *the immersion is immediately effective, as it says: '[He who covers up his faults will not succeed;] he who confesses and gives them up will find mercy' [Proverbs 28:13]. And it says, 'Let us lift up our hearts with our hands to God in heaven' [Lamentations 3:41]."*

CONTEXT

The Tractate *Ta'anit* deals with fasts that were undertaken by entire Jewish communities as a response to severe droughts. Many Jews believed that God was punishing the people for their sins by withholding the rains. During such a crisis, fasting, prayer, and acts of charity were considered the best ways to plead with God to relent and send rain.

In our section, the Rabbis ponder the question of what constitutes true repentance. Rav Ada bar Ahava believes that while confessing one's sins is an important first step in the process of repentance, it cannot be the only step. One must also stop committing the sin. Rashi, in his commentary to the Gemara, explains that the sin in question here is theft. Thus, merely admitting that one had stolen something would not be a sufficient act of repentance. The thief must also return the stolen item to its rightful owner.

The Talmud drives this point home by reference to a graphic analogy connected to the ritual of immersion. A person had to be in a state of ritual purity in order to enter the Temple and participate in the sacrificial cult. One became ritually impure by contracting the skin disease known as *tzara'at,* through discharge from the sexual organs, through contact with the carcass of certain animals (such as reptiles, listed in Leviticus 11) or contact with a dead body. Someone who was impure had to go to the mikveh and immerse in water.

A mikveh, literally "collection" of waters, is either a natural pool or an artificially constructed one

The Rabbis then considered the theoretical case of a person who immersed in the mikveh while still holding a reptile. They concluded that until the reptile was released, all the *built in a prescribed way and holding at least forty* seahs *of naturally accumulated water. (One interpretation calculates forty* seahs *as the equivalent of 151 gallons.) Following the immersion, the person was again ritually pure. A mikveh is still used today in the Jewish community by those converting to Judaism, by brides prior to their weddings, by Jewish women following their monthly menstrual cycle, and by many as a way of achieving spiritual purification.* •

water in the world would not make the immersion in the mikveh effective. Similarly, until a person stopped the sinful behavior, the act of confessing was, by itself, meaningless.

Two verses from the Bible are brought to reinforce the dual aspect of true repentance. In the first one, from Proverbs, the Rabbis note that a person will find mercy (in other words, receive God's forgiveness) by both "confessing" sins and "giving them up," giving back the stolen property. Both acts—admitting one's errors and then changing one's ways—are required for repentance to be complete. In the second verse, the Rabbis interpret "lifting our hearts to God" as referring to prayer and confession; the "lifting of our hands," a more physical activity, is understood to mean that we have given back anything our hands may have stolen from others.

D'RASH

A man returned to his doctor, six months after being diagnosed with emphysema caused primarily by smoking. Although his condition had improved somewhat after the initial diagnosis and treatments, the painful symptoms, including the difficult breathing, had recently returned. During the course of the examination, the doctor found that the patient had, in the past two months, taken up smoking again.

"Doc, you've got to help me. I can hardly catch my breath, and the coughing is torture."

"John, I've explained this to you before: Until you stop the smoking, there's nothing that I can do to help you. It's really up to you. You want to get better? First get rid of the cigarettes."

Before we can move ahead and try to become better, we need to get rid of the bad and leave it behind. This law of nature apparently applies not only to the ritual of mikveh and to the science of medicine, but also to the realm of ethics as well. The Rabbis teach us that the power of Yom Kippur, the Day of Atonement, is such that if we seek God's forgiveness for sins we have committed against God, we are automatically forgiven. However, all the crimes and transgressions we have committed and all the wrongs we have done to our fellow human beings in the past year are not forgiven unless and until we go to those we have hurt and offended and make restitution to them. Admitting our errors is the first step but it, by itself, is not sufficient. If we have broken something, we need to replace it. If we have humiliated another person, we need to find a way to restore his or her dignity. To do any less would be the equivalent of immersing in the mikveh with a reptile still in our hands.

לְעוֹלָם יְהֵא אָדָם רַךְ כְּקָנֶה
וְאַל יְהֵא קָשֶׁה כְּאֶרֶז

A person should always be as bending as a reed, not as rigid as the cedar.

TEXT

Ta'anit 20a-b

A story: Rabbi Elazar son of Rabbi Shimon came from his master's house in Migdal Gedor, riding on a donkey, travelling by the river. He was extremely happy, very taken with himself after having learned so much Torah. He came upon a very ugly man who said to him: "Shalom, Rabbi." He did not return his greeting. He then said [to the ugly man]: "You nothing! How ugly that man is! Are all the people of your town ugly like you?" He answered: "I do not know, but why don't you go and tell the Craftsman who made me?" When he [Rabbi Elazar] himself realized that he had sinned, he got off his donkey and bowed before him and said to him: "I have spoken improperly to you. Forgive me!" He said to him: "I will not forgive you until you go and tell the Craftsman who made me 'How ugly is this thing You have made!'" He [Rabbi Elazar] followed him until he reached his town. The townspeople came out to greet him, saying: "Shalom, Rabbi, Rabbi! Master, Master!" He [the ugly man] said to them: "Who are you calling 'Rabbi, Rabbi'?" They said: "This man, walking behind you." He said to them: "If this is a Rabbi, may there not be more like him in Israel!" They said to him: "Why?" He said to them: "This is what he did to me. . . ." They said to him: "Nevertheless, forgive him, for he is a great man of the Torah." He said: "For your sakes, I will forgive him, on the condition that he not do this again." Immediately, Rabbi Elazar son of Rabbi Shimon came in and preached: "A person should always be as bending as a reed, not as rigid as a cedar. Therefore has the reed merited to be used for the quills with which we write the Torah scroll, tefillin, and mezuzzot."

On the Gemara, Rashi comments: "There are books in which it is written that it was Elijah, may his memory be for a blessing, and his intention was to reprove him so he would not do this again." •

CONTEXT

The Gemara notes the similarities of the Jews to the reed: Both desperately need water in order to survive. In addition, the Jews were simple, weak, and humble like the reed. The strong, tall, and noble cedar tree was seen as symbolic of the nations of the world and, specifically, the Romans. Yet, the poor reed was the ultimate survivor. It was able to bend and give in the face of a strong wind or a storm. The mighty cedar, because it was not as pliant, was more likely to be uprooted. This message was to become an important strategy in coping with persecution.

Because of its "easy-going" nature and its willingness to show flexibility, the reed was, according to tradition, rewarded with the privilege of being used in the holy task of writing Torah scrolls, tefillin and mezuzzot. (Tefillin are the two boxes strapped on to the arm and head during the morning weekday service; the boxes contain parchment on which sections from the Torah are written; mezuzzot are containers attached to the doorpost which also contain selections of the Torah written on parchment.)

D'RASH

Our story highlights the paradox that weakness and strength are not always what we expect them to be: The teacher, it turns out, is the one who needs to learn the lesson; the one presumed least worthy of instructing us is the one who has the most to teach. The mighty, tall cedar tree is the first to be toppled by the wind, while the small, meager reed is able to survive almost any assault.

Strength is often not defined in the conventional terms of size, might, power, resolve, or immutability. The classic Jewish story to show this is, of course, that of David and Goliath. The Israelite shepherd boy is too young, he is too small, he comes without armor, and with no battle experience—and yet he walks away the victor. His courage, his agility, his resourcefulness, and his faith in God are enough to enable him to defeat the giant warrior. In many ways, that has also been a recurrent theme of Jewish history: Time and time again, the Jewish people were outnumbered by a more powerful enemy, yet they managed to survive and prevail, while the enemy was ultimately vanquished and disappeared. The nation of Israel was able to outlast the Egyptians, the Canaanites, the Babylonians, and the Syrian-Greeks; the Rabbis of the Talmud believed, correctly so, that the Romans, too, would eventually go the same way.

Our tale reminds us that what was true on a national scale is also true on a personal level, as well. Real strength is not measured by how big someone's muscles are and not by how many people one has beaten up or killed. Ben Zoma asks the question: "Who is mighty?" and gives an unexpected answer: "One who controls his own impulses" (Avot 4:1). A man has been insulted to his face, but instead of striking the offender, he chooses to teach him the meaning of dignity and Godliness. The Rabbi has had a lapse of moral judgement. Instead of trying to make excuses or look for someone else to blame, he steps forward and says: "I did a terrible thing to you. Please forgive me." These are examples of strength, at least as the Rabbis defined it. Often, we try to resist, to stand up to pressure, to remain steadfast. At times, those are admirable qualities. However, if we became inflexible in the hope that we can remain unmovable, we may find ourselves knocked down and even uprooted. From a law of nature, the Rabbis derive a law of human relations: Learn when to bend, or you will break.

אִם יֹאמַר לְךָ אָדָם
יָגַעְתִּי וְלֹא מָצָאתִי אַל תַּאֲמֵן

If a person says to you:
"I have labored but did not find,"
do not believe it!

TEXT

Megillah 6b

> *Rabbi Yitzḥak said: If a person says to you: "I have labored but did not find," do not believe it! "I did not labor and I found," do not believe it! "I labored and found," believe it! These words refer to matters of Torah. But in matters of business, help is from Heaven! And in matters of Torah, this refers only to acumen, but for maintaining learning, help is from Heaven!*

CONTEXT

Rabbi Yitzḥak's words are a straightforward attempt on the part of one Talmudic sage to define the rabbinic approach to success. In the eyes of Rabbi Yitzḥak, success in life is, plain and simple, the result of hard work. One who claims to have succeeded effortlessly should not be believed. And one who claims to have worked diligently without achieving is probably not telling the truth either. All this, of course, is the view of one sage, Rabbi Yitzḥak. He seems to be teaching about life in general, since the Hebrew word *matzati,* "I found," can refer to many different realms and have various different meanings.

As is usually the case in the Gemara, when a generalized statement like this is made, a clarification is necessary. Can this really be saying that hard work *always* produces success? Is life as black-and-white as Rabbi Yitzḥak would paint it to be? The later discussion will limit and qualify the earlier generalization (earlier both in the order of the text and chronologically). Thus, the Gemara says that Rabbi Yitzḥak is correct that work produces results but (and this is the limitation) only in the area of study. In other areas of our lives, it is, in rabbinic terms, "in the hands of Heaven," beyond our control. And in matters of Torah, effort pays off only relative to comprehension. One who studies hard will ultimately understand. However, that person may soon forget what was learned, for memory is beyond our control and is from Heaven.

Some later commentators ask: Are there not times when we do *not* see results, even if we work hard in studying and trying to understand? They answer that even partial results

*The Rabbis of the Talmud, Rabbi Yitzḥak among them, were well aware that good things happen to bad people and that the righteous sometimes struggle while the wicked not only avoid suffering but even thrive. There are numerous discussions and debates in the Gemara on how to deal with wickedness and the wicked, both from a philosophical viewpoint (Why does it even exist in God's world?) to very practical concerns (How should we respond to the wicked?). Elsewhere in the Talmud (*Berakhot *7b), Rabbi Yitzḥak is involved in one such debate. Rabbi Yoḥanan, his teacher, quotes a verse from Proverbs as proof that we should fight the wicked: "Those who forsake instruction [Torah] praise the wicked, but those who heed instruction [Torah] fight them" (Proverbs 28:4). However, Rabbi Yitzḥak takes a different approach, teaching: "If you see the wicked having his hour, do not argue with him, as it says: 'His ways prosper at all times' (Psalms 10:5); and even more so, he may win in court, as it says: 'Your judgments are far beyond him' (ibid); and even more so, he may see his enemies' defeat, as it says: 'He snorts at all his foes' (ibid)." The* in study have a reinforcing effect; it sharpens our minds. Just *trying* to understand text is worthwhile, even if we think we are not successful. We are laying the foundation to build on later. Despite this, the simple explanation of Rabbi Yitzḥak's view is a very general rule that hard work is the key to success.

Talmud solves the contradiction between the view of Rabbi Yitzḥak (to leave the wicked alone) and that of Rabbi Yoḥanan (to fight the wicked): One (the view of Rabbi Yitzḥak) refers to personal matters like commerce, while the other (the view of Rabbi Yoḥanan) refers to "matters of Heaven," that is, religious issues. Jews have been arguing over such questions ever since. ●

D'RASH

The Gemara itself already saw that Rabbi Yitzḥak's words are, to a large degree, an overgeneralization, perhaps even a bit naive. Work pays off—*usually.* There is a certain amount of what we would call luck, or what the Rabbis of the Talmud would call "divine help," in most spheres of life. We might even add: It is true in the study of Jewish texts as well. We may slave over a chapter, a source or a book, only to find it beyond our comprehension.

The Gemara's limitation of Rabbi Yitzḥak's words is a good reminder that in commerce, as much as hard work and perseverance count, a great deal also depends upon luck and timing. A person may slave, year after year, on an invention that will revolutionize life, only to find the country not ready for this gadget. Yet another inventor, with only a fraction of the effort, will earn millions of dollars and become an overnight sensation for a device that is only half as innovative and hardly as functional or worthwhile.

In the education sphere, however, Rabbi Yitzḥak's general principle is a sound one. Few learning endeavors produce results effortlessly. One who desires to study a text or learn a skill will likely have to invest a great deal of effort in order to be intellectually satisfied and rewarded with competence. Rabbi Yitzḥak's principle is no less true in Jewish education. Various organizations offer "crash courses" in Jewish studies. These may help overcome fears and stimulate interest. They can produce a fundamental knowledge base and increased interest in study. Nonetheless, knowledge of and intimacy with Jewish life and practice are the product of ongoing, concerted effort, years and even decades of training, repetitive endeavors, and hard work.

Some, especially those who have not been fortunate in business, may be angry or disappointed with this reality. After all, in business, it *is* possible to "strike it rich." Furthermore, those who study are sometimes disappointed with their learning. One may labor and still feel uneducated or frustrated. On the whole, though, Rabbi Yitzḥak's dictum is a sound one for much of life, especially Jewish living. Without the effort, we are unlikely to see the rewards.

מִלָּה בְּסֶלַע מַשְׁתּוּקָא בִּתְרֵין

A word costs a *sela,* silence goes for two.

The Prayer, ha-Tefillah *in Hebrew, refers to the* Amidah, *the "standing" prayer, which is also known as the* Shemoneh Esrei, *the "eighteen," because there were originally eighteen sections and concluding blessings in the prayer. It is the central unit of the standard worship service. There are at least two traditions concerning its origin:*

> *The* Amidah: *Where is it from? As it has been taught: Shimon ha-Pakuli arranged the eighteen blessings in order before Rabban Gamliel in Yavneh. Rabbi Yoḥanan said (and others say it was taught in a* baraita): *"One hundred and twenty elders—and among them several prophets—established the eighteen blessings in their proper order." (*Megillah *17b)* •

TEXT

Megillah 18a

If one hundred and twenty elders—and among them several prophets—already established the Prayer [Amidah] *in its proper order, what was it that Shimon ha-Pakuli did? They [the blessings] had been forgotten, and he came back and set them in their order. From that point on, it was forbidden to [further] tell the praises of the Holy One, blessed be He, for Rabbi Elazar said: "What is the meaning of the verse: 'Who can tell the mighty acts of the Lord, proclaim all His praises?' [Psalms 106:2]. Who is worthy of telling the mighty acts of the Lord? One who is able to proclaim* all *of His praises."*

Rabbah bar bar Ḥana said in the name of Rabbi Yoḥanan: "One who speaks too much in praising the Holy One, blessed be He, is uprooted from the world, as it says: 'Is anything conveyed to Him when I speak? Should a man wish to be swallowed up?' [Job 37:20, author's translation]." Rabbi Yehudah of K'far Giboriya, and some say of K'far Gibor Ḥayil, preached: "What is the meaning of the verse: 'To You, silence is praise' [Psalms 65:2, author's translation]? The best medicine is silence." When Rav Dimi came he said: "In the West, they say: 'A word costs a sela, *silence goes for two.'"*

CONTEXT

The Gemara first attempts to reconcile two different traditions concerning the origin of the *Amidah,* "the Prayer." The point is then made that once the text had been established and fixed, it was no longer possible to add extemporaneous praises of God. (Apparently, at one point in the development of the *Amidah,* new words were added quite often to the prayer; each leader or worshiper was expected to express the fixed themes of the prayer in a personal way.) One reason for this change is that the Rabbis felt that, ironically, by saying more and more about God, we were, in effect, diminishing God's greatness. God is so great that any new attempt to praise God by specific adjectives only serves to define, and thus confine, the divine.

Rabbi Elazar's clever twist on the verse from the Psalms makes the point that only someone capable of proclaiming *all* of God's praises is allowed to add to the fixed prayers. Of course, no such human being exists; Rabbah bar bar Ḥana's interpretation of the quote from Job shows what will happen to a person who tries. Rabbi Yehudah offers the wisdom that sometimes saying nothing is better than saying too much. Silence shows our inability to respond to a power so much greater than ourselves. Rav Dimi's folk saying from the West (Israel) makes the same point. A *sela* was a common coin. Thus, the price of silence is twice that of words.

D'RASH

A friend has just sustained a terrible personal loss. At the funeral, there were so many people, we barely had a chance to say more than "I'm so sorry." A day or two have passed, and we need to go make a condolence call, but we are very anxious about the visit. It is extremely uncomfortable to have to deal with death. We don't know which words we should use to express our feelings, and we are at a total loss in terms of what to say to the mourner to try and heal her pain and bring her comfort.

There are certain standard phrases that are suggested by social custom: "I was so sorry to hear about your loss." "If there is anything that we can do for you, please let us know." Jewish tradition offers its own formula: "May God comfort you among the other mourners of Zion and Jerusalem."

But sometimes, we find that the *more* we say, the *less* helpful we are. Some people offer platitudes or clichés ("Don't worry, time heals all wounds"). Others focus inappropriately on themselves ("After *my* husband died, I was a basket case for the longest time"). Still others say the most insensitive things ("You're still young, you can have *another* child").

Tradition—social or religious—may be very wise in providing us with short, standard phrases. Our attempts to improve on them, or add to them, may turn out to actually diminish the good we are trying to do. Our kind intentions do not count for much when we end up hurting people already in great pain.

It may very well be that the words we say are not as important as we might think. It often turns out, in fact, that our presence is much more significant than any utterances that we might make. One of the best things that we can do is ask about the person who has died, and then sit back and listen attentively. Some mourners need to talk much more than they need to hear someone else's wisdom. At other times, we may sense that our friend is not up to listening *or* to talking, but they desperately need someone to be with. Holding a hand, giving a hug, or lending a shoulder to cry on may be all that is needed.

Knowing just what to say, or what not to say, in a given situation is a sign of wisdom. Knowing that a word costs a *sela,* but that silence is worth twice as much, is a sign of even greater understanding.

כָּל מָקוֹם שֶׁאַתָּה מוֹצֵא גְבוּרָתוֹ
שֶׁל הַקָּדוֹשׁ בָּרוּךְ הוּא
אַתָּה מוֹצֵא עַנְוְתָנוּתוֹ

Wherever you find the strength of the Holy One, praised be He, you find His humility.

TEXT

Megillah 31a

On Yom Kippur, we read "After the death" [Leviticus 16] and we conclude with "For thus said He who high aloft forever dwells" [Isaiah 57:15]. At Minḥah, *we read about forbidden relations [Leviticus 18] and we conclude with Jonah. Rabbi Yoḥanan said: "Wherever you find the strength of the Holy One, praised be He, you find His humility." This is written in the Torah, repeated in the Prophets, and reiterated in the Writings. It is written in the Torah: "For the Lord your God is God supreme and Lord supreme" [Deuteronomy 10:17] and it says right after that "but upholds the cause of the fatherless and the widow." It is repeated in the Prophets: "For thus said He who high aloft forever dwells, whose name is holy" [Isaiah 57:15] and it says right after "yet with the contrite and lowly in spirit." It is reiterated in the Writings, as it says: "Extol Him who rides the clouds; the Lord is His name" [Psalms 68:5] and it says right after that "the father of orphans, the champion of widows."*

The Tractate Megillah *discusses not only the reading of the Megillah, that is, the scroll of Esther on Purim, but also many of the laws of reading from the Torah (Pentateuch or Five Books of Moses) and haftarah (readings from the Prophets on Shabbat and holidays). The Mishnah preceding this section of Gemara outlines the Torah readings for holidays like Pesaḥ and Rosh Hashanah. The Gemara expands upon the theme, giving not only the Yom Kippur morning Torah reading (from Leviticus 16) but also the haftarah (from Isaiah 57). The expression "we conclude with,"* maftirin, *is from the same Hebrew root as haftarah. After the Torah is read, the haftarah, a* concluding *section of Bible from the Prophets, is chanted.* •

CONTEXT

In a discussion on which Torah reading is read and which haftarah is chanted on certain holidays, Rabbi Yoḥanan notes that each mention of God ("the Holy One, praised be He") extols not only God's strength but also God's humility and compassion for humanity. Thus, the mention of the haftarah for Yom Kippur morning, taken from Isaiah and referring to God as the high and mighty King, reminds Rabbi Yoḥanan of this rule: God's strength and humility are always intertwined in the biblical text. Rabbi Yoḥanan, being a master teacher and scholar, easily finds three verses where both God's strength and concern for people go hand-in-hand.

According to Rabbi Yoḥanan's Midrash, God is supreme in power and might, riding the clouds, yet also humble—down to earth and caring for those human beings who need a champion for their cause. God's strength and concomitant kindness are written in Torah, repeated in the Prophets, and reiterated in the Writings, proof positive that wherever we find the strength of the Holy One, we also find God's humility.

The Hebrew words for "written," "repeated" and "reiterated" are interesting terms. "Written" is *katuv,* a fairly common Hebrew word. "Repeated" is *shanui,* from the same root as the Hebrew number two (and the word mishnah, a teaching that is "repeated"). What we translate as "reiterated" *(meshulash)* is from the Hebrew root for "three." Thus, God's strength and humility are written, repeated, and reiterated throughout the three parts of the Bible—Torah, Prophets, and Writings.

D'RASH

Often, we think of God in terms of overwhelming power—the Creation, the splitting of the Sea of Reeds, the revelation at Sinai. Rabbi Yoḥanan's explanation reminds us that the rabbinic view of God's greatness is more inclusive. God exhibits not only strength and grandeur in divine transcendence, but also unending concern for humanity and love, in divine imminence.

Perhaps Rabbi Yoḥanan's words, and his attempt to expand our view of God's attributes, can help us refocus our view of greatness—not only God's, but also our own. If we are to follow God's ways and imitate God's attributes, then we have to understand real stature. True greatness is powerful, expansive, and broad-based, yet it is also quiet and understated. Wherever there is strength, there should also be compassion.

Recent studies of successful businesses have made this exact point. Those companies that excel are not only strong, powerful corporations but, more often than not, businesses that show care and concern for people. They are in the forefront of providing child-care for employees, of listening to customer suggestions and acting on them, of making people, even the lowliest employee on the corporate ladder, feel both needed and welcome.

Sam Walton, founder of Wal-Mart, turned a small store into a nationwide chain, becoming one of the richest men in America. Some have explained Walton's success in his concern for each employee. A story demonstrates this: One night, he could not sleep. After driving to an all-night bakery at 2:30 A.M., Mr. Walton brought donuts to the workers at a Wal-Mart distribution center, chatting with them at this late hour. In so doing, he found out that the employees wanted a new shower installed at work, which he arranged for. Sam Walton's greatness was not only in selling $2 billion of merchandise a year, but also in caring for the lonely employee who worked the late night shift at one of his stores.

This is what Rabbi Yoḥanan's words are saying to us today: Just as God's greatness comes from strength combined with compassion, we humans, created in God's image, must show both strength *and* compassion, hand-in-hand. Thus, a business executive can have a high-powered career, earning lots of money and wielding strength; that executive must also care for the human beings who are touched by the company. Powerful politicians can win votes and elections, but the real challenge is often winning the hearts of the people whom they represent. We have to earn money to support our families, but we cannot forget to spend time with them.

If the common person, even the most unfortunate member of society like the widow or orphan, is constantly the focus of God's attention, then don't we human beings have an equal responsibility of never forgetting them? This, in Rabbi Yoḥanan's eyes, as well as in the view of Judaism, is true greatness.

אֵין מְעָרְבִין שִׂמְחָה בְּשִׂמְחָה

One does not mix one happy occasion with another.

TEXT

Moed Katan 8b

Mishnah *(1:7): One does not marry a woman during a festival, be she a virgin or a widow, nor does one effect a levirate marriage, because it is a happy occasion. . . .*
Gemara: *So what if it is a happy occasion? Rav Yehudah said in the name of Shmuel, and so too Rabbi Elazar said in the name of Rabbi Oshiya, while others say Rabbi Elazar said in the name of Rabbi Ḥanina: "Because one does not mix one happy occasion with another." Rabbah bar Rav Huna said: "Because he would set aside the rejoicing in the festival and busy himself with rejoicing with his wife." Abaye said to Rav Yosef: "What Rabbah bar Rav Huna said is the same as Rav said, for Rav Daniel bar Katina said in the name of Rav: 'From where do we learn that one does not marry a woman during a festival? As it says: "You shall rejoice in your festival" [Deuteronomy 16:14]. In your festival, not with your wife.'" Ulla said: "Because of all the trouble." Rabbi Yitzḥak Nappaḥa said: "Because of the neglect of reproduction."*

The Gemara goes on to ask if there is a biblical source for the principle of not mixing one happy occasion with another. It is found in the account of Solomon's dedication of the Temple which took place on the seven days following the festival of Sukkot:

> *So Solomon and all Israel with him—a great assemblage, [coming] from Lebo-hamath to the Wadi of Egypt—observed the Feast at that time before the Lord our God, seven days and again seven days, fourteen days in all. (I Kings 8:65)*

The Rabbis note that it would have been easier and more convenient for the people to have celebrated the dedication of the Temple during *the holiday of*

CONTEXT

One is immediately struck by the large number of Rabbis mentioned in this short piece. Trying to establish the correct source of a teaching is a very important characteristic of rabbinic literature. Attributing a quote to its original author, or bringing alternative claims of authorship, account for the many names here. Mentioning the correct source helps to establish the authority of a particular teaching; it also bestows a kind of immortality on the author.

The levirate marriage referred to in the Mishnah is when a man marries his childless dead brother's widow, in order to continue the family line (Deuteronomy 25:5–6). Four reasons are presented by the Gemara to explain the prohibition of marriage during a festival. Rabbah bar Rav Huna is concerned that a man would spend time with his new wife and neglect the celebration of the holiday. Rav derives the prohibition from a very literal reading of a biblical verse. Ulla worries that a wedding requires a great deal of preparation, and work of many kinds is forbidden on a holiday. Rabbi Yitzḥak Nappaḥa notes that weddings cost a good deal of money, as did holiday preparations. If weddings were permitted on a festival, many people might postpone their marriages until the festival, so they would have to prepare only one banquet for both. Rabbi Yitzḥak fears that by putting off weddings, ultimately there would be a decrease in the number of children born.

Sukkot. The justification for imposing upon the nation to spend an additional week in Jerusalem is that both the festival and *the dedication were considered happy occasions, not to be mixed.* •

D'RASH

According to a Yiddish proverb, "You can't dance at two weddings." The problem is not only a physical one—being in two places at one time—it is also a psychological one. Human beings are generally able to focus on only one thing at a time. If we attempt to do two things at once, one of the two will ultimately give way to the other. When both are of critical importance, something of great value will be lost.

Rabbah bar Rav Huna saw this principle at work in the conflicts that Jews faced in their public and private lives. The festivals of the Jewish calendar punctuated the seasons and gave character to the months of the year. They also served to unite the entire Jewish nation by enabling Jews to recall and relive their mutual history. The folkways, traditions, customs, and laws gave the nation a common practice and a shared set of values. No matter where Jews lived throughout the world, the festivals enabled them to dwell together in the dimension of time.

Whereas a holiday was observed by all, a wedding was seen by most people as a private celebration of two individuals and their immediate circle of family and friends. Holidays came year in and year out; miss a holiday this year and you can always celebrate it again next year. Weddings, on the other hand, were hopefully once-in-a-lifetime events. Everything else was to be put aside to celebrate this most joyous *simḥah*.

Imagine a wedding scheduled during Passover. There are so many preparations necessary to celebrate both events. Trying to do both would become a logistical nightmare. The individuals involved would in no way be able to enjoy either occasion. The other possibility, of course, is that the family would choose to concentrate on one and thus neglect the other. In such a conflict, most people would choose the private and personal over the public; weddings would take place at the detriment of the festival. Holidays would no longer be universally observed, and the community would be split apart and divided, each family going its own way, doing "its own thing."

As many Jewish couples have found out, there are many days during the year when weddings cannot be held. In addition to the festivals, marriages traditionally do not take place during all or part of the *sefirah* period in the spring (between Pesaḥ and Shavuot) and during "the Three Weeks" in the summer (between the seventeenth of Tammuz and the ninth of Av). All these restrictions are hard to comply with and sometimes difficult to understand. What the Rabbis had in mind, among other things, was simply to protect the integrity of the sacred days of the Jewish year and to preserve the unity and integrity of the Jewish people. In doing so, they were also conveying another critical message: The welfare of the community, of the group, of the nation takes precedence over the interests of the individual. There is one corollary to this approach: We are taught that true happiness is to be found not alone, by ourselves, but with others.

מִקְצַת הַיּוֹם כְּכֻלּוֹ **Part of a day is like a whole day.**

TEXT

Moed Katan 20a-b

> *When Rav, the son of the brother of Rabbi Ḥiyya, who was also the son of the sister of Rabbi Ḥiyya, went there, he said to him: "Is father alive?" He said to him: "Mother is alive." He said to him: "Is mother alive?" He said to him: "Father is alive." He [Rabbi Ḥiyya] said to his attendant: "Take off my shoes and follow me to the bathhouse." From this we learn three things: A mourner is forbidden to wear shoes; [mourning upon hearing] delayed news is practiced for only one day; and part of a day is like a whole day.*

CONTEXT

This section of Gemara deals with laws of mourning, specifically *sh'muah r'ḥokah,* "delayed news," news of the death of a close relative that is received more than thirty days after the fact. In such a case, the thirty-day mourning period would have been over. The Gemara attempts to teach us a lesson about delayed news from the actions of Rabbi Ḥiyya. In the conversation above, Rabbi Ḥiyya has returned "there," to Israel. (It is "there" to the compilers of the Talmud Bavli or Babylonian Talmud.) Rabbi Ḥiyya seeks to find out about his parents while his nephew Rav—in attempting to be gentle and not tell his uncle sad news—answers about his own parents, also relatives of Rabbi Ḥiyya. Through a series of marriages, Rabbi Ḥiyya was doubly related to his nephew Rav: He was both his *paternal* uncle and his *maternal* uncle. There are several possible interpretations of the dialogue; for our purposes, we will assume that the following is what Rabbi Ḥiyya and Rav are saying to each other (with our interpretation added in parentheses):

> Rabbi Ḥiyya: "Is (my) father (Aḥa) alive?"
> Rav: "(My own) mother is alive."
> Rabbi Ḥiyya: "Is (my) mother (who is also your grandmother) alive?"
> Rav: "(My) father (Aybu, your half-brother) is alive."

Rabbi Ḥiyya correctly interprets his nephew's intent to break the news of the death of Rabbi Ḥiyya's mother, Aḥa's wife, kindly and gently. Rabbi Ḥiyya immediately begins the period of mourning. But he has been away from Israel for quite some time, and this subtle announcement that Rabbi Ḥiyya's mother has died is "delayed news." Rabbi Ḥiyya's words to his attendant (perhaps the student attending to his needs, rather than a porter or slave)—"Take off my shoes and follow me to the bathhouse"—teach us three things:

1) A mourner is not allowed to wear leather shoes, a practice still followed today. Even in the case of "delayed news," wearing of shoes is prohibited.
2) Bathing is also not allowed to a mourner. Since Rabbi Ḥiyya tells the attendant to meet him at the bathhouse, it is clear that Rabbi Ḥiyya's mourning period will end shortly, because "delayed news" requires only one day of mourning. And,
3) Since he will go directly to the bathhouse, it is clear that, where mourning is involved, "part of a day is like a whole day." Once Rabbi Ḥiyya has mourned for a token amount of time on that one day, his entire mourning period—one day because of the "delayed news"—has been completed.

These three mourning practices are still in effect today. A mourner does not wear leather shoes, which are considered a luxury; a mourner does not bathe; and we count part of a day as a whole day. In fact, in all *cases of mourning, whether for timely news or for delayed news, part of a day is like a whole day. Thus, we count the first day of* shivah *(the seven-day mourning period) which is the day of the burial, as a whole day even though mourning rituals were observed for only part of that day (from after the burial until sunset). Similarly, the last day of* shivah *is always a shortened day. After the* Shaḥarit *service on the morning of the seventh day, the* shivah *mourning period ends.* ●

Nowadays, because communications are so superior to those in second-century Israel and Babylonia, delayed news of a death is less common. Nonetheless, there are still cases where one does not find out about a death until much later. If the delay is less than a month, it is considered "timely news," and all of the mourning rites are observed. If, however, one finds out about a death more than a month afterwards, the case is *sh'muah r'ḥokah,* "delayed news." The mourner is required to observe only one hour, a token amount or "part of a day" of mourning, during which time he or she sits on a low stool and, as a symbol of bereavement, removes leather shoes.

D'RASH

We have all been to a wedding, concert, or play that we just did not want to end. We have all said to ourselves, at one time or another: "That celebration was so joyous, I wish it could have gone on forever." (Or, as they sang in *My Fair Lady,* "I could have danced all night!") We have been to a concert where the music was so inspiring and lively that it reverberated in our heads for hours. We may have seen a play in which the acting was so moving and the plot so thought-provoking that we kept it in mind for days afterwards. These feelings are common and expected, and these occasions are times to stretch, to add, and to increase, as we attempt to prolong these happy occasions, to extend them as much as possible, as well we should.

However, we know that life gives us sad times as well. As Longfellow wrote:

> Into each life some rain must fall,
> Some days must be dark and dreary.

At one time or another, each of us will have reason to grieve and mourn. The Jewish tradition, in the principle "part of a day is like a whole day," is trying to remind us not to extend mourning or overdo sadness.

When a president of the United States dies (especially when one dies in office), there are many ceremonies to mark the passing of a great leader. Offices are closed; flags remain at half staff for an extended period. Then the country must move on. Many Americans will think of the President and will privately mourn as they conduct their everyday affairs. Even if we inwardly feel sad and grieve, outwardly we must return to our daily routine, ever aware of the precarious nature of life and the memories of those who are no longer among the living.

Similarly, Jewish tradition requires us to mourn the death of certain relatives. We must set aside time, a week known as *shivah,* for this most intense period of grieving. Even then, the law is that seven *full* days may be too much. Thus, no *shivah* is really seven complete days. The first day (the day of the burial) and the last day are always partial days, perhaps a reminder that we must face bereavement with the right attitude. Just as there is a time for mourning, there is a time to end our mourning. *Shivah* traditionally concludes with a walk around the block, symbolic of a return to society and to everyday living, despite our personal loss.

The Talmud is teaching us that if we can curtail our mourning a bit by observing only part of a day as a whole day for sad times, then well and good. Happiness should be prolonged; sadness can be cut short.

חַיֵּי בָּנֵי וּמְזוֹנֵי
לָא בִּזְכוּתָא תַּלְיָא מִלְּתָא
אֶלָּא בְּמַזָּלָא תַּלְיָא מִלְּתָא

Life, children, and food
are matters that depend
not on merit, but on luck.

TEXT

Moed Katan 28a

Rava said: "Life, children, and food are matters that depend not on merit, but on luck, for Rabbah and Rav Ḥisda were both righteous rabbis. One would pray and rain would fall, and the other would pray and rain would fall. Rav Ḥisda lived ninety-two years; Rabbah lived forty. In the house of Rav Ḥisda there were sixty weddings; in the house of Rabbah, sixty funerals. In the house of Rav Ḥisda, there was bread of the finest flour for the dogs, and it was not wanted; in the house of Rabbah, there was only barley bread for the people, and it was in short supply."

CONTEXT

In the section immediately preceding ours, a discussion is found that attempts to understand the meaning of premature death. Some Rabbis believed that if a person died at an early age, it was a sign of God's disfavor with them. One viewpoint held that if a person died before reaching fifty, it meant that the punishment of *karet,* "being cut off," had been visited upon that person; if one died at sixty, it was another category of punishment, "death at the hands of Heaven."

Rava comes to dispute this. His position is that the length of a person's life is not determined by righteousness or piety. It is, in the end, a matter of luck. As proof, he brings the case of the two well-known Rabbis, Rav Ḥisda (Rava's own teacher) and Rabbah. Both men were known for their righteousness. During a drought, either man was able to pray for rain, and God would immediately answer their prayers, ending the drought and sending the rain. Yet one lived a life of tragedy, the other of blessing. Rava can explain the differences only as a matter of luck.

*Rav Ḥisda was sitting in the school of Rav, and the Angel of Death could not come close to him, for his mouth did not cease repeating Torah. He sat upon a cedar bench in Rav's school. The cedar cracked, Rav Ḥisda stopped talking, and the angel overpowered him. (*Makkot *10a)* •

Rabbah bar Naḥmani died because of the religious persecutions. Someone informed on him to the king. They said: "There is a man among the Jews who removes 12,000 Jewish men from the royal tax rolls one month every summer and one month every winter. [Rashi explains these months to be Nisan, when they would come in to hear his lectures about Pesaḥ, and Tishrei, when they assembled for his teachings about the festivals. When the tax collectors came, they did not find these people at home and could not collect the monies due the king.] The king's troops were sent after him . . . The Angel of Death could not come close to him for his mouth did not cease repeating the Torah. In the meantime, a wind blew

D'RASH

What do you do when following the rules and doing the right thing gets you nowhere?

A student in school studies hard and does her homework every night. She then watches as half the class uses stolen answers to take the course final. She scores a B, while the cheaters "ace" the exam.

A storekeeper tries to maintain his business by offering quality items and friendly service to his customers. The competition down the street seems intent on doing everything, legal or otherwise, to capture the entire market and drive him out of business. Despite the inferior quality of its product and its reputation for not caring about its customers, it seems to be succeeding.

A family is very involved in their synagogue and extremely generous to numerous charities. Despite devoting themselves religiously to God and to their fellow human beings, they suffer one tragedy after another.

*and rustled the reeds. He thought it was a band of horsemen. He said: "Let me die at the hands of the Angel of Death and not be given over to the King." (*Bava Metzia *86a)* •

Many of us expect that good people will be rewarded for their goodness, and bad people will be punished for their evil. We would anticipate that religious teachers would reinforce that expectation and exhort us, accordingly, to be good. Experience shows us that life is often not as it should be or as we might expect it to be. Rava, in our section, has the courage to admit that there is a wide gap between what should be and what is.

There is an unasked question that is at the center of Rava's admission: If being good is no guarantee that good things will happen to you—as was the case with Rabbah—then why bother being good? What is the point? Whether you are rich or poor, live long or die young, celebrate many weddings or attend too many funerals is all a matter of luck, says Rava. Why should anyone care about following the rules or doing the right thing?

Perhaps one response to this question is to be found in what we learn from Rabbah's own life. We are told that, in times of drought, he would pray to God for rain, just like Rav Ḥisda, and he would be answered. We have to imagine that the same Rabbah who turned to God when his people were in trouble also turned to God when he and his family were in difficult straits. Yet God apparently answered only this righteous man's communal prayers, not his personal ones. If there is any logic here, it is beyond our comprehension. What is instructive is that Rabbah *continued* to turn to God, using his powers to help whomever he could. The negative answer to his personal prayers did not prevent him from turning to God to seek help for others. Perhaps, then, it is not simply luck that determines what happens to us. It is the presence of good, decent people like Rabbah who help to make the lives of others better, richer, and happier. Their prayers and their good deeds benefit us even if they are incapable of doing the same for themselves. So it is not just luck that affects life, children, and food, but *people* who are willing to give of themselves, not because they will be rewarded for it, but because it *is* the right thing to do.

רִמּוֹן מָצָא
תּוֹכוֹ אָכַל קְלִפָּתוֹ זָרַק

He found a pomegranate: The inside he ate; its peel he threw away.

TEXT

Ḥagigah 15b

Rava explained: "What was the meaning of the verse: 'I went down to the nut grove to see the budding of the vale' [Song of Songs 6:11]? Why are scholars compared to a nut? To tell you that just as the nut is dirtied by mud and filth yet its contents are not spoiled, so too scholars—even though they have sinned—their Torah remains unspoiled."

Rabbah bar Shela met Elijah. He said to him: "What is the Holy One, blessed be He, doing?" He said: "He is uttering traditions in the name of all the Rabbis, but traditions in the name of Rabbi Meir He is not uttering." He said: "Why not?" "Because he learned the tradition from Aḥer." He [Rabbah] said: "Why not? Rabbi Meir found a pomegranate: The inside he ate; its peel he threw away."

Aḥer [Rabbi Elisha ben Avuyah]—what happened to him? There are those who say he saw the tongue of Ḥutzpit the translator being dragged by a pig. He said: "The mouth that uttered pearls now licks the dirt." He went out and sinned. (Kiddushin *39b)*

He went out and found a prostitute. He propositioned her. She said: "Are you not Elisha ben Avuyah?" He pulled a radish out of the ground on Shabbat and gave it to her. She said: "He is Aḥer [someone else]." (Hagigah *15a)* ●

CONTEXT

Elisha ben Avuyah was a contemporary of Rabbi Akiva and a teacher of Rabbi Meir. Some time during the second century, he became a heretic and turned his back on the Jewish people. There are several stories that try to explain this radical change: Some say he was attracted to the ideas of other religions or philosophies; others show how he was deeply troubled by the seeming lack of justice in a world in which righteous individuals suffered terribly. He is referred to in the Talmud by the name Aḥer, meaning "someone else" or "the other one." While most of the Jewish world turned against him, his student Rabbi Meir remained committed to bringing his teacher back into the fold.

Rava begins the discussion by interpreting a verse from the Song of Songs to mean that even though teachers may sin, what they taught us still remains valid. As if to refute this, at least with respect to Elisha ben Avuyah, we are told that another Rabbi, Rabbah bar Shela, once happened upon Elijah the prophet. (According to tradition, Elijah never died. He often appeared to the Rabbis as a person with knowledge of what God in Heaven was thinking or doing.) Elijah tells Rabbah that Rabbi Meir is not held in esteem by God because he learned his teachings from Aḥer. Rabbah comes to Rabbi Meir's defense by saying that Meir took only the valid teachings from Elisha ben Avuyah; the heretical beliefs and views he discarded like the bitter peel of a sweet pomegranate.

D'RASH

A mother came home late from work and found her three young children, ages six, nine, and twelve, "glued" to the television screen. To her horror, she discovered they were watching an R-rated movie on cable in which a particularly violent rape had been graphically depicted. When her husband came home a little later, a big argument ensued.

"I want that television out of this house!" she yelled.

"Hold on, honey, I understand you're upset; *I'm* upset too. But getting rid of the TV is a little drastic, don't you think? We can get one of those channel blockers for the cable movies."

"No! You don't understand," she replied. "It's not just the cable movies that are the problem. It's the whole TV thing! The kids watch too much television. There's an hour before school, and the damn thing is on from the time they get home until they go to sleep! Do you have any idea of the number of violent killings they see each week? What is that doing to their minds and to their souls? You can't watch a sitcom today without sexual innuendos and double-entendres. Most of what they watch is just stupid junk. And then there are the commercials brainwashing them 'Buy this' or 'You gotta have that.' We don't talk any more as a family; we just watch TV in the same room. I've had it up to here! I want that thing out!"

Pretty compelling arguments. Yet one thing that was forgotten in the heat of the argument is that there is also much of worth on television—educational shows, cultural programs, coverage of historical events, to name a few. Getting rid of television altogether from the home might very well be a positive for this family. However, it would come with a price, throwing away some of the positive things that TV brings into the home.

It's a difficult decision. Most people don't even bother to struggle with it. They mindlessly take in everything and anything that is offered. Television is used as a babysitter and has taken the place of real conversation in many families. A few parents react like this mother and decide that the only way to protect and preserve their families is by getting rid of the TV altogether.

There is a third approach, one offered by Rabbi Meir: Hold on to the good, while discarding that which is bad. This is a difficult path to follow. It requires a lot of thinking and some very hard choices. Every decision brings a plus, as well as a minus. We have to be eternally vigilant, aware of what we are being offered and discriminating about what we choose. It is a lot easier to take an all-or-nothing approach, but it is more honest to do what Rabbi Meir did. He understood that there is some truth and some good everywhere. It is extremely rare to find a mentor, role model, or source that is always good, always positive, always full of merit. Trying to find perfection is foolish; it does not exist (except in God). The secret is to find someone, or something, that has much to offer us and take it in, while rejecting that which is lacking in worth. In the words of the Gemara, we should eat the inside and throw away the peel.

תָּפַשְׂתָּ מְרֻבֶּה לֹא תָּפַשְׂתָּ

If you grab too much, you haven't grabbed a thing.

TEXT

Ḥagigah 17a

Rabbi Elazar said: "Rabbi Oshiya said: 'From where do we learn that [the missed sacrifices of] Shavuot can be made up any time during the seven days [following the festival]?' As it says: 'On the Feast of Unleavened Bread, on the Feast of Weeks and on the Feast of Booths' [Deuteronomy 16:16]. It juxtaposes the Feast of Weeks to the Feast of Unleavened Bread: Just as [the missed sacrifices of] the Feast of Unleavened Bread can be made up any time during the seven days [following the festival] so too [the missed sacrifices of] Shavuot can be made up any time during the seven days [following the festival]."

Why not say: "It juxtaposes it to the Feast of Booths: Just as [the missed sacrifices of] the Feast of Booths can be made up any time during the eight days [following the festival], so too [the missed sacrifices of] Shavuot can be made up any time during the eight days following the festival"? Because the eighth day of the Feast [of Booths] is considered a holiday unto itself.

When we say that the eighth day of the Feast [of Booths] is a holiday unto itself, we mean with reference to P.Z."R. K.S."B. But regarding the making up [of missed sacrifices] it [the eighth day] serves to make up for [the missed sacrifices of] the first day, as it was taught: "One who did not offer the sacrifice on the first day of the festival may bring it any time during the festival, or on the last day of the festival." If you grab too much, you haven't grabbed a thing; if you grab a little, you have grabbed something.

Three times a year—on the Feast of Unleavened Bread, on the Feast of Weeks, and on the Feast of Booths—all your males shall appear before the Lord your God in the place that He will choose. They shall not appear before the Lord empty-handed, but each with his own gift, according to the blessing that the Lord your God has bestowed upon you. (Deuteronomy 16:16–17) •

On the fifteenth day of this seventh month there shall be the Feast of Booths to the Lord, [to last] seven days. The first day shall be a sacred occasion: you shall not work at your occupations; seven days you shall bring offerings by fire to the Lord. On the eighth day you shall observe a sacred occasion and bring an offering by fire to the Lord; it is a solemn gathering: you shall not work at your occupations. (Leviticus 23:34–36) •

CONTEXT

The Rabbis raise the question of what is to be done when a person neglected to bring the prescribed sacrifices on the first day of any of the three pilgrimage festivals: The Feast of Unleavened Bread (Pesaḥ), the Feast of Weeks (Shavuot), and the Feast of Booths (Sukkot). Since all three are mentioned in one sentence (Deuteronomy 16:16), the Rabbis assumed that they must share something in common: Just as the Passover sacrifices can be brought on any of the seven days of the festival, so too the Shavuot sacrifices can be brought on the seven days *following* the festival. (Shavuot is a one-day holiday in the Torah.)

Another possibility is raised: If we can learn the procedures for Shavuot from its proximity to Pesaḥ in the same verse, why not learn the procedures for the festival of Sukkot, which is *also* mentioned in the same sentence? And since Sukkot is an eight-day festival, perhaps the Shavuot sacrifices could be brought on any of the *eight* days that follow the festival.

The Gemara first says no: Sukkot, while ostensibly an eight-day holiday, is really a seven-day festival with a special eighth day called Shemini Atzeret, both a part of Sukkot and a separate holiday unto itself. The Gemara then ultimately rejects this suggestion, stating that only for six things is Shemini Atzeret separate. However, regarding the issue of making up a missed sacrifice, we learn that the eighth day *is* considered a part of Sukkot. Consequently, the missed Shavuot sacrifice *can* be brought for an additional eight days.

The six areas which characterize Shemini Atzeret as a holiday unto itself are noted in the Gemara by a two-word mnenomic (P.Z."R. K.S."B). The abbreviations stand for:

P. (*Payis* = Lottery): On the first seven days of Sukkot, the twenty-four groups of *kohanim* officiated in order; on the eighth day, a lottery determined who would officiate.

Z. (*Z'man* = Time): A separate *she-he-ḥeyanu* blessing was recited on Shemini Atzeret.

R. (*Regel* = Festival): The eighth day has its own separate name—Shemini Atzeret— and is not called Sukkot.

K. (*Korban* = Sacrifice): The offering on this day was different from that offered on the seven days of Sukkot.

S. (*Shir* = Song): The Levites recited a special song, Psalm 12, on Shemini Atzeret.

B. (*Berakhah* = Blessing): The people recited a special blessing for the King on this day. (See I Kings 8:66.)

The Gemara's final answer to this question comes in the form of a maxim: "If you grab too much, you haven't grabbed a thing." Everyone agrees that the missed Shavuot sacrifice can be brought on any of the *seven* following days. The disagreement is whether it can be brought on the *eighth* day. Therefore, we are told, to be on the safe side we should offer the sacrifice only on one of the seven days following the festival. If we wait until the disputed eighth day, we may end up offering the sacrifice one day too late.

D'RASH

Kids used to flock to a general store and spend hours around the candy barrels, dreaming of how they would spend their precious pennies and which of the sweets they would choose. One particular merchant had a clever way of teaching the children a lesson about greed. Instead of weighing out the candy by the pound, he offered a new method: "All you can grab for one penny!" The kids could not believe their ears. "It's not a joke; pay me one penny and then stick your hand into the barrel, palm side down. Whatever you can grab, you can keep!"

The kids were delighted. This was a dream come true. They lined up, eagerly waiting for their turn to grab the treasure. The children stuck their hands into the barrel; they stretched their tiny fingers as far apart as possible, then closed them into a fist to capture the candy. But before pulling out their hands, each one thought: "Am I getting as much as I can? Let me try to grab a little more." So they relaxed their grasp to grab again; in doing so, they lost control of whatever it was that they had already captured. By trying to grab more, the kids always ended up with less. The merchant watched and smiled, wondering how long it would take the children to figure out this lesson of life.

Some of us never grow up. As adults we continue to grab for more and more. Material possessions, power and control, honors: We never seem satisfied no matter how much we have. But there ultimately comes a point when we stop to assess what we have attained in life, and we are overcome by a terrible sense that we may have allowed all that *really* matters to slip through our fingers.

Rest Stop

"They set out from Elim and encamped by the Sea of Reeds." (Numbers 33:10)

Words of Torah are compared to water, as it says: "Ho, all who are thirsty, come for water." [Isaiah 55:1] . . . Just as water comes down drop by drop and forms many rivers, so too with Torah: One learns two laws today and two tomorrow until it becomes a mighty river. (*Song of Songs Rabbah* 1, 3)

Rabbi Zusya of Hanipol once started to study a volume of the Talmud. A day later, his disciples noticed that he was still dwelling on the first page. They assumed that he must have encountered a difficult passage and was trying to solve it. But when a number of days passed and he was still immersed in the first page, they were astonished, but did not dare to query the master. Finally one of them gathered courage and asked him why he did not proceed to the next page. And Rabbi Zusya answered: "I feel so good here, why should I go elsewhere?" (Abraham Joshua Heschel. *The Earth is the Lord's.* New York: Harper & Row, 1966, p. 50)

At times you should study one page of Gemara ten hours, and at times ten pages of Gemara one hour. (Ḥayyim ben Yitzḥak, *Geklibene Shritfn* I, 36, quoted in Joseph L. Baron, *A Treasury of Jewish Quotations,* Aronson/B'nai B'rith, 1985, p. 480)

Seder Nashim

Introduction to Seder Nashim

The third Order of the Mishnah is *Nashim,* meaning "Women." The seven tractates in this Order cover the crucial issues of marriage (including marriage documents and levirate marriage, where a man was obligated to marry the childless widow of his dead brother), divorce, adultery, and the tangential topics of vows and the institution of the *nazir.* (The *nazir* was a person who vowed not to cut his hair, drink wine, or come in contact with the dead, as an act of piety and devotion to God.)

יֵשׁ נָאֶה דוֹרֵשׁ
וְנָאֶה מְקַיֵּם

There are those who preach well and practice well.

TEXT

Yevamot 63b

It was taught: Rabbi Eliezer says: "Anyone who does not engage in increasing the species is like one who sheds blood, as it says: 'Whoever sheds the blood of a man, by man shall his blood be shed' [Genesis 9:6], and it is written after that: 'Be fertile, then, and increase' [Genesis 9:7]." Rabbi Yaakov says: "It is as if he diminished the image [of God], as it says: 'For in His image did God make man' [Genesis 9:6], and it is written after that: 'Be fertile, then, and increase' [Genesis 9:7]." Ben Azzai says: "It is as if he sheds blood and *diminishes the image [of God], as it says: 'Be fertile, then, and increase.'" They said to Ben Azzai: "There are those who preach well and practice well; those who practice well, but do not preach well. You preach well, but do not practice well!" Ben Azzai said to them: "What can I do? My soul is in love with the Torah. It is possible for the world to be carried on by others."*

According to other traditions in the Talmud, Ben Azzai did *marry:*

> *Rabbi Akiva was a shepherd of Ben Kalba Savua. The daughter saw that he was modest and noble. She said to him: "If I were to become betrothed to you, would you go to study?" He answered: "Yes." (*Ketubbot *62b)*
>
> *The daughter of Rabbi Akiva did the very same thing with Ben Azzai. (*Ketubbot *63a)*
>
> *If you wish, you can say that he [Ben Azzai] had been married, but then separated from her. (*Sotah *4b)* •

CONTEXT

There are in the Torah, according to the Rabbis, 613 commandments. The very first one, given to Adam and Eve and again later to Noah and his family after the flood is: Be fertile and increase (or, in the well known phrase, "Be fruitful and multiply"). The Rabbis took this commandment very seriously. Not to marry and bring children into the world was likened by Rabbi Eliezer to murder: Both acts had the effect of decreasing the population in the world. Though this may sound foreign to our ears, we need to remember that two thousand years ago, our modern concerns about a population explosion were nonexistent. In addition, infant mortality was extremely high and many children never grew to adulthood. There were real concerns as to whether individual families, or the Jewish people as a nation, would survive.

Rabbi Yaakov goes even further than Rabbi Eliezer: He believes that not bearing children actually reduces the very presence of God in the world. Human beings are created in the image of God; fewer people means God's manifestation on earth is diminished.

Shimon Ben Azzai believes so strongly in the need to bring children into the world that he agrees with both Rabbi Eliezer and Rabbi Yaakov. However, the Rabbis then turn on

Ben Azzai, who himself was single and childless, and accuse him of hypocrisy: How could he preach something but not do it in practice? He answers that he indeed has fallen short of the ideal but that because of his desire and love for the Torah, he never had the time to be a husband and father.

D'RASH

During "Drug Awareness Week," a high school schedules a guest speaker to address the students. He is a drug addict who has been in and out of rehabilitation programs for ten years. The speaker describes his background, which is remarkably similar to that of many of the students. He recounts how he first began to experiment with drugs in high school and how he later became hooked. Then he tells the harrowing story of his descent into the hell that drugs made of his life. He honestly explains to the audience that he cannot really say he has kicked the habit completely; every so often, he is drawn back to the world of the "quick high." He ends his talk by making a very strong appeal to the teenagers: "Stay away from drugs. If you haven't tried them, don't. If you have, don't go back. And if you're hooked, then go and get help. But stay away from drugs!"

The principal opens the session up to questions. There is silence for a few moments. Then one student raises his hand and, with some indignation, attacks the speaker: "Who are *you* to come and tell us to stay off drugs? By your own admission, you *still* do drugs now and then! As far as I'm concerned, you lost your credibility. Man, if you can't practice what you preach, then you have no business telling us what to do!"

The student's attitude represents a common viewpoint today: One who does not practice what he preaches is a hypocrite, and a hypocrite has absolutely no moral authority to tell anyone else what to do.

Shimon Ben Azzai would have us take a position that is a little more tolerant and understanding of the frailties of human nature. There are very few people who are completely consistent in what they do and what they say. Truth can come from many places and many sources. We should not be so quick to turn off the messages of "hypocrites." They, too, might have a great deal to teach us if we are willing to listen. We assume Ben Azzai was *unwilling* to have children; it is also possible that he was a man *unable* to have children. Perhaps he spoke out of anguish and pain. He would tell us: Even if I don't practice, I still have the right to preach; I still have something of value to share.

The addict was not put off by the student's attack. He simply sat back and smiled. "Hey, you can listen to me, or not. It's no skin off my nose. But if you look at me and what I've been through, and if you take my message to heart, you can save yourself a lot of grief. Nobody is more of an expert than I am on the hell that drugs can put you through. But hey, listen to me, or not: It's up to you."

שִׂפְתוֹתָיו דּוֹבְבוֹת בַּקֶּבֶר

His lips whisper from the grave.

TEXT

Yevamot 96b-97a

Rav Yehudah said in the name of Rav: "Why is it written: 'O that I might dwell in Your tent forever [le-olamim]*' [Psalms 61:5]? Is it possible for a man to dwell in two worlds? Rather, David said before the Holy One: 'Lord of the World! May it be Your will that they say what they heard from me in this world,' as Rabbi Yoḥanan said in the name of Rabbi Shimon ben Yoḥai: 'Every scholar who is quoted in this world, his lips whisper from the grave.'"*

CONTEXT

Rav Yehudah's interpretation makes little sense without a pun which occurs in the Hebrew. "Forever" is *le-olamim,* which is taken from the word *olam,* meaning "world." The meaning of *le-olamim,* literally "for worlds," is perhaps best captured in the English phrase "for eternities," each eternity being a world. The Hebrew plural is interpreted by the Rabbis to mean "this world and the next world." Since Psalm 61 is ascribed to King David, its explanation in the Gemara is put into David's mouth. The king pleads with God to let him live in two worlds. However, this is not simply an appeal for resurrection. King David—according to the Gemara—is referring to the concept that whenever a scholar is quoted in *this* world, the lips of the original teacher move in the *next* world. Thus, David asks that after his own death, his words from the Psalms be quoted in this world so that he will receive the benefit in the next world.

Rabbinic Judaism has a strong belief in the afterlife. Nonetheless, the major emphasis of this story, like that of Jewish life since the Talmud, is this-worldly. Even if King David's lips will move in the next world, the major impact will still be on the students here on earth.

In the Bible, there are few, if any, clear references to the afterlife. However, by the rabbinic period there was a strong belief in an existence beyond this world. Though there is much discussion of the afterlife in the Talmud and Midrash, the topic is not given uniform and deliberate treatment in rabbinic literature. On the contrary: There are many divergent and often contradictory views of the afterlife. This is similar to rabbinic discussions on many other controversial topics.

Some Rabbis believed strongly in the physical resurrection of the dead. In an intriguing passage in Berakhot *18b, there are various graveyard stories which attempt to show that the souls of the dead, while in the* next *world, have knowledge of* this *world. Elsewhere in the Talmud, various Rabbis describe in detail what heaven will be like and who will receive the various rewards there. Rabbah says that "Jerusalem of the world to come" will be unlike Jerusalem of this world, where any who want can enter. In the next world, only those who are invited or called will be allowed in. Just as there are talmudic stories about heaven and the*

D'RASH

In *The Brothers Karamazov,* Dostoevsky wrote:

> *If you were to destroy in mankind the belief in immortality, not only love but every living force maintaining the life of the world would at once be dried up.*

Dostoevsky's view is an extreme one, but it seems clear that most human beings are looking for a kind of immortality, something that lives on forever. Many people are quite literal about the soul living on, accepting religious beliefs that promise immortality through faith in a certain god or *many boons that the righteous will find there, so too there are views of hell and the punishment of the wicked.*

Many of these stories and beliefs attempt to deal, in one way or another, with the theological problems of good and evil. Why do the righteous suffer? Why do many wicked prosper? Though the Bible does not deal with these problems directly, it does suggest answers, explanations which themselves lead to more philosophical problems. The Rabbis often found their own answers, as well as their comfort, in concepts like the World-to-Come and the Resurrection of the Dead. The rewards in the next world *are reserved for those who had suffered in* this world. *To find prooftexts for this thinking, they sometimes interpreted verses in ways that were clearly not the original intent.* ●

prophet. The Indian ruler Shah Jahan built the Taj Mahal as an eternal memorial to his favorite wife; she would not die but would live on in this majestic structure. Some bequeath large estates, with specific instructions on how to use only the interest so that the principal will remain in perpetuity.

To the traditional Jew, eternal life can be simpler. It does not require a system of beliefs, but one of actions. No great monument has to be erected; no trust funds need be established. The Jew sees eternity through the ongoing teachings of the tradition. The words of the Bible and Talmud are ageless and timeless. When we quote them, we attain a degree of immortality. When we live our lives by their values and traditions, we connect ourselves with an "eternal people" and an undying tradition. Individual Jews die; Judaism lives on. And, more important, many of the ideals and patterns of behavior of Judaism are so old and time-tested that even if their origin is in a specific era in the ancient past, they are called "eternal."

The Rabbis were very aware that when a teacher is invoked by name by a student or by the student's student, the master's words continue to live, the lips "whispering from the grave." Therefore, there was an accepted practice of quoting what one learned *b'shem om'ro,* "in the name of the one who said it." Teachers today also find great comfort in knowing that their lessons continue to educate and inspire beyond the point when the student leaves the classroom, even beyond the point when the teacher leaves this world.

When we quote our mentors and loved ones, their lives continue through us. True immortality comes not from statues or inheritances but from statutes and heritages that live beyond the grave. Edgar Lee Masters wrote:

> Immortality is not a gift,
> Immortality is an achievement;
> And only those who strive mightily
> Shall possess it.

Centuries before, Rav Yehudah and Rabbi Yoḥanan taught this same concept on two levels. First, when we invoke our ancestors, they live on in us and through us. Second, and equally important, we have to live our lives in such a way that future generations will call on us. It is ours to strive mightily to achieve immortality by living out those ageless values that were passed on to us. Then, some day in the future, our lips, too, may whisper from the grave.

כּוֹפִין אוֹתוֹ עַד שֶׁיֹּאמַר רוֹצֶה אֲנִי

We force him until he says: "I want to!"

TEXT

Yevamot 106a

The Rabbis taught: Deceptive ḥalitzah *is valid; a deceptive* get *is invalid. Forced* ḥalitzah *is invalid; a forced* get *is valid. How is this so? If he said: "I want to," even for* ḥalitzah, *if he did not say: "I want to," even for a* get, *it is so. No, this is what it means: Deceptive* ḥalitzah *is always valid, and a deceptive* get *is always invalid; forced* ḥalitzah *or a forced* get, *sometimes it is valid and sometimes it is invalid. In one case, he said: "I want to," in another case he did not say: "I want to." And it is taught: "He shall make his offering" [Leviticus 1:3], teaching us that we force him. Can this mean even against his will? The text says "by his will" [ibid., author's translation]—we force him until he says "I want to!" And similarly we find with a woman's* get, *we force him until he says "I want to!"*

CONTEXT

In order to understand this section of text, we must have a clear picture of two laws relating to marriage and divorce. In the first, the Torah (Deuteronomy 24) says that if a man finds something that he dislikes about his wife, he may write a bill of divorcement for her. Thus, a formal document, called a *get* in rabbinic literature, is required to end the marriage. The first question of the Gemara, above, is whether a *get* given under coercion or based on deception is valid.

The second law is outlined in Deuteronomy 25. If a man died without having fathered a child but he left a surviving brother, then that brother is obligated to marry his deceased brother's widow in order to carry on the family line. This is called "Levirate marriage" or *yibum* in Hebrew. However, if the brother refuses to marry his widowed sister-in-law, a ceremony called *ḥalitzah,* "removing" the shoe, is performed: The widow takes her brother-in-law to the elders at the city gate, where his refusal is publicly acknowledged. She then removes his sandal, spits in his face and says: "Thus shall be done to the man who will not build up his brother's house!" The second question of the Gemara is whether an act of *ḥalitzah* done under coercion or based on deception is valid.

Thus, the Gemara is asking a number of critical questions: What if the *get* was forced on the husband (for example, by a court)? Does this fulfill the obligation? Or what if

A man takes a wife and possesses her. She fails to please him because he finds something obnoxious about her, and he writes her a bill of divorcement, hands it to her, and sends her away from his house; she leaves his household and becomes the wife of another man; then this latter man rejects her, writes her a bill of divorcement, hands it to her, and sends her away from his house; or the man who married her last dies. Then the first husband who divorced her shall not take her to wife again, since she has been defiled—for that would be abhorrent to the Lord. You must not bring sin upon the land that the

Lord your God is giving you as a heritage. (Deuteronomy 24:1–4) •

When brothers dwell together and one of them dies and leaves no son, the wife of the deceased shall not be married to a stranger, outside the family. Her husband's brother shall unite with her: take her as his wife and perform the levir's duty. The first son that she bears shall be accounted to the dead brother, that his name may not be blotted out in Israel. But if the man does not want to marry his brother's widow, his brother's widow shall appear before the elders in the gate and declare: "My husband's brother refuses to establish a name in Israel for his brother; he will not perform the duty of a levir." The elders of his town shall then summon him and talk to him. If he insists, saying: "I do not want to marry her," his brother's widow shall go up to him in the presence of the elders, pull the sandal off his foot, spit in his face, and make this declaration: Thus shall be done to the man who will not build up his brother's house! And he shall go in Israel by the name of "the family of the unsandaled one." (Deuteronomy 25:5–10) •

the *ḥalitzah* was performed through an act of deception? For example, what if the deceased husband's brother is unacceptable to the widow, and her family offers him money to choose *ḥalitzah* (the refusal to marry her) rather than *yibum* (the obligation to marry his brother's wife)? And what if this money has not yet been paid, but the *ḥalitzah* has already taken place? Is this *ḥalitzah* valid, or is it deceptive because the money was promised but not yet delivered?

At least one opinion of the Gemara says that we can coerce a man into doing these acts. "We force him until he says 'I want to!' " Some later commentators explain that such coercion is allowed because the husband is being forced to do his obligation under the law. Thus, it is only partial coercion. In simpler terms, the husband is saying: "I *want* to do the upright and proper thing, even if I have to be forced to admit it."

D'RASH

All of us, at one time or another, have been forced to do things that we do not want to do. The government obligates us to pay taxes. While we may argue about the specific amount and type of taxes, we somehow know that, on the whole, taxes are a positive since they allow the government to provide services for us. We feel forced—until we enjoy a park, police protection, public library, or interstate highway system. Then, we feel as if we *want* the services and are willing to pay for them, rather than feeling *forced* to do so.

We are required, because of professional responsibilities and job expectations, to attend social functions that we would much rather say no to. Our feeling of obligation often ends when we realize that our jobs provide us with the lifestyle that we have grown accustomed to. No obligations would mean no pleasures either.

There are times when others—especially parents—are too pushy. Yet often, the push is just what is needed, even if the "I want to" is not heard for many years and is not expressed in so many words. The child who would rather play outside but instead is cajoled into taking music lessons may not jump up and shout "Thanks, Ma!" Yet, as that child grows to appreciate music and become an accomplished musician, the strains of "I want to!" can often be heard between the notes.

A young adult is looking to her parents not only for love but also for structure to help make sense of her chaotic teen years. The parent who lovingly yet firmly imposes rules actually understands the child's genuine needs. The rebellious teenager who is forced to accept parental regulations may come to appreciate a parent's concern years later, when she has a family of her own.

There are times when each of us has been pushed into a situation that makes us say: "Okay, I'll do it!" After the resentment dies down and the bitterness passes, we are able to look at the situation in its proper perspective. We then come to realize and appreciate that we were forced to do something that was for our own good.

בָּרִי וְשֶׁמָּא—בָּרִי עָדִיף

"Sure" or "maybe"
—"sure" is better.

TEXT

Ketubbot 12b

> *It was stated: [One says:] "You have a* maneh *of mine," and the other says: "I do not know." Rav Yehudah and Rav Huna say: "He is obligated to pay," and Rav Naḥman and Rabbi Yoḥanan say: "He is exempt." Rav Huna and Rav Yehudah say: "He is obligated; in a case of 'sure' or 'maybe'—'sure' is better." Rav Naḥman and Rabbi Yoḥanan say: "He is exempt; the money stays in the possession of the one who has it."*

CONTEXT

One person (let's call him Reuven) says to another (named Shimon): "You owe me one *maneh* (an amount of money, probably equal to one hundred *zuz* or *dinars*)." Shimon replies that he does not remember if he borrowed such a sum from Reuven. What is the law in this situation? Two possible answers are offered, based on very different legal principles. Rav Yehudah and Rav Huna hold that in a case where Reuven is sure of the facts and Shimon is not certain, the law supports Reuven, and Shimon must repay the money: In a case of "sure" or "maybe," "sure" is better.

Rav Naḥman and Rabbi Yoḥanan take the opposite viewpoint which is similar to our expression "Possession is nine-tenths of the law." In other words, the person who has it keeps it unless convincing evidence can be brought to show why the money should be taken away and given to someone else.

Later Jewish law codifies which of these two views is followed: [One says:] "You have a maneh *of mine that I lent you, or that I left for safekeeping with you", and the other says: "I do not know if you lent it to me, or left it with me for safekeeping"—he [the latter] swears an oath of inducement that he does not know of it, and he is exempt from having to pay.* (Shulḥan Arukh, Ḥoshen Mishpat *75:9)* •

D'RASH

A friendly game of basketball at the playground has degenerated into a huge shouting match. Robert, on defense, accuses Steve of stepping out of bounds while dribbling. "I saw it clearly," Robert yells, "you stepped over the line! It's our ball!" Steve isn't sure one way or the other. "Did anybody else see it?" he asks. There is silence. "Then I'm not giving up possession, just because you say so." Robert is furious. "But I saw it! You were out!" And the argument goes on and on . . .

Rabbis Huna and Yehudah deal with a similar, though somewhat more serious, situation. Their response is that in the absence of better evidence, we do the best with what we have. A decision needs to be made and in a choice of one person who is certain, versus another person who is unsure, we go with the former over the latter. There is, of course, an underlying principle in this course of action: We take people at their word, trusting that they are telling us the truth. Rav Huna and Rav Yehudah will probably argue that it is a rare circumstance when we have clear, documented, objective evidence from a neutral outsider that will enable us to render a totally just verdict. And in the absence of that, we need to make decisions; life (and the game) must go on. We do the best we can, and trust that people will be honest.

Rabbis Naḥman and Yoḥanan are troubled by such an approach. First of all, how do we know that a person is telling the truth? When a game is on the line, or a lot of money is at stake, it may be very difficult for a person to be completely honest. Emotions or greed can sometimes get in the way of telling what really happened. But even if a person *is* telling the truth, how can we be sure that what he saw, or remembers, is actually what happened? Eyesight or memory can both be very deceiving at times. Rabbi Naḥman and Rabbi Yoḥanan would counsel us to require more compelling evidence before taking the ball from Steve or the money from Shimon. Witnesses or documentation are necessary; otherwise, we leave things the way they are. Jewish law takes the more demanding approach. And yet, there is still sound wisdom in what Rabbi Yehudah and Rabbi Huna teach us: In a case of "sure" or "maybe," "sure" is better. Too often in life we take the easy way out. We rely on information that has not been verified, or rumors that have not been substantiated. We seem to feel: "What difference does it make?" We settle for "This is good enough." In a friendly game at the playground, it may not matter so very much. But with a doctor treating a patient, or a lawyer defending a client, or a architect designing a skyscraper, the difference between "sure" and "maybe" can mean the difference between life and death. We must always strive, to the best of our ability, for certainty and truth.

לֹא כָחָל וְלֹא שָׂרָק וְלֹא פִּרְכּוּס וְיַעֲלַת חֵן

Neither paint, nor rouge, nor hair dye, yet radiating charm.

TEXT

Ketubbot 17a

> *When Rav Dimi came, he said: "This is what they sing before the bride in the West: 'Neither paint, nor rouge, nor hair dye, yet radiating charm.'" When the Rabbis ordained Rabbi Zeira, they sang this to him: "Neither paint, nor rouge, nor hair dye, yet radiating charm."*

An alternative translation: "Neither powder, nor paint, nor waving of the hair, yet still a graceful gazelle." Keḥal *is a powder that is used on the eye lids;* serak *is a paint for the cheeks;* pirkus *can refer to making the hair pretty by dyeing or "waving" it into locks;* ya'alah *is a gazelle. The root can also be from* alah, *meaning "to go up," "give off," or "radiate."* •

*Rabbi Zeira used to hide, so he would not be ordained, for Rabbi Elazar said: "Stay in the dark and stay alive." When he heard another teaching of Rabbi Elazar—"A person cannot rise up to greatness unless he is forgiven of all his sins"—then he strove to attain it. (*Sanhedrin *14a) The implication of Rabbi Elazar's second teaching is that public office would lead one to seek forgiveness for one's sins.* •

CONTEXT

In the section just prior to ours, the Rabbis discuss the appropriate words that one should say to a bride on her wedding day. Rav Dimi, a teacher of the fourth century, traveled a great deal between Babylonia and Israel. On many occasions in the Talmud, he reports on the customs of the Jews "in the West," that is, in Israel, which is west of Babylonia.

One of the songs of praise that was uttered at a wedding was also applied to a Rabbi on the occasion of his ordination. The stories about Rabbi Zeira inform us that he was quite short, disfigured from a fire, and perhaps somewhat crippled, with a physically unattractive face. No doubt, he was painfully aware of these attributes. Yet, when the Rabbis came to ordain him and looked to find one sentence that would summarize who he really was, they chose to emphasize that there *was* something very beautiful about him. Despite the external characteristics, his teachers found in him wonderful internal qualities that shone through the outer ugliness.

D'RASH

The story is told (*Avodah Zarah* 20a) of Rabbi Shimon ben Gamliel who once noticed a beautiful woman walking by. Seeing her, he quoted the verse in the book of Psalms (Psalms 104:24): "How great are the things You have made, O Lord! [author's translation]" Jewish law, in fact, later prescribed a blessing to be recited upon seeing a person of extraordinary beauty or handsomeness: "Blessed is God Who has created such as these in His world." The Rabbis were not oblivious to beautiful people. Where the Greeks saw beauty and worshiped and valued it, the Jews were prompted by beauty to worship God, Who created it.

The world we live in is more beholden to Greek values than rabbinic ones. In our society, a tremendous emphasis is placed on how a person looks. Being beautiful or handsome is often more prized—and praised—than being smart (and certainly more than being good). The Rabbis tried to teach that outward appearances are often deceptive.

"Rabbi [Yehudah ha-Nasi] says: 'Do not look at the vessel, but rather what is in it. There may be an new vessel filled with the old [wine], and an old vessel that does not even contain the new [Avot 4:27]." Or as we say today: "You can't judge a book by its cover."

There is another blessing the Rabbis teach us to recite, upon seeing someone of exceptional ugliness: "Blessed is God Who has created all different kinds of beings." Some people might recoil in horror at seeing deformity or ugliness; others might scream or make a face. The Rabbis teach us to recite a blessing, one that reminds us that this person, too, is a creature of God. Beneath the outward ugliness there is to be found a person who was created by and in the image of God.

This very same attitude is found in the origin of our phrase. This maxim was a wedding song sung to a bride. In the Gemara, it follows a disagreement between Bet Hillel and Bet Shammai: The former believe we should praise *all* brides as beautiful, while the latter hold that we can do so only if she is indeed beautiful; otherwise we would be lying. Our wedding song brings another opinion altogether: Tell her that even without makeup she radiates an *inner* beauty and charm that makes her special and attractive.

There is something else that is fascinating about this text: The wedding song usually sung in praise of a bride is also used on another occasion to praise a *man* as he is about to be ordained a rabbi. We often have very different ways of judging (and praising) men and women: The former are expected to be smart and strong, the latter to be pretty and sweet. The Rabbis here find a unique praise that fits both sexes in all situations: You have no superficial mask; you don't pretend to be someone you are not; you have an inner beauty that shines through.

How refreshing a way to "look" at someone! And how refreshing that it applies to both men and women.

כֵּיוָן שֶׁהִגִּיד שׁוּב אֵינוֹ חוֹזֵר וּמַגִּיד Once he spoke, he cannot revoke!

TEXT

Ketubbot 18b

> Mishnah (2:3): *If witnesses said: "This is our handwriting, but we were forced [to sign]," "We were minors," or "We were ineligible," they are believed. If there are other witnesses that it is their handwriting, or their handwriting can be identified from another place, they are not believed.*
> Gemara: *Rami bar Ḥama said: "We were taught this [they are not believed] only in the case of 'We were forced [to sign] because of money,' but 'We were forced because of our lives,' they are believed." Rava said: "Is his [the witness's] claim accepted? Once he spoke, he cannot revoke!"*

CONTEXT

The previous Mishnah gave certain rules of testimony. Our Mishnah continues this theme. Two witnesses sign the *ketubbah,* the document which attests that a wedding ceremony took place. However, certain people are invalid witnesses, for example (the cases in our Mishnah) (1) someone who is forced to sign, (2) a minor, and (3) a relative. If the witnesses who signed a document like a *ketubbah,* upon later questioning by the court, make one of these three statements—"We were forced," "We were minors," or "We were ineligible"—they are believed. The document is invalid, and, in the case of a *ketubbah,* the legitimacy of the marriage is suspect. The reason for believing them is that they are both the signataries *and* the initiators of the question regarding their signatures.

If, however, another set of witnesses comes forward and attests that these are the witnesses' valid signatures, or if their signatures can be checked and certified from another document, then the signatures are considered legitimate, the witnesses' protestations to the contrary. The independent proof is relied upon for authentication; the witnesses' words are of no import. Outside evidence is stronger than internal evidence.

In the Gemara, Rami bar Ḥama tries to limit the case of disbelieving the witnesses' claim to financial coercion. In a matter of life and death ("We were forced because of our lives"), Rami bar Ḥama holds that we do believe the witnesses that these are not their valid signatures. Rava objects to Rami bar Ḥama's reasoning: There is an overriding rule that once

One who marries without witnesses, we do not even consider it a marriage. (Arukh ha-Shulḥan, Even HaEzer, Hilkhot Kiddushin *42:18)*

When he marries before one witness, it is also of no legal import, according to the Rif [Rabbi Isaac Alfasi, eleventh century, North Africa], the Rosh [Rabbi Asher ben Yeḥiel, thirteenth and fourteenth centuries, Germany/Spain], the Rambam [Rabbi Moses Maimonides, twelfth century, Spain/Egypt] and most of the decisors. There are those who were stringent on this and wrote that we are suspicious of such a marriage, and so our rabbi the Rema [Rabbi Moses Isserles, sixteenth century, Poland] was suspicious according to the stringent position. Where there is not a case of iggun *[when a husband has left a wife who is technically still "bound" to him while awaiting a* get*]* testimony is given, it cannot be retracted. Their signatures themselves declare that the document is valid. *Any* claim to the contrary is "speaking after the fact" and automatically discounted, for once they spoke, they cannot revoke.

and urgency, we should rely on the lenient position [that there is a marriage even without two witnesses], which is the majority of opinions. (Arukh ha-Shulḥan, Even HaEzer, Hilkhot Kiddushin *42:20)*

D'RASH

A politician addresses his constituency: "My fellow Americans, when I spoke last week in the public forum, I mentioned certain facts and figures about the issue at hand. Clearly, I was emotional about this topic and did not fully research it. Since then, it has come to my attention that some of the statistics I used were based on outdated studies. Other information was supplied to me by an interested party who was biased. Thus, my presentation was one-sided and unfair. I apologize if I have offended any of my constituents, and I ask you, the voters of this great state, to give me a second chance."

As critical as we may be of such a politician, forced to "eat his words," we also have a certain empathy for him. After all, every one of us, at one time or another, has had to take back a statement that we made. It may not have had major political ramifications or been so public, but we know that it was harmful and had to be retracted. We turn to a person—a family member, fellow worker, even a total stranger—and ask for a second chance.

The problem is that some words cannot be retracted and certain actions are irrevocable. Once the damage is done, there is no opportunity for a second chance. Think, for example, what might happen if a parent publicly criticizes a child. Even if the criticism was reasonable, the time and place may not have been. The parent may feel guilty afterwards. As many times as the parent apologizes and explains, the damage has been done. A loved one has been publicly humiliated. The wound may never heal.

What is true of words also applies to actions: Late one night while home alone, a teenager hears noise downstairs. He knows that his parents are away on vacation and his sister is staying at a friend's house. He calls out—"Who's there?"—but there is no answer. Fearful that there might be a burglar in the house, he removes the gun from his father's dresser drawer. "Who is it?" he shouts again, but there is no answer. A figure moves toward him in the dark; he raises the gun and pulls the trigger. Someone drops to the floor. As this young man turns on the light, he is shocked to see that he has shot his own sister. She lies near him in a pool of blood, suitcase still in hand. Apparently, hoping not to bother her brother, she snuck into the house to retrieve some clothes. What has been done cannot be undone.

While most mistakes can be corrected, some cannot be taken back. Rava's saying should serve as a warning to us. There are some words and certain actions that, once taken, cannot be revoked.

לֹא רָאִינוּהָ אֵינָהּ רְאָיָה **"We did not see her" is no proof.**

TEXT

Ketubbot 22b–23a

Our Rabbis taught: If two [witnesses] say she was betrothed, and two say she was not betrothed, she may not marry, and if she does marry, we do not force her to divorce. If two say she was divorced and two say she was not divorced, she may not marry, and if she married, we force her to divorce. What is the difference between the first case and the second case? Abaye said: "Explain it using only one witness. If one witness says she was married and one witness says she was not married, both testify against an unmarried woman, but the one who testifies 'she was married' is only one, and the word of one does not stand up against the word of two! In the second case: One witness says she was divorced and one witness says she was not divorced, both testify against a married woman, and the one who says 'she was divorced' is only one, and the word of one does not stand up against the word of two!" Rav Ashi said: "This certainly deals with two witnesses in each case, and it's the opposite! If two say: 'We saw that she was betrothed,' and two others say: 'We did not see that she was betrothed,' then she may not marry, and if she does marry, we force her to divorce." This is obvious! "We did not see her" is no proof.

The idea of two corroborating witnesses goes back to the Torah, specifically to capital cases. The book of Deuteronomy specifies two witnesses in the case of idolatry, a capital crime:

> *If there is found among you, in one of the settlements that the Lord your God is giving you, a man or woman who has affronted the Lord your God and transgressed His covenant—turning to the worship of other gods and bowing down to them . . . —and you have been informed or have learned of it, then you shall make a thorough inquiry. If it is true, the fact is established, that abhorrent thing was perpetrated in Israel, you shall take the man or the woman who did that wicked thing out to a public place, and you shall stone them, man or woman, to death.—A person shall be put to death only on the testimony of two or more witnesses; he must not be put to death on the testimony of a single witness. (Deuteronomy 17:2–6)* •

CONTEXT

The Gemara is dealing with proofs of whether or not a woman is allowed to marry based on various testimonies. If, for example, she says of herself: "I was married and divorced"—as we have in the case on the previous Mishnah on *Ketubbot* 22a—she is believed, "for the mouth that forbade is the mouth that permits." "The mouth that forbade" is her own; she declared herself married and therefore forbidden to other men. "The mouth that permits" is also her own; she declared herself divorced and thus permitted to other men. Since we believe her on one account ("the mouth that forbade") we likewise believe her on the other account ("the mouth that permitted").

In the first case of our Gemara, there are conflicting testimonies. One set of witnesses claims that she did not marry, while another asserts that she did marry. She should not marry again, since her status is doubtful, but if she did nonetheless marry, she is allowed to remain with that husband, since there was testimony that she was not previously married. If, however, there is conflicting testimony over whether or not she divorced, there is the possibility that she is still another man's wife. In such a case, she is forced to divorce the new husband.

Abaye, however, understands the Gemara's case as involving only one outside witness. In the case of the death of a man whose wife is then allowed to remarry, the testimony of one witness, even of the wife herself, is accepted. According to Abaye, this one witness, plus the wife, form a pair of witnesses. Their testimony outweighs that of a conflicting, single witness. Thus, if the wife plus one witness say she was not married, then their testimony is superior to that of another witness who claims that she did marry. Similarly, if the wife and one witness claim that she was not divorced, then their testimony is superior to that of a lone witness to the contrary.

Rav Ashi sees the Gemara is a different light. He assumes that we are dealing with two outside witnesses (and not the wife as witness). In such a case, evidence that an event occurred carries more weight than *lack of* evidence that it occurred. The Gemara's answer to this is: "This is obvious!" "We did not see her" becomes a non-proof. Perhaps this latter pair of witnesses was unaware; maybe they did not see but it happened nonetheless. We accept the testimony of the two who *did* see something. The Gemara does not make decisions based on incomplete evidence or testimony to the negative. It is obvious that "We did not see her" is no proof.

D'RASH

"You ran the red light!" "I did not. You're a liar!" Two men, involved in a traffic accident, bring different perspectives to what happened. Shouting and pushing ensue as each accuses the other of lying. Within a few minutes, a police officer arrives and starts to sort out the details. One man says: "I was driving behind a sixteen-wheeler. When I saw this guy making a turn, I slammed on my brakes but it was too late. If he had been looking where he was going, I wouldn't have hit him."

The other responds: "It didn't happen that way. I was waiting at the intersection, and the light had turned yellow when the tractor trailer made the turn. I clearly saw that his light had turned red by the time he made the turn." After a lengthy discussion with the two drivers, the police officer ascertains that one man saw the accident happening, while the other only claims that he did not cause the accident. He cannot recall when the light changed; in fact, he can't even remember seeing the traffic light, since his vision was partially obscured by the truck.

Here is a modern example where "We did not see it" is no proof! The police officer is likely to write up his report based on the first driver's version, since he saw what happened. The second driver's account is based on his claim that he was innocent. His supporting evidence is what he *did not* see. Negative evidence, what was not seen, carries less weight than positive testimony, what was seen.

The teaching of the Gemara points not only to testimony but also our ability as humans to see others and be aware of them. Our individual, subjective experience is only part of reality. Yet, we often hear the words "I didn't see it" as an excuse for our selfishness, callousness, or egocentricity. A generation ago, those living in Europe maintained exemption from some of the blame for the Nazi atrocities by claiming ignorance. The world said: "How could you let that happen?" Many in Europe answered: "We did not know what was happening. We did not see!" The world answered: "'We did not see it' is no excuse!"

The inability to see human ills, though they exist just under the surface of society, is common in our day and age as well. There are beggars and the homeless in every metropolitan area of our country. Nonetheless, when we are in a city, we may walk by them and not, in our indifference, really see them. Their numbers are too great. Their clothes are too shabby. Their misfortune is too sad for us really to pay attention, and we let them become nonhumans. It would hurt us so if we truly saw their poverty, broken lives, and desperation. Thus, we pass them by—on foot, in our cars, by train, even when their stories are told on television or in the newspaper—and we choose not to see. But "We did not see them" is no excuse. It holds no weight in the eyes of the Jewish tradition, which puts the burden of proof on those who could see but choose not to.

We have an obligation to delve, to find out, to see more of the world than that which we want to see. If we do not, if we ignore the ugly truth, we ultimately bear some of the guilt and part of the blame, for "We did not see" is neither proof nor excuse.

הַכֹּל כְּמִנְהַג הַמְּדִינָה

Everything is according to local custom.

TEXT

Ketubbot 66b

Mishnah (6:4): *If she agreed to bring in money,* selas *are equal to six* dinars. *The husband undertakes ten* dinars *of pocket money for each* maneh *for the box. Rabban Shimon ben Gamliel says: "Everything is according to local custom."*

Gemara: *But this is the same as "He must agree to bring fifteen* maneh"! *First it was taught about major trade, then about minor trade. And we need both: For if it was taught only about major trade, it might apply only to major trade where the profit is great, but not to minor trade where the profit is less. And if it was taught only about minor trade, it might apply only to minor trade where administrative costs are incidental, but not to major trade where administrative costs are great. Thus, we need both.*

CONTEXT

Tosefta or "Addition" is a collection of rabbinic laws from the time of the Mishnah, roughly the third century C.E. *It is divided into the same six orders as the Mishnah, with almost every tractate having its Tosefta. The Tosefta is roughly four times the size of the Mishnah and, therefore, often presents not only parallel teachings but new material not mentioned in the Mishnah. For the student of rabbinic literature, the Tosefta's additions often clarify issues in the Mishnah. For example, the Tosefta on* Ketubbot *describes specific marriage practices that were common in Judea and the Galilee in the first two centuries of the Common Era. Some of these are not mentioned in the Mishnah.* •

The section from the Mishnah, like the Tosefta which parallels it in the sixth chapter of *Ketubbot,* teaches about the amount that a husband and wife agree to bring into the marriage. The wife's dowry ("she agreed to bring in money . . .") is assigned a value different from its usual rate, for the Rabbis are intentionally overvaluing the dowry: First, the *sela* is a coin usually worth four *dinars,* but in this case, the Rabbis assign it a value of *six dinars.* Second, the *maneh* is a coin usually worth one hundred *dinars,* and for each *maneh* she brings into the marriage, he must bring in ten *dinars.* These will insure the wife of sufficient funds from "the box," what is sometimes referred to as "pin money," that is, funds for the wife's own use.

The Gemara then asks: Isn't this rule the same as what we learned in the previous Mishnah, that if she brings in 1,000 *dinars,* "he must agree to bring fifteen *maneh*"? The Gemara then proceeds to explain the difference between this Mishnah and the previous one, since in each case, the husband adds fifty percent valuation over the usual rate. The reason we need each Mishnah is to teach about both large sums and small sums. If we had only the previous Mishnah, we would think that the husband adds fifty percent in the case of large-money transactions, but in the case of pocket money, the exchange rate is usual. And if we had only this Mishnah, we might think that we inflate the rate only where this increase is incidental, in the case of the wife's money "from the box," but where a fifty percent surcharge would be a huge sum, perhaps there is no overvaluation. Thus, we need both teachings.

The Mishnah and Gemara teach us that a husband may not decrease from the customary amount brought into a marriage, nor may he increase that amount. In a male-oriented society, it would certainly be to the wife's disadvantage for her husband to reduce his financial commitment to the marriage. In the future, she may not have that to live on. What is less easily understood is how *increasing* that amount would be a disadvantage. Would it not be to the woman's benefit for him to increase certain financial contributions? Our Mishnah is based on the concept that not every act of generosity is truly beneficent or desirable. The Mishnah assumes that this couple does not live in a vacuum but as part of a society with certain roles and expectations. If this specific husband gives the wife more by increasing his financial contribution to the marriage, he may simultaneously be harming other brides. What happens to the next bride, whose husband cannot increase the amount? Will many more brides be hurt because they cannot receive the additional sum? Will the very institution of marriage be impaired, since other husbands cannot increase their base amount to this new, higher standard? Every time we "up the ante" and attempt to establish a new, stricter norm of behavior—ostensibly a positive and favorable action—we must carefully consider the impact on those for whom the new standard will be a burden.

D'RASH

"Everything is according to local custom" sounds very much like "When in Rome do like the Romans." The difference, of course, is that the talmudic dictum speaks not only to the practices of Rome but of each and every community, not only to the money of the bride and groom but to many other everyday Jewish practices and habits as well. There *are* laws which are constants, transcending time and space. (Thus, the word "everything" is an exaggeration.) Yet, there are also customs which depend upon the will and practices of the people in the local community.

The way Jews dress for the synagogue is, to a large degree, a matter of local custom. In Israel, people tend to be much less formal even on Shabbat, often wearing sandals and (for the men) open-collar shirts to services. In America, the local custom is more formal, especially for the men. At times, we see shock on the face of an American tourist, on a first trip to Israel. Unaware of the local customs, he enters an Israeli synagogue, appropriately dressed for Shabbat *in the United States:* a suit and tie. How out of place he probably feels! Yet, we also see many an Israeli man attending Shabbat services for the first time in an American synagogue, dressed as if he were back in Israel: slacks, short-sleeve white shirt, collar open, sandals on his feet. He feels equally uncomfortable. Perhaps the *most* uncomfortable should be the American man who, after a stay in Israel, walks into an American synagogue in slacks and sandals—while everyone else is dressed in suits—and announces: "*This* is how they dress in Israel!" We can easily answer him: "Yes, in Israel, that would be proper Shabbat synagogue dress. But you're not in Israel any more. You're back in America. So come to the synagogue properly dressed for *this country.*"

Thus, the appropriate way to dress for Shabbat services depends less on formal regulations or our personal preferences and more on where we are. In Israel, it is one way, while in America, it is often quite different. And there are even regional differences throughout America, between one community and the next, between one area and another. In some places, it is considered proper, even fashionable, for women to attend services in slacks. In other communities, it would be highly inappropriate to enter a synagogue in even the most fashionable pants outfit. What we like to wear and what we feel like doing are less relevant than the practices customary in that area. After all, "everything is according to local custom."

דְרָחֵם לֵיהּ לָא חָזֵי לֵיהּ חוֹבָה
דְסָנֵי לֵיהּ לָא חָזֵי לֵיהּ זְכוּתָא

A loved one—one does not see his faults; a hated one—one does not see his merits.

TEXT

Ketubbot 105b

> *Rava said: "What is the reason for [the prohibition against a judge receiving] a gift? Once he receives a gift from him, his opinion draws closer to his, and he becomes like him, and a man cannot see guilt in himself. What is* 'shoḥad *[a gift]?'* 'Sheh-hu ḥad'*—'he is one [with the gift giver].'" Rav Papa said: "A person should not judge a case of someone he loves, nor of someone he hates, for a loved one—one does not see his faults; a hated one—one does not see his merits."*

CONTEXT

Rava and Rav Papa teach about judicial impartiality. Rava bases himself on the verse in Deuteronomy that prohibits a judge from receiving a gift from the people who will come before him. He uses a word play to emphasize his point: The word for a gift or a bribe is *shoḥad.* He breaks the word up into two words that sound similar to the original. This well-known rabbinic methodology is called *notarikon,* from the Greek word that refers to a stenographer's method of shorthand.

The Talmud goes on to show the lengths to which some judges went in order to remain impartial. Shmuel was once crossing a river on a ferry. As he went to step onto land, a man approached and offered Shmuel his hand to assist him. Shmuel asked: "Who are you?" The man replied: "I have a case in court before you." Shmuel then disqualified himself from acting as judge in the case. "Gifts" was understood not only as bribes but also as any act or words that might cause the judge to show one party any preferential treatment.

You shall not judge unfairly: you shall show no partiality; you shall not take bribes, for bribes blind the eyes of the discerning and upset the plea of the just. (Deuteronomy 16:19). •

*Moses Maimonides codifies the law: "It is forbidden for a judge to try a case of a person he holds dear—even if it is not a best friend or someone who is a very close friend, nor should he try a case of someone he hates—even if is not an enemy or someone who seeks to do him evil, but rather it must be that the two litigants are equal in the eyes and hearts of the judges. And if he did not know either one of them nor knew of their deeds, there is not a judge of righteousness better than this." (*Mishneh Torah, Sefer Shoftim, Hilkhot Sanhedrin *23:6)* •

D'RASH

A father who has been coaching Little League for several years gets his own son on his team. Several friends suggest that it is not the best of situations to be your child's coach, but the father thinks he can handle it. In a critical game, with the championship on the line, the coach picks his son to be starting pitcher, despite the boy's mediocre record. The child has a bad outing; the opposition hits practically everything he throws. Despite the unhappiness of the other team members, and over the complaints of many parents in the stands, the coach refuses to take his son out and put in a new pitcher. Later, he blames the defeat on the bad calls of the umpire and the poor fielding of the players. What the coach-father refused to acknowledge is that it is so very difficult to see the shortcomings of those we love. A coach has to treat all his players equally; a father has to show special attention to his own child. Sometimes these two roles are mutually exclusive.

A supervisor at work is asked to put together an evaluation of one of the firm's employees who is being considered for a promotion. Just last year, however, the two women fought bitterly over the way a job was being handled. Harsh words were exchanged, and feelings were hurt. The employee questioned the supervisor's competence and submitted a complaint to the boss. The supervisor has never forgotten, or forgiven. Now, *she* will have the last word, making sure that the employee pays for what she did to her. Despite the fact that everyone else values the employee and raves about her work, the supervisor cannot find anything positive to say about her.

Rav Papa would remind us that we all have our prejudices. Honesty demands that we recognize them and admit them; fairness requires that we not allow them to influence how we behave in certain situations. Some people are able to perform the difficult balancing act that is required of a coach and parent. Some people can give an objective evaluation of another person's work, even though they may dislike that individual intensely. Most of us, however, can not. Rav Papa suggests we acknowledge this and step aside, allowing someone more objective and less involved to judge the situation and make the difficult decisions. The Torah already warned us that bribes and other influences can blind us from making the right choices. The key question is whether we are willing and able to see this when issues touch close to home.

אַל יִשְׁתֶּה אָדָם בְּכוֹס זֶה
וְיִתֵּן עֵינָיו בְּכוֹס אַחֵר

A man should not drink from one cup while looking at another cup.

TEXT

Nedarim 20b

> *"So that you do not follow your heart [Numbers 15:39]." Based upon this, Rabbi said: "A man should not drink from one cup while looking at another cup." Ravina said: "This is necessary even if both of them were his wives."*

CONTEXT

This text appears in the third chapter of *Nedarim*, where there is a long excursus on permitted and prohibited sexual relations between husband and wife. The author of this saying is Rabbi Yehudah ha-Nasi, the third century C.E. leader of the Jewish community in the land of Israel. He was such a central rabbinic figure that the Talmud simply called him "Rabbi."

It is clear that the Rabbis of the Talmud assumed that Jewish law or halakhah, which is ultimately God's law, should control every action of the Jew. There is nothing beyond the purview and the value system of the halakhah. For example, the Talmud describes the proper way for us to eat, drink, sleep, and even relieve ourselves. Each of these reflects a set of values based on a total world view. Included in this system and these values are human sexual relations. The Rabbis were not afraid to talk about sexual intimacy or to describe what halakhah allowed between a husband and his wife. Nonetheless, the Rabbis often employed euphemistic language. In this case, "drinking from a cup" is a rabbinic metaphor for having sexual relations with one's wife.

Thus, "looking at" would probably best be understood as "fantasizing about," rather than *physically* peering at with one's eyes. The Talmud teaches that a man should not think of another woman, even if that woman is a second wife of his. The Rabbis did not see this as being within the Jewish ideal of sexual relations. During the talmudic era, few Jewish men actually had more than one wife at a time. Even though there was little possibility of fantasizing about a second wife, Jewish sexual ethics nevertheless applied the same principle to all relationships. Rabbi Nissim Gerondi, from eleventh century North Africa, known by the acronym "Ran," offers the following commentary on this section of Talmud:

*The Rabbis of the Talmud often employed metaphors and euphemistic language. There are numerous reasons for this. The Rabbis were concerned that Jews use respectable language. Hence, pubic hair is called "the lower beard" and sexual intercourse "use of the bed." Their use of euphemisms in part reflects a belief that sexual relations are holy yet private, sacred to the point of being personal. In addition, some subjects are extremely sensitive, and the Rabbis tried to avoid hurting anyone when discussing these issues. Thus, there is a moving story in the Talmud (*Berakhot *58a) about Rav Sheshet who was blind and how he outsmarted a certain sectarian. Rav Sheshet is called* sagi nahor, *Aramaic for "an abundance of light" or "much light." This is the talmudic euphemism for one who is blind. In fact, euphemistic language in general is called* leshon sagi nahor, *the "language of much light."* ●

> *At the hour when he is engaged [in sex] with his [first] wife he should not look at another woman, even if she is his [second] wife.*

A Biblical basis for this is given by Rabbi in the verse from Numbers, that one not "follow his heart" and the fantasies of his imagination. Note that the discussion is largely directed to the man, perhaps reflective of the limited access that women had to the world of talmudic learning.

D'RASH

Many contemporary sex experts posit that fantasy is a healthy part of a couple's sex life. Fantasizing is seen as a normal, even expected, behavior. Dr. Ruth Westheimer, in *Dr. Ruth's Guide for Married Lovers,* writes that "for good sexual functioning this ability to make images, fantasies, is as important as having genitals or being alive." This seems to be the modern wisdom.

The Talmud takes a slightly different approach. On one level, Rabbi is offering a preventive measure against adultery. If a man does not *think* about other women, then he will not be tempted to have relations with another woman. Thus, we might say that improper thoughts can lead to inappropriate and forbidden actions.

Yet, the case that Rabbi and Ravina deal with is *not* one of adultery. The man in this Gemara is married to two women; therefore, thoughts about his *other* wife are permitted. Nonetheless, Rabbi Yehudah ha-Nasi discourages such thoughts during intercourse with the first wife. To Rabbi and Ravina and their colleagues, pleasure *is* an important part of married life. The Rabbis went so far as to prescribe how often a wife could demand sexual relations with her husband. Yet, the bottom line for the Rabbis is not pleasure but holiness. We may even speculate that Rabbi and Ravina would add that a man who finds physical satisfaction with one woman while thinking of another woman will really not find the experience as *fully pleasing* as possible, for sexual pleasure is more than physical proximity and sensual satisfaction, even more than "something in the mind."

This Gemara directly contradicts the teachings of many modern sex therapists that fantasy about someone other than your spouse is healthy. The bottom line for much of American society is pleasure, whatever the price or action. The Rabbis of the Talmud disagree (at least to this kind of fantasy). Instead of the American ideal of "safe sex," the Rabbis affirm "sacred sex," for without the focus of holiness, sex is, in the eyes of the Talmud, an incomplete experience.

כָּל מִי שֶׁאֵינוֹ מְבַקֵּר חוֹלִים
כְּאִלּוּ שׁוֹפֵךְ דָּמִים

Anyone who does not visit the sick is like one who spills blood.

TEXT

Nedarim 39b–40a

Rav Ḥelbo took sick. Rav Kahana went and announced: "Rav Ḥelbo is sick!" No one came. He said to them: "Wasn't there an incident with a student of Rabbi Akiva who was sick and the Sages did not come to visit him; Rabbi Akiva went to visit him and because they swept and cleaned up before him, he got well? He [the student] said to him [Rabbi Akiva]: 'You have given me life!' Rabbi Akiva went out and explained: 'Anyone who does not visit the sick is like one who spills blood.'" When Rav Dimi came, he said: "Whoever visits the sick causes him to live, and whoever does not visit the sick causes him to die!" What is the cause? Shall we say that anyone who visits the sick begs mercy that he live, and anyone who does not visit the sick begs mercy that he die? Do you really think "that he die"??!! Rather: Anyone who does not visit the sick does not beg for mercy that he should either live or die!

The Gemara's phrase "they swept" is kib'du, *a word from the same root as the Hebrew term* kavod, *or honor. Why do both words come from one root? What connection is there between cleaning and honoring? Perhaps an answer can be found from another use of the same root elsewhere in the Talmud. In* Pesaḥim *7a, the Gemara says, in commenting on money found in a public place: "The streets of Jerusalem used to be swept every day." Thus, money found on the streets could not have been there long. When we speak of Jerusalem, the holy city, the connection between honor and sweeping becomes clearer. Because Jerusalem had a special status, the city was kept extra clean, even to the point of sweeping its streets each and every day. Similarly, we honor Shabbat by cleaning ourselves and our homes. A great scholar like Rabbi Akiva would deserve similar respect, and accordingly, the room was swept before his arrival.* •

CONTEXT

This section explains the importance in rabbinic Judaism of visiting the sick with an incident that occurred to the famous Rabbi Akiva. Despite the fact that Rav Ḥelbo was one of the regular students at the study house, no action was taken by his fellow students when his illness was announced there. To show how wrong this is, Rav Kahana reminds them of a time when Akiva personally visited one of his own students, after which the student soon recovered. The Talmud's explanation for the recovery is that because the room was cleaned up to honor Rabbi Akiva, the sick student benefited from this honor and was healed.

Rabbi Akiva then offers a pronouncement: Not visiting the sick is tantamount to causing their death! Rav Dimi, visiting Babylonia from Palestine, brings a similar statement with him from the Sages of Israel: Visiting the sick makes them live, and not visiting them contributes to their dying. It is not clear what the causative factor is. That is, what about a visit makes a person better? We would likely answer that the concern of others is what makes the patient feel better. The Rabbis, however, assume that it is the prayer that accompanies a visit. If that is so, the Rabbis ask, might we then assume that one who neglects to visit the sick is praying that a person should die? No, they answer, one who does not visit does not pray *for* the person or *against* him; he simply does not include the person in his prayers at all.

D'RASH

In a famous Willy Nelson song, the singer apologizes for all the wrongs he did to a lover with the excuse: "You were always on my mind." Even if I did not write or call, at least I thought of you, that is, I did not do something to hurt you, but simply had no opportunity to do something to help you or our relationship. To the singer, this is a less malicious sin, one of omission rather than commission.

Theodore Tronchin, a physician writing in an eighteenth century journal of medicine, held that "In medicine, sins of commission are mortal, sins of omission, venial." In other words, what the doctor *does* can hurt someone, but what he misses or forgets to do is benign. Though this line of reasoning is understandable and undoubtedly true in many situations, few us of would accept such medical practices. We have heard about and seen too many people who were hurt by medical sins of omission.

Are Willy Nelson and Theodore Tronchin right, that less fault can be assigned for action not taken than for action taken? Can we say that a person had intention or design through *in*action? Rabbi Akiva and Rav Dimi would take a skeptical view of this approach. Perhaps we should as well. One who has the opportunity to help a fellow human being but does not help is, in a way, choosing not to be involved.

Being "actively uninvolved" is something we do all the time. When the former friend, who has become an annoyance, calls, we tell a family member to say that we're not there. This deception takes a great deal of effort on our part, even though we never talk on the phone. Those of us who have passed beggars and panhandlers on the street know that it is a very active and a very conscious choice not to give them a handout. There may be good reason for not giving them, but it is an act of neglect. Every act of omission is also one of volition.

There are, admittedly, times when we will not notice one who needs help. We cannot be faulted for these. It is the other opportunities that Rabbi Akiva is referring to. Poet Marianne Moore spoke to these in the revision of her *Complete Poems*. She deleted several lines from a poem, adding a personal note that "Omissions are no accident." In so many cases, they are not.

בִּנְיַן יְלָדִים סְתִירָה
וּסְתִירַת זְקֵנִים בִּנְיָן

The building up of children is really tearing down, while the tearing down of elders is really building.

TEXT

Nedarim 40a

Rav said: "One who visits the sick is saved from the punishment of Gehinnom, as it says: 'Happy is he who is thoughtful of the wretched; in bad times may the Lord keep him from harm [Psalms 41:2].' 'Wretched [dal]' *can refer only to the sick, as it says: 'He will cut me off from sickness* [dalah] *[Isaiah 38:12, author's translation].' And also from this verse: 'Why are you so dejected* [dal], *O prince, morning after morning [II Samuel 13:4]?' 'Harm' can refer only to Gehinnom, as it says: 'The Lord made everything for a purpose, even the wicked for an evil day' [Proverbs 16:4]." If he visits [the sick], what is his reward? What is his reward?! It was said: "He is saved from the punishment of Gehinnom!" But what is his reward in* this *world? "May the Lord guard him and preserve him and may he be thought happy in the land. Do not subject him to the will of his enemies [Psalms 41:3]." "May the Lord guard him"—from the evil inclination. ". . . and preserve him"—from suffering. ". . . and may he be thought happy in the land"—everyone will be honored through him. "Do not subject him to the will of his enemies"—that he may chance upon friends like Naaman's who healed his leprosy, and not chance upon friends like Rehoboam's who divided his kingdom.*

It is taught: Rabbi Shimon ben Elazar says: "If children say to you 'Build!' and elders [say] 'Tear down!' listen to the elders and do not listen to the children, for the building up of children is really tearing down, while the tearing down of elders is really building. An example of this is Rehoboam, son of Solomon."

Naaman, commander of the army of the king of Aram, was important to his lord and high in his favor, for through him the Lord had granted victory to Aram. But the man, though a great warrior, was a leper. . . . Elisha sent a messenger to say to him, "Go and bathe seven times in the Jordan, and your flesh shall be restored and you shall be clean." . . . So he went down and immersed himself in the Jordan seven times, as the man of God had bidden; and his flesh became like a little boy's, and he was clean. (II Kings 5:1, 10, 14) •

CONTEXT

Rav begins our section by talking about the mitzvah of *bikkur ḥolim,* visiting the sick. It is considered a very important act of kindness; the reward for this mitzvah is that after death, a person would be spared the punishments of "Gehinnom." The name Gehinnom originally derived from "the valley of the sons of Hinnom," south of Jerusalem, where children were offered in fire to the god Moloch. Because of this, it later came to mean the place where the

... Jeroboam and all the assembly of Israel came and spoke to Rehoboam as follows: "Your father made our yoke heavy. Now lighten the harsh labor and the heavy yoke which your father laid on us, and we will serve you." ... King Rehoboam took counsel with the elders who had served his father Solomon during his lifetime. He said, "What answer do you advise [me] to give to this people?" They answered him, "If you will be a servant to those people today and serve them, and if you respond to them with kind words, they will be your servants always." But he ignored the advice that the elders gave him, and took counsel with the young men who had grown up with him and were serving him. ... And the young men who had grown up with him answered ... "Say to them, 'My little finger is thicker than my father's loins. My father imposed a heavy yoke on you, and I will add to your yoke; my father flogged you with whips, but I will flog you with scorpions.'" (I Kings 12:3–4, 6–8, 10–11) •

dead were sent to receive punishments for their sins. (The concept of "burning in Hell," common in literature including rabbinic texts, is not referred to in the Bible.) Rav brings several verses to prove his assertion; because the same key word *dal* (sick, wretched, poor) appears in them all, the context of one is applied to the others.

The question is asked about the reward in *this* life for performing the mitzvah of visiting the sick. The final answer is that such a person will be *given* friends like those of Naaman and will be *spared* friends like those of Rehoboam. Rehoboam succeeded his father Solomon as king. Solomon had heavily taxed the people, and they were deeply concerned about Rehoboam's policies. Because the king followed the bad advice of his young friends to be harsh with the people, the ten northern tribes broke away and founded their own kingdom, known as Israel and ruled by Jeroboam. Rehoboam was left ruling only the two southern tribes, known as Judah.

D'RASH

Many people think that youth is synonymous with energy and growth and is entirely positive, while age implies weakness and decay and is to be shunned or avoided. Rabbi Shimon ben Elazar tells us not to be so quick in our judgements. Youth can bring with it immaturity and impatience; unbridled energy acting on momentary whims can lead to terrible and costly mistakes. On the other hand, age often has the benefit of wisdom that is born of experience and reflection.

There is another assumption that Rabbi Shimon is challenging: Building is always good, while tearing down must, by definition, always be bad. Architects and city-planners understand that too much building can create overcrowding. Building in the wrong place can leave people without access to shopping, work, or recreation. Shoddy building can be a major safety hazard. Building without concern for esthetics can have a major negative impact on how people see their environment and how they feel about themselves. Building more is not always better.

What is true of the physical realm is often true in the social sphere as well. Involvement with people and causes is a good thing, but many of us make the mistake of assuming that more is always better. There are many individuals who are so active in work or organizations that they are busy to the point of dysfunction. Spreading themselves too thin by their relationships, involvements, or obligations, they have no time left for the things that truly matter.

On the other hand, destruction can sometimes lead to unexpected, but very constructive, consequences. Destruction is often the first step in the process of change, renovation, and revitalization. Tearing down makes for breathing room and allows for new growth. Scientists have observed that a fire in a forest, while being very destructive, actually lays the foundation for more fertile soil and eventual rebirth of an ecosystem that is stronger and healthier than it was before. In the eighteenth century, medicine took a giant leap forward by suggesting that inoculating people with a disease could prevent a more severe case of that disease in the future. Imagine the initial response of most people to the suggestion that smallpox could be eliminated if you first gave a patient a mild dose of the plague. It must have seemed madness! Yet sometimes, what seems like destruction can actually lead to something very positive.

A good football coach knows that punting on fourth down is not always a sign of failure. It can be a part of a larger strategy to give the other team the ball with very poor field position. It is a way of building up an eventual score, even though at the moment it looks destructive to the goal of putting points on the board.

Rabbi Shimon would counsel us: Don't be so quick to judge things by who is doing them or by how they appear at first glance. What seems vibrant and constructive may not be. What seems destructive and old may actually lead to something good and lasting.

גְדוֹלָה עֲבֵרָה לִשְׁמָהּ
מִמִּצְוָה שֶׁלֹּא לִשְׁמָהּ

A sin done for the right reason is better than a mitzvah done for the wrong reason.

TEXT

Nazir 23b

> *Rav Naḥman bar Yitzḥak said: "A sin done for the right reason is better than a mitzvah done for the wrong reason." But did not Rav Yehudah say in the name of Rav: "A person should always occupy himself with Torah and mitzvot even if they are done for the wrong reason, for by doing them even for the wrong reason he will eventually come to do them for the right reason"? Therefore, say: [A sin done for the right reason is]* like *a mitzvah done for the wrong reason, as it is written: "Most blessed of women be Jael, wife of Heber the Kenite, most blessed of women in tents [Judges 5:24]." Who are the women in tents? Sarah, Rebekah, Rachel, and Leah.*

CONTEXT

The sin done for the right reason is Jael's killing of the Canaanite general, Sisera. After suffering a terrible defeat on the battlefield at the hands of the Israelites, Sisera fled and sought refuge with Jael. According to the biblical story, she offered him a place to hide, but after he fell asleep, she killed him, destroying an enemy of the Israelites and bringing about a period of peace and security. According to the Midrash, Jael not only gave him a place to sleep, she had sex with him in order to make him go to sleep, so that she could kill him.

He asked for water, she offered milk;
In a princely bowl she brought him curds.
Her [left] hand reached for the tent pin,
Her right hand for the workmen's hammer.
She struck Sisera, crushed his head,
Smashed and pierced his temple.
At her feet he sank, lay outstretched,
At her feet he sank, lay still;
Where he sank, there he lay—destroyed. (Judges 5:25–27)

The mitzvah done for the wrong reason was when each of the Matriarchs presented her husband with a handmaiden who was to become his concubine. Ostensibly, this was done because the matriarch was barren and wanted to make certain that her husband would have a child, so the family would increase and multiply. But according to the Rabbis, the Matriarchs had ulterior motives. They were really interested in engendering jealousy among their rivals. The gift was not about survival of the family; it was motivated by ego and selfishness.

D'RASH

Sarai, Abram's wife, had borne him no children. She had an Egyptian maid

What is more important: What we do, or why we do it? Rav Yehudah takes the standard Jewish view: actions are what count the most. It is better to do the right thing, even if it is for the wrong reason. The boss is in the hospital. We don't really like him all that much, and if we had our choice, we would rather not go to see him. If we do pay him a visit, it would only be as a way to get on his good side and "score points": Thinking of asking him for a raise, we were hoping that this little visit might make him think more favorably of us. Rav Yehudah would say: "Go see him; it's a mitzvah to visit the sick. Deeds are more important than intentions. Better to live in a world filled with people doing good deeds even if for all the wrong reasons."

Rav Naḥman takes a very different approach: "It's the thought that counts. Don't judge people by what they accomplish; judge them by what they intend." Imagine a mother who comes home from work and finds her kitchen a shambles. The sink is filled with running water cascading onto the floor. Dishes are broken. Sugar is spilled everywhere. The refrigerator is left wide open. The mother is furious at her children, whose footprints she can see in the mess. Just as she is about to yell and scream at them, they surprise her with the birthday cake they have made for her, from scratch. Even though the kitchen—and the cake—are disasters, she now considers this one of the most precious gifts she has ever received.

The examples Rav Naḥman brings are rather startling, as they deal with sexual ethics. They remind us of the proverb found in the Midrash: "She sells her body for apples, and then gives them away to the sick" (*Leviticus Rabbah* 3, 1). It is quite daring of the Rabbis to question—and condemn—the motives of Sarah, Rachel, and Leah, and at the same time to praise Jael for her seduction of Sisera.

Ultimately, both Rav Naḥman and Rav Yehudah teach us to try to do the right thing for the right reason, to combine good deeds *with* good intentions. Knowing human nature, they were willing to settle for only half. We struggle throughout our lives to achieve the ideal and to add the other half.

servant whose name was Hagar. And Sarai said to Abram, "Look, the Lord has kept me from bearing. Consort with my maid; perhaps I shall have a son through her." (Genesis 16:1–2)

When Rachel saw that she had borne Jacob no children, she became envious of her sister; and Rachel said to Jacob . . . "Here is my maid Bilhah. Consort with her, that she may bear on my knees and that through her I too may have children." (Genesis 30:1, 3)

When Leah saw that she had stopped bearing, she took her maid Zilpah and gave her to Jacob as concubine. (Genesis 30:9) •

בְּמִדָּה שֶׁאָדָם מוֹדֵד
בָּהּ מוֹדְדִין לוֹ

By the measure that a person measures, so is he measured.

TEXT

Sotah 8b

> Mishnah (1:7): *By the measure that a person measures, so is he measured. She dressed herself up to sin, the Holy One dressed her down. She exposed herself to sin, the Holy One exposed her. She started to sin with the thigh, and afterwards the belly; therefore, the thigh suffers first and the belly afterwards. And the rest of the body does not escape punishment.*
> Gemara: *Rav Yosef said: "Even though the measure is abolished, 'by the measure' is not abolished."*

CONTEXT

The Mishnah here is expanding on the case of the "straying wife," the woman suspected of adultery, as the Torah delineates the law in Numbers 5: 11–31. In fact, the name for this entire tractate of Talmud is *Sotah,* "[the woman] who has gone astray," the technical name for the woman who is suspected of being unfaithful to her husband. The Torah describes the ritual to which she had to submit. The woman is brought to the *kohen,* where she drinks "water of bitterness," whereupon the *kohen* recites a formula: "If you have been faithful to your husband, may nothing happen to you because of these waters; if you have not been faithful, may the Lord curse you with sickness." It is possible that the effect of the ritual is for a woman guilty of adultery to suffer a self-induced illness. The specific nature of this illness is not known, though some scholars believe "thigh" to be a euphemism for genitals. Thus, this curse would impair her reproductive abilities, a severe curse in biblical times and even today.

The principle of "measure for measure" in the text assumes a symmetry between the sin and the punishment: The woman sinned by trying to look beautiful for her paramour; she is punished by being made to look ugly in the eyes of the onlookers: Her hair is shaven; she is dressed in ugly clothes; and her jewelry is removed. And just as she exposed herself to attract the man, God exposes her by having her disgrace made public, in the eyes of all onlookers. Since her sin was with her sexual organs, her punishment (in the words of the curse) should be on these very same reproductive organs.

The Lord spoke to Moses, saying: Speak to the Israelite people and say to them: If any man's wife has gone astray and broken faith with him in that a man has had carnal relations with her unbeknown to her husband, and she keeps secret the fact that she has defiled herself without being forced, and there is no witness against her—but a fit of jealousy comes over him and he is wrought up about the wife who has defiled herself; or if a fit of jealousy comes over one and he is wrought up about his wife although she has not defiled herself—the man shall bring the wife to the priest. . . . The priest shall bring her forward and have her stand before the Lord. . . . After he has made the woman stand before the Lord, the priest shall bare the woman's head and place upon her hands the meal offering of remembrance, which is a meal offering of

In the Gemara, Rav Yosef explains that even though we no longer punish according to the actual measure, since capital punishment had been abolished by the time of the Gemara, "by the measure," apparently a reference to divine retribution, has not been abolished. Though *we* cannot be strict in meting out punishment, we can rest assured that justice will, in the end, prevail.

D'RASH

The biblical ordeal, as described in the Torah and explained in the Mishnah and Gemara, sounds to the modern ear harsh and biased. We believe in the rights of the accused. We hold that a person is innocent until proven guilty, while the woman in Numbers 5 and our Mishnah is exposed to public humiliation based solely on her husband's accusation. And what if the jealous husband's accusation is unfounded? "But if the woman has not defiled herself and is pure, she shall be unharmed and able to retain seed" (Numbers 5:28). The end of the test may yet prove her innocence, but only after undergoing this entire public ordeal!

While few of us would ask that guilty people be publicly disgraced for what they did wrong, we would ask that people be punished for their crimes. We feel satisfaction when there is "measure for measure": A tax cheat falls victim to bankruptcy. The man who derides others is insulted himself. The woman who never had time to help out others is at wit's end when she needs someone to lean on in an emergency—and there is no one to help her.

Yet, we also know that the world is not always so symmetrical and fair. People get away with murder, literally and figuratively. As Rabbi Yannai teaches in *Pirkei Avot* (4:19): "We cannot explain the tranquility of the wicked or the suffering of the righteous." The problem of good and evil has plagued humankind since people began to think.

Thus, we may not be able to see "measure for measure" on a cosmic level. Nonetheless, we usually can have it function on the interpersonal level. People respond "measure for measure" to the way they are treated. As we notice people dealing kindly with us, we usually respond to them with kindness. A congenial saleswoman smiles at you as you pay her for a purchase; you, in turn smile back, and you smile at the next few people you encounter.

Similarly, if we give off hostility, we are likely to face a hostile, angry reaction. What we may call "getting out of the bed on the wrong side" is often simply a chain reaction of

jealousy. And in the priest's hands shall be the water of bitterness that induces the spell. The priest shall adjure the woman, saying to her, "If no man has lain with you, if you have not gone astray in defilement while married to your husband, be immune to harm from this water of bitterness that induces the spell. But if you have gone astray while married to your husband and have defiled yourself, if a man other than your husband has had carnal relations with you"—here the priest shall administer the curse of adjuration to the woman, as the priest goes on to say to the woman—"may the Lord make you a curse and an imprecation among your people, as the Lord causes your thigh to sag and your belly to distend. . . ." (Numbers 5:11–16, 18–21) •

scowls. You're not feeling too well, and you bark out an order to the first person you meet. He, in turn, responds by thundering back at you. Soon, you notice that everyone around you is speaking in loud, angry tones. "What's going on today?" you think. "Why are people yelling at me?"

On the universal level, "measure for measure" is beyond our control, but on the interpersonal measure, in people we see, day in and day out, the Golden Rule of giving and receiving usually applies. Every day, people await the tone that we will set before they respond to us. If we measure the world positively, if we greet everyone cheerfully, if we act honestly towards others, we can be reasonably sure that most others will respond in kind.

אֵין אָדָם עוֹשֶׂה בְּעִילָתוֹ בְּעִילַת זְנוּת

A man would not have casual sex.

TEXT

Gittin 81a–b

> Mishnah (8:9): *He who divorced his wife and spent the night with her at an inn—Bet Shammai says she does not need a second* get *from him, but Bet Hillel says she needs a second* get *from him. Under what circumstances? If she was divorced from marriage, but everyone agrees that if she was divorced from betrothal, she does not need a second* get*, because he is not yet intimate with her.*
> Gemara: *Rabbah bar bar Ḥana said in the name of Rabbi Yoḥanan: "The disagreement is only if she was seen having sex. Bet Shammai thinks that a man would have casual sex, while Bet Hillel thinks that a man would not have casual sex. But where she was not seen having sex, everyone agrees that she does not need a second* get*."*

CONTEXT

A *get* is a Jewish divorce document, given by the husband to the wife to end their marriage. In talmudic times, a *get* was also used to end a formal engagement or betrothal. In this Mishnah, both Bet Hillel and Bet Shammai (the "everyone" in this argument) agree that a man would not have sex with his former fiancée, and we may therefore assume that there were no sexual relations between them, even if they spent a night together at an inn. Thus, a second *get* would be unnecessary. Were we to assume that the couple *did* have sexual relations, then a second *get* would be necessary, since the Rabbis of the Mishnah teach that intercourse is one way of formalizing the relationship between a man and a woman. This is taught in the first Mishnah of *Kiddushin:* A woman is married in one of three ways—money (the husband gives her a gift), a contract, or sexual intercourse. In our case in the Mishnah above, the couple's intercourse would reestablish their marriage bonds to each other.

We should note that our Mishnah assumes that a couple would not engage in *pre*-marital sex but might engage in *post*-marital sex, as exemplified by the case of a formerly married couple. If, after their divorce, a couple spent the night together at an inn, what should we assume about their behavior and actions? Does their act of cohabitation constitute a reaffirmation of the original marriage bond to each

Bet Hillel and Bet Shammai are two talmudic schools following the teaching of the great sages Hillel and Shammai who lived at the end of the first century B.C.E. *and the beginning of the first century* C.E. *Bet Hillel and Bet Shammai each have characteristic ways of thinking and deciding Jewish law, often disagreeing with the other. The Talmud records many of their disagreements. Some scholars used to explain the differences between Bet Hillel and Bet Shammai in light of the characteristics of their founders: Hillel was known as a gentle, kindly, and open teacher, while Shammai was apparently very stern and strict. Other scholars used to trace the two schools to economic and social differences, Bet Shammai representing the rich upper class and Bet Hillel representing the need of the common folk. Thus, Bet Shammai required a cup of wine in each house for* havdalah *(the ceremony that ends Shabbat), which was not a particular problem for the rich, while Bet Hillel ruled that* havdalah *in the synagogue exempted the individuals in the house, where an additional cup of wine might be a real hardship. Modern scholarship is not sure of the original or exact nature of the differences between the two schools. Rabbinic sources, however, traced the development of normative law to Bet Hillel and its earthy kindness, generosity, and concern for human welfare.* •

other? If so, "she needs a second *get* from him." This is the view of Bet Hillel. As is common, the Gemara not only explains the Mishnah but also limits the applicability of the law: It refers only to a case where someone actually *saw them* having sexual relations, that is, they were not simply sharing a room and we *assume* that they had intercourse.

The Rabbis of Bet Hillel presume that men would not have casual sex. Thus, the intercourse between the man (the former husband) and the woman (his former wife) cannot be a random affair but must be seen as an act of recommittal, even without the couple's saying so, for no man would have casual sex.

The Rabbis of Bet Shammai take the other view. A man can have sex for a variety of reasons. Sometimes, he wants to establish a relationship, but at other times, there is no intention other than physical gratification. Bet Shammai assumes that the latter is what happened at the inn. The husband and wife, already familiar with each other, had sex with no commitment. Following Bet Shammai's view, we cannot assume any more than what we see. Without the husband's explicit declaration ("I am marrying this woman through this act of sexual intercourse"), there is no reaffirmation of their original marriage, and no *get* is required.

The difference between Bet Hillel and Bet Shammai, as often happens between these two schools of thought, goes beyond the specific issue to encompass assumptions about people and world views. Bet Shammai seems to be saying that people do things for the reasons they articulate. Lacking proof, we cannot assume any positive motivation for actions. Bet Hillel, however, takes a different view of human nature, assuming that people act for the most positive, healthy, and religiously sound reasons possible, even if reality seems to conflict with this assumption. This is not based on the naiveté of Bet Hillel but on a rather sophisticated reworking of reality. Bet Hillel appears to be constructing a world view based on its own idealized perspective on human behavior. Thus, Bet Hillel cannot view a couple's sex as purely casual, promiscuous, or recreational.

D'RASH

We are not the first era to be concerned with casual sex. Knowing that people engage in sex for a variety of reasons, the Rabbis of the Talmud tried to teach that we should sanctify sexual relations. Very specific rules were drawn up to increase modesty and sanctity in sex and to insure that relations would not be immoral or crude.

Nonetheless, it is clear that people were having sexual relations outside the parameters of these teachings. The very discussion is proof. The question then becomes: What do we assume about people's motivations, purposes, and intentions? Bet Shammai and Bet Hillel have two different views, not only about sex but also about human behavior in general.

The Rabbis of Bet Hillel were aware that people's motivations are not always pure, in sex as in much of life. Nonetheless, they seem to have chosen to assume the best about people, facts aside, in the hope that the world would soon become closer to this ideal. Reality, they are saying, is what we make of it. If we assume the best about people, the world will begin more closely to reflect our ideal.

Every one of us can think of examples of others who have questionable motivations. How do we respond to them? For example, what should we think if a new employee speaks to a supervisor about certain work conditions? If we assume the worst, we think that he is trying to get in good with the boss, to promote himself at the expense of the group. We surmise that the newcomer is out only for himself.

A Bet Hillel approach, though, asks us to act based on our most positive assumptions about others, to be more trusting of their motivations. With no evidence to the contrary, we should assume the best about others. In this situation, if we act according to Bet Hillel, we may assume that this new employee has seen certain conditions that can be improved; perhaps he can demand changes, because of his new status, which veteran employees could not. The employee may very well be acting in everyone's best interest and may actually help those around him.

Our finding a more positive way of looking at reality is based not on naiveté but on a genuine desire to create a better world. Just as Bet Hillel assumes (even with facts to the contrary) that the "a man would not have casual sex," so too we can make positive, optimistic assumptions about our world and the people in it. This is often a way of finding the best in others. Our optimistic assumptions may be wrong at times, but often we will find people living up to our ideal. As we start to view the world more positively, it may begin to look a little more like the ideal place we envision.

גָּדוֹל מְצֻוֶּה וְעוֹשֶׂה
מִמִּי שֶׁאֵינוֹ מְצֻוֶּה וְעוֹשֶׂה

One who is commanded and acts is more praiseworthy than one who is not commanded and acts.

TEXT

Kiddushin 31a

Rav Yehudah said in the name of Shmuel: "They asked Rabbi Eliezer: 'What is the limit for honoring one's parents?' He said to them: 'Go see what a certain idol worshiper in Ashkelon named Dama son of Netina did. Once, the Sages sought to buy gems for the ephod from him at 60,000 profit—Rav Kahana taught 80,000—but the key was under his father's head and he would not disturb him. The next year, the Holy One rewarded him when a red cow was born to his herd.' When the Sages came to him, he said to them: 'I know that if I were to ask for all the money in the world, you will give it to me, but I am asking only for the money I lost by honoring my father.'" Rabbi Ḥanina said: "If someone who is not commanded and acts [is considered praiseworthy], how much more so one who is commanded and who acts!" For Rabbi Ḥanina said: "One who is commanded and acts is more praiseworthy than one who is not commanded and acts."

Honor your father and your mother, that you may long endure on the land that the Lord your God is assigning to you. (Exodus 20:12) •

The Lord spoke to Moses and Aaron, saying: This is the ritual law that the Lord has commanded: Instruct the Israelite people to bring you a red cow without blemish, in which there is no defect and on which no yoke has been laid. (Numbers 19:1–2) •

CONTEXT

How far does one have to go to fulfill certain mitzvot? When asked this question concerning honoring one's parents—a well-known mitzvah mentioned in the Ten Commandments—Rabbi Eliezer responds with a story. The Rabbis approach a non-Jew named Netina in the hope of buying from him jewels for the ephod, one of the vestments that the *Kohen Gadol* wore while serving in the Temple. They are not greeted by Netina but by his son, Dama. As a non-Jew, Dama is not required to observe the mitzvah of honoring one's parents. However, he does respect his father who at the time is sleeping, with the key to the jewelry under his head. Dama's actions cause his father to lose 60,000 (or 80,000) profit. (We are never told 60,000 or 80,000 *what,* but it is apparently coins.) The reward that Dama receives is a "red cow," that prized animal mentioned by the Torah in Numbers 19 and used in rituals of purification. This animal was extremely rare and, thus, quite expensive (worth more than 60,000 coins!). Dama apparently knows enough about Judaism to realize that he had been rewarded with an exceptional prize. Nonetheless, he asks only for repayment of the

Next you shall instruct all who are skillful, whom I have endowed with the gift of skill, to make Aaron's vestments, for consecrating him to serve Me as priest. These are the vestments they are to make: a breastpiece, an ephod, a robe, a fringed tunic, a headdress, and a sash. (Exodus 28:3–4) •

amount he lost by not making the original sale the year before (60,000 or 80,000 coins).

The entire section is based on the assumption of Rabbi Ḥanina that one who acts because he is commanded by a mitzvah is considered more praiseworthy than someone who is not commanded. Thus, if Dama ben Netina, a non-Jew who is *not* required to fulfill the mitzvah of honoring one's parents, takes this obligation so seriously and is praised by the Rabbis, imagine how far a Jew who *is* commanded to honor his parents must go in order to fulfill the mitzvah, and how great his or her reward will be!

D'RASH

Every day, we hear stories of people who volunteer and who do great good in the world. These accounts are inspiring, and the Rabbis would have only praise for those people who act, care, and help, though not required to. Our text does not take away anything from these men and women. Volunteers are, indeed, praiseworthy. This Gemara, however, sings the praises of people who *have to* act, those who simply do what is expected of them, day in and day out. Their actions are not glorious or newsworthy, but they are commendable and praiseworthy.

Each and every day, people go to work and earn an honest living, supporting their families and paying their taxes. They do so, in part, because it is expected and required of them. There is little distinction in their actions—other than the fact that they are doing precisely what they should be doing, day in and day out.

Every day, most parents impart positive values to their children through hard work and honest living, often holding down more than one job. These are people for whom making ends meet may be a struggle, but for whom cheating and fraud would be unthinkable ways of making a living. The newspapers will carry stories both of the mother who stole to feed her drug habit but not her children, and of the father who refused to work to support his family. The everyday heroism of honest, hard-working folk does not make the news, but it is worthy of praise.

A single mother rears her children without benefit of spouse, teaching her youngsters love and pride. When parents have no time or interest in religion, a grandparent may be the one who brings the child to synagogue and helps keep tradition alive. A widow or widower manages to remain involved and active despite the fact that it's a "paired-off" world; widows and widowers overcome sorrow and loneliness, creating new, active lives for themselves. Parents take a firm stand against dishonesty in schoolwork, even though it means bucking the trend and swimming upstream. A family gives charity generously, though money is tight and so many of their peers are selfish.

There are these and hundreds of other examples of simple people who live honest, genuine yet ordinary lives. Rabbi Ḥanina speaks to everyday responsibilities and mundane living, not to the generals of our society but to the foot soldiers. We should not relegate them to mediocrity or dismiss them as unimportant, even though they will not get their names into "Who's Who" or receive a medal for their actions. These people are the salt of the earth, and their strength and endurance makes them true heroes of life today.

הָרַב שֶׁמָּחַל עַל כְּבוֹדוֹ
כְּבוֹדוֹ מָחוּל

The rabbi who gave up his honor,
his honor is given up.

TEXT

Kiddushin 32a–b

> *Rav Yitzḥak bar Shelah said in the name of Rav Matneh, who said in the name of Rav Ḥisda: "The father who gave up his honor, his honor is given up. The rabbi who gave up his honor, his honor is not given up." But Rav Yosef said: "Even the rabbi who gave up his honor, his honor is given up, as it says: 'The Lord went before them in a pillar of cloud by day' [Exodus 13:21]." Rava said: "Is this [the same case as] that?* There, *with the Holy One, blessed be He, the world is His, and the Torah is His; He can give it up.* Here, *is the Torah his?" Rava came back and said: "Yes, the Torah* is *his, as it is written: 'In his Torah he studies day and night' [Psalms 1:2, author's translation]."*

*A person must be very careful about the honor and the reverence due his father and mother. What is reverence? . . . Not to sit in their special place, not to contradict their words . . . not to call them by their names. . . . What is honor? To give them food and drink, to dress them, to help them come and go. (*Shulḥan Arukh, Yoreh Deah *250:1, 2, 4)* •

*A person is obligated to respect and honor his rabbi even more than his father. It is forbidden for a student to call his rabbi by his name. . . . He should not greet his rabbi, nor return his greeting the way he would with anyone else, but must do so with respect and reverence. . . . It is forbidden to walk next to him; he should rather distance himself somewhat behind him. He should not sit in his presence until he tells him to sit. He should not sit in his [teacher's] place, nor contradict his words. (*Shulḥan Arukh, Yoreh Deah *252:1, 15, 16)* •

CONTEXT

Jewish tradition demands that a child, as well as a student, must show respect and reverence to a parent and a teacher. Our section raises the question as to whether that parent and teacher (or rabbi) may dispense with the formalities that tradition requires. The first conclusion is that a parent may do so. The Gemara goes on to bring in a disagreement between Rav Yitzḥak bar Shela and Rav Yosef: The former holds that a rabbi is different; the formal relationship between master and disciple must always be maintained. The latter believes that a rabbi, like a parent, is able to relax the rigid rules of behavior expected of his student. Rav Yosef brings proof for this point of view from a verse in Exodus that describes God acting as a guide for the Israelites as they wandered through the desert for forty years. At night, God became a pillar of fire; in the daylight, God was a pillar of cloud. Foregoing greatness, God became a mere pillar in order to help and guide the Israelites. If God could forgo honor to help a student, then certainly a rabbi of flesh-and-blood could do the same.

Rava questions whether this analogy is really apt: God can forgo honor, because the honor was God's to do with as God pleased. But is the honor due a rabbi really the rabbi's to do with as he pleases? Rava is at first inclined to believe that the honor accorded to a rabbi is given to him because of mastery of the Torah, and the Torah belongs to God! Hence, the rabbi has no right to dispense with something that is not truly his own. Later, apparently, Rava rethinks this opinion and changes his mind, basing himself upon an interpretation of a verse. Psalm 1 refers to a righteous man (a rabbi): "The teaching of the Lord is his delight, and in his Torah he studies day and night." The first half of verse 2 refers to the "teaching of the Lord," "*torat Adonai.*" But the second half speaks ambiguously of *torato,* which can be translated as "his teaching" or "His teaching." Rava chooses to interpret the word *torato* as referring to the teaching of the righteous. Therefore, since the Torah does belong to the rabbi, he can choose to forgo the honor ordinarily due him.

D'RASH

A first-year high school teacher, just out of college, finds himself in a deep philosophical conflict with his principal, a veteran administrator of the "old school." The teacher sees his role not as disciplinarian, not as authority figure, but as a mentor and guide who can best achieve results by being a friend to his students. He dresses informally—in jeans and a sweat shirt. He insists that his students call him by his first name. And he tries to spend time interacting socially with the students, both during school hours and after.

The principal is certain that this is an approach that is sure to lead to chaos and disaster. She insists that teachers wear a jacket and tie and use the title "Mr.," and suggests that faculty and students not socialize at all. The teacher, however, believes strongly that he can best succeed by having his students relate to him as a person, and by relating to them as individuals, virtually on an equal par. The formality of dress and title only serve to distance his students from him. He demands that the principal allow him to dispense with the formalities in an attempt to bring the two sides closer together. The principal believes just as strongly that school, and most of society, functions because there are well-accepted rules of relationships. Students know how they are supposed to behave. It is that expectation, from both sides, that enables one teacher to teach and control thirty children who would, by desire or disposition, rather talk or play. The teacher feels that the students' respect for him will be earned by treating them as equals. The principal is sure that respect is first imposed by adhering to accepted norms; later, it can be earned as students get to know the teacher. The teacher pleads: "I'm an individual. Let me do what I can do best!" The principal answers: "You are a teacher and a member of the faculty. What you do affects not only your own class but every other class and every other teacher as well!"

The debate of the Rabbis about the "honor" due certain individuals is actually over a much more fundamental question: "Who are we, really?" All of us play many roles in life—"child," "sibling," "friend," "pupil," "spouse," "parent," and "employee" or "boss." Into each role we infuse different elements of our personalities. Sometimes, those roles impose upon us very rigid modes of behavior that leave little room for individuality. It is only when we discover where the self ends and the role begins that we have started to define who we really are.

אֵין שָׁלִיחַ לִדְבַר עֲבֵרָה

There is no agent for wrongdoing.

TEXT

Kiddushin 42b

It has been taught: One who causes a fire to break out through the agency of a deaf-mute, an insane person, or a minor is not liable by human law, but is liable by Heaven's laws. If one caused it through the agency of a person in possession of all his faculties, the person in possession of all his faculties is liable. Why is this so? Can we not say that a person's agent is considered like the person? That case is different, for there is no agent for wrongdoing, as we say: "The words of the Master, and the words of the disciple: Whose words do we obey?"

The ḥeresh *(deaf-mute),* shoteh *(insane person) and* katan *(minor) are three groups of people who, because of their limited intellectual capacity, are not held responsible for their actions and are not obligated to perform the* mitzvot. Ḥeresh *is someone who can neither speak nor hear. The Rabbis bring examples of the behavior that characterizes a* shoteh: *going out alone at night, sleeping in a cemetery, ripping his clothing, and losing all personal possessions. A* katan *is someone who has not reached the age of maturity, thirteen years and one day.* •

CONTEXT

The Gemara begins by quoting a Mishnah (*Bava Kamma* 6:4) that lays down who is responsible for damage done by fire to someone else's property. In the first case, someone of diminished mental capacity blows on hot coals and causes a fire. The person who gave the coals is not legally responsible ("by human laws"), though is morally liable ("by Heaven's laws") for the damage. But if the person given the coals is of normal mental capacity, that person (and not the one who gave him the coals) is legally responsible for any damage.

The question is then raised concerning this second case: Why blame the one given the coals? Why not blame the person who gave the coals in the first place? Isn't *that* person ultimately responsible for the fire and for the damage done? This line of reasoning follows the legal principle "*sh'luḥo shel adam k'moto,*" "a person's agent is considered like the person." The Talmud rejects this approach, relying on another principle, "There is no agent for wrongdoing." The person given the coals, being of sound mind, knew right from wrong and knew the potential damage that hot coals could do. Therefore once that individual had possession of the coals, the responsibility for them and for destruction done to any property falls on the recipient, not on the one who gave them. Blame or liability cannot be shifted.

In the final question of our piece, the "words of the Master" refer to God's teaching; the "words of the disciple" are instructions given to us by human beings (in our case, the potentially dangerous order to take hot coals through a neighbor's property). The moral imperative to do the right thing takes precedence over anything else someone may tell us to do.

D'RASH

Harry Truman had a famous sign on his desk in the White House Oval Office: "The Buck Stops Here." He was reminding himself, and those who worked for the people, that if something went wrong, they were responsible. There were to be no excuses, no looking for a scapegoat, no shifting of blame.

That willingness to shoulder responsibility is becoming rarer in our society. More and more, we see a trend emerging of people looking for an excuse for their misconduct. A most extreme example was the so-called "Twinkie Defense," where a man who murdered two San Francisco politicians blamed his actions on "junk food," which had caused him to lose control of himself. This approach of "I'm not to blame" is all around us. A drunk driver blames alcoholism for the death of the pedestrian he ran down. A pedophile blames his crimes on his father, who sexually abused him when he was a child. A mugger points a finger at poverty and the society that forced him into a life of crime. A gunman opens fire in a crowded train, and his lawyers explain that the rage came because their client was a victim of racism. A woman sustains serious burns when she spills coffee on herself in a restaurant and sues the fast-food chain, claiming that they made the drink too hot. A rapist blames the victim, saying she was "asking for it."

Imagine a defendant standing up in court and just pleading guilty. "Your honor, I did it. I know I was wrong. I did a terrible thing. I feel sick about what I've done, and about the suffering that I've caused. I'm here to admit my guilt, to take responsibility for my actions, and to say that I am deeply, deeply sorry. I'm ready to accept my punishment." How absurd such a statement sounds in our society. And how refreshing.

The Rabbis teach us that there is no agent for wrongdoing, that we should not look for someone else to blame: "You know right from wrong. You know that there are consequences to your actions. Take responsibility for what you do!" Three times a day in the *Amidah,* a traditional Jew "confesses" his or her sins: "Forgive us, our Father, for we have sinned; pardon us, our King, for we have transgressed." These lines are punctuated by many people with two symbolic taps on the breast, over the heart. They are a daily reminder that we should not waste our time looking for excuses or other people to blame for what we ourselves have done. There is no agent for wrongdoing; *we* are responsible.

אֵין אָדָם טוֹרֵחַ בִּסְעוּדָה וּמַפְסִידָהּ A person does not prepare a meal to ruin it.

TEXT

Kiddushin 45b

> *A certain man said, "[Let our daughter be married]* to my *relative," while she said, "*To my *relative." She pressured him until he agreed to* her *relative. When they were eating and drinking,* his *relative went to the roof and married her. Abaye said: "It is written: 'The remnant of Israel shall do no wrong and speak no falsehood' [Zephaniah 3:13]." Rava said: "It is presumed that a person does not prepare a meal to ruin it." Where do they differ? They differ about a case where one did not prepare.*

The Jewish wedding of today is actually two ceremonies. In the days of the Talmud, these two ceremonies were separated by a period of time, often a year. In the first ceremony, Kiddushin *or* Erusin, *often called "betrothal," the groom handed the bride an object of value (like a ring) and said to her, in the presence of two witnesses: "Behold, you are consecrated to me by this ring in accordance with the law of Moses and Israel." Two blessings were also recited over a cup of wine. The couple was then consecrated to each other, though cohabitation was not yet allowed. At a later date, the* Nissuin *or ḥuppah took place. At this time, seven blessings were recited over a cup of wine and the marriage was consummated. Probably in the twelfth century, the two ceremonies were joined together as one (as they are today) under the ḥuppah. The perilous conditions of medieval Jews is usually given as the cause*

CONTEXT

A father (the "certain man") and mother argue. Each says: "Let our daughter be married to *my* relative!" The father finally agrees to allow his daughter to be married to the wife's relative. The festive wedding banquet is prepared, but before the actual betrothal can take place (at the preliminary festivities), the father's relative grabs the bride-to-be, takes her up to the roof and marries her there. We can imagine how the mother would feel; how would the father, who had promised that his daughter could marry the *mother's* relative, react?

Abaye and Rava agree that the father would disapprove of what has happened, but their reason for the disapproval differs. Abaye, basing himself on a verse from the prophet Zephaniah ("The remnant of Israel shall do no wrong and speak no falsehood") assumes that the father was not lying when he made the promise to his wife. He had indeed agreed to have his daughter married to the mother's relative and is now upset at his own relative's actions. Rava also thinks that the father would be upset, but not because of Abaye's moral concerns. Rava takes a much more cold, practical approach: A person is not going to spend a large amount of money on a wedding banquet if he knows that the wedding would not take place as planned. It is because of this monetary consideration that Rava holds that we should believe the father when he claims that he had nothing to do with his relative's plan to marry the daughter and elope.

Is there any *practical* difference between the opinions of Abaye and Rava? ("Where do they differ?") Yes, but only in a situation where *no* wedding feast had been prepared. In such a case, according to Abaye, the father would still be upset, since "the remnant of Israel shall . . . speak no falsehood," i.e., Jews do not lie, and he had intended the daughter to marry her relative. Both the father and the mother would be upset, and even though his relative was deceptive, the mother has no complaint against the father. Rava, however, believes that the father's main concern was the money. Where no meal had been prepared and no money spent, the father would have no defense against his wife's suspicion of his complicity.

for this change. In addition, it likely was difficult for the couple to have all the stringencies of marriage with none of the benefits. Thus, the difficulty of waiting a year was alleviated by bringing the two ceremonies together under the ḥuppah. The Jewish wedding festivities are traditionally a week-long celebration. Each day, the Shevah Berakhot, *the Seven Blessings of the original ḥuppah, are repeated at a festive meal.* ●

D'RASH

There is a stop sign at a busy intersection. Three cars stop. Are we correct in assuming that each driver has the same motivation? Hardly. The first driver stops because of the law: it says you're supposed to stop, and he respects rules. The second driver stops because she has previous moving violations and is afraid of permanently losing her license to operate a motor vehicle. The third driver stops because of memories of a cousin, injured by a careless driver who ran a red light. Each of these people stops at the corner, but their reasons for stopping are not at all the same.

The disagreement between Abaye and Rava goes to the very question of motivation. What causes people to act in the way that they do? Is it honesty and virtue, respect of laws and the affect that breaking them has on others around us? Or is it self-interest and ulterior motives like money?

In many cases, we are motivated by both views. Rava is correct to assume that we would not want to sacrifice money, waste time, lose a profit, or cause ourselves some other disadvantage. We would surely be angered if any of these happened to us.

The challenge for us is not to choose between the moral idealism of Abaye, where Jews "speak no falsehood," and the realism of Rava, where people are motivated by materialistic concerns, even when their closest family members are involved. In a world of tight money and limited resources of all kinds, most of us have a good portion of Rava in us. Our challenge is to incorporate a bit of Abaye's sanguine viewpoint into our lives.

Few of us are motivated only by principle. We, like the father, may have financial worries, social pressures, time constraints. We recognize that many of the motivations that Rava alludes to impel us. The message of the Gemara is not to choose one or the other. Rather, we need to recognize the selfish and self-centered reasons that we act and strive to incorporate the idealistic into our lives as well.

The reality is that we will act for Rava's reasons. We can also choose to act for Abaye's ethical goals.

דְּבָרִים שֶׁבַּלֵּב אֵינָם דְּבָרִים

Words that are in the heart are not words.

TEXT

Kiddushin 49b–50a

There was a man who sold his possessions with the intention of going to the land of Israel, but at the time of the sale he said nothing [of this intention]. Rava said: "These were words that were in the heart, and words that are in the heart are not words." From where did Rava [learn this]? Shall we say from that which has been taught: "[If his offering is a burnt offering from the herd, he shall make his offering a male without blemish.] He shall bring it [to the entrance of the Tent of Meeting, for acceptance in his behalf before the Lord]" [Leviticus 1:3]. This teaches that they [the court] can force him to bring it. Shall we say against his will? *The text says "for acceptance in his behalf." How can this be? They force him until he says: "I want to." How can this be, since in his heart he did* not *want to? Thus, is it not because of what we have said: "Words that are in the heart are not words"?*

Rashi: And subsequently, he was prevented from going. ●

In a slightly different case (Kiddushin *50a*), *Rava ruled as follows: There was a man who sold his possessions with the intention of going to the land of Israel. He left, but was not able to settle there. Rava said: "Anyone who leaves goes with the intention of settling, and this man did not settle." [Rashi: And is therefore like one who could not leave; thus the sale is reversed.] There are those who say: "He left with the intention of going, and he did go [and therefore the sale is legally binding]."* ●

CONTEXT

The man who sold his land had in mind this condition: "The sale will be final only if I indeed go to Israel. If my plans fall through and I cannot go, then the sale will not be considered binding." Rava comes to teach that a mental stipulation has no legal force. The Talmud finds the basis for this principle in an interpretation of a verse in the first chapter of Leviticus. The apparently redundant use of the words *yakrivenu/ yakriv*—"he shall make his offering/he shall bring it"—is interpreted as meaning that the court must pressure a man to bring a sacrifice that he had promised to offer. However, this would then conflict with the notion that sacrifices must be brought willingly. This is resolved by the principle that a court can pressure a man until he says "I am willing." Yet someone who is pressured outwardly to do something may still have an inner mental reservation. The Rabbis ruled: Inner mental reservations—words in the heart—are not considered of substance. Rava based his ruling on this earlier teaching.

D'RASH

A couple sits in a therapist's office; they are there for marriage counseling. The wife complains bitterly about her husband's lack of showing her affection. "I'm always telling him how much I love *him.* When we go out, I always reach for his hand, to hold it as we walk. At home, I'll come over and for no reason at all just give him a hug or a kiss on the top of his head. But I get nothing in return! The only time he'll tell me he loves me is when we're in bed, or maybe on my birthday, or before he goes on a trip. When we're out together, he won't hold my hand, or even let me put my arm around him. It's like I'm poison. Doesn't he know how that's bound to make me feel? I need more affection from him. I need him to let me know that he loves me. Sometimes lately, I begin to wonder if he even loves me at all any more."

The husband breaks in. "How can you say that? I show you all the time how I feel about you. Maybe not in words, but that doesn't mean the feelings aren't there. No matter what I say, you are always in my thoughts." The therapist interjects, "What *is* on your mind? How *do* you feel about her? *Do* you love your wife?"

"Of course I do! How can she question that?" the husband answers.

"I question it because I just don't know. You don't tell me. Sometimes I need to hear you say it. *In words!*"

Rava uses the principle "Words that are in the heart are not words" in a legalistic sense, but it is clear that the principle has validity in other spheres as well. It teaches us the importance of communication, of letting people know what we are thinking and feeling. Some people believe: "It's the thought that counts." Rava does not. To him it is not enough to leave thoughts in our hearts or minds. They must be expressed, they must be shared with others. If they are not, if they are left unsaid, then often we are left to explain, too late, "But what I really meant was . . ." How sad.

Rest Stop

From there they set out and encamped at the wadi Zared. (Numbers 21:12)

Words of Torah are compared to water, as it says: "Ho, all who are thirsty, come for water." [Isaiah 55:1] . . . Just as water is not to be found in a golden or silver vessel, but rather in the lowliest of vessels, so too Torah is not to be found except in one who makes himself like an earthen vessel. (*Song of Songs Rabbah* 1,3)

A rabbi fell asleep and dreamed that he had entered Paradise. There, to his surprise, he found the sages discussing a knotty problem in the Talmud.

"Is this the reward of Paradise?" cried the rabbi. "Why, they did the very same thing on earth!"

At this, he heard a voice chiding him, "You foolish man! You think the sages are in Paradise. It's just the opposite! Paradise is in the sages."

(Nathan Ausubel. *A Treasury of Jewish Folklore.* New York: Crown Publishers, 1960, p. 55)

Seder Nezikin

Introduction to Seder Nezikin

The fourth Order of the Mishnah is *Nezikin,* or "Damages." There are ten tractates that discuss civil and criminal law cases. The first three tractates were originally one long section; they were broken up into more manageable size and given the names "First Gate," "Middle Gate," "End Gate" (in Aramaic *Bava Kamma, Bava Metzia,* and *Bava Batra*). Two tractates of this Order have no Gemara. One of them is *Pirkei Avot,* "the Chapters (or Ethics) of the Fathers," a book of ethical maxims that is among the most well known and popular sections of all rabbinic literature.

אָדָם מוּעָד לְעוֹלָם

A man is always forewarned.

TEXT

Bava Kamma 26a

> Mishnah (2:6): *A man is always forewarned, whether inadvertently or deliberately, whether awake or asleep. If he blinded the eye of another, or broke his utensils, he must pay full damages.*

CONTEXT

The Mishnah, both here and in previous chapters, is defining categories of living things and objects as to their culpability in the case of damages. Some are "blameless" (in Hebrew, *tam*), that is, there are no damages assessed when they injure. Others are called "forewarned" (in Hebrew, *muad*). Caution must be taken and, where it was not, the responsible party can be assessed damages.

Thus, for example, if a person's ox gores another's animal, how much is the ox's owner responsible for those damages? It is well known that oxen gore, and the ox's owner must take necessary precautions to protect others from his animal's habits. If he does not, then he is liable for damages. As far as goring by an ox is concerned, the owner is "forewarned" (or, to be technical, the animal is in the category "forewarned").

Domesticated animals are different. If a cow bites, kicks, or pushes, the owner cannot be assessed damages. None of these is a normal habit or expected behavior of a cow. The owner can be expected to take precautions only against the animal's regular habits and common forms of damage. In such a case, the owner is not forewarned and is blameless, because it was unlikely that such damages would occur. The Mishnah does not expect the owner of the cow to go to extraordinary lengths to prevent every conceivable damage.

What about damages caused by people? The Mishnah text above from *Bava Kamma* tells us that, relating to damages, a person is always "forewarned." This means that, "whether inadvertently or deliberately, whether when he was awake or asleep," a person who caused harm to another would be required to pay damages. For example, while Reuven is sleeping, Shimon lies down next to him. In his sleep, Shimon pokes out Reuven's eye. Shimon is liable to Reuven damages for having caused harm, though inadvertently and while asleep, because "a man is always forewarned" concerning damages.

When an ox gores a man or a woman to death, the ox shall be stoned and its flesh shall not be eaten, but the owner of the ox is not to be punished. If, however, that ox has been in the habit of goring, and its owner, though warned, has failed to guard it, and it kills a man or a woman—the ox shall be stoned and its owner, too, shall be put to death. (Exodus 21:28–9)

As has been previously noted, Jewish law has an extensive literature on damages, found in the section of Talmud called Nezikin, *"Damages." The Midrash tells the story of how* Masekhet Nezikin *came to be divided: There was one student who was so overwhelmed by the prospect of having to study thirty chapters of* Nezikin *(for one tractate or subject was studied each year) that the tractate was divided into three, each containing ten chapters. The practical nature of* Nezikin*—injuries, damages, real estate, and inheritance—makes these three tractates popular among Talmud students and teachers.* ●

D'RASH

A woman, walking down the street, trips and falls on a crack in the sidewalk and breaks her leg. Who is the responsible party? Should her insurance company, which has charged her hefty premiums for its coverage, pay for her medical care? Or should the owner of the house and his insurance company be assessed damages, since it was on his sidewalk that this woman fell?

In contemporary America, such a case might end up in court, where the arguments will likely focus on who was *wrong,* not on obligation but on fault: Was the crack in the concrete new, or had the town issued a citation for a broken sidewalk in the past? Was the house owner aware of the problem with his sidewalk? Could the woman just as easily have walked around the crack? Was the woman wearing her glasses when she fell? Had she drunk any alcoholic beverages before her walk? It is conceivable that this case will fill the court docket for weeks or months, as the sides attempt to assign blame for the accident and, in turn, responsibility for the medical bills.

The Rabbis of the Mishnah would likely be able to determine responsibility and fault in such a case. Yet, their entire approach to damages is quite different from that of our society. The Mishnah speaks about the social contract with society and the implicit responsibility each of us has to those around us. By telling us that "a man is always forewarned," the Mishnah reminds us of this obligation. We do not need specific and advanced notice not to harm another.

In our day and age, this social contract is often obscured, and we may take this communal responsibility less than seriously. The Rabbis would likely say that if our sidewalk is cracked, it is our obligation to fix it, even if no one ever trips on it, regardless of citations, lawsuits, and petitions.

This is a Jewish response to the "Ignorance is bliss" theory that many people work under. People claim "I didn't know" as the excuse for a host of faults and transgressions.

"Young man, you have to pay for the candy. You just can't stick your hand in and grab it!" "There was no sign that I couldn't!"

"What were you thinking when you didn't pay your income taxes for twelve years?" "Your honor, I didn't know I had to pay taxes."

"Why were you riding your bicycle on the crowded sidewalk? Didn't you realize that you could hurt someone?" "No one said I couldn't."

It is unsettling when people act irresponsibly, causing injury or damage. Thus, we have the right to demand and expect responsible behavior from others, to assume that those around us do their utmost to protect our safety. Most important, though, that burden falls on *our* shoulders. We are the ones who must ultimately assure the welfare of society. It is our actions, within the implicit responsibility of one member of society to the others, that assures the well-being of those around us.

כֵּיוָן שֶׁנִּתְּנָה רְשׁוּת לַמַּשְׁחִית	Once permission has been given to the Destroyer,
אֵינוֹ מַבְחִין	it does not differentiate
בֵּין צַדִּיקִים לִרְשָׁעִים	between righteous and wicked.

TEXT

Bava Kamma 60a

> *Rabbi Shmuel bar Naḥmani said in the name of Rabbi Yoḥanan: "Punishment comes upon the world only when there are wicked people in the world, but it begins with the righteous, as it says: 'When a fire is started and spreads to thorns' [Exodus 22:5]. When does a fire start? When there are thorns around. It only begins with the righteous, as it says: 'so that stacked . . . grain is consumed' [ibid]. It does not say: 'so that stacked grain* will *be consumed' but rather 'is consumed'—meaning that it already had been consumed."*
>
> *Rav Yosef taught: "What is the meaning of the verse: 'None of you shall go outside the door of his house until morning' [Exodus 12:22]? Once permission has been given to the Destroyer, it does not differentiate between righteous and wicked. Moreover, it* begins *with the righteous, as it says: 'I will wipe out from you both the righteous and the wicked' [Ezekiel 21:8]."*

CONTEXT

Just prior to our section, the Mishnah and the Gemara discuss the legal issue of who is responsible for damage caused by a fire set by an individual. The basis of the law is the verse from Exodus 22 about a fire that spreads to thorns. The Rabbis then interpret that verse homiletically: The thorns represent the wicked, and the stacks of grain are the righteous people. The good are the first victims of the fire, which the Rabbis view as the Destroyer, the destructive angel or force sent by God to exact punishment on the world.

Rav Yosef brings the story of Pesaḥ to support the assertion that the righteous are usually the first to suffer when destruction is unleashed; an innocent Israelite who left home the night of the tenth plague in Egypt would have fallen victim to the Destroyer, even though it was only the Egyptians who were guilty. The Rabbis quote the verse in Ezekiel as a further proof, noting that it mentions the righteous *before* the wicked in a context of destruction; consequently, the innocent suffer before the guilty.

Moses then summoned all the elders of Israel and said to them, "Go pick out the lambs for your families, and slaughter the passover offering. Take a bunch of hyssop, dip it in the blood that is in the basin, and apply some of the blood that is in the basin to the lintel and to the two doorposts. None of you shall go outside the door of his house until morning. For when the Lord goes through to smite the Egyptians, He will see the blood on the lintel and the two doorposts, and the Lord will pass over the door and not let the Destroyer enter and smite your home." (Exodus 12:21–23) •

D'RASH

At the onset of the AIDS epidemic, many people believed that those afflicted with the disease were "getting exactly what they deserved." Drug-users who shared dirty needles or homosexuals who engaged in risky and promiscuous behavior were reaping what they themselves had sown. Many saw the virus as God's punishment for sinful behavior. As long as one did not commit the sins, one had nothing to fear from the punishment. But it soon became clear that this black-and-white view of AIDS was not accurate. A young boy, a hemophiliac, contracted the disease from a blood transfusion. The same thing happened to a superstar tennis player during a heart operation, and to the wife of a well-known television actor. All three were to die of AIDS. Faithful wives were infected by their husbands who, unbeknownst to them, were leading secretly promiscuous lives. "Once permission has been given to the Destroyer, it does not differentiate between righteous and wicked."

We would like to think that technology has brought us to the point where we can fight "clean" wars. The nation watched television during the Gulf War, enthralled by the "smart bombs" that could be directed to a specific target and even guided through a chosen window or door. We came to believe that only the target would be hit, leaving no "collateral damage." But our assumptions about the new warfare proved illusory. Some of the smart bombs malfunctioned; others were adversely affected by wind or weather conditions. And of course, there was always human error. The truth is that innocent civilians who happen to be in the wrong place at the wrong time continue to die in war. It is in the very nature of bombs and warfare itself to be indiscriminate. "Once permission has been granted to the Destroyer, it does not differentiate between righteous, and wicked."

Two people are sharing some juicy gossip. One says to the other: "Can you keep a secret? I've just got to tell you what I heard yesterday, but you've got to promise me that you won't breathe a word of this to anyone!" The next day, the person sworn to secrecy has "just got to tell" someone else, who will also be told to keep it confidential. Pretty soon, the secret is public knowledge and is not only being passed from one person to another but also being embellished. Whether it is true or false, whether it was supposed to be private or not is now irrelevant. Several people will be deeply embarrassed; reputations may even be ruined. Someone may be fired; another person's marriage may be destroyed. Once the genie is let out of the bottle, it cannot be put back in. That is the nature of gossip. "Once permission has been given to the Destroyer, it does not differentiate between righteous and wicked."

Knowing that this is true, we need to be extremely careful that we ourselves are not the ones who give "permission" to the various "destroyers" of life and human dignity.

קֵרֵחַ מִכָּאן וּמִכָּאן

Bald from both sides.

TEXT

Bava Kamma 60b

> *Rav Ammi and Rav Assi were sitting in front of Rabbi Yitzḥak Nappaḥa. One said: "Tell us a law!" The other said: "Tell us a legend!" He started to say a legend but was not allowed to. He started to tell a law but was not allowed to. He said to them: "I will tell you a parable. To what can it be compared? To a man with two wives, one young, one old. The young one pulls out his white hairs, while the old one pulls out his black hairs, and thus he becomes bald from both sides!"*
>
> *He said to them: "If so, I will tell you one thing that is good for both of you: 'When a fire is started and spreads to thorns' [Exodus 22:5]. 'Is started'—by itself—'[so that stacked, standing, or growing grain is consumed,] he who started the fire must make restitution.' The Holy One, blessed be He, said: 'I must make restitution for the fire I started. I started a fire in Zion, as it says: "He kindled a fire in Zion which consumed its foundations" [Lamentations 4:11], and I will one day rebuild it by fire, as it says: "And I Myself . . . will be a wall of fire all around it, and I will be a glory inside it" [Zechariah 2:9].' A law: The verse begins with property damage and ends with personal damage, to show that fire is his responsibility."*

The Rabbis of the Talmud felt free to cite and quote not only God's words but also God's thoughts and intentions. There are times, though, when the Rabbis went even further, taking a verse out of context or quoting only the part of the verse that suited their own purposes. The verse from Zechariah is a classic example. It would be awkward, redundant, and contradictory to have God quote the entire *verse, saying:*

> *And I Myself—declares the Lord—will be a wall of fire all around it, and I will be a glory inside it.*

Therefore, the verse is quoted in the Gemara without the two Hebrew words n'um Adonai, *"declares the Lord." It is*

CONTEXT

In this Gemara, Rav Ammi and Rav Assi, two sages often quoted together, are studying with Rabbi Yitzḥak Nappaḥa. Each student wants his mentor to teach the material that he enjoys most: One asks for legend/midrash, the other for law/halakhah. Rabbi Yitzḥak is caught in a bind. When he starts to teach midrash, one student interrupts and asks his teacher for law. But when Rabbi Yitzḥak switches to law, the other student prevents him from continuing, for he prefers legend.

Being a master teacher, Rabbi Yitzḥak resorts to the use of a parable to explain his predicament: A man with two wives, one young and one old, would have one of them wanting him to look more youthful and the other desiring a more mature husband. (It seems that Rabbi Yitzḥak did not really consider the possibility that a young wife might want an older man, or that an older woman might prefer a more youthful husband.) Each wife pulls out only *some* of his hair, but nonetheless, the result is that the man is left "bald from both sides." Thus, the expression is roughly equivalent to our English "no-win situation" or the more contemporary "Catch-22."

Rabbi Yitzḥak is such an expert teacher that he finds one biblical verse that serves the purpose of both a midrash/legend and a halakhah/law, thus satisfying both students. The midrash is that if the person who started the fire must make restitution, then even God will do so. God had caused Jerusalem to be destroyed by fire (as the verse from *Eikha,* or Lamentations, attests), and God will accept the responsibility and cause Jerusalem to be rebuilt by fire (the verse from Zechariah). The law that Rabbi Yitzḥak teaches is that both property damage and physical damage are referred to in the verse from Exodus. Property damage is from the words "When a fire is started and spreads to thorns," while personal damage is implied in "he who started the fire," that is, someone started it (as opposed to the beginning of the verse, where it appears as if the fire started on its own). Even though the fire may appear to have started by itself, there is still a responsible party who must pay.

In the Hebrew, what is translated as "fire is his responsibility" is literally "fire is his arrow," meaning that it is something that the man himself did. Just as shooting an arrow can start an entire process that may have been unintended and unexpected, but is nonetheless the responsibility of the marksman, so too the one who started a fire which spread to another's field is responsible.

likely that the Rabbis saw no problem with this truncated reading of the verse, taking the words and putting them back in God's mouth in a totally different context. In order to accomplish this, the Rabbis had to leave out two words to make God sound sensible.

D'RASH

A middle-age woman decides to spend much of her day with her mother. She feels guilty for having ignored Mom of late and for not having spent more time with her. As she has been focusing more of her attention on her children and her career, her own mother has become less a part of her everyday life. The woman finally decides to right the wrong by spending a day with her mother, but the day turns out to be most difficult. It's been a while since the two spent so much time with each other, and even though there is a great deal of love, there is also tension. The relationship has changed, and their day together is less rewarding than expected.

As this woman returns home, she finds her children needy and clingy and her husband resentful and jealous that Grandma received so much attention today. "When is the last time *we* spent an entire day together?" he complains, noting that the babysitter arrived late and one of the children got sick while his wife was away. Before they can talk about the family situation, the phone rings. It's the woman's boss at work, calling with an office crisis that only she can handle. With children screaming and husband pouting, she works furiously to solve the emergency at hand, knowing full well that she will be faced with a family crisis when she hangs up.

The feeling of being "bald from both sides" is typical of people in the "sandwich generation," trying to cope with both parents and children, juggling career and family, obligations to and love for parents and responsibility to and love for children. Such people are like the husband in Rabbi Yitzḥak's story, beleaguered from two sides by different generations and differing needs. It is often difficult—if not downright impossible—to please everyone and not to end the day feeling guilty for having hurt *both* sides.

How can we learn to cope with such a situation? First, Rabbi Yitzḥak Nappaḥa admits that some situations are "no-win." His students will never be fully satisfied if he teaches *only* legend or *only* law. In such a predicament, this admission is an important first step.

Rabbi Yitzḥak, in his genius, finds a verse that satisfies both sides, if not perfectly, then at least adequately. Perhaps those of us in the sandwich generation can emulate his genius. Next time, the woman in the incident above might bring the whole family together for part of the day, so that everyone receives a bit of Grandma's attention and no one at home feels resentful and cheated of Mom's love.

It is clear, however, that not every conflict can be solved so cleverly. What if Rabbi Yitzḥak Nappaḥa had not been so creative? What if he could not think of that one verse? At one point or another in life, each of us will find ourselves in a Catch-22. If we are blessed with a flash of genius, we may create an escape. If not, we have to admit to one side or another (and to ourselves as well) that we cannot fully satisfy everyone. One day, we may have to say: "Kids, today Grandma needs me, and even though I love you and I want to spend time with you, I can't do it right now." At another time, we might want to say, "Mom, I wish that I could go with you tomorrow, but I really have to spend the day with the children. They see precious little of me as is, and I promised them long ago that we would share tomorrow."

Sometimes, the situation may truly be no-win. The best we can hope for is to cut our loses. At such times, it may be helpful to remind each party of the story told by Rabbi Yitzḥak: Neither wife wanted her husband to be bald. Each woman pulled out only *part* of the husband's hair, with the result that he became totally bald. Acknowledging a no-win situation may help us move on and put this crisis in perspective.

כַּד הֲוֵינַן זוּטְרֵי לְגַבְרֵי
הַשְׁתָּא דְקַשִׁישְׁנָא לְדַרְדְּקֵי

When we were young,
[we were treated] like grown-ups;
now that we are elderly,
[we are treated] like children.

TEXT

Bava Kamma 92b–93a

Rava said to Rabbah bar Mari: "What is the source of what they say: 'If you lift up the burden, I will lift it, and if not, I won't lift it'?" He said to him: "As it is written: 'But Barak said to her, "If you will go with me, I will go; if not, I will not go"' [Judges 4:8]."

Rava said to Rabbah bar Mari: "What is the source of what they say: 'When we were young, [we were treated] like grown-ups; now that we are elderly, [we are treated] like children.'?" He said to him: "First it is written: 'The Lord went before them in a pillar of cloud by day, to guide them along the way, and in a pillar of fire by night, to give them light' [Exodus 13:21], but afterwards it is written: 'I am sending an angel before you to guard you on the way.'[Exod, 23:20]."

Deborah, wife of Lappidoth, was a prophetess; she led Israel at that time. . . . She summoned Barak son of Abinoam, of Kedesh in Naphtali, and said to him, "The Lord, the God of Israel, has commanded: Go, march up to Mount Tabor, and take with you ten thousand men of Naphtali and Zebulun. And I will draw Sisera, Jabin's army commander, with his chariots and his troops, toward you up to the Wadi Kishon; and I will deliver him into your hands." But Barak said to her, "If you will go with me, I will go; if not, I will not go." "Very well, I will go with you," she answered. "However, there will be no glory for you in the course you are taking, for then the Lord will deliver Sisera into the hands of a woman." (Judges 4:4, 6–9) •

CONTEXT

These two short sections of Gemara are from a longer series of queries from Rava to Rabbah bar Mari on the origin of various aphorisms. In each case, Rava asks for a biblical verse for the derivation of a popular saying. Every time, Rabbah provides Rava with a scriptural illustration of the maxim.

In the first inquiry above, Rava asks for the biblical basis of the adage "If you lift up the burden, I will lift it, and if not, I won't lift it." Apparently, this was a popular maxim and was taken to refer not only to physical burdens but also to military endeavors and business ventures as well. Rabbah cites a verse from Judges in which the Israelite general Barak tries to convince Deborah to fight Sisera and the enemy forces. If two are willing to carry the burden—in this case, the battle against the enemy—it can be done. If only one is willing to bear the burden, it is impossibly heavy.

In the second question, Rava asks for the origin of the phrase "When we were young, [we were treated] like grown-ups; now that we are elderly, [we are treated] like children." Rabbah explains its origin in two verses that the Torah uses to describe God's protection of the Israelites as they left

Egypt. When they were a young people and needed God's close attention and protection, God (apparently complimenting them) treated them as if they were older and more mature, sending only a pillar of cloud by day and pillar of fire by night. However, later in the story, when they presumably needed less help and guidance, a more protective angel was nonetheless sent to guard them on the way.

D'RASH

There is an apocryphal tale of a woman who, thinking that she had become pregnant the night before, rushed to make an early morning phone call—*not* to her obstetrician or to a family member but to the local nursery school to sign up her "child" for kindergarten. She was afraid that her "baby" would be closed out of class five years hence.

Whether this story is factually true or not, it does reflect a reality about children in our contemporary world: They are rushed through life. In his book *The Hurried Child,* psychologist David Elkind outlines examples of youngsters pushed to grow up too fast and forced to live adult lives before they are physically or psychologically ready. We, too, can think of dozens of examples of children who are hurried through life and are not allowed, slowly and patiently, to mature:

> The child who does not excel in kindergarten and who, at age five, is labeled a problem child for the rest of life. If the label sticks, the youngster may never have the opportunity to overcome these obstacles.
>
> The Little League team members whose coach forces a win-or-lose mentality on them, turning the game from fun into a battlefield. They may grow up *playing* team sports but not *enjoying* them.
>
> The child of divorce who is thrust into adult roles—cooking, caring for infants—and adult responsibilities at an early age. Unfortunately, the need for another set of hands in the home may make the extra pressure on this youngster unavoidable.

Elkind cites the example of a seven-year-old who left school because of a nervous breakdown, who was a weak student with no friends and a poor athlete with odd mannerisms. At a young age, he was labeled a problem child. It is conceivable that such a youngster would lose out on the opportunity to overcome adversity and become a worthwhile member of society. Fortunately, in this case, the young man surmounted all of these negative stereotypes and matured into the great physicist Albert Einstein.

Often, the negative effects on youngsters come about as by-products of positive intentions. We want our children to get ahead, and consequently we buy them (and ourselves) books, videos, and even computer programs that help get an "edge" on life—"Toilet Training in One Day!" or "Calculus for Preschoolers."

There *are* times when our youngsters are ready to handle more, when they will demand to be challenged. Yet, we often fall into the trap of hurrying our children (and our grandchildren) beyond what they can handle. We do this out of both love and fear. We love them and want the best for them. We are afraid that they will fall behind in an ever-changing world. We want them to succeed in life, and rather than choosing time-honored values and slowly reinforcing methods of teaching, we opt for quick fixes and fads.

Similarly, there are times when we infantilize our elderly, treating them like children. We assume that someone who is getting hard of hearing also cannot think so well. We imagine that those who were born many years ago cannot cope with change, when the reality is that they have had to manage change repeatedly in their lives. We may assume, incorrectly, that those who are retired and no longer have a job likewise no longer have a purpose in life. Each of these instances treats the elderly like children.

While some believe that youth is wasted on the young, we know that youth is *for* the young, just as the older years are for the elderly. Treating our youngsters like children and our seniors like elders is exactly what we *are* supposed to do. In the case of our children, it allows them the pleasure, the opportunity, and the privilege of growing up, a process that truly cannot be hurried. In the case of our elders, it confers upon them the dignity and honor they deserve.

כְּלִי שֶׁנִּשְׁתַּמֵּשׁ בּוֹ קֹדֶשׁ יִשְׁתַּמֵּשׁ בּוֹ חֹל

Should a vessel that was used for holy be used for everyday?

TEXT

Bava Metzia 84b

As he was about to die, he [Rabbi Elazar son of Rabbi Shimon] said to his wife: "I know that the Rabbis are angry with me and will not treat me well. Lay me out in the loft and do not be afraid of me." Rabbi Shmuel bar Naḥmani said: "Rabbi Yonatan's mother told me that the wife of Rabbi Elazar son of Rabbi Shimon told her: 'I kept him in the loft no less than eighteen years and no more than twenty-four years. When I went up there, I would check his hair, and when hair fell out, blood would flow. One day, I saw a worm come out of his ear, and I became weak. He came to me in the dream and said to me: "This is nothing! One day I heard a scholar insulted and I did not protest it as I should have." When two came for judgment, they stood at the entrance, each one making his case, and a voice came forth from the loft, saying: "So-and-so, you are guilty! So-and-so, you are innocent!"'" One day, she was arguing with a neighbor who said to her: "May you be like your husband, unworthy of burial!" The Rabbis said: "This is not the right way." Some say that Rabbi Shimon ben Yoḥai appeared to them in a dream, telling them: "There is a single pigeon of a pair among you, and you won't let him come to me?" The Rabbis went to take care of him, but the people of Akhbariya would not let them, for all the years that Rabbi Elazar son of Rabbi Shimon rested there, no wild animal came to them. One Yom Kippur eve, when they were busy, the Rabbis sent word to the residents of Biri to carry out his bier. They carried him to the burial cave of his father, but they found a snake encircling it. They said: "Snake! Snake! Open your mouth and let a son enter with his father." It opened for them. Rabbi sent to speak [of marriage] to his [Rabbi Elazar's] wife. She sent back to him: "Should a vessel that was used for holy be used for everyday?"

CONTEXT

This story tells of the death of Rabbi Elazar ben Shimon, a scholar who was seen by many as a traitor for the help he gave the conquering Roman army during its occupation of Israel. Rabbi Elazar may have been fearful of his colleagues' reaction to his death, afraid that they would not treat him respectfully. He therefore asked his wife that, upon his death,

The Talmud is not ashamed to present unpopular and even derogatory views of the

Rabbis. Some scholars suggest that the purpose of such stories is not to show off the fine qualities of one rabbi as opposed to those of another, or to advocate a specific position. Most likely, these stories attempt to teach the reader a lesson about the world around them.

This is probably the case in our Gemara from Bava Metzia, *for even though Rabbi Elazar is portrayed as a righteous man by his widow, we know that there are places in the Talmud where he was seen as a traitor. Rabbi Elazar ben Shimon lived in the second-century* C.E. *and was the son and student of the famous Rabbi Shimon bar Yoḥai. Together, we are told, they hid in a cave for thirteen years to escape punishment from the Romans for having taught Torah. Yet, while the father, Shimon, continued to defy Rome, the son, Elazar, later worked for the Roman administration, becoming an official responsible for reporting on thieves. This put him in a position of conflict with many of the Rabbis of the time, leading his teacher Yehoshua ben Korḥah to condemn him: "Vinegar son of wine (i.e., a spoiled son of a vintage master)! How long will you continue to hand over the people of our God to be killed?" Despite his association with the Romans, Rabbi Elazar is pictured as a saint and martyr in the narrative which follows our text.* •

his body not be buried but left in a loft or upper chamber of their house. This she did. Not only did she keep the body there, but it kept its original, natural state, even producing blood (after all the years) when hair fell out.

Once, she felt guilty for not having buried her husband properly, but he reassured her that the worm coming forth from his ear was punishment for not having stood up for a fellow rabbi when he was being insulted. Even more amazing than the lack of decomposition of the body is the fact (according to the story) that Rabbi Elazar issued judicial rulings even after his death. People would present their cases at his doorway, and a voice would be heard announcing the verdict.

However, when a neighbor mocked the wife, she knew it was time to have her husband buried. One tradition says that the Rabbis wanted to bury Rabbi Elazar. Another tradition holds that his father, Rabbi Shimon, appeared to them in a dream. His words—"There is a single pigeon of a pair among you, and you won't let him come to me?"—mean "My son and I are a pair. I am already in the World-to-Come, and you will not allow my son to join me here?" The people of Akhbariya feared that his burial would mean the end of the protection that they had been given while Rabbi Elazar's body remained in his loft. Still, the Rabbis sought to bury Elazar. The next obstacle to overcome was a snake, blocking the entrance to the burial cave.

Some time after the burial, Rabbi Yehudah ha-Nasi ("Rabbi") sent emissaries to Rabbi Elazar's widow ("his wife"). The message they brought was a proposal for marriage: Now that your deceased husband has been buried, you can marry me. She rebuffed Rabbi, and her response "Should a vessel that was used for holy be used for everyday?" has become a classic. The unnamed wife means: Are you worthy to take the place of such a holy man? While Rabbi Yehudah ha-Nasi was one of the greats of his day (and of any day in Jewish life, seen both from his title and his status), the widow of Rabbi Elazar considered Rabbi Yehudah as ordinary compared to her beloved, holy husband.

D'RASH

On a practical level, "Should a vessel that was used for holy be used for everyday?" has been interpreted to refer to any object that is used for sacred purposes. Our Jewish tradition considers it improper to use this sacred object afterwards for secular or mundane purposes. Thus, the bag used to hold a tallit or a pair of tefillin in it, while only cloth and of no true ritual value (as opposed to the tallit and tefillin themselves, which do have religious significance) would nonetheless not be used afterwards for a secular purpose. Once the object attains a degree of sanctity, by holding tallit or tefillin, it retains that holiness.

Of course, we can apply the rule that a vessel used for holy should not be used for everyday on a metaphoric level as well. We accord the president of the United States a certain degree of honor and deference even after having left office. For example, a former chief executive of the country is still referred to as "Mr. President," as a sign of respect. Similarly, on an organizational level, a president or committee chairperson is given a degree of honor that should follow them throughout life. We may at times forget this, causing hard feelings, since one grows accustomed to the honor and glory that goes with a public office. A person who retires should receive the same honor that was given during tenure, if not more. A retired professor or rabbi is given the title "emeritus" as a symbol of this honor.

Even in an area as commonplace as baseball, we do not entirely "throw out" the old players just because they no longer throw out batters. Most teams have an annual "Old Timers Day," where those who *used* to be great are accorded the status and homage that once was theirs. Many hold on to the tassel that once adorned their graduation mortarboard not only as a reminder but also as a symbol: This tassel was used for a special day and is a reminder of that time. It should not be discarded or used for a routine purpose but should be saved, retaining some of its special status.

We live in a very informal world. The sacred is indeed rare. Yet those objects—and especially those people—who achieve a degree of honor and sanctity should not lose their status, because a vessel that was used for holy should not be used for everyday.

גָּדוֹל הַמְעַשֶּׂה
יוֹתֵר מִן הָעוֹשֶׂה

One who causes others to do is greater than one who does.

TEXT

Bava Batra 9a

Rabbi Elazar said: "One who causes others to do is greater than one who does, as it says: 'For the work of righteousness shall be peace, and the effect of righteousness, calm and confidence forever' [Isaiah 32:17]. If he is deserving, 'It is to share your bread with the hungry' [Isaiah 58:7], if he is not deserving, 'and to take the wretched poor into your home' [ibid.]." *Rava said to the people of Maḥoza: "I beg of you: Act towards one another so that you will have good relations with the government." Rabbi Elazar also said: "When the Temple stood, a man weighed out his* shekel *and atoned. Now that the Temple no longer stands, if they do acts of charity, good; but if not, the nations of the world come and take them forcibly. Even so, it is seen as charity, as it says: 'Prosperity as your officials' [Isaiah 60:17]."*

For the work of righteousness shall be peace, and the effect of righteousness, calm and confidence forever.
Then my people shall dwell in peaceful homes,
In secure dwellings,
In untroubled places of rest.
(Isaiah 32:17–18). •

Is such the fast I desire,
A day for men to starve their bodies?
Is it bowing the head like a bulrush
And lying in sackcloth and ashes?
Do you call that a fast,
A day when the Lord is favorable?
No, this is the fast I desire:
To unlock fetters of wickedness,
And untie the cords of the yoke
To let the oppressed go free;
To break off every yoke.
It is to share your bread with the hungry,
And to take the wretched poor into your home;
When you see the naked, to clothe him,
And not to ignore your own kin. (Isaiah 58:5–7) •

Whereas you have been forsaken,
Rejected, with none passing through,
I will make you a pride everlasting,

CONTEXT

Rabbi Elazar's idea is fairly straightforward: There are people who themselves do good, and there are people who *cause others* to do good. The former are praiseworthy, but the latter are much more exemplary. However, much of the proof for Rabbi Elazar's axiom is through a Midrash based on Hebrew words in the biblical text. Rabbi Elazar's axiom speaks of "the one who causes others to do." This long English phrase is actually only one word in Hebrew, *ha-measeh*, an intensive verb. One who "causes others to do" is greater than one who simple does. Rabbi Elazar connects his idea with the verse from Isaiah 32 using a word play. In Isaiah, "the work of righteousness" is, in Hebrew, *ma'aseh tzedakah*. Rabbi Elazar associates the two words with the same Hebrew root, *measeh*, meaning "the doer" and *ma'aseh*, meaning "the work," since they have the same Hebrew letters, though with different vowels.

The verse from Isaiah is then introduced to show that if you are fortunate enough to have money and if you do good to others, then "it is to share your bread with the hungry." If you do not help others voluntarily and out of conviction, then you will have to "take the wretched poor into your home." The "wretched poor" may refer either to the needy themselves or to the government's tax collectors who will come and take your money from you.

Rava reinforces this idea by asking the residents of Maḥoza, a town on the Tigris River in Babylonia, to help themselves out, for if they do not, the government will step in and will take care of their needy for them. Rabbi Elazar is quoted again to reiterate the point. When the Temple stood, people could give directly to the *kohanim*. This was *measeh*, an intensive and thoughtful act of giving. Rabbi Elazar offers two forms of consolation. First, to those who cannot give directly to the Temple, he teaches that their voluntary contributions to the poor are still considered positive acts of charity. And he offers comfort even to those whom the government forces to give and help others: Their helping is still considered *tzedakah*, translated as both charity and prosperity, as Isaiah says: "*Tzedakah*/Prosperity as your officials." Even the government's forcibly taking your money and distributing it to the poor is considered an act of *tzedakah*.

A joy for age after age.
You shall suck the milk of the nations,
Suckle at royal breasts.
And you shall know
That I the Lord am your Savior,
I, the Mighty One of Jacob, am your Redeemer.
Instead of copper I will bring gold,
Instead of iron I will bring silver;
Instead of wood, copper;
And instead of stone, iron.
And I will appoint Well-being as your government,
Prosperity as your officials.
(Isaiah 60:15–17) •

D'RASH

We usually think of great philanthropists as the most generous people in the world. A wealthy person who endows an entire university, a medical school, or a library is to be praised for generosity—and there is no argument with this. Yet, Rabbi Elazar is proposing that one who causes others to do is even greater than one who does. This means that the fundraiser who secured the grant deserves more credit than the actual donor. The financial advisor who counseled that the rich, childless widow leave her assets to the local library is greater, in certain respects, than the benefactor. The savvy clergyperson who suggested that the wealthy congregant would be best remembered through a chair at the seminary can find comfort in the words of Rabbi Elazar. Each of these advisors is even greater than the contributor, for each caused others to act.

We can take this one step further, for Rabbi Elazar's words refer not only to financial giving and acting. We may not notice the biology teacher who encouraged that special student, pushing him to work hard and giving him the confidence to go on in science. We should, however, notice and praise that teacher for ultimately causing the student to make a great medical discovery. The English professor who spent time with a struggling author, helping her years later to have the ability to write a famous novel, should get some of the fame associated with the novel. The high school coach whose protégé becomes a well-known sports star may be mentioned rarely in the athlete's biography, but deserves a large share of the accolades.

Many a time, we are disheartened that the rich and famous get all the credit, that the tedious, not so glorious work of the common folk goes unnoticed. This type of effort is cited less often in the newspapers and in Nobel Prizes. Nonetheless, Rabbi Elazar's words, exaggerated as they might be, remind us that the successes of great people would be impossible without the behind-the-scenes work of others. Rabbi Elazar's teaching should give encouragement to those of us who don't win prizes or garner headlines but who nonetheless cause others to do great things.

קִנְאַת סוֹפְרִים תַּרְבֶּה חָכְמָה

Jealousy among teachers will increase wisdom.

TEXT

Bava Batra 20b, 21a

Mishnah (2:2) *[If one opens] a shop in the courtyard: One may object and say to him: "I cannot sleep because of the noise of those coming and going." But he can make utensils and sell them in the marketplace, and one cannot object and say: "I cannot sleep because of the noise of the hammer, the millstone or the children."*

Gemara: *Come and hear: If two live in a courtyard and one wants to become a physician, an artisan, a weaver or a teacher of children, the others can prevent him. But this deals with non-Jewish children! Come and hear: He who has a place for rent in the courtyard should not rent it to a physician, an artisan, a weaver, a Jewish teacher or a non-Jewish teacher. This is the case we are dealing with: A town teacher. Rava said: "Given the ruling of Yehoshua ben Gamla, we do not send students from town to town, but we do send them from synagogue to synagogue. If there is a river in between, we do not send them; if there is a bridge, we send them, but not if it is only a board." Rava also said: "The number of schoolchildren for one teacher is twenty-five. If there are fifty, we appoint two. If there are forty, we appoint an assistant, at the expense of the town." Rava also said: "If there is a teacher who gets them to study and one who gets them to study better, we do not replace him lest he get discouraged." Rav Dimi from Nehardea said: "He will get them to study even more, for jealousy among teachers will increase wisdom."*

Is it possible that two seemingly contradictory sources are both correct and accurate teachings? For example, in this Gemara, one source says that others cannot prevent a person from teaching in their courtyard, while a second source holds that one should not rent to a teacher! How can this be? In reality, these may be independent oral teachings that were handed down via different traditions. They may, in fact, contradict each other. However, the talmudic mind would prefer to accept both teachings as genuine. This is where the expression "This is the case we are dealing with" becomes a useful tool. By limiting the situation the contradiction is eliminated. We only thought *that these texts were contradictory, that one text says "One cannot object to a teacher in the courtyard" while another says the opposite: "Do not rent a room facing the courtyard to a teacher."*

CONTEXT

This chapter of *Bava Batra* deals with laws of the free marketplace. Talmudic law controls territorial rights based on established claims: One may not simply open a new store, set up a craft shop, or operate any other kind of business just anywhere because a new craftsperson may put a veteran out of business. In addition, there are rules and regulations intended to protect the community. A tannery smells; a new dovecote may steal the doves from adjoining nests.

Thus, our Mishnah teaches that one who sets up a shop in a common courtyard can be stopped because the comings and goings of customers will disturb the neighbors. The Gemara reiterates this concept with examples from an out-

In reality, there is no such contradiction at all, since the specific case we are dealing with, as the later Rabbis interpret it, is only that of a town *teacher. An ordinary teacher would have little traffic in and out, while the master teacher of the area would have many more students each day. Therefore, we may refuse renting to such an individual.* •

side source, and it is the example of the "town teacher" who would apparently have many students coming and going that becomes the focus of the discussion.

Rava credits Yehoshua ben Gamla with requiring each town to appoint a local professional teacher at the town's expense. Until this time, teaching children had been seen as the father's responsibility. What, then, constitutes a "school district"? How far do we send a child to study? And how many students can one teacher handle? Rava passes down a tradition that the acceptable ratio is twenty-five students per teacher.

This leads Rava to comment on teachers' qualifications. What if a better teacher can be found? Should we replace the first teacher who does not motivate the students as well? There are two opinions. Rava holds that replacing this teacher might demoralize him. This group of students might be helped, but the teaching profession—and, more important, the study of Torah—will be harmed in the process. Rav Dimi, however, holds to the contrary. He feels that competition is good. The jealousy that a teacher feels towards a colleague who teaches better will not be demoralizing but will serve as motivation to excel.

D'RASH

What ultimately motivates people to change? Rava and Rav Dimi have two different conceptions. To Rava, the catalyst for change is internal: People change because they want to improve, and external comparisons only serve to heighten their sense of inadequacy. We do best, in Rava's eyes, when we are judged against our personal standard rather than against external paradigms.

Rav Dimi conceives of motivation as something quite different, involving a kind of "creative tension." When we see how someone else is doing, we are pushed to improve ourselves, trying to reach that ideal and standard that the other has presented.

Each approach has its positives, as seen in the tenure system for university faculty. Some say that tenure gives faculty the sense of security they need to excel in their academic work. A professor with tenure will not have to worry about the "publish or perish" of university life, a system that heightens nervousness more than it heightens scholarship. Others hold that faculty should never be beyond review, that constant pressure is a positive force, generating creativity and learning. Without this tension, professors would tend to be laid-back and complacent.

We see a corollary of Rav Dimi's approach in the push for legislative term limits. Proponents of this position believe that only by holding legislators constantly accountable can we see any positive results. Incumbents who seem to have a permanent appointment eventually slouch off and do not do their jobs well. Opponents say that it takes years to learn the legislative system. Veteran representatives not only know the ropes but also can call in favors and in other ways use their seniority to the benefit of their constituents.

Just as the Talmud brings in different approaches to the topic, we too can often benefit from both viewpoints. Some people who work with us or for us will be motivated by competition. The friction of working against others causes them to work harder. Others do better in a cooperative setting. Often, these people find rivalry between colleagues detrimental and even threatening. At times, *we ourselves* will be motivated by an internal urge to excel, while at other times, it will be competition with a friend or colleague: "*She's* not going to outperform me!"

There is no absolute right or wrong for personal motivation with every person or in every situation. We need to know what motivates others—and ourselves—so that a suitable atmosphere can be set and appropriate methods utilized.

אֵין גּוֹזְרִין גְּזֵרָה עַל הַצִּבּוּר
אֶלָּא אִם כֵּן רֹב הַצִּבּוּר
יְכוֹלִין לַעֲמֹד בָּהּ

A decree should not be imposed
upon the community
unless the majority
of the community can follow it.

TEXT

Bava Batra 60b

Our Rabbis taught: When the second Temple was destroyed, the number of ascetics in Israel who would not eat meat or drink wine increased. Rabbi Yehoshua met with them. He said to them: "My children, why are you not eating meat or drinking wine?" They said to him: "Shall we eat meat that used to be offered on the altar that is no longer functioning? Shall we drink wine that used to be poured on the altar that is no longer in use?"

He said to them: "If that is so, we should not eat bread, because the Meal Offerings have ceased. What about fruit? We should not eat fruit, because the First Fruit offerings have ceased. . . . We should not drink water because the Water Libations have ceased." They were silent. He said to them: "My children, come and I will speak to you. Not to mourn at all is impossible, because the decree has already been set down. But to mourn too much is impossible, for a decree should not be imposed upon the community unless the majority of the community can follow it, as it is written: 'You are suffering under a curse, yet you go on defrauding Me—the whole nation of you' [Malachi 3:9]. Rather, this is what the Sages said: 'When a person plasters his home, he leaves a small section undone.' (How much? Rav Yosef said: 'A square cubit.' Rav Ḥisda said: 'It should be by the door.') When a person prepares a meal, let him leave something out. (What? Rav Papa said: 'A dish of hors d'oeuvres.') When a woman is putting on her jewelry, she should leave something off. (What? Rav said: 'She should not remove the hair from her temples.')"

The Talmud goes on to praise those who mourn (in an appropriate way) for the destruction of the Temple: All those who grieve over Jerusalem will merit to see her rejoicing, as it says: "Rejoice with Jerusalem and be glad for her, all you who love her! Join in her jubilation, all you who mourned over her . . ." (Isaiah 66:10). The Rabbis

CONTEXT

The first Temple built by Solomon was destroyed by the Babylonians in the year 586 B.C.E. The second Temple was built about a century after that and was destroyed by the Romans in the year 70 C.E. The Temple was not only the center of Jewish religious life, it was the symbol of Jewish nationhood and independence. Its destruction led to severe mourning by Jews. Some individuals became ascetics, believing that life could not go on as it had before the tragedies. These Jews, called *perushim,* or "those who set themselves apart," began refraining from pleasurable activities that would have reminded them of the Temple. Eating meat brought to their minds the animal sacrifices where a portion of the offering was given to the worshipper to eat in the city of Jerusalem. Drinking wine caused them to recall the *nisukh ha-yayin,* the libation of wine accompanying some sacrifices that was poured out at the base of the altar.

read the beginning and the end of the verse not as two separate clauses, but rather as one interdependent unit: Only those who have mourned will one day rejoice. •

Rabbi Yehoshua challenged these restrictive practices by taking the arguments of the *perushim* to their logical conclusion: Bread should also not be eaten, because bread and meal offerings were brought in the Temple. Fruits should not be eaten, because they were offered to the *kohanim* during the harvest season. Even water should be avoided, because the pouring out of water was central to the Temple ritual during the festival of Sukkot.

Rabbi Yehoshua argued that the restrictions of the *perushim* were more than the people could bear. He derived the principle "A decree should not be imposed upon the community unless the majority of the community can follow it" from his reading of the verse in Malachi: The entire nation has made a vow to bring the *ma'aser*—a tenth of the harvest—to God. Failure to do so would have resulted in a self-imposed curse falling upon the people. According to Rabbi Yehoshua, such a vow with its harsh accompanying curse was valid only because "the whole nation" had accepted it upon themselves. Instead of the harsh restrictions of the *perushim,* the Talmud suggests three other alternative expressions of mourning that the majority of the people would have been able to follow.

D'RASH

The story of Rabbi Yehoshua and the *perushim* shows us a critical moment in the development of Judaism and also teaches us an important lesson about religion in general. Jews in the first century were searching for a way to respond to the trauma of the destruction of the Temple. One group of people began taking upon themselves a number of restrictions that were seen by many to be rather severe. No doubt those who could not follow this path felt very guilty, wondering about their own weaknesses or their apparent lack of devotion to their God.

Rabbi Yehoshua was troubled by the particular response of these *perushim* and the effect it was having on the Jews.

Here was a unique and ironic situation: A religious leader going to his followers and telling them, in essence, "You're being *too religious!*" It's usually the opposite message that we expect to hear from a rabbi, priest, minister, or imam; but in rebuking the *perushim,* Rabbi Yehoshua teaches them, *and us,* a great deal about the meaning and purpose of religion. We can almost imagine him using words like these:

"Your heart is in the right place, but you haven't brought your *head* into the equation in dealing with this problem. That is a fatal flaw that can turn religion from a positive force into a negative one. God gave us hearts *and* minds, and expects that we use our emotions *and* our intelligence in the choices and decisions that we make.

"First of all, your ideas are not thought through: Why have you taken on these particular restrictions and not others? What logic underlies your choices? There is a lack of consistency that makes your decisions seem arbitrary. Other people will have a hard time being convinced that yours is the right way.

"Second, you haven't taken into consideration anyone else! *You* may be able to follow this path, but most people will not. Religion will become a burden and a hardship instead of a boon and a comfort. And just at the time we need unity to bring us together, you will be creating a wedge that will drive us further apart and split us into factions. You have forgotten that as much as a religion is about relating to *God,* it is also about relating to *other people!*"

In every generation, religious zealots arise in response to the crisis of that time and place. Most people are unable to follow their example of fervent piety. Many people are afraid to challenge them because of their intense devotion to what they believe in. Though in the minority, these zealots are able to establish for everyone else what is forbidden and what is permitted. More often than not, their brand of religion emphasizes the former over the latter. Rabbi Yehoshua brings us a very different idea of what religion is all about. He also serves as a model of a courageous religious leader, willing to stand up to extremists on behalf of the tradition and the community.

אוֹי לִי אִם אֹמַר
אוֹי לִי אִם לֹא אֹמַר

Woe to me if I speak, woe to me if I don't speak.

TEXT

Bava Batra 89b

Our Rabbis taught: "The levelling rod may not be made thick on one side and thin on the other side. One may not level with one quick movement, for leveling with one quick movement is bad for the seller and good for the buyer. Nor may one level very slowly, for this is bad for the buyer and good for the seller." Concerning all of these, Rabban Yoḥanan ben Zakkai said: "Woe to me if I speak, woe to me if I don't speak. If I speak, perhaps deceivers will learn; if I don't speak, perhaps the deceivers will say: 'The scholars are not experts in what we do!'" The question was raised: "Did he speak or not?" Rav Shumel bar Rav Yitzḥak said: "He did speak, and he based himself on this verse: 'For the paths of the Lord are smooth; the righteous can walk on them, while sinners stumble on them' [Hosea 14:10]."

*Rabban Yoḥanan ben Zakkai's concern with fraudulent business practices was not merely an academic subject. For many years he was a part of the business world: "It has been taught: The years of Rabban Yoḥanan ben Zakkai's life were one hundred and twenty. Forty years he engaged in business, forty years he studied, and forty years he taught." (*Rosh Hashanah *31b)* •

CONTEXT

The levelling rod was an instrument used for measuring out quantities of grain. Our section is concerned both with how the rod was made and how it was used. Apparently, there was a great deal of fraud going on in the buying and selling of grain, and the Rabbis were interested in setting up ethical business standards for people to follow. A thin-sided rod would be more precise in its measurements, and thus advantageous to the seller who wanted to give as little of the product as he had to. The thick-edged rod, on the other hand, would work to the buyer's advantage. Some people had rods with two different sides, which they would use depending on whether they were buying or selling. The Rabbis insisted that the rod be of two equal sides, thin or thick, depending on local custom. Similarly, using the rod with a quick single stroke would result in more grain being measured which would favor the customer. On the other hand, merchants liked to measure with several small, slow strokes that would leave no extra grain for the buyer.

Rabban Yoḥanan ben Zakkai was deeply torn over whether to discuss such matters in public. He feared that he was in a no-win situation: If he spoke about such matters, he might be giving some people ideas of how to defraud others. On the other hand, if he did not address these practices, he thought that people would assume that the Rabbis were naive and unaware of what went on in the marketplace. This might lead people to lose their respect for—and fear of—the Rabbis and their mission to impose higher ethical standards. In the end, Rabban Yoḥanan opted to discuss the fraudulent practices. He based this decision on his interpretation of a verse from the prophet Hosea: Righteous people will learn right and wrong from the discussion; the sinners might learn or be encouraged to deceive others, but ultimately they will stumble and be punished.

D'RASH

Rabban Yoḥanan ben Zakkai finds himself in the classic no-win situation: "Damned if you do, damned if you don't." He is faced with two choices, and no matter which one he makes there is a serious down side. What does one do in such a predicament?

At another juncture in his life, Yoḥanan ben Zakkai was faced with another such choice, only this time, the very fate of the Jewish people lay in the balance. According to the Talmud and Midrash, the Romans had set up a siege against the city of Jerusalem. The Zealots inside the city were prepared to fight the Romans to the death. Yoḥanan ben Zakkai saw that Jerusalem was doomed. He felt that the best hope for the future lay in abandoning the city, acknowledging the Romans as victors, and trying to sue for peace by negotiating with the enemy. Imagine how prospects must have looked at that critical moment: No matter what he did, he would lose. If he stayed in the city and fought with the Zealots, all the Jews would most likely be killed. If he fled the city and dealt with the Romans, he would probably be branded a collaborator and a traitor. What choice does one make in such a critical moment?

In both cases—what to teach the people about business ethics, and how to deal with the Roman threat—Rabban Yoḥanan ben Zakkai looked beyond the moment to the future. He believed that what really mattered was not what happened in the short term, but what was better for his people in the long run. He taught about the seamy side of the marketplace, even though some people might use his words and go out and defraud others. And after having been smuggled out of Jerusalem in a coffin, he went to the Roman general and asked for the town of Yavneh as a new base of study; it was from Yavneh that Rabban Yoḥanan and the other Rabbis began to rebuild the Jewish religion and the

Jewish people. Although at the time both of these options must have seemed to Yoḥanan ben Zakkai like no-win situations, history looks back upon him as a great hero who made the right choices.

In both cases, Yoḥanan ben Zakkai did not hesitate to confront the seamy side of life and to make the difficult compromises that were necessary. He could have remained in his ivory tower and lectured only about the ideals of Jewish business ethics, without describing the tricks that the deceivers used. Or he could have remained within the city of Jerusalem and fought heroically to the death with the Zealots. But he recognized that both of these choices were inadequate. Life has a dark side. Unless we acknowledge that and confront it, we are only deceiving ourselves. Rabban Yoḥanan ben Zakkai teaches us to deal with reality but always to strive to do the very best we can. When confronted by two terrible options, we first accept the fact that with our choice we will pay a great price. Then we look beyond the present, try to regroup, and begin to build for a better future.

כִּי רְחִימְתִּין הֲוָה עַזִּיזָא	When our love was strong, we
אַפּוּתְיָא דְסַפְסֵרָא שְׁכִיבַן	could sleep on the edge of a sword;
הַשְׁתָּא דְלָא עַזִּיזָא רְחִימְתִּין	now that our love is not strong,
פּוּרְיָא בַּר שִׁתִּין גַּרְמִידֵי לָא סַגֵּי לָן	a bed sixty cubits wide
	is not big enough for us.

TEXT

Sanhedrin 7a

> *There was a man who used to say: "When our love was strong, we could sleep on the edge of a sword; now that our love is not strong, a bed sixty cubits wide is not big enough for us." Rav Huna said: "This is found in verses. Of the early time, it is written: 'There I will meet with you, and I will impart to you—from above the cover' [Exodus 25:22], and it is taught: The Ark was nine [handbreadths] and the cover, one handbreadth, making ten, and it is written: 'The House which King Solomon built for the Lord was 60 cubits long, 20 cubits wide, and 30 cubits high' [I Kings 6:2]. Of the later time, it is written: 'Thus said the Lord: The heaven is My throne and the earth is My footstool: Where could you build a house for Me?' [Isaiah 66:1]."*

The cover of pure gold, known as the kaporet, *was placed on top of the Ark in the Sanctuary and the Temple. The Ark contained the two stone tablets, on which was engraved the Ten Commandments.* ●

A tefaḥ, *or handbreadth, was a basic standard of length, measuring across a clenched fist, or approximately 3 1/2 inches.* ●

The amah, *or cubit, was the distance from the elbow to the tip of the middle finger, or approximately 18 inches.* ●

CONTEXT

Our epigram was originally meant to convey a description of human love. Rashi comments: "'When our love was strong'—between myself and my wife." But the verses brought by Rav Huna show that he applied this statement to the relationship between God and the Jewish people. "Of the early time" refers to the beginning of the relationship, during the forty years when the Israelites were in the desert, having just been liberated from Egypt. Of this period, the prophet Jeremiah spoke nostalgically when he quoted God: "I accounted to your favor the devotion of your youth, your love as a bride—how you followed Me in the wilderness" (Jeremiah 2:2). During the wilderness period, the Israelites built the portable Sanctuary, and according to Exodus 25, God spoke to Moses from a position just on top of the *kaporet,* the cover of the Ark. The Rabbis figure this distance to be ten *tefaḥim* (or handbreadths) from the ground. The idea that God's presence was about a yard off the ground shows how close God was to the people. In the analogy, this is the period of great love, when the husband and wife could share a very small space together.

Later, when Solomon built the Temple in Jerusalem, the dimensions of "God's abode" grew. The size of the Temple was approximately ninety feet long, thirty feet across, and forty-five feet high. Finally, we have a verse from the days of the prophet Isaiah, after the destruction of the Temple (which according to rabbinic theology took place because the people sinned and were estranged from God). Here, God says that *no* Temple could possibly hold God. In our analogy, this is the husband and wife no longer in love, uncomfortable being together on a bed some ninety feet wide.

D'RASH

A personal ad in the newspaper reads: "Professional woman, 32, never-married, non-smoker, 5'2", seeking man for romantic candlelight dinners, walks on the beach at sunset, cruises under a full moon, fireworks and violins every time we kiss." It's a dream that many of us have at one time or another, encouraged and sustained by romance novels and movies. In life, however, it is very rare that such dreams become reality. We have to wonder if the idyllic, impossible expectations that we have for love and romance don't somehow contribute to the terrible disappointments, unhappy marriages, and high divorce rates that are so common today.

Imagine another personal ad: "Man seeking woman willing to put up with: my sometimes forgetting to put the toilet seat down; Sundays in front of the TV watching football; occasional burping out loud; leaving wet towels on the bathroom floor; and my being able to walk by a sink full of dirty dishes without washing them." One cannot imagine many people being attracted to *that* description. The irony is, however, that it is much closer to everyday reality than the first one is.

The anonymous author of our maxim reminds us that true love is not dependent upon the superficial things that popular culture always associates it with. We do not fall in love because of moonlight or violins. We fall in love with a real person, one with imperfections, faults, and weaknesses. If we are blessed with such a love, then we are able, together, to overcome the obstacles and problems that beset every relationship. A man and a woman in love are somehow able to manage even when poverty gives them a little more room than "the edge of a sword"; they are able to survive if they are in the precarious predicament of "lying on the razor-sharp edge of a blade." For two people for whom love has died, the seductive atmosphere of a roaring fireplace or of a tropical island is not enough to rekindle romance. For two people who care deeply for one another, even the edge of a sword is enough space—so long as they are together.

אָדָם קָרוֹב אֵצֶל עַצְמוֹ

A person is related to himself.

TEXT

Sanhedrin 9b

> *Rav Yosef said: "If the husband brought witnesses that she was adulterous, and her father brought witnesses that his witnesses conspired, the husband's witnesses are slain, and no money is paid. If the husband returns with witnesses that the father's witnesses conspired, the father's witnesses are slain; they pay money to this one and capital punishment to them." Rav Yosef also said: "'So-and-so sodomized him,' he and another combine to slay him. 'It was consensual,' he is evil, and the Torah says: 'You shall not join [. . .] a malicious witness [Exodus 23:1]." Rava said: "A person is related to himself, and a person cannot incriminate himself."*

The tractate Sanhedrin *deals with matters of testimony. For capital cases, two corroborating witnesses are needed, based on the verse from Deuteronomy 17:6: "A person shall be put to death only on the testimony of two or more witnesses." But what if the witnesses conspire to give false testimony? Such witnesses are called* edim zommemim, *"scheming witnesses." The Torah requires the conspiring witnesses to receive the punishment they sought to inflict, in this case, death. "If a man appears against another to testify maliciously and gives false testimony against him, the two parties to the dispute shall appear before the Lord, before the priests or magistrates in authority at the time, and the magistrates shall make a thorough investigation. If the man who testified is a false witness, if he has testified falsely against his fellow, you shall do to him as he schemed to do to his fellow. Thus you will sweep out evil from your midst; others will hear and be afraid, and such evil things will not again be done in your midst. Nor must you show pity: life for life, eye for eye, tooth for tooth, hand for hand, foot for foot." (Deuteronomy 19:16–21)* •

CONTEXT

A husband brings charges of adultery against his wife, with accompanying witnesses. This case differs from the biblical ordeal of *Sotah* where the husband has only suspicions, but no witnesses. A second set of witnesses is brought by the wife's father; they charge the husband's witnesses with conspiracy and falsehood. The husband's false witnesses receive the death penalty, the punishment that would have been imposed upon the wife had their (false) testimony been accepted. In this case, the wife does not receive the usual compensation of the money listed in her *ketubbah*, or marriage agreement. Thus, "no money is paid" to the wife, because this would be a second punishment for the same crime.

However, what happens if a *third* set of witnesses is brought by the husband? They testify that the wife's father's set of witnesses, the second set, were lying. Thus, we have a first set of witnesses charging adultery, a second set testifying that the first set conspired to lie, and a third set asserting that the second set is itself lying! In such a scenario, the conspiring second set is sentenced to death *and* pays the wife money for her *ketubbah*. Each of these is considered a separate punishment, one for a wrong committed against the first set of witnesses (falsely accusing them of lying), one for a wrong against the wife (falsely accusing her of adultery).

Homosexual rape ("So-and-so sodomized him") is also a capital crime and, thus, requires two witnesses. In this instance, the victim-accuser and a second witness together become a set to testify against the accused. This is the meaning of "he (the accuser) and another (an independent witness) combine." The language "So-and-so sodomized *him*" may simply be the Talmud's polite way of saying "So-and-so sodomized *me.*" The accuser uses the third person to depersonalize a painful charge.

But what if the accused answers: "This was not rape, but a consensual act!"? In this case, we apply Rava's rule against self-incrimination. Since homosexual acts, whether consensual or forced, are themselves prohibited by traditional Jewish law, the accused's answer—"It was not forced but by mutual consent"—is *ipso facto* invalid. In so testifying, he is admitting to a wrongdoing. Just as one may not testify either for or against a relative in court, one may not testify against himself in a court, for "a person is related to himself, and a person cannot incriminate himself." Later commentators will limit this principle to capital crimes, while in financial matters, one *can* self-incriminate. Nonetheless, the testimony "It was consensual" is invalid.

The verse from Exodus—"You shall not join [. . .] a malicious witness"—is creatively misquoted by the Gemara. The full verse from Exodus 23 (in translation) is:

> *You must not carry false rumors; you shall not join hands with the guilty to act as a malicious witness.*

The Gemara has left out parts of the verse: "You shall not join [hands with the guilty to act as] a malicious witness" (Exodus 23:1). Rashi, knowing that the Gemara has used the term "and the Torah says" without giving the exact verse, comments succinctly in an apparent apologetic: "As it is written, 'You shall not join hands etc.'"

D'RASH

"Let the mouth of another praise you, not yours" (Proverbs 27:2). Thus, we are not allowed to lavish praise on ourselves. Yet, Jewish law frowns upon self-deprecation as well. It is not only wrong but also unbecoming and improper for us to put ourselves at a disadvantage. The concern we show for others, especially for our relatives, must also be shown to ourselves. This is the traditional interpretation of "a person is related to himself."

Our text reminds us that we have to watch out for ourselves in a positive sense. In American jurisprudence, there is a similar concept in the Fifth Amendment's protection against self-incrimination. Our assumptions about a person who "pleads the Fifth" are negative; that person is *guilty,* and the constitutional immunity protected that individual from self-incrimination. However, there is a very positive side to the Fifth Amendment, as well as to our rule that "a person is related to himself." Even a guilty individual is protected by the Fifth Amendment from lying and thus compounding the wrong.

As much as we have to attend to the needs of others, those entrusted to our care, we also have to think of the needs of the caregivers, ourselves. How often have we seen a devoted mother strap her child in an automobile seat belt yet not put one on herself? Isn't that mother "related to herself"? Shouldn't she show the same concern for her child's mother as she shows for her child? Similarly, we buy our children new clothes for a special occasion but deny ourselves that luxury. Aren't we "related to ourselves"? We consider it important for our parents to concern themselves with health and medicine, but not for us to do the same. Or we make sure that our children have a religious education, but then somehow cannot find the time for one ourselves. All that we desire for those closest to us, all the positives that we do for them and promote in them, we have to do for ourselves as well, for "a person is related to himself," that is, we are our own first and primary relatives.

"Love your neighbor as yourself" is usually interpreted in Jewish sources as meaning "Only if you love *yourself* can you love your neighbor." Rava's words are not intended to justify excessive narcissism or self-indulgence. Rather, they should prevent self-martyrdom. Each of us who cares for relatives must begin that concern with the one who is most closely related—himself or herself.

אַף עַל פִּי שֶׁחָטָא יִשְׂרָאֵל הוּא

Even though he sinned, he is still "Israel."

TEXT

Sanhedrin 44a

> *"Israel has sinned!" [Joshua 7:11]. Rabbi Abba bar Zavda said: "Even though he sinned, he is still 'Israel.'" Rabbi Abba said: "This is as people say, 'A myrtle that stands among the willows is still a myrtle, and a myrtle it is called.'"*

CONTEXT

Before leading the Israelites into battle against the city of Jericho, Joshua had warned the people not to take spoils of war. "If you take anything from that which is proscribed, you will cause the camp of Israel to be proscribed; you will bring calamity upon it" (Joshua 6:18). One man, Achan son of Carmi of the tribe of Judah, took some of the forbidden items for himself. When the Israelites next went to war against the town of Ai, they suffered a terrible defeat. Joshua complained to God: "Why did You lead this people across the Jordan only to deliver us into the hands of the Amorites, to be destroyed by them?" (Joshua 7:7). God answered: "Israel has sinned! They have broken the covenant by which I bound them. They have taken of the proscribed" (Joshua 7:11).

Then Joshua said to Achan, "My son, pay honor to the Lord, the God of Israel, and make confession to Him. Tell me what you have done; do not hold anything back from me." Achan answered Joshua, "It is true, I have sinned against the Lord, the God of Israel. This is what I did: I saw among the spoil a fine Shinar mantle, two hundred shekels of silver, and a wedge of gold weighing fifty shekels, and I coveted them and took them." . . . And Joshua said, "What calamity you have brought upon us! The Lord will bring calamity upon you this day." And all Israel pelted him with stones. (Joshua 7:19–21, 25) •

The Rabbis noted God's use of the term Israel here. (Rashi, in his commentary, points out that we might have expected God to say "*The people* have sinned.") Since Israel is a name of honor, the question is raised why God would use this particular name even when the context refers to a dishonorable act. The answer is that even when the people do wrong, even when they commit a sin, they still retain the honor and uniqueness that the name Israel carries with it.

A folk saying is brought to support this concept. The myrtle is a beautiful and fragrant shrub with rich green leaves. Even when surrounded by the ordinary willow (as during the festival of Sukkot, when the palm branch of the *lulav* has myrtle and willow branches attached to it), the myrtle stands out and maintains its uniqueness and its name. Just as the myrtle is always a myrtle, no matter where or when, so too the people of Israel always remain "Israel" no matter where or when.

D'RASH

In certain religions, a person can be excommunicated—expelled from the fellowship of the church—because of committing a serious sin or breach of canon law. In Judaism, by contrast, there is virtually nothing a Jew can do that would result is his or her being cast out of the religion. "Even though he sinned, he is still 'Israel.'" Should a Jew become an apostate, denounce Judaism and convert to another faith, he or she is still considered a Jew in many respects. While there were categories of excommunication once practiced by the Jewish community (such as *ḥerem* and *niddui*), they were used merely as a means of social pressure to get an individual to change behavior. Others cannot take away our Jewishness; we ourselves are unable to renounce it. Criminals and heretics still remain Jews, no matter what they have done.

Why is this so? True love does not come with conditions or with strings attached. While respect and admiration have to be earned, love is freely given. When a child does something wrong, it may be difficult for a parent to like the youngster at that moment, but a father's or mother's love is never withdrawn. The same is true of divine love for God's children. God may be angry with us and may even chastise us for doing wrong. But God never disowns us. We have to *earn* the titles of "*mensch*," a decent human being, or "*tzaddik*," a righteous person, but no matter what we do, the title "Israel" is always ours. A priest can be defrocked; a lawyer can be disbarred, a soldier can be dishonorably discharged. But a Jew can never be denied the honor of the name "Israel."

That special honor entails special responsibility. We have to think twice before we do wrong, because our actions will always reflect on the rest of our people. Like Achan, what we do can adversely affect other Jews. The concept that "Even though he sinned, he is still 'Israel'" also implies that there is always the possibility of return and reconciliation. No matter what we may have done, we can always redeem ourselves and "come home" again. We always carry within us the "holiness" (to use Rashi's term) of the name Israel. We can always reach within us and draw on that holiness, and in doing so, make ourselves worthy of the honor that the name carries.

חֻצְפָּא אֲפִלּוּ כְּלַפֵּי שְׁמַיָּא מְהַנֵּי

Audacity even towards Heaven is effective.

TEXT

Sanhedrin 105a

["The elders of Moab and the elders of Midian, versed in divination, set out. They came to Balaam and gave him Balak's message. He said to them, 'Spend the night here, and I shall reply to you as the Lord may instruct me.'] So the Moabite dignitaries stayed with Balaam" [Numbers 22:7–8]. Where had the elders of Midian gone to? Once he had said to them, "Spend the night here, and I shall reply to you," they said to themselves: "Is there a father who hates his son?" Rav Naḥman said: "Audacity even towards Heaven is effective." In the beginning it is written: "Do not go with them" [Numbers 22:12], but in the end it is written: "Go with them" [Numbers 22:20].

There are other cases in the Bible of people who exhibit audacity towards Heaven with the same good intentions as Abraham and Moses but which inexplicably do not result in the same happy ending. The most striking example is in II Samuel 6, the story of King David moving the Ark of God. David has chosen Jerusalem as his capital city, and the Ark of God must be brought there.

> *They loaded the Ark of God onto a new cart and conveyed it from the house of Abinadab, which was on the hill, and Abinadab's sons, Uzzah and Ahio, guided the new cart. They conveyed it from Abinadab's house on the hill, [Uzzah walking] alongside the Ark of God and Ahio walking in front of the Ark. Meanwhile, David and all the House of Israel danced before the Lord to [the sound of] all kinds of cypress wood [instruments], with lyres, harps, timbrels, sistrums*

CONTEXT

In the eleventh chapter of *Sanhedrin,* there is a lengthy interpretation of the story of Balak and Balaam, found in Numbers 22-24. In the biblical account, Balak, king of Moab, wants to hire Balaam, a famous prophet, to curse the Israelites. Balaam tries to refuse, but Balak won't take no for an answer. King Balak sends emissaries to convince Balaam. These are "the elders of Moab and the elders of Midian." Thus, the opening question of the Gemara focuses on the difference between the beginning of verse 7, where both "the elders of Moab and the elders of Midian" are mentioned, and the end of verse 8, where only "the Moabite dignitaries" are cited. What happened to the Midianite elders? The answer is that once Balaam asked them to await God's reply, the Midianite elders knew that their cause was in vain: The father (the Father in Heaven) always loves his child (the children of Israel) and will display this love by preventing Balaam from harming the Israelites. Thus, there was no need to waste the night in anticipation, waiting for a negative reply from God.

With Balak's dignitaries spending the night under Balaam's roof, Balaam awaits God's instruction. God tells Balaam: "Do not go with them. You must not curse that people, for they are blessed." What should Balaam do? We would expect Balaam to send the emissaries on their way, for God has already made the answer known. Yet this is not what Balaam does. He tells the elders: "So you, too, stay here overnight, and let me find out what else the Lord may say to me." This is what the Talmud calls "audacity even towards Heaven," that is, flagrantly ignoring God's specific command not to go with the elders. Once God had said no, and Balaam tried to obtain a different answer, he has exhibited "audacity towards Heaven."

Despite the fact that it is impudence towards God, it works! God allows Balaam to go with Balak's messengers. The word translated as "audacity" is, of course, *ḥutzpah,* one of the Hebrew words that is best known to the Western world. One cannot hold God hostage, but one may, at times, challenge God and win. The guidelines of this *ḥutzpah* toward Heaven are not clear. In the story of Sodom (Genesis 18), Abraham argues with God, lowering the number of righteous required to save the city from fifty to ten. This is certainly audacious, since "the outrage of Sodom and Gomorrah is so great, and their sin so grave" (Genesis 18:20)! In the aftermath of the Golden Calf, Moses puts his own life on the line. He tells God either to forgive the sin of the people, or "erase me from the record which You have written" (Exodus 32:32), that is, take my life away. This would seem to be *ḥutzpah* towards Heaven, yet it is audacity that works, for God backs down from destroying the entire Israelite nation.

and cymbals. But when they came to the threshing floor of Nacon, Uzzah reached out for the Ark of God and grasped it, for the oxen had stumbled. The Lord was incensed at Uzzah. And God struck him down on the spot for his indiscretion, and he died there beside the Ark of God. (II Sam. 6:3–7)

To our minds, Uzzah acted justly, trying to stop the cart with the Ark on it from tipping over. Yet, Uzzah's actions are strangely seen as an affront to the Lord. What appears as obedience is taken as overstepping. Uzzah pays with his life. Sometimes, ḥutzpah *towards Heaven does not work and can even result in the most extreme consequences.* ●

D'RASH

We can learn from Rav Naḥman's observation that, in the Jewish tradition, *ḥutzpah* towards God is not always seen as heresy or rebellion. On the contrary, the examples from the stories of Abraham, Moses, and Balaam show that "God's will" is often malleable. The negative things that we are certain will happen to us can often be averted. We need not say that the future is predetermined, for we can, at times, exhibit the *ḥutzpah* to challenge God's decree and alter it.

We often hear the predestiny theology couched in simplistic axioms like: "If God had wanted people to fly, we would have been given wings." Human beings have the potential to fly not because God gave us wings, but simply because we have used our God-given talents to innovate and overcome the forces of gravity. This faulty line of thinking may then be stretched to read: "If God had wanted us to be healthy, we would have been created immune to illness." Judaism says that God and humans are partners in this world. It is less a matter of what God wanted for us, and more a matter that God endowed us with the power to help ourselves.

In our day and age, medicine, science and technology have created amazing new drugs and therapies. Smallpox has been eradicated from the earth. Major illnesses have been cured, and remedies for other illnesses are being discovered every day. Does this challenge Heaven? On the contrary: It is the work of Heaven! If there seems to be any audacity towards a divinely written script, it is only in our minds.

In the end, "God's will," "God's decree," or "fate" are really relative terms. What we think to be predetermined is actually changeable. Since God is, by definition, constant and immutable, can we then say that the evil was by divine decree? It seems more likely, from a traditional Jewish viewpoint, that we are supposed to argue with God on issues of morality, to show a certain measure of audacity towards Heaven by not accepting fate but challenging it. It is part of the divine plan that we try to change God's mind, to avert the evil decree, to tempt fate and alter it. At times, *ḥutzpah* towards Heaven can be effective.

אַהֲבָה מְבַטֶּלֶת שׁוּרָה שֶׁל גְּדֻלָּה

Love cancels out the dignified conduct expected of the great.

TEXT

Sanhedrin 105b

It was taught in the name of Rabbi Shimon ben Elazar: "Love cancels out the dignified conduct expected of the great. We learn this from Abraham, as it is written: 'So early next morning, Abraham saddled his ass' [Genesis 22:3]. Hatred disrupts the normal order. We learn this from Balaam, as it says: 'When he arose in the morning, Balaam saddled his ass' [Numbers 22:21]."

CONTEXT

Abraham is commanded by God: "Take your son, your favored one, Isaac, whom you love, and go to the land of Moriah, and offer him there as a burnt offering on one of the heights that I will point out to you" (Genesis 22:2). Despite this being the most difficult command that a parent would ever have to obey, Abraham hastens to carry it out because of his devotion to and love of God. The Rabbis note that the text says that he set out without delay early the next morning. They also note that Abraham saddled the ass himself. This is strange, since Abraham was quite old and quite wealthy. We know he had servants (two of them accompany him on the journey). It does not seem right for a rich, elderly, important man like Abraham to do such menial tasks. Therefore, Rabbi Shimon ben Elazar taught, love (in this case, Abraham's love of God) can cause people to do things that are out of character.

Balaam, a Midianite prophet and soothsayer, is hired by Balak, king of the Moabites, to put a curse upon the Israelites as they wander through the desert. A delegation comes to escort Balaam so he can execute the curse. "When he arose in the morning, Balaam saddled his ass and departed with the Moabite dignitaries" (Numbers 22:21). Once again, the Rabbis note that Balaam was a very important person, and it was quite unusual for him to saddle his own animal. The explanation given is that Balaam, an enemy of the Israelites, was so full of hatred for these people that he could not wait to go out and curse them. He prepared his own ass so he could begin his mission without further delay. Hatred, like love, can make us do things that normally we just would not do.

An expanded version of this teaching is also found in the Midrash, Bereshit Rabbah *55,8, where it is attributed to Rabbi Shimon bar Yoḥai, not Shimon ben Elazar. In the Midrash, a fascinating prayer of Rabbi Shimon bar Yoḥai concludes the text: "May one saddling come and override the other saddling! May the saddling of Abraham our father, done in order to fulfill the will of He who spoke and the world came into being, come and override the saddling done by Balaam, who was on his way to curse Israel."* •

We cannot help but admire Rabbi Shimon's keen eye for reading and remembering stories in the Torah. He brings together two tales with significant similarities and contrasts: A great man, in the morning, saddles his ass. But Abraham does it to carry out the will of God, while Balaam does it in an attempt to disobey God's word: "But God said to Balaam . . . 'You must not curse that people, for they are blessed'" (Numbers 22:12).

D'RASH

On the highway, there is an overpass: Spraypainted across the concrete is the message "John loves Mary." We are either annoyed or amused by the graffiti. Then, we suddenly consider "how" this was done, and we realize that John was probably hanging upside down, thirty feet over busy traffic as he scrawled this letter to Mary. Of course, we know "why" he wrote the message; it was love.

There is a well-known story of a man who left a strange stipulation in his will: "My son will not inherit a penny from me until he has gone crazy." No one could figure out what the deceased could possibly have had in his mind when he wrote such an unusual condition. Finally, the mystery was solved when someone came into the son's home and saw him, on the floor, on his hands and knees, pretending to be a horse, neighing and galloping around the room, with his little boy riding on his back. It was suddenly clear: The old man wanted his own son to become a parent before he inherited the estate. The old man understood that parenthood—and love of all kinds—causes us to be a little crazy at times.

Hatred can do the same thing to us. A man discovers that his wife has been having an affair, and their marriage breaks up. Yet instead of burying the past and making a new life for himself, he becomes obsessed with trying to punish her for her betrayal. Years later, he continues to spend a great deal of time, money, and energy in vindictively trying to get even. His friends tell him: "You're only making a fool of yourself," but he cannot hear them. Hatred has taken over his life.

Swastikas and messages of hate are painted all over a synagogue. The quiet community is shocked. Then the police arrest two teenagers, former Boy Scouts, bright, clean-cut, all-American types. The neighborhood is stunned. How could these boys have done such a terrible thing, not only to a House of God, but also to their neighbors? Given the shame and the criminal record they will now carry with them, how could they have done this to their own families, and to themselves? Hatred, too, can make us do things that are out of character and that do not make much sense.

Love and hatred are powerful emotions that can radically change the way we see the world. They can also drastically alter the way that we behave. It is important for us to understand these different factors and how they affect us. Whenever possible, we must strive to control them so that they don't control us. And like Rabbi Shimon bar Yoḥai, we also pray that in our personal lives, as well as in the larger world around us, the power of love be strong enough to overcome the power of hate.

יֵשׁ קוֹנֶה עוֹלָמוֹ
בְּשָׁעָה אַחַת

There are those who achieve their world in a single hour.

TEXT

Avodah Zarah 17a

It was taught: They said of Rabbi Elazar ben Dordia that there was not a single prostitute in the world that he had not gone to. Once, he heard that there was a prostitute in the towns by the sea who took a purse of dinars *as her payment. He took a purse of* dinars *and crossed seven rivers to get to her. While having sex, she passed wind. She said: "Just as this wind will not return to its place, so too Elazar ben Dordia will not be accepted if he returns in repentance."*

He went and sat between two great mountains and hills. He said: "Mountains and hills! Plead for mercy on my behalf!" They said to him: "Before we can plead on your behalf, we have to plead for ourselves, for it says: 'For the mountains may move and the hills be shaken' [Isaiah 54:10]."

He said: "Heaven and Earth! Plead for mercy on my behalf!" They said: "Before we can plead on your behalf, we have to plead for ourselves, for it says: 'Though the heavens should melt away like smoke, and the earth wear out like a garment' [Isaiah 51:6]."

He said: "Sun and Moon! Plead for mercy on my behalf!" They said: "Before we can plead on your behalf, we have to plead for ourselves, for it says: 'Then the moon shall be ashamed, and the sun shall be abashed' [Isaiah 24:23]."

He said: "Stars and planets! Plead for mercy on my behalf!" They said to him: "Before we can plead on your behalf, we have to plead for ourselves, for it says 'All the host of heaven shall molder' [Isaiah 34:4]."

He said: "The matter depends on me alone." He put his head between his knees and wept until his soul departed. A voice from heaven proclaimed: "Rabbi Elazar ben Dordia is invited to life in the World-to-Come." Here is a case where he died committing a sin. There, it was because he was so addicted to immorality that it was similar to heresy. Rabbi cried and said: "There are those who achieve after many years, and there are those who achieve their world in a single hour." Rabbi said: "Not only are those who return accepted, they are also called by the title 'Rabbi.'"

CONTEXT

The story of Elazar ben Dordia comes as part of a discussion of the meaning of a verse in Proverbs: "All who go to her cannot return and find again the paths of life" (2:19). The Rabbis interpret "her" as referring to *minut* or heresy, by which they generally meant those Jews who were attracted to a variety of different religious groups. These particular Rabbis took a very hard line towards those Jews: Anyone who joined these sects was unable to return to the Jewish fold; what is more, those who tried to return to normative Judaism after having flirted with heresy would die as a result of their sin. The vehemence of the Rabbis towards apostasy hints at how great a threat they felt it was to first- and second-century Judaism, and why they were willing to go beyond the usual principle that even a sinning Jew is still Jewish.

You will recall from above in the text from Sanhedrin *44a that Rabbi Abba bar Zavda said: "Even though he sinned, he is still 'Israel.'" Our text seems to contradict what was taught there. It is quite common to find contradictory opinions in the pages of the Talmud. These divergences reflect differences of time, place, and philosophy. Jews have taken this diversity not as a sign of weakness but of strength.* •

The Gemara then goes on to ask whether there are other sins that carry the same severe penalty as heresy does. The answer seems to be that heresy is unique; for it alone would the sinner suffer death and be unable to return. But then the case of Elazar ben Dordia is brought up. He was guilty of sexual immorality, not apostasy. He attempted to repent, but he died, without being given additional years of life. This objection to the Gemara's point (made by reference to a story that seems to contradict it) is answered by the Rabbis: the case of Elazar ben Dordia is unique. He was *so* addicted to his sin that it was equated with heresy. (One could say that he committed it "religiously.") Yet even in his case, we are told, his repentance *was* effective: A *bat kol,* or voice from heaven, assures us that he was invited into the World-to-Come. Sincere, heartfelt contrition does make a difference.

At the beginning of the story, we are led to believe that Elazar ben Dordia is a Rabbi. At the end of the tale, we learn that the title "Rabbi" is conferred upon him only *after* his death. He has become a Rabbi, a teacher, because he showed us that it is never too late to repent. The prostitute's interpretation of the verse in Proverbs, "all who go to her"—to a woman like me—"cannot return" is proved to be wrong.

The other Rabbi in our story is Rabbi Yehudah ha-Nasi ("the prince"), the great sage and leader of the Jewish people in the third century C.E. We wonder why he weeps at the end: Is it because he is so moved by Elazar ben Dordia's act of contrition, his acceptance to heaven, and his being given the title "Rabbi"? Or is it out of jealousy and frustration, that such a scoundrel could achieve in one hour what it would take another individual (Rabbi Yehudah ha-Nasi?) an entire lifetime to achieve? Being human, perhaps he felt a little of both.

D'RASH

The National Football League record for most points scored in a lifetime is held by George Blanda. The kicker broke into the sport in 1949, with the Chicago Bears, and retired after the 1975 season with Oakland. Over the course of twenty-six years in the game, Blanda scored 2,002 points. This incredible number was composed of 9 touchdowns, 335 field goals, and 943 points after touchdown.

Roger Bannister is also listed in the sports record book, in the category of track and field. On May 6, 1954, Bannister achieved sports immortality by being the first person to break the "four-minute mile." His record time was 3 minutes, 59.4 seconds.

One man achieves fame after more than a quarter of a century; the other, in just a few minutes. The same thing happens off the sports field all the time. One man spends his entire life working hard to support his family, twelve hours a day, six days a week, fifty-two weeks a year, for almost fifty years. Only upon retirement is he able to relax and begin to enjoy the remaining few years of his life. Another man goes into a store, pays a dollar for a lottery ticket, and wins ten million dollars the next day. One person achieves his world after many years, another in a single hour.

Like Rabbi Yehudah ha-Nasi, perhaps we too want to cry when we are confronted by the quick success of others, while we struggle and work hard just to get by. In an ideal world, fame, fortune, and success would be available to anyone willing to work hard. But our experience teaches us that we do not live in an ideal world. It is not within our power to explain these discrepancies and why they occur.

The comforting part of our story, however, is the teaching that it is never too late to achieve something important. It is possible, even in a single hour, to accomplish what is vital and crucial. And it is never too late to turn our lives around.

מַמְזֵר תַּלְמִיד חָכָם קוֹדֵם לְכֹהֵן גָּדוֹל עַם הָאָרֶץ

A *mamzer* who is a scholar takes precedence over a High Priest who is an ignoramus.

TEXT

Horayot 13a

Mishnah (3:8): *A* kohen *takes precedence over a Levite, a Levite over an Israelite, and an Israelite over a* mamzer, *and a* mamzer *over a* netin, *and a* netin *over a proselyte, and a proselyte over a freed slave. When? When they are all equal. But if the* mamzer *was a scholar and the High Priest was an ignoramus, a* mamzer *who is a scholar takes precedence over a High Priest who is an ignoramus.*
Gemara: *"When? When they are all equal." From where do we derive this? Rabbi Aḥa son of Rabbi Ḥanina said: "As it says in Scripture: 'She is more precious than rubies* [mip'ninim]' *[Proverbs 3:15], more precious than the High Priest who enters the Innermost* [lifnei v'lifnim]."

The Bible describes the kohen *as follows: "Aaron was set apart, he and his sons, forever, to be consecrated as most holy, to make burnt offerings to the Lord and serve Him and pronounce blessings in His name forever" (I Chronicles 23:13). Thus, one is a* kohen *if his father was a* kohen *before him, tracing the lineage back to Aaron and his sons.* •

The Levite is mentioned in the Torah often: "At that time the Lord set apart the tribe of Levi to carry the Ark of the Lord's Covenant, to stand in attendance upon the Lord, and to bless in His name, as is still the case" (Deuteronomy 10:8). The Levites trace their lineage back to Moses. •

Unfortunately, there are many confusing translations of Hebrew terms, and this Mishnah has two words that are commonly translated in English terms that do not reflect Hebrew concepts. Kohen *has often been translated as "priest," a word with a very different meaning in the Christian religion.* •

Similarly confusing is mamzer, *often translated as "bastard." The term does not mean what the English word denotes. A* mamzer *is*

CONTEXT

This Mishnah—the last in the Order *Nezikin*—is speaking of matters of honor and rescue. Who should be honored first? And in the case of an emergency, who should be rescued first? In other words, who has the highest status in the community? The Mishnah then lists an order—*kohen*, Levite, Israelite, *mamzer*, *netin*, proselyte, freed slave. Before we can understand the Mishnah, we must define a few terms: *kohen* is one descended from Aaron. The *kohanim* (plural of *kohen*) functioned in the Tabernacle, and later the Temple, in special public roles. For this reason, they are given special status in the Mishnah. Today, we still follow this practice by giving a *kohen* the first *aliyah* to the Torah. The *levi* or Levite was the helper in the Tabernacle and later in the Temple. The plural is *levi'im*, or Levites in English. They sang the Temple liturgy as well. These are next in order of honor. Israelites refers to the common people at that time, the majority of the people who were neither *kohanim* nor Levites. A *mamzer* is the offspring of an incestuous or adulterous relationship; his honor would be even less.

Netin is traditionally understood as a descendent of the Gibeonites, a nation described in the book of Joshua, chapter 9: The Gibeonites disguised themselves as foreigners to avoid attack by the Israelites. Upon learning of this ruse, Joshua spared their lives but made them "hewers of wood *the offspring of a forbidden relationship, that is, an incestuous or adulterous one (as opposed to an illegitimate child, a concept not known in Jewish law). The* mamzer *bears a strong stigma and may marry only another* mamzer. •

An aliyah, *from the root meaning "to go up," is the honor of being "called up" to the Torah.* •

and drawers of water . . . for the community and for the altar of the Lord." That is, they accepted a low status in the Israelite community in exchange for their lives. Their low status is reflected in their coming after *kohen*, *levi* and Israelite.

"Scholar" and "ignoramus" are general translations for words that may be technical terms in the Mishnah. *Talmid ḥakham,* the "scholar," is actually one who studies with a master-teacher. *Am ha-aretz,* translated as "ignoramus," likely refers to one who was suspect of not having properly observed tithes and ritual cleanliness rules. Later Hebrew uses the expression *am ha-aretz* for an ignoramus, and this is how it is used in modern Hebrew.

In the Gemara, Rabbi Aḥa seeks to find a biblical source to support this order, especially for the fact that a *mamzer* who is a scholar takes precedence over a High Priest who is an ignoramus. He finds his proof in a verse from Proverbs. The entire chapter speaks of the value of wisdom:

> Happy is the man who finds wisdom,
> The man who attains understanding.
> Her value in trade is better than silver,
> Her yield, greater than gold.
> She is more precious than rubies;
> All of your goods cannot equal her.
> (Proverbs 3:13–15)

Rabbi Aḥa makes a play on the letters in the two Hebrew words, saying that wisdom is more precious, *mip'ninim,* than rubies, even greater than the one who enters *lifnei v'lifnim,* literally, the most inside place, that is, the Holy of Holies in the Temple. If wisdom is greater than priesthood, then the respect we give to the scholar outweighs that which we give to the *kohen.*

D'RASH

The story is told of a man who offered a rabbi ten thousand dollars to make him a *kohen.* "You cannot buy that," the rabbi responds. The man returns later, offering the rabbi one hundred thousands dollars. "I'm sure that you very much want to become a *kohen,*" answers the rabbi, "but it's not something I can sell to you." A week later, the same man returns. "Look, rabbi, it'll put me in hock forever, but I'll give you a million dollars to make me a *kohen.*" The rabbi is dumbfounded. "Okay, if it will make you happy, I'll make you a *kohen.* But tell me: Why is it so important?" "Well, rabbi, my father was a *kohen,* and his father, and his father before him!"

Of course, the humor here is from the fact that one becomes a *kohen* automatically. The priesthood in the Bible is through lineage. One needs no qualification other than a father who is a *kohen.* Until recently in Jewish history, and still today in some quarters, *yiḥus*—lineage or family background—was extremely important. Marriages were arranged based on one's lineage. A poor young man who was descended from a distinguished sage was a great catch, for he had *yiḥus.*

In our egalitarian world, we might dispute the validity of this hierarchy and genealogy, claiming that it creates a caste system. Yet, throughout much of Jewish history, some hierarchy has always been accepted. The biblical ideal based on lineage (*kohen, levi,* Israelite) was eventually replaced by one founded on knowledge (scholar, student, ignoramus). The latter half of this Mishnah presages the development from a lineage-centered hierarchy to a meritocracy based on scholarship.

Today, we might wish to expand on the Mishnah's words. Jewish leadership must be based on Jewish knowledge. Unfortunately, many of us, the descendants of knowledgeable Jews, often rest on our ancestors' laurels. How often have we heard it said, "My grandfather was a rabbi in Europe"? Yet how sad it is when the speaker is so far removed from Jewish life, learning, and observance. That one's *grandfather* sat and studied all day is interesting. That one's *grandchildren* become committed, educated Jews is crucial.

We now know that it is not lineage, but learning, that is the key to the continuity of Jewish life in the future. If we remain unschooled in Judaism, then even if we have good *yiḥus,* we are easily surpassed both in honor and communal prestige by a learned person with no background, and even by one with impaired background like a *mamzer.* This is a strong motivation to check not only our lineage, where we came from, but also our Jewish learning, where we are going.

Rest Stop

From there they set out and encamped beyond the Arnon. . . . And from there to Beer, which is the well where the Lord said to Moses, "Assemble the people that I may give them water." (Numbers 21:13, 16)

Words of Torah are compared to water . . . as it says: "Ho, all who are thirsty, come for water" [Isaiah 55:1]. . . . And just as with water, a great man is not ashamed to say to a child: "Bring me a drink of water," so too with Torah—a great man is not embarrassed to say to a child: "Teach me a chapter, or a verse, or a word, or even a letter." (*Song of Songs Rabbah* 1,3)

Once upon a time, there lived a man, who during his whole life studied nothing but the treatise of Hagigah. When the man died and was about to be buried, a woman dressed in white came up to the corpse and stood in front of it. When the people saw her, they asked her who she was and what was her name. And she replied: "I am Hagigah and I am praying for this man in the other world, for he studied nothing but the treatise Hagigah all his life, and therefore he deserves that I should plead for him in the other world." In the same way, all other good deeds which a man performs in this life plead for him in the world to come. (*Ma'aseh Book: Book of Jewish Tales and Legends,* translated by Moses Gaster. Philadelphia: Jewish Publication Society, 1981, p. 648)

Seder Kodashim

Introduction to Seder Kodashim

The fifth section of the Mishnah is *Kodashim,* or "Holy Things." Its eleven tractates cover the sacrifices that were offered in the Temple in Jerusalem. Interestingly, by the time of the editing of the Mishnah, the Temple had been destroyed for over a century. Nevertheless, the Rabbis of Babylonia saw fit to create a Gemara for nine of these tractates. Perhaps they felt that the Temple would some day be rebuilt, and it was thus critical to lay out the proper procedures for the time when the sacrifices would be reinstituted. Or it is possible that they felt that in the absence of the ability to offer the sacrifices, the best that could be done by Jews was to *remember* the sacrifices and discuss their details.

אַלְקַפְטָא נַקְטַן
רֵיחָא אָתֵי לַהּ לְיָד

The nobleman has taken us [by the hand], and his scent lingers on the hand.

TEXT

Zevaḥim 96b

> *Rav Yitzḥak son of Rav Yehudah used to come regularly before Rami bar Ḥama. He left him and went to Rav Sheshet. One day, he [Rami bar Ḥama] met him [Rav Yitzḥak]. He said to him: "The nobleman has taken us [by the hand], and his scent lingers on the hand. Because you went to Rav Sheshet, do you think you will become like Rav Sheshet?" He [Rav Yitzḥak] said to him: "It was not for that reason! When I asked a question of the Master, you answered me from logic. If I came across a Mishnah, it refuted it. But with Rav Sheshet, if I asked a question of him, he answered me with a Mishnah, so that even if I came across a Mishnah that refuted it, it was only one Mishnah against another Mishnah."*

Rav Sheshet especially disparaged those schools which taught students to come up with forced conclusions that were based on hair-splitting logic known as pilpul. *In one particular case, Rav Sheshet decided an issue (as was his custom) according to what was taught by "tradition" in a Mishnah. Rav Amram came to offer another interpretation based on forced logic. Rav Sheshet said to him: "You must come from the study house of Pumbeditha, where they pull an elephant through the eye of a needle!"* ●

CONTEXT

The Rabbis of the Talmud understood that there were two major sources for their teachings. The first was tradition, which included (1) verses from the Bible, (2) rabbinic lessons found in the Mishnah or *baraitot,* or (3) precedent. The second source was reason or logic. Tradition was considered by the above text to be a stronger authority than reason.

Rav Yitzḥak had been a student of Rami bar Ḥama; he left his study house and went to stay with Rav Sheshet. Rami bar Ḥama was offended that his pupil had left him for another teacher. Rami accused Rav Yitzḥak of being attracted to Rav Sheshet because of his fame and reputation. He sarcastically tells his former student: You think that when the great man touches you, his scent will linger on your hand. By being with Rav Sheshet, you think you will become *like* Rav Sheshet. (The word in the folk-saying, translated as "nobleman," *alkafta* or *arkafta,* is the title of a high Persian dignitary.)

Rav Yitzḥak replies that it was not Rav Sheshet's fame, but his teaching methodology, that was so attractive. Rav Sheshet insisted on finding the traditional sources for his teachings. Rami, on the other hand, favored logic. Rav

Yitzḥak explains that in a conflict between one teaching based on tradition and another teaching based on logic, the former takes precedence. Thus, the methodology of Rav Sheshet is superior to that of Rami. Rav Yitzḥak adds that where traditions, such as two sections of the Mishnah, conflict, it is acceptable to maintain one teaching over the other since they are both of equal authority. Either way, Rav Sheshet's methodology, based on tradition rather than logic, proves to be superior.

D'RASH

While walking down the street, we see someone who looks very familiar. It's not a friend or an acquaintance, we realize, but a famous celebrity, perhaps an athlete or a politician or a movie star. We find ourselves drawn to him, following his every motion, unable to walk away. He seems larger than life, somehow very special and unique. We long to establish a connection with him in some way. We would love to talk to him, but we cannot imagine what we would say. We might even be hesitant to just say hello, fearing that we would be disturbing this great person, afraid that we will come off looking silly or acting like a pest. Many of us, if we have the presence of mind, and a pen and a piece of paper handy, might ask for an autograph. If we are lucky enough to get it, we would cherish that bit of barely legible scrawl as one of our most prized possessions.

Why is this so? Perhaps it is because we live in a huge, complex world, and so often we feel small and insignificant. In addition, so much of life is mundane and ordinary. It is quite natural for us to dream of a different reality where we are important and each moment is exciting. Popular culture exploits our boredom and unhappiness, transferring our fantasies to certain individuals who we assume must live charmed lives. In our desire for wealth, power, and excitement, we buy into the myths of the "rich and famous." Little do we realize that the actual lives of these people are, for the most part, not too different from our own. But it is one thing to dream, from time to time, about living a life of glamour. It is quite another thing to let these occasional dreams become obsessions and for us to live vicariously through the lives of others.

Rami bar Ḥama was responding to what he feared had become an obsession in one of his students. He reminds us that we can shake hands with a great person, but all that sticks is their scent. In a moment, even that is gone. Nothing of a lasting value comes from "hanging around" or worshiping celebrities. Rami would teach us that greatness is achieved by doing great things. Merely being in the company of the great is no substitute. We are challenged not to feed off someone else's accomplishments but to strive to be great ourselves.

תֶּבֶן אַתָּה מַכְנִיס לַעֲפָרַיִם You're bringing straw to Afarayim.

TEXT

Menaḥot 83b, 85a

Mishnah (8:1): *All of the [meal] offerings of the community or of the individual are brought from the land [of Israel] or from outside the land, from the new or from the old, with the exception of the Omer and the Two Loaves, which must be brought from the new and from the land. All the offerings must be from the choicest. What constitutes "the choicest?" Mikhmas and Zanoaḥ are first for fine flour. Second, behind them, is Afarayim in the valley. All lands were kosher [for this], but they used to bring it from here.*

Gemara: *"All the offerings must be from the choicest." Yoḥna and Mamra said to Moses: "You're bringing straw to Afarayim!" He said to them: "It is just as people say: 'To the place of vegetables—bring vegetables.'"*

Beginning on the second day of Pesaḥ, a sheaf [Omer] of newly harvested grain was offered each day for seven weeks: "When you enter the land that I am giving to you and you reap its harvest, you shall bring the first sheaf of your harvest to the priest." (Leviticus 23:10) •

The two loaves were brought on the festival of Shavuot: "Then you shall bring an offering of new grain to the Lord. You shall bring from your settlements two loaves of bread as an elevation offering; each shall be made of two-tenths of a measure of choice flour." (Leviticus 23:16–17) •

CONTEXT

The Mishnah begins a discussion of what kind of flour was appropriate for the *Minḥah* meal-offerings. These offerings were made of flour and oil and cooked in various ways. They were brought in addition to the animal sacrifices or, on occasion, by themselves. With two exceptions, the flour could be either from new or old produce. The exceptions were the Omer and the Two Loaves.

The Mishnah then defines "choicest"; only this quality was acceptable for the meal-offerings. We are told that the towns of Mikhmas and Zanoaḥ had the reputation for producing the best flour in Israel; the next best flour was to be found in Afarayim.

The Gemara adds a piece of folklore associated with the town of Afarayim. This town apparently was well known for its abundant supply of straw. When Moses first came to Egypt to demand that Pharaoh let the Israelites go, he brought with him an arsenal of signs and wonders that were supposed to convince the Egyptians of God's power. For example, Moses would change his staff into a serpent; he could make his hand turn white with leprosy; and he could turn the waters of the Nile blood-red. Two of the Egyptian magicians, Yoḥna and Mamra (also referred to in other sources as Jannes and Jambres) came to meet him and ridiculed him. "Egypt is famous for its magicians who can perform many wonders. Your coming here with your tricks is like bringing straw to Afarayim!" Moses answers them with a folk saying: "If you want to sell vegetables, go to the place where people look to buy them—in the vegetable market!" In other words: I can play your game—doing magic—and beat you at it!

D'RASH

A young woman, in her senior year of college, wants to apply to law school. But her friends and advisors are telling her she is making a big mistake: "There is a glut of lawyers in America now; we have more lawyers per capita than any other country in the world! The field is just too crowded. You'll never find a decent position. Look for some other line of work. You'll be doing yourself a real favor."

The woman is determined. "I love the idea of becoming a lawyer. I love the logic of it, and the challenge of it. And I believe that through the law, I can really make a difference—either in government and public service, or in representing people who otherwise don't have a voice in our society. And I think I'm bright enough, and motivated enough to make a place for myself. If you are good at what you do, there will always be room for you."

When the Egyptian magicians told Moses that he was bringing straw to Afarayim, they were basically telling him: "There's already too many people here who do what you want to do. There's no more room for you. You won't succeed. Find something else to occupy your time. Here you will just be another small fish in a big pond. Go away!!" But Moses refused to take "No!" for an answer. He was not afraid of the competition, not afraid of being put to the test. He believed in himself and in what he was able to accomplish. His response to "You're bringing straw to Afarayim" (which is similar to the expression "You're carrying coals to Newcastle") was "You bring vegetables to where the vegetables are." Yes, in the produce market, there will be scores of other merchants all selling the same product. Yet, it is the market where people go to when they want to buy their vegetables. We prove ourselves by showing that what we have to offer is just as good as or better than what the next person is selling.

Moses was not afraid to be put to the test. The signs and wonders that he brought to Egypt were more powerful than anything the magicians there could do. His self-confidence and courage were liberating—both for the Israelites and for us, who learn from him not to be scared away by a challenge or competition.

חֲמִירָא סַכַּנְתָּא מֵאִסּוּרָא

Concerns about danger are more severe than ritual prohibitions.

TEXT

Ḥullin 9b–10a

Come and hear: If a person left a jar uncovered and came back and found it covered, it is impure, for I would say that an impure man entered and covered it up. If a person left it covered and came back and found it uncovered—if a weasel was able to drink out of it (or, according to Rabban Gamliel, a snake) or if dew fell into it over night, it is invalid.

Rabbi Yehoshua ben Levi said: "What is the reason? Because it is the way of reptiles to uncover; it is not their way to cover." (You could say that this reason applies when he left it uncovered; but if he found it just as he had left it, it is neither impure, nor invalid.) But if there is any doubt about water that was left uncovered, it is forbidden. We learn from this that concerns about danger are more severe than ritual prohibitions.

The Bible speaks about ritual impurity, which is imparted to a person who has been in contact with the dead. Someone who was ritually impure was unable to participate in the Temple sacrificial service until undergoing ritual purification. In the rite, the ashes of a "Red Heifer" were mixed with water: "Some of the ashes from the fire of cleansing shall be taken for the unclean person, and fresh water shall be added to them in a vessel. A person who is clean shall take hyssop, dip it in the water, and sprinkle on the tent and on all the vessels and people who were there, or on him who touched the bones or the person who was killed or died naturally or the grave. The clean person shall sprinkle it upon the unclean person on the third day and on the seventh day, thus cleansing him by the seventh day." (Numbers 19:17–19) •

CONTEXT

The Talmud is discussing what happens if there is suspicion that the water to be mixed with the ashes of the Red Heifer for the purification ritual may have been tampered with in some way. In the first case, a jar of the water was left uncovered and open, but it was later found closed, the lid having been put on it. It is clear that an animal could not have done this; it could have been done only by a person. If that person was himself ritually impure, he will have rendered the water ritually impure as well. The water may then not be used in the purification ritual. Since we do not know who did this or their status, we have to assume that it might have been done by someone ritually impure, and therefore we may not use the water.

In the second case, a jar previously left covered is now found with the lid off. If there is a possibility that a weasel or a snake knocked off the lid and drank from the water, or if dew might have fallen into the open jar, we consider the water *pasul,* invalid for use in the ritual. (Invalid is different from *tameh,* impure. While invalid is considered ritually impure, it cannot convey ritual impurity to something else, like something *tameh* can.) In general, animals drinking from a jar would not render the water impure because they suck up the liquid. Weasels are different; they lap the water and therefore their saliva will drip back into the jar. Rabban Gamliel includes snakes because they spew back what they drink. Any other liquid, including dew, that comes into the jar will render the standing water as ritually invalid.

Since in this case there are three possibilities of how the lid came off (a pure person took it off, an impure person took it off, or a reptile knocked it loose) and, in two of these three, the water remains pure, the Rabbis decided to "follow the majority" (two possibilities that it is pure as against one possibility that it is impure) and declared that the water was pure. In the third case, the jar is found exactly as it was left. Consequently, it is neither impure nor invalid.

The Gemara concludes by adding that in a situation where we suspect that the water may have been tampered with or has been poisoned (for example by a venomous insect or animal), the water is considered *asur,* forbidden, a category much more restrictive than either *tameh,* impure or *pasul,* invalid.

D'RASH

Jason and Jessica were driving to the beach for a day of sunning and swimming. Along the way, Jessica kept a sharp eye on the speedometer. Every time that the needle went above 55, she would let Jason know that he was speeding and that he had better ease up on the gas pedal. "What's the problem?" he asked. "The roads are empty . . . I'm not putting us in any danger by driving at 60!" Jessica was not impressed by the argument. "I don't care! It's against the law to drive over 55, so don't do it! I don't want us to get stopped by the police. Slow down!"

When they arrived at the beach, Jason noticed that the lifeguard stations were empty. Signs were posted everywhere: "Danger! No lifeguard on duty. Swim at your own risk." Jason was very nervous about going into the water. "Don't be a scaredy-cat" Jessica yelled. "Come on in! The water's fine!" "But there's no lifeguard," Jason answered. "And there are all those danger signs! I don't think we should swim today." Jessica shook her head: "We're not breaking any law. . . . We'll be fine. Let's swim!"

Many people make the same mistake as Jessica. They think that because something is not illegal, it must be safe. The truth is that there are many things which are legal but still dangerous. Smoking cigarettes may be the most common example in our society today.

We all know that it is important to heed the warnings that various authorities give us; they can literally save our lives. But we also need to learn that while others may look out for our welfare much of the time, there are countless situations each and every day when we are left on our own. At these instances, we have to depend not upon someone else to protect us but upon our own good common sense.

אֶפְשָׁר לִשְׁנֵי מְלָכִים
לְהִשְׁתַּמֵּשׁ בְּכֶתֶר אֶחָד

Is it possible for two kings to share one crown?

TEXT

Ḥullin 60b

Rabbi Shimon ben Pazi contrasted two verses. It is written: "God made the two great lights. . ." [Genesis 1:16] and it is written: ". . . the greater light [to dominate the day] and the lesser light [to dominate the night]. . ." [ibid]. The moon said to the Holy One, blessed be He: "Master of the World! Is it possible for two kings to share one crown?" He said to her: "Go, and make yourself smaller!" She said to Him: "Master of the World! Just because I said to You the correct thing, I have to make myself smaller?" He said to her: "Go, and rule over the day and the night." She said to Him: "What is so special about a lamp in the daylight? What purpose does it serve?" He said to her: "Go, Israel will calculate by you the days and the years." She said to Him: "But they cannot calculate the seasons without the sun, as it is written: 'They shall serve as signs for the set times—the days and the years' [Genesis 1:14]." "Go, the righteous shall be called by your name: Jacob ha-Katan [the lesser], Shmuel ha-Katan, David ha-Katan." When He saw that this did not console her, the Holy One, blessed be He said: "Bring a sacrifice of atonement for Me, for having made the moon smaller," and this is as Rabbi Shimon ben Lakish said: "What is different about the he-goat brought on Rosh Ḥodesh? As it says concerning it: '[And there shall be one goat as a sin offering] for the Lord' [Numbers 28:15, author's translation]. The Holy One, blessed be He said: 'This goat will be atonement for My having made the moon smaller.'"

"O Lord God, pray forgive. How will Jacob survive? He is so small." (Amos 7:2) •

"The three oldest sons of Jesse had left and gone with Saul to the war. The names of his three sons who had gone to war were Eliab the first-born, the next Abinadab, and the third Shammah; and David was the youngest [smallest]." (I Samuel 17:13–14) •

Shmuel ha-Katan was a leader and teacher in first century Israel. He was asked by Rabban Gamliel of Yavneh to compose a special prayer against the minim, *the sectarians, and this paragraph became a standard part of the* Amidah. *According to one interpretation, he was known as ha-Katan because he was so humble, lessening his own importance.* •

CONTEXT

Rabbi Shimon ben Pazi is intrigued by the fact that the sun and moon are first described by the Torah as equals ("the two great lights"), but are then characterized as a "greater" and a "lesser." This change is explained by a legend. Originally, the sun and moon *were* of equal size but after the moon complained that "two kings cannot share one crown," God reduced the moon in size. In other versions of this Midrash, the moon was punished for the sin of pride; here there is no logical reason why God should have made the moon smaller.

In trying to console the moon, God tells her that the title *ha-Katan* ("the lesser") is actually one of honor. Two great biblical figures, Jacob and David, and a great rabbinic personality, Shmuel, are all referred to by this same title.

The end of this piece pictures God deeply distressed over having made the moon smaller. To atone for this, God asks that a sacrifice be brought for this "sin" (!) on Rosh Ḥodesh (the festival of the New Month, which is marked by the virtual disappearance of the moon from the heavens). This incredible notion, that God committed a sin, comes from a clever reading of a Hebrew word in the list of sacrifices to be brought on the holidays. On Rosh Ḥodesh, the sacrifice is to be brought "*la'donai.*" This can be read either as "*to* the Lord" (obviously, the intended meaning) or "*for* the Lord" (as Rabbi Shimon ben Lakish suggests). The latter reading implies that God must have done something wrong that required the bringing of an offering to atone for a mistake.

D'RASH

The president of the United States is wounded by an assassin's bullet. He is rushed to a hospital where doctors work frantically to save his life. The vice president, in the meantime, is on board Air Force Two, thousands of miles away. The president's chief of staff rushes into the White House press room and informs the country: "I'm in charge here . . ." Fortunately, the president recovers, the vice president returns to Washington, and the chief of staff continues his normal duties. But for several hours, there is total confusion. What if there were a world crisis that required an immediate decision? Who was empowered to make those critical choices? Who was really in charge? In every bureaucracy, there has to be a decision-making process, and there must be, ultimately, one person who has the final responsibility. Two kings cannot share one crown because the people need to know who is in charge, whom to obey, and whom to listen to.

What is true of kings of flesh and blood is also true of Heavenly Kings: In the Midrash, the Rabbis often use the figure of a king as a metaphor for God. By telling us that two kings cannot share one crown, perhaps they were also attacking the philosophy of Dualism that was prevalent in the ancient world. Dualism held that there were two great equal forces in the universe, the power of light, or goodness, and the power of darkness, or evil. These two opposing forces were constantly at war with one another. Consequently, the adherents of Dualism believed that conflict was at the heart of all existence and were never quite sure which power to turn to for help. The Rabbis rejected this notion. They believed that there was but one God, one King to wear the crown, one authority to go to with our prayers. This meant that unity, not divisiveness, was the central principle of existence. It also meant that there was hope of bringing all peoples together as one. God may have sinned, according to Rabbi Shimon ben Lakish, by being too quick to make sure that two kings didn't share one crown. However, we can understand God's concerns—both here on earth as well as in Heaven; there is just too much at stake.

הָלְכָה חֲמוֹרְךָ טַרְפוֹן There goes your donkey, Tarfon!

TEXT

Bekhorot 28b

> Mishnah (4:4): *It once happened that a cow had its womb removed, and Rabbi Tarfon fed it [the cow] to the dogs. The incident came before the Sages in Yavneh and they permitted it. Todos the physician said: "No cow or pig leaves Alexandria without their cutting out its womb so that it will not give birth." Rabbi Tarfon said: "There goes your donkey, Tarfon!" Rabbi Akiva said to him: "Rabbi Tarfon, you are a court expert, and every court expert is exempt from repayment."*
> Gemara: *Let him [Rabbi Akiva] derive it from the fact that he had erred in a matter of Mishnah, and an error in a matter of Mishnah can be retracted! He [Rabbi Akiva] gave a first reason and then a second: First, an error in a matter of Mishnah can be retracted, and second, even if your mistake was in a case of opposing views, you are a court expert, and every court expert is exempt from repayment.*

CONTEXT

A cow that was born without a womb would be *treif*, literally "torn," that is, ritually unfit and not allowed for consumption by Jews. Thus, when Rabbi Tarfon determined that this particular cow was *treif* because it had no womb, he fed it to dogs, in fulfillment of the admonition in Exodus (22:30): "You must not eat flesh torn *[treifah]* by beasts in the field; you shall cast it to the dogs." However, when this case was brought before the Rabbis in Yavneh, the seat of learning at the time, it became clear that Rabbi Tarfon had erred. This was not an instance where a cow had been born without a womb and was therefore defective, but rather one in which the cow's womb had been surgically removed. This was probably done because Alexandrian animals were highly regarded; removal of the womb would prevent breeding of these cattle elsewhere and would keep the monopoly on this prized breed in Alexandria.

When Rabbi Tarfon realized what he had done, he exclaimed: "There goes your donkey, Tarfon!" As Rashi explains this idiom, Rabbi Tarfon thought that he would have to sell his donkey in order to pay for the damage he had caused the owner of the cow by rendering an incorrect decision. We know that people often speak of themselves or to themselves in the third person, especially in anger or surprise.

Rabbi Tarfon was a great tanna, *a teacher from the time of the Mishnah. The Talmud relates that Rabbi Tarfon was a man of great wealth and kindly character. Upon scaring off a thief eating from his vineyard, Tarfon was distressed that he had used his rabbinic title, thus diminishing the Torah. Rabbi Abahu, in the name of Rabbi Ḥananiah ben Gamliel, commenting on this incident, said: "All his life, that righteous man [Rabbi Tarfon] was saddened over this incident!"*

Elsewhere, the generous character of Rabbi Tarfon is illustrated with a story of his saving three hundred poor women by marrying each of them. (Polygamy was still permitted in talmudic times.) This occurred during a drought, when these women otherwise might have starved to death. By marrying Tarfon, who was a kohen, *they would be allowed to eat from* terumah, *the portion of grain harvest brought to the* kohanim *in the Temple. Thus, while it may be surprising that this scholar made such an error in judgment concerning the cow, it is not surprising—*

given the many stories of his generosity and kindness that appear in the Talmud—that Rabbi Tarfon felt that, as both a judge and a man of considerable means, he should repay the cow's owner for his error in judgment. •

Rabbi Tarfon is no different. His words are similar to the English-language phrase "You've cooked your own goose."

The Mishnah ends with Rabbi Akiva reminding Rabbi Tarfon that he, as a recognized expert in legal matters, is under a court exemption and will not have to repay. The Gemara then asks why Rabbi Akiva uses this line of reasoning, since there is another teaching that would just as easily exempt Rabbi Tarfon: He had erred in a matter of Mishnah, and an error in a matter of Mishnah can simply be retracted! The answer from the Gemara is: He, Rabbi Akiva, really gave *two* reasons why Rabbi Tarfon is exempt: first (not recorded in our Mishnah), a Mishnah mistake can be retracted, and second (recorded in our Mishnah), even if he did render a wrong decision, he is not required, as a court expert, to make amends.

D'RASH

A number of years ago, a well-known college football coach told the story of receiving three envelopes when he started his tenure. They were from his predecessor, given to the new coach with a note: "When things get bad, open the first envelope. When things get worse, open the second envelope. When things get really awful, open the third envelope." The new coach and his team struggled during the first season, hardly able to put any points on the scoreboard. He opened the first envelope and found a note inside: "Blame the players." In the off-season, he spoke about how the players were not motivated enough and how they lacked the necessary discipline to become winners. The second season, the team continued to lose, and as the season drew to a close, the coach opened the second envelope. In it was a note that read: "Blame the alumni." And the coach spoke about how critical the alumni had been of the college's football program, how the school could have a winning record with everyone behind the team. The third season was not much better, and as the team wrapped up another losing season, the coach opened the third and final envelope. In it were these words: "Prepare three envelopes."

This story points to the reality that responsibility means something more than words which, as we know, can be cheap. In saying "There goes your donkey," Rabbi Tarfon is acknowledging this fact. Admitting that we are wrong, apologizing to the person we have hurt, and feeling a sense of remorse are steps taken to begin the appeasement process. However, there are times when "I'm sorry" is not enough, where one must make amends as well.

We are pleased when the president of the United States admits: "I take full responsibility for this mistake." In the end, though, his words fall short of what we are looking for. The apology does not cost him anything except, perhaps, face. Nonetheless, in our day and age, taking a fall and admitting wrongdoing and responsibility have not only become widespread but even are seen by some as a sign of strength and maturity. Rabbi Tarfon and Rabbi Akiva are saying that words by themselves are not enough. This attitude toward responsibility helps not only the injured party, but also the one who did the injury, Rabbi Tarfon himself, for he will never feel as if he fully made amends until he does something to help the one he hurt.

If we hurt someone and cause a loss, shouldn't we both apologize *and* compensate them for their loss? At times, we let others—the community, friends, an insurance company—take care of the compensation. Rabbi Tarfon is saying that we, the offending individuals, must involve ourselves in the restitution process, for with every privilege comes responsibility. We should not exempt ourselves from it or leave it to others.

Centuries later, Thomas Paine wrote: "What we obtain too cheaply, we esteem too lightly." Rabbi Tarfon would certainly agree and would add: "In a situation where words are cheap, or just less than adequate, deeds must be added to them."

לְשׁוֹן תְּלִיתָאי קָטֵל תְּלִיתָאי The third tongue kills three.

TEXT

Arakhin 15b

The school of Rabbi Yishmael taught: "Anyone who gossips is considered as having committed the grave sins of Idolatry, Sexual Immorality, and Murder. It is written here: 'Every tongue that speaks arrogance [gedolot]*' [Psalms 12:4], and concerning Idolatry it is written: 'Alas, this people is guilty of a great* [gedolah] *sin' [Exodus 32:31]. Concerning Sexual Immorality it is written: 'How then could I do this most* [gedolah] *wicked thing?' [Genesis 39:9], and concerning Murder it is written: 'My punishment is too great* [gadol] *to bear' [Genesis 4:13]. You could say* gedolot *[in Psalms 12:4] refers to two [sins]! Which one [of the three] would you then eliminate?" In the west they say: "The third tongue kills three." It kills the one who tells, the one who hears, and the one they talk about."*

Men speak lies to one another; their speech is smooth; they talk with duplicity. May the Lord cut off all flattering lips, every tongue that speaks arrogance. (Psalms 12:3–4) •

Idolatry:
The Lord spoke to Moses, "Hurry down, for your people, whom you brought out of the land of Egypt, have acted basely. They have been quick to turn aside from the way that I enjoined upon them. They have made themselves a molten calf and bowed low to it and sacrificed to it, saying: 'This is your god, O Israel, who brought you out of the land of Egypt!'" (Exodus 32:7–8) •

Sexual Immorality:
After a time, his master's wife cast her eyes upon Joseph and said, "Lie with me." But he refused. (Genesis 39:7, 8) •

Murder:
. . . and when they were in the field, Cain set upon his brother Abel and killed him. (Genesis 4:8) •

CONTEXT

Our section discusses the sin of *leshon ha-ra,* literally "evil speech," otherwise known as gossip. Many people do not even consider gossip as a sin, let alone a serious one. The Rabbis take a very different view. They equate gossip with three sins that are traditionally considered the most grievous: Idolatry (in Hebrew "worshiping stars"), Sexual Immorality ("uncovering nakedness") and Murder ("spilling blood").

The Rabbis arrive at their teaching of the power of language through a careful analysis of the language used in the Bible. The Rabbis were very sensitive to words and how and where they were used. The repetition of the same word in different places was seen as a hint that the separate sections were in some way related. This is the basis for the Rabbis' startling claim that gossip is on the par with Idolatry, Sexual Immorality, and Murder. They observed that the word "great" appears in a verse in the Psalms (12:4) that discusses sins of speech, and is also found in the verses that speak about the three most serious sins. The example of Idolatry is the story of the Israelites' worshiping the Golden Calf. Sexual Immorality is seen in the attempt of Potiphar's wife to seduce Joseph. Murder is in the tale of Cain and Abel.

The Rabbis note that the word in Psalms, referring to gossip, is in the plural, *gedolot.* Usually, an unspecified plural is understood by the Rabbis to imply *two.* Thus, "every tongue that speaks arrogance *[gedolot]*" equates gossip with *two* capital crimes. This interpretation undermines the Gemara's notion that the sin of gossip is equal to *three* sins. The Talmud responds to the arithmetic objection by asking "which of the three would you drop?" In other words, the Rabbis say, we prefer to ignore the usual methodological approach in order to focus instead on the content of the message.

This teaching is a serious one: Gossip can destroy three lives. Many would interpret this literally: The person gossiped about may attack the person who defamed him. Both may die in the violence that ensues, and their relatives may then seek vengeance against the person who initiated the slander.

D'RASH

Children often respond to a taunt with the rejoinder: "Sticks and stones may break my bones, but names will never hurt me." The Rabbis disagree. Names *can* hurt us, much more deeply than sticks and stones can. Words have incredible power. They can heal, or they can destroy. "Death and life are in the power of the tongue" (Proverbs 18:21).

The saying from the west, "The third tongue kills three," reminds us of a very important ethical principle: Our actions have far-reaching effects. Simple words can destroy a reputation or a life.

A group of high school students sit around complaining about their teacher who has given them low grades on a final. They make fun of his manner of talking and even of the way he walks. Someone suggests that maybe he is a homosexual. Another student speculates that he became a teacher because he likes young boys. A third wonders out loud if perhaps the teacher has molested some students in the past. Idle talk born out of resentment and anger. The next day, the "theory" is flippantly repeated throughout the halls of the school. Within a week, the "scandal" has caused the teacher to be fired and then arrested. Even if the teacher is cleared of all charges, the rumors may follow him around for the rest of his life.

We can understand how gossip can destroy the victim of the lies; we can even see that the purveyors of the gossip are hurt, legally or otherwise, by the things that they say. But rabbinic belief that the third party, the listener, is also destroyed is rather surprising. The Talmud seems to be suggesting that, in this matter, there is no such thing as an innocent bystander. Listening quietly as another person is "trashed" demeans us. It means that we stood by and did nothing to defend them. By not chastising and silencing the gossiper, we become enablers. We give our tacit approval, and thus encourage the gossiper to continue. It is the people who sit back and do nothing who are ultimately responsible for allowing evil to be committed. The Rabbis teach us that saying "But I did nothing!" is no excuse. It is an admission of guilt of another kind.

סִמָּנָא מִלְּתָא הִיא

Omens are significant.

TEXT

Keritot 5b-6a

Our Rabbis taught: "Kings are anointed only near a spring, so that their rule shall endure, as it says: 'Then King David said . . . bring him down to Gihon . . . [and] anoint him there . . .' [I Kings 1:32-34]." Rav Ammi said: "A person who wants to know if he will survive the year or not should bring a torch during the ten days between Rosh Hashanah and Yom Kippur and hang it in a house where the wind does not blow; if the torch burns itself out, he knows that he will survive the year. A person who is about to engage in business and wants to know if he will succeed or not should get a rooster; if it grows fat and attractive, he knows that it will succeed. A person who wants to go on a trip and wants to know if he will return to his home should go up to a dark room; if he sees the shadow of his shadow, he knows that he will come back home. But he should not do these things lest he be frightened and his luck turn bad." Abaye said: "Since we have said that omens are significant, a person should make it a custom on Rosh Hashanah to eat gourds, fenugreeks, leeks, beets and dates."

Then King David said, "Summon to me the priest Zadok, the prophet Nathan, and Benaiah son of Jehoiada." When they came before the king, the king said to them, "Take my loyal soldiers, and have my son Solomon ride on my mule and bring him down to Gihon. Let the priest Zadok and the prophet Nathan anoint him there king over Israel, whereupon you shall sound the horn and shout, 'Long live King Solomon!' Then march up after him, and let him come in and sit on my throne. For he shall succeed me as king; him I designate to be ruler of Israel and Judah." (I Kings 1:32–35) •

CONTEXT

The anointing of the king was to take place by the Giḥon spring for symbolic reasons: "May the King rule as long as the spring flows!" Rav Ammi brings three other cases where "signs" were said to be significant in predicting the future: Fire was seen as a symbol of life, and the days between Rosh Hashanah and Yom Kippur were when God decided who would live and who would die; the rooster was a symbol of sexuality and aggressiveness and thus the ability to sustain oneself; a shadow represented a person's essence, and seeing it (or not) was a sign if that person would survive.

Abaye adds that since symbolic signs are considered meaningful, it is the custom to eat certain foods on Rosh Hashanah. Today, we are familiar with the custom of dipping an apple into honey as a way of asking for a sweet year. Here, five other foods are mentioned because their names bring to mind sweetness and abundance or the destruction of our enemies. Gourds are *kara* which calls to mind the word *kera,* "torn": We pray that all evil decrees against us be torn up. Fenugreeks are *ruvia,* reminding us of the blessing *p'ru u'rvu,*

"Be fruitful and multiply." Leeks are *karti,* which sounds like *karet,* "cut off": May all those who hate us be cut off! Beets are *silka,* similar to the Aramaic word for "end" and the basis for a pun on *yistalku:* May God bring an end to our enemies! A date is *tamar* and evokes the word *y'tamu:* May there be a "finish" to those who hate us!

D'RASH

A woman walks out of her house early in the morning, on her way to work. She's thinking about all the things she has to do and wonders if this will be a good day or a bad one. Suddenly her eye catches a shiny spot by the curb; something is gleaming in the sunlight. She goes over to examine it and finds a penny. She smiles as she stoops down to get it, saying to herself, "Find a penny, pick it up, all the day, you'll have good luck!" The day, by the way, turns out to be an incredible one for the young woman: She finishes a major project she has been working on; the boss compliments her on her work; and at lunch she literally bumps into a handsome young man who asks her to the movies on Saturday night.

Two weeks later, as she leaves her home once again in the morning, a black cat ominously darts across her path. Her eyes widen in horror, and deep down she wishes she could just go back home and crawl into bed. She knows that bad things will happen today. A few hours later, at work, she slips down the steps and, trying to brace herself, fractures her wrist.

Are there really such things as omens? Rav Ammi seems to believe that "omens are significant," that they can indeed be indicators of what the future holds. He also adds that we should not use these tests. It's not that they are not true; we should avoid them precisely because they *do* contain the truth. He is worried that if we get a "bad sign," it would weigh so heavily on us that we might bring the bad things upon ourselves.

The Rabbis believe very strongly in free will. They reject the notion that life is all predetermined. They teach that the individual has the power, to a great extent, to determine his or her own future. Yet they also understood human nature well enough to know that most prophecies are self-fulfilling. If we believe good things will happen, very often they do. If we expect bad to come, more often than not, it will. Perception is reality: The way we look at something is the way it is. We eat sweet foods on the first day of the New Year not because we are trying to manipulate fate; by doing so we adjust our own attitudes, beginning the new year on a positive, upbeat note. Sometimes, that is enough to make all the difference.

Some people seem to go through life with a black cloud hanging over their heads. Are these people really unlucky? Or is it possible that some people *believe* they are unlucky, and subconsciously go through life living out their self-image? On the other hand, people with cancer who focus on positive thoughts and deeply believe they will get well seem to do so at a higher rate than those who give up and believe they are doomed. Athletes who focus on images of success are often much more successful than those who worry about failure.

Omens can be significant, not so much in telling us what *will* be, but in helping us to focus on what *might* be.

אָדָם נֶאֱמָן עַל עַצְמוֹ
יוֹתֵר מִמֵּאָה אִישׁ

A man is believed about himself more than a hundred men.

TEXT

Keritot 11b, 12a

Mishnah (3:1): *If two say "He ate," and he says "I did not eat," Rabbi Meir makes him liable. Rabbi Meir said: "If two can bring him to death, which is harsh, can't two bring him to a sacrifice, which is mild?" They said to him: "If he wants, he can say: 'I did it on purpose'!"*
Gemara: *It was asked of them: What is the Rabbis' reasoning? Is it because a man is believed about himself more than a hundred men?*

The Tractate Keritot *deals with the thirty-six sins for which one receives* karet, *a punishment mentioned in the Bible for certain deliberate sins like eating leaven on Pesaḥ or eating prohibited fat of otherwise kosher animals.* Karet *means "cutting off," and it is often assumed that the punishment is a divine one, God's "cutting off" the sinner from the Israelite nation. Some interpret this to mean dying before one's time. This Mishnah is teaching not about a deliberate offense but, rather, where one* inadvertently *committed one of the thirty-six sins and is required to bring a sin offering.* •

CONTEXT

The question here is one of a sin offering that would have to be brought if someone inadvertently committed a certain transgression, for example, if he accidentally ate forbidden fat and only later realized it. But what if two witnesses say, "We saw you eating forbidden fat. We know that you would never eat forbidden fat *intentionally,* but we want you to know that you *accidentally* ate it and now must bring a sin offering"?

To this, the person answers, "I did not eat. I appreciate your concern, but I know that I did not eat any forbidden fat." What should a person do in such a case? And what should the Rabbis assume about such a person?

There are two viewpoints. Rabbi Meir believes that, in this instance, one is liable for a sacrifice. After all, two witnesses could testify against him that he committed murder, and even if he protested "I did not do it," he would be guilty of a capital crime nonetheless! How much more so should we believe two witnesses who testify against him in the case of an accidental, non-capital sin.

However, the Rabbis disagree. The accused man is putting himself at a disadvantage by saying that he did not eat. The accused can quickly end the discussion by simply admitting: "Yes, I did it—and on purpose!" In this case, the punishment would be shifted from an earthly one (a sin offering for accidental transgression of eating) to a punishment in the hands of Heaven (*karet* for an intentional sin). Since this man did not offer this excuse, and did not shift the punishment, we assume that he is telling the truth and that he did not eat any forbidden fat. Furthermore, as the Gemara explains, one possible reason we can add to the Rabbis' argument is that people know themselves best. Individuals would know if they ate forbidden fat, and one who claims not to have eaten any is believed.

D'RASH

"If you want to feel better, you should. . . ." "You'd enjoy the program better if you would. . . ." Every one of us has been in a situation where others give us advice: "*You* should do this. *You* should feel that." Those who counsel us usually do so with every good intention. However, they are on the outside looking in. They may *think* that they know how we feel, or what happened to us, or who we want to be close with, but in the end, each of these is a very personal, subjective decision.

"A man is believed about himself more than a hundred men" still applies today to medical care. When we enter a doctor's office for an examination, the physician will start by asking why we are there. If there is a specific complaint, the doctor will make note of it and will conduct the examination accordingly. A physician can tell us what causes our pain, what appears on the tests, and what treatments are available. Only *the patient* can tell the doctor what really hurts, when the ache started, and if the prescribed therapy is effective in relieving the symptoms. Medical practitioners are being trained more and more to consider the patient's mental state and emotional stability as well as the description of the illness and concerns about the healing process. Unfortunately, we periodically hear of a case where the patient's worries were ignored by a doctor, resulting in dire consequences.

Jewish law takes note of the personal perspective and how outsiders may not know what is best for us. "A man is believed about himself more than a hundred men" about whether to be permitted to eat on Yom Kippur. While the Torah prohibits eating on Yom Kippur and the Talmud elaborates on these rules, a sick person is allowed to eat on the advice of a physician. What if the doctor says that the illness is not that severe and the sick person can fast despite the illness, while that sick person insists on eating? Jewish law then returns the decision to the sick person, on the theory that "a man is believed about himself more than a hundred men." An outsider can comment on general medical implications of fasting, but they cannot tell us how difficult it is for *us* to fast. A third party can give a general comment about fasting on those who are ill but cannot fully comprehend the affects of fasting on *us*.

Especially when we're feeling down on ourselves, we are often willing to accept advice from others, even if it's not in our best interest. Others can know a lot about us, but ultimately we—each and every one of us individually—know our own selves best. This is not to say that we should reject all guidance from others. Rather, we have to sift through the advice and suggestions of others, to test if it is applicable to us, and to be strong enough to believe in ourselves even if a hundred others believe otherwise.

Rest Stop

The Israelites then marched on and encamped in the steppes of Moab, across the Jordan from Jericho. (Numbers 22:1)

Words of Torah are compared to water . . . as it says: "Ho, all who are thirsty, come for water" [Isaiah 55:1]. . . . And just as with water, a person who does not know how to swim will in the end drown, so too with Torah—a person who does not know how to swim in it and to learn from it will in the end drown. (*Song of Songs Rabbah* 1, 3)

When I started to study Talmud at the age of 10 or 11, I had to go to a teacher who was extremely poor and who lived in a one-room apartment with his two older daughters. When I came in he asked me, "Why do you have two hands?" I had never asked myself the question, and so it was a matter of "Why shouldn't I have two hands?" I said, "What is the answer?" He said, "With one hand you point into the text, and the other hand you put on the commentary. Once you do that you will never get lost. You know what the text means."

Well, of course, I considered this childish. I was already studying at the gymnasium. But later I really understood why we have two hands. With one hand we point to our tradition, the text, which accompanies us through the centuries; with the other hand, we have to look for the meaning. What does this text mean to us today? One hand is not enough. We need the other hand in order to explore what the text means. (Nahum N. Glatzer, "What I Have Learned," *Jewish Heritage* summer/fall 1993)

Seder Teharot

Introduction to Seder Teharot

The sixth and final Order of the Mishnah is *Teharot,* or "Clean Things." It details the very complex laws of ritual purity which were in effect during the period that the Temple stood. Of the twelve tractates in the Mishnah, only one contains Gemara. This tractate is *Niddah,* which discusses the rules of "family purity," that is, a woman's menstrual cycle and how it impacts on her ability to have intimate relations with her husband. Traditionally observant Jews continue to follow these laws to this day.

הַכֹּל בִּידֵי שָׁמַיִם
חוּץ מִיִּרְאַת שָׁמַיִם

Everything is in the hands of Heaven, except for the fear of Heaven.

TEXT

Niddah 16b

Rabbi Yoḥanan said: "It is forbidden for a man 'to use his bed' [to have sex] during the daytime." What is the verse [that proves this]? As it says: "Perish the day on which I was born, and the night it was announced, 'A male has been conceived" [Job 3:3]. Night was thus set aside for conception, but daytime was not set aside for conception. Resh Lakish said: "It [scriptural proof] comes from here: 'He who is heedless of his ways will die'" [Proverbs 19:16]. How does Resh Lakish interpret the verse cited by Rabbi Yoḥanan? He needs it in the same way that Rabbi Ḥanina bar Papa explained: "The angel in charge of conception is named 'Lailah' [night]. He takes a drop [of sperm] and places it before the Holy One, blessed be He, and says to Him: 'Master of the World! This drop: What will become of it? Strong or weak? Wise or stupid? Rich or poor?' But 'wicked or righteous' is not said, following Rabbi Ḥanina, for Rabbi Ḥanina said: 'Everything is in the hands of Heaven, except for the fear of Heaven, as it says: "And now, O Israel, what does the Lord your God demand of you? Only this: to revere the Lord your God"' [Deuteronomy 10:12]."

He who has regard for his life pays regard to commandments; he who is heedless of his ways will die. (Proverbs 19:16) ●

And now, O Israel, what does the Lord your God demand of you? Only this: to revere the Lord your God, to walk only in His paths, to love Him, and to serve the Lord your God with all your heart and soul, keeping the Lord's commandments and laws, which I enjoin upon you today, for your good. (Deuteronomy 10: 12-13)

Interestingly, these two quotations have four key roots or words in common, though in English translation they are rendered somewhat differently:

shomer/lishmor—*pays regard/keeping*

CONTEXT

The notion that sex was to take place at night—in the dark—may derive from the Jewish value of *tzni'ut* or modesty. While it may seem a rather puritanical idea to most of us, we need to remember that in pre-modern times, and certainly in antiquity, privacy was very rare. Many houses consisted simply of a cooking/eating area, and a living/sleeping area. Restricting sex to the night time was often the only way to make certain other people weren't able to watch a couple during intimacy.

Rabbi Yoḥanan and Resh Lakish both attempted to back up this teaching with the authority of a biblical verse. Rabbi Yoḥanan looks to the Book of Job, and places great emphasis on the fact that the verse connects conception to the night. A modern reader, of course, would probably see this connection merely as the author's poetic expression. To the Rabbis of the Talmud, however, every nuance of the text is there for a specific purpose, and the connection is read literally.

Resh Lakish agrees with Rabbi Yoḥanan's teaching, but disagrees with his choice of verses to prove it. Instead of Job, he looks to the Book of Proverbs. The key word he focuses on in the verses he chooses is "ways." Perhaps he connected this word (*derekh,* in Hebrew) with the same word, also found in Proverbs, that speaks of the intimate relationship between a man and a woman: "Three things are beyond me; four I cannot fathom: How an eagle makes its way over the sky; how a snake makes its way over a rock; how a ship makes its way through the high seas; how a man has his *way* with a maiden. Such is the *way* of an adulteress: She eats, wipes her mouth, and says, 'I have done no wrong'" (Proverbs 30:18–20, emphasis added). Being "heedless of his (or His, that is, God's) ways" (i.e., having sex during the daytime) can lead to death according to the verse and is thus proof that such behavior is to be avoided.

The Gemara then asks: If Resh Lakish uses Proverbs 19:16 to prove that sex is forbidden during the day, what does he say that Job 3:3 (Rabbi Yoḥanan's verse) comes to teach? The answer is that it tells us an angel named Lailah is present just prior to conception to question God about the future of the child to be born from the act of sexual union. This bit of folklore derives from reading the word *Lailah* not as a *common* noun (meaning night: ". . . the night it was announced: 'A male has been conceived'") but as a *proper* noun ("Lailah announced: 'A male has been conceived'").

Finally, the close reading of verses concludes with Rabbi Ḥanina interpreting Deuteronomy 10:12 to mean: Since only *one* thing was asked of Israel (that they revere God), the implication is that *that alone* is out of God's hands; everything else (whether a person is rich or poor, weak or strong, wise or stupid) *is* decided by God.

nafsho/nafshekha—
his life/your soul
mitzvah/mitzvot—
commandment/commandments
derakhov/derakhov—
his ways/his paths
Thus one verse comes to strengthen the themes of the other. We imagine that Resh Lakish, or the editors of the Gemara, were aware of these affinities when putting these texts together. •

D'RASH

During the Second World War, an Austrian psychiatrist, Dr. Viktor Frankl, was among those Jews arrested and sent to the Auschwitz concentration camp. During the three years of his incarceration, Frankl paid careful attention to how human beings reacted to the most horrid examples of "man's inhumanity to man" in modern history. His observations became the basis for his book *Man's Search for Meaning* and a new school of psychiatric thought, "logotherapy." Frankl wrote:

> *We who lived in concentration camps can remember the men who walked through the huts comforting others, giving away their last piece of bread. They may have been a few in number, but they offer sufficient proof that everything can be taken from a man but one thing: the last of the human freedoms—to choose one's attitude in any given set of circumstances, to choose one's own way. (p. 104)*

The Nazis could dictate and determine every single aspect of a person's life, except for one: how that person would *respond* to what the Nazis did.

The same lesson applies to a person who is the victim of a debilitating disease or of a terrible accident. Much may have been taken away from them: their mobility, their health, even their future. But one thing remains: *How* they will react to the terrible blow. Some people become bitter and spend their days striking out at everyone who tries to come near—doctors, friends, even loved ones. There are those who choose to pull away from others, withdrawing into a world of their own, overcome by sadness or self-pity. But there are also those who choose a different path: They decide to make the most out of every day that remains to them. Instead of obsessing on what they cannot do, they concentrate on what they *are* able to accomplish, and then go out and do it.

It's no different with the mundane or ridiculous problems that each and every one of us faces every single day. So much of what happens to us is out of our control. We are all, in one sense or another, victims of fate, circumstance, and bad luck. We cannot pick the cards that life deals us. But once dealt a mediocre, or even a terrible hand, there are still options and choices we have. We can give up and quit, or we can make the best of a less than perfect situation. As Victor Frankl came to see, the choice we make under such situations tells a great deal about character and inner strength.

Rabbi Ḥanina taught the very same lesson from a religious perspective: "Everything is in the hands of Heaven, except for the fear of Heaven." God determines everything, except for one thing: What we feel about God. We have been given the power to say "Yes" or "No" to God . . . and to life. All else can be taken from us and decided for us, but never that.

אֲפִלּוּ בַּעַל הַנֵּס
אֵינוֹ מַכִּיר בְּנִסּוֹ

Even the one who has a miracle happen to him does not recognize his own miracle!

TEXT

Niddah 31a

> *Rav Yosef expounded: What does this text mean: "I give thanks to You, O Lord! Although You were wroth with me, Your wrath turned back and You comfort me" [Isaiah 12:1]? What is the text speaking about? Two men who set out to trade. One of them got a thorn, and he started to revile and blaspheme. After a while, he heard that his friend's ship had sunk in the sea; he began to thank and praise. Therefore it is written: "Your wrath turned back and You comfort me." And this is what Rabbi Elazar said: "What does it mean: 'Who alone does wondrous things; blessed is His glorious name forever' [Psalms 72:18-19]? Even the one who has a miracle happen to him does not recognize his own miracle!"*

CONTEXT

This homiletical explanation comes in a series of expositions contrasting God and human beings. People have the ability to do certain things, while God, with infinite power, has the ability to outperform humans. Several examples are given, and our text is one of them.

The explanation by Rav Yosef starts with a person who is initially angered but subsequently becomes comforted. This proves the point that a person cannot see even one's own miracle. Rav Yosef uses a story of two traders to explain his approach. One trader is angered that he is prevented from traveling on the ship because of a thorn in his foot. However, he is actually the fortunate one: The friend's trip will continue with his taking the boat on an ill-fated voyage. The thorn in the foot turns out to be a fortuitous accident, saving the first man's life. This, says Rabbi Elazar, shows that one does not even recognize a miracle as it is happening.

Rabbi Elazar uses the verses from Psalm 72 to prove his point, though he quotes only the second half of the first verse and the first half of the second verse. The verses in their entirety read:

> Blessed is the Lord God, God of Israel,
> who alone does wondrous things;

Three times a day in the Amidah, *we acknowledge the miracles that God performs for us:*

> *We proclaim that You are the Lord our God and God of our ancestors throughout all time. You are the Rock of our lives, the Shield of our salvation in every generation. We thank You and praise You morning, noon and night for Your miracles which daily attend us and for Your wondrous kindness. Our lives are in Your hand; our souls are in Your charge. You are good, with everlasting mercy; You are compassionate, with enduring lovingkindness. We have always placed our hope in You. (Translation,* Siddur Sim Shalom*)* •

> Blessed is His glorious name forever;
> His glory fills the whole world.
> Amen and Amen.

If we read the first verse with the emphasis on *alone,* we understand better Rabbi Elazar's point: God *alone* does miracles. We cannot do them; we usually do not even see them. Often, what we think of as a bad turn of events is, in reality, an auspicious one. We human beings are left to thank God after the fact.

D'RASH

The words of Rav Yosef and Rabbi Elazar, cynical as they may sound, are nonetheless a good reminder not to let the amazing go unnoticed. How many wondrous things have we let slip by? How many events have we only later said, "Wow, that was a miracle!"? Yet, the exposition can also be seen as a more general reminder not to overlook the extraordinary and the positive in events as they are happening. Undoubtedly, each of us has been guilty of this at one time or another.

Imagine that we are driving down the street, trying to get somewhere in a hurry. We are running late, and then we get stuck at a corner while a man, slowly and meticulously, crosses the street. Our first reaction may be, "Why me? Why now? Why couldn't this slow-poke choose to cross somewhere else? I'm going to be late because he's taking forever!" Just as we are about to lose our cool, we see that this man is blind, and we begin to reevaluate the situation. Thank God, we have our eyesight. We are capable of driving here and there, even rushing around, even if we *are* a bit late at times. The situation really isn't as bad as we assumed it was a few minutes ago. In fact, on second thought, we are extraordinarily lucky just having the ability to see. In perspective, being late turns out to be a minor inconvenience.

Psychologist Martin E.P. Seligman, in his book *Learned Optimism,* asserts that people who are optimistic, who see the best in every situation, are ultimately more successful. Seligman proposes that we look at every situation critically, thinking of alternative ways of interpreting events. Does it have to be as negative as we initially thought? Is there only the one way of looking at it? Finding the optimistic and optimal way of construing situations is, according to Seligman, in our own best interest, leading to greater happiness and a fuller, richer life.

Centuries ago, Rav Yosef and Rabbi Elazar were trying to get us to look optimistically at the world and be thankful for what we have. They knew how difficult it is for us to appreciate the miracles around us. Their words remind us to acknowledge the many positives in life. We are required, by Jewish tradition, to thank God three times every day for "Your miracles which daily attend us." We begin to realize that our lives are really quite amazing and that we have a great deal for which to be thankful. We understand that the splitting of the sea was a monumental miracle long ago; however, there are miracles all around us every single day—the birth of a baby, the constant beating of our hearts, the daily renewal of nature, and even the ability to awaken and experience all of these. For some of us, this may be an acquired skill. For all of us, this appreciation makes life so much richer.

מִצְווֹת בְּטֵלוֹת לֶעָתִיד לָבֹא

Mitzvot will be annulled in the World-to-Come.

TEXT

Niddah 61b

You shall observe My laws. You shall not let your cattle mate with a different kind; you shall not sow your field with two kinds of seed; you shall not put on cloth from a mixture [kilayim] *of two kinds of material. (Leviticus 19:19)*

You shall not wear cloth combining wool and linen. (Deuteronomy 22:11) •

I am numbered with those who go down to the Pit;
I am a helpless man abandoned among the dead,
like bodies lying in the grave of whom You are mindful no more,
and who are cut off from Your care.
(Psalms 88:5–6) •

The Rabbis taught: "A garment in which kilayim *was lost should not be sold to an idolater or made into a saddle-cloth, but it can be made into a shroud for the dead." Rav Yosef said: "This proves that mitzvot will be annulled in the World-to-Come." Abaye (and some say Rav Dimi) said to him: "Didn't Rabbi Manni say in the name of Rabbi Yannai: 'This [that we can use* kilayim*] was taught only to lament him, but to bury him, it is prohibited'?!" He [Rav Yosef] said: "But wasn't it taught that Rabbi Yoḥanan said: 'Even to bury him'? And Rabbi Yoḥanan is consistent, for Rabbi Yoḥanan said: 'What does it mean when it is written: "free among the dead" [Psalms 88:6, author's translation]? As soon as he dies, a man becomes free from the mitzvot.'"*

CONTEXT

The Torah specifically prohibits certain mixtures called *kilayim*—different types of animals while plowing, different types of seeds while sowing a field, and wool and linen in cloth (called *sha'atnez* in Deuteronomy). This Gemara discusses the case of a garment that may have become prohibited by having both wool and linen in it. This piece of cloth is only possibly *kilayim,* since a thread of wool may have been woven into a linen garment—"lost"—or a thread of linen in a woolen garment. The thread cannot be found and removed from the cloth. The opening of this Gemara deals with the case of such a piece of cloth.

The Rabbis taught that it should not be sold to a non-Jew who, while not subject to the laws of *kilayim,* might nonetheless inadvertently sell that cloth back to a Jew. Neither should the cloth be made into a garment which, while not worn, will still be sat upon (a "saddle-cloth") and used by a Jew. However, the Rabbis teach it may be made into a shroud. From this, Rav Yosef deduces that the mitzvot are no longer incumbent on those who have died; its use as a shroud proves that the dead no longer have to observe the mitzvah of *kilayim* and, hence, all the mitzvot. However, Abaye (or Rav Dimi) argues that there is a tradition that teaches us that we can use *kilayim* only during the mourning process, but for the burial, we are prohibited from using this cloth. Rav Yosef answers this objection with another tradition from Rabbi Yoḥanan: He taught that this cloth with *kilayim* is allowed even to bury a person in. Rabbi Yoḥanan finds proof in a verse from Psalm 88. The psalmist uses the expression *ḥofshi* which can be translated as either "free/released" or "abandoned" ["among the dead"]. Rabbi Yoḥanan understands the verse to mean that the person among the dead is "freed" from the worries and responsibilities of this world, specifically the mitzvot.

D'RASH

In the Bible, references to the afterlife and the "World-to-Come" are few and far between. Even in Psalm 88, the section used by Rabbi Yoḥanan to prove his point, the psalmist cites "the Pit" and "Sheol" (the dark underworld) but does not describe it. This is in sharp contrast to the Talmud, where there are many references and complete descriptions of *olam ha-ba,* "the World-to-Come." The Rabbis foresaw a time in which the righteous would sit beneath God's throne, would dine luxuriously on the most sumptuous foods and would be privileged to study all the time.

Nonetheless, the Rabbis also knew that the emphasis of the Torah and of Jewish life is *this* world. The World-to-Come was described in detail, in part, to reflect an ideal. Everything they envisioned for the next world was a goal, a vision for this world, the world of reality. Thus, they constructed a system of practices and rites that would reflect some of the ideals of the next world in this one. If in the next world, material possessions would not be a worry, then in this world, they should not be our ultimate concern. What activity would be more worthwhile than study of Torah day and night? Therefore, they strove to combine the concern for worldly possessions and our daily needs with daily study of Torah. Few could exempt themselves from the struggle for sustenance; none could be exempted from daily study.

If the system worked to perfection, this world would become a reflection of the next world. If everyone observed the mitzvot, then strife and warfare would end. If nothing else, this world would be elevated and beautified. That the ideal could never be achieved was not a concern to the Rabbis. The ideal itself would become a paradigm for how a person should conduct everyday life. Ironically, if every person lived out all of these ideals—the mitzvot being a crystallization of God's vision of a perfect world—then there would no longer be a need for the mitzvot, for the next world would be achieved.

This irony was not lost on the Rabbis. They knew that we often strive to leave an inheritance (in Hebrew, *yerushah*) after we die, something tangible and physical that our children and grandchildren can possess, when we should really be working to leave a heritage (*morashah,* from the same Hebrew root), something that enriches life before we die. If our Sages were to look at our world today, they might tell us: "You may think that you can gain immortality through stock futures, annuities, and insurance policies. These are ephemeral—important, but fleeting. If you want to leave something that will live on forever, turn this world into a reflection of the next. Be concerned with something even greater than yourselves, something more lasting than tomorrow."

As we complete our study of Talmud texts, this remains our challenge.

PART

Select for Yourself a Teacher, Acquire for Yourself a Colleague

We can imagine what Akiva, the 40-year-old novice student, must have felt like, some eighteen centuries ago. We can visualize how, as Akiva began his first lesson, he must have felt overwhelmed! He may have said to himself: "I don't belong here. Maybe I made a terrible mistake. I don't know what any of this means, I *certainly* don't know how it applies to me!" It took a great deal of commitment for him to decide that study was important, just as it required tremendous courage to actually go and learn.

We can't know what Akiva's study began with, but we can imagine that Akiva's teacher anticipated his student's fears and chose a very special instruction for that day. Perhaps the lesson came from the words of Yehoshua ben Peraḥiah, two centuries earlier:

> *Select for yourself a* rav/*teacher;*
> *Acquire for yourself a* ḥaver/*colleague.* (Pirkei Avot *1:6)*

A wise yet caring teacher would have been concerned that Akiva have both a teacher and a friend; these two needs are very much our essentials as well.

The *rav* or rabbi is a teacher who explains the text to us. Often, a page of Talmud is incomprehensible without a rabbi, even if we understand all of the words. (How much more so when we do not understand the words, or when we read the work in translation!) Our focus is generally limited to the particular chapter or issue we are dealing with, while the teacher sees the totality of the Talmud and helps us understand broader concepts, ideas, and approaches as they apply to this text.

A teacher cites traditional interpretations, linking us with the Jewish past. Before we can bring our own interpretations and insights to the page, we should appreciate and understand the *traditional* Jewish readings of the Talmud text.

Only then can we disagree with them and, perhaps, even expand upon them.

For some of us, the need for a teacher may not be obvious. After all, we Americans are used to "rugged individualism," doing something on our own and without help. We live in a culture of "do-it-yourself" books and "self-actualization." Relying on others is often seen as a sign of weakness. Jewish tradition takes a radically different approach. We do not have to "go it alone." "Doing it yourself" may be unhealthy and may lead us to err in our interpretation of the text. We may find ourselves in totally over our heads, unable to comprehend.

In addition, some of us—especially those who are knowledgeable and used to instructing others—may find it difficult to rely on others. Letting a teacher guide us means admitting that while we may know a great deal about medicine, law, stocks, soybean futures, plumbing fixtures, or any other topic—there is still much that we do not know about the Talmud. It requires the ego strength to let others instruct us and a willingness to admit that even if we know a little, someone else knows a little more.

A mentor challenges us to see the text from another viewpoint. He or she questions whether our outlook is justified based on the material we are studying. Yet, this teacher knows not only text, but also *us.* The rabbi or *rav* understands that the challenge is not only to the subject taught, but also to a human being, a student with mind, habits, and personality. Thus, the teacher understands how far to push us—when we are being lazy and falling back on pat answers, and when we have stretched our minds to their limit and need time to assimilate the material. He or she knows how and when to criticize us, as well as how and when to encourage.

An effective teacher knows whether to respond to specific questions or to broader and more general issues. Our ideal teacher realizes that the student's question may have to deal solely with the text at hand; yet, the inquiry may reflect other concerns and necessitate answers that go far beyond this page of Talmud (though not beyond the purview of the Talmud as a whole). Hence, this teacher can put the subject-at-hand into a context, bringing the text to bear on all of life itself.

A rabbi helps us to grow—and to continue growing. Thus, even a teacher needs a *rav;* even one with knowledge requires his or her own guide for all the very same mentoring and growth reasons as the less knowledgeable student.

The Hebrew phrase *"Aseh lekha rav,"* "Select for yourself a teacher," could also be translated "*Make* for yourself a teacher." It is clear from the Hebrew that the teacher referred to is not found overnight or stumbled upon accidentally; he or she is *made*. The teacher may be the rabbi at the local synagogue, a Jewish studies professor at a nearby university, or a friend with a good traditional Jewish education. *Making* a teacher implies an ongoing process of give-and-take, as well as effort on behalf of the student. It is not only the teacher who must push the student; the student has to respectfully challenge the *rav*. Hopefully, this will result in a warm, lasting and developing relationship.

The second half of the equation is *K'neh lekha ḥaver,* or "acquire a colleague for yourself." The word *ḥaver/ḥavera,* a friend, colleague, or study partner, comes from a Hebrew root meaning "joined together." With a friend, there is a coming together of concerns for each other and a joining together of each other's strengths. This is why traditional Jewish study is often in *ḥavruta* (from the same root), a pair of students learning together. *Ḥavruta* provides for give-and-take with a peer. While a student cannot give that much to a teacher, one peer can give tremendously to another. They can also receive from each other on a social, as well as an intellectual, level.

In a *ḥavruta,* one *ḥaver* will see the other outside the formal boundaries of classroom study. The concerns of a *ḥaver* will thus extend beyond the fixed curriculum to all of life itself. One traditional source asks: "Why do we need a *ḥaver?*" The answer is: "He is the one who corrects your halakhah" (*Avot derabbi Natan* 8). Many understand the word from the root *halakh,* meaning "walk" or "go," and referring not only to Jewish law but also a person's practice or actions. There are certain necessary criticisms and suggestions that are embarrassing when coming from a teacher, but more tolerable when coming from a peer. The *ḥaver,* being an equal, shares similar experiences and similar feelings. Each partner in a study group or *ḥavruta* brings his or her own strengths and personal perspectives. Each challenges the other with a fresh outlook and a different approach. Thus, it is considered healthy to study with a colleague. A *ḥaver* assures us that we will be in touch with other Jews, both for a sense of community and for a periodic "reality check." In a famous talmudic story, Ḥoni ha-Me'agel returns home after seventy years of sleep. To his chagrin, the new generation of Rabbis in the study house do not recognize him. Despondent, he prays for his own death. Rava comments: "This is why people say: 'Either companionship *[ḥavruta]* or death *[mituta]*'" (*Ta'anit* 23a). While this may be an exaggeration, it gives us a sense of the difficulty of trying to study alone.

Yehoshua ben Peraḥiah knew that we need both a *rav*/teacher and a *ḥaver*/colleague. Each provides something unique. The same places we found a *rav,* the synagogue or university or even closer to home among family or friends, may be the very areas we find a *ḥaver.* We may find a *ḥaver* in someone who is already a friend socially but not yet a study-partner. The *ḥaver* may be assigned to us by a teacher, or we may search out another person, unknown to us, who is simply looking for a partner to study with. Just as the relationships with teachers are made over time, colleagues become joined together through prolonged sharing. The Rabbis knew that study is difficult and that the tools for learning take both time and effort. Just as a "swimming buddy" can keep an eye on us and help us when we find ourselves in over our heads, so too a *ḥaver* can assist us when things get particularly difficult in the sea of Talmud.

Occasionally, a book may have to substitute for a *rav* until a personal teacher can be found. A group may study together for a period of time while searching for a compatible mentor. Similarly, one may have to study alone with a teacher until a *ḥaver* can be found. Hopefully, while we learn, we also become more fluent in the methods of Jewish study, how and where to continue learning. We may find out that even with a weaker background, we have a great deal to offer others and to contribute to the material being studied. This reflects the sentiments of another talmudic sage, Rabbi Ḥanina, who remarked: "I have learned a great deal from my teachers, more from my colleagues than from my teachers, and even more than all from my students" (*Ta'anit* 7a). In other words, he learned more from his students than from anyone else. Each individual is unique and has his or her own insight and something of value to contribute.

Having entered the sea of Talmud, we may still feel a bit frightened or overwhelmed. One way to overcome these feelings is with a *ḥaver*/friend or a *rav*/instructor. This will undoubtedly make entering the sea easier. Hopefully, this book will have served as a *rav* and *ḥaver* to you, smoothing your entry into the sea of Talmud.

EPILOGUE

TEXT

Menaḥot 29b

> *Rav Yehudah said in the name of Rav: "When Moses went up on high, he found the Holy One, blessed be He, attaching little crownlets to the letters [of the Torah]. He said: 'Master of the World! What is taking You so long?'*

Moses was (like many of us) impatient when it came to wanting to acquire the Torah (and to learn the Oral Traditions of the Torah, the Talmud). He couldn't understand the delay. He wanted it *now*, not later. He (like many of us) thought that desire alone was all that was necessary.

But Moses, and we ourselves, have come to understand the complexity and the depth of Torah and Talmud. We have learned, with Akiva, that water *can* bore a hole in solid rock, but only after quite some time and only by being determined and persistent.

> *He [God] said to him: 'In the future, at the end of many generations, there will be a man, Akiva ben Yosef is his name. One day he will come and teach mountains of laws from each of these little crownlets.'*

There is an old saying: "God is in the details." Here, in an interesting twist on that idea, we see *God* focusing great attention on the most minute details of the Torah—the tiny decorative marks that always appear on the tops of seven Hebrew letters. Because of their shape and position, they are called "crownlets." (They are also known as "jots and tittles.")

Moses, at first, could not fathom that there was any significance to these seemingly insignificant scribbles. God here explains to him that what initially appears to be of little importance will actually be the basis for "mountains of laws." Even in the crownlets there is much to learn.

One of the things that exasperates the newcomer about the Talmud is the endless concern with minutiae. We often wonder: "How could such great thinkers and teachers constantly get bogged down in such small details and concerns?" Hopefully, we have come to understand that in discussing the specific, the Rabbis were really dealing with the general; while focusing on the particular, they were ultimately looking at the universal.

Moses and Akiva were similar in many ways: Both were shepherds; both had their lives changed after coming upon a phenomenon in nature (a burning bush, a hole cut into a rock by dripping water); both went on to become great teachers of Torah to their people. Yet what Moses initially saw as a waste of time, Akiva found to be the fertile source of incredible inspiration. How do we account for this difference?

Much of it has to do with knowing what to look for. When we approach the Talmud from a western, logical framework, we are puzzled, lost, or turned off. But when we view the Mishnah and the Gemara in the context of the world they came from, we begin to understand things differently. Hopefully, seeing that God spends time on the crownlets, we learn that this is a worthy and an important thing to do.

He [Moses] said to Him: 'Master of the World! Show him to me!' He [God] said: 'Turn around, behind you!' He [Moses] went and sat at the back of the eighth row.

Jewish learning does not take place merely in the here and now; it crosses all boundaries of time and space. God teaches Moses that in order to truly understand Torah, one has to look to the past, as well as see into the future. We cannot study the Talmud as outside observers reading ancient history. Instead, we must become the colleagues and disciples of the Rabbis mentioned on the pages, learning not just about them, not even *from* them, but rather *with* them!

The Talmud often reports a teaching in the present tense: "Rabbi Akiva says" (not "said"). Some might explain this merely as a quote from a contemporary source. But there is a deeper way to understand this phrase. In a real sense, Rabbi Akiva is still alive, and he is talking and teaching *now.* We go back into the past and sit on a bench in his study house, learning at his feet as he lectures to us. Or Rabbi Akiva, like Moses, moves forward in time, dwelling with us, today, counseling us how to apply the ancient teachings to our time and place.

He could not understand a thing they were saying and became very despondent.

What an irony: Moses, the Lawgiver, *Mosheh Rabbenu* (Moses our Rabbi), not able to understand anything that was being discussed in Rabbi Akiva's class! The additional irony is that we can recall the time when *Akiva* knew next to nothing and had to begin his education as a forty-year-old man sitting in with the kindergarten children, learning the alphabet.

Akiva and Moses both went through experiences of being totally overwhelmed, of feeling out of place, of wanting to quit and forget about the whole idea of learning. Yet both overcame these feelings of inadequacy, rising to become, respectively, the greatest biblical and talmudic figures. There is a message of comfort here for us: No matter how overwhelmed we may occasionally feel by the sea of Talmud, we should remember we are in good company. And we must also recall that if those before us struggled and achieved, we can do so as well.

When they reached a particular matter, his [Akiva's] student said to him: 'Rabbi, where do you know it from?' He said to them: 'It is a law that goes back to Moses at Sinai,' and he [Moses] was comforted.

In studying Talmud, there are moments when we are lost and overwhelmed and may feel very depressed; there are also great moments of exhilaration when we achieve significant breakthroughs and enlightenment. Sooner or later, like Moses, we all hear our names called: Because the Talmud is so deep, because it encompasses virtually every aspect of life experience, eventually each of us will find that there is a realm that we recognize, an area that speaks to our own individual circumstances. Mysteriously, that moment often comes just when we least expect it, and precisely when we need it the most. Part of the secret of Talmud study is sticking with it long enough. Another part of the secret is learning how to listen for our name—recognizing our own story in the pages of the Talmud.

He returned and came before the Holy One, blessed be He. He said to Him: 'Master of the World! You have such a man, and you gave the Torah through me?'

To be a Jew is to question God. From Abraham, who argued with God over the morality of destroying Sodom and Gomorrah, to Moses, who here challenges God's choice of lawgiver, it has always been our right (and even responsibility!) to stand up to God and ask "Why?" or say

"No!" That reverent irreverence is found on every single page of the Talmud. Everything and everyone—including God—is questioned. Every position offered is challenged and taken apart. Nothing is taken for granted, nothing is assumed, nothing is accepted unless it passes rigorous tests. Intellectual integrity is prized above almost everything else. We are never afraid of asking a question, because that is the only sure way to get an answer.

He [God] said to him: 'Silence! This is how I planned it to be. . .'"

Humility is a crucial requirement for a student of Talmud: Recognizing our own limitations, understanding that, alone, we cannot become masters of the text. No matter how wise we may be in other readings, we still need guidance and help in order to swim in *this* sea. Paradoxically, it is Moses' recognition of his unworthiness that makes him truly worthy of passing on the Torah. As always, God has the last word in all arguments: Moses may be right, but God has chosen him nevertheless. And therefore, with God's help, he will succeed.

May the same be true of us.

הַדְרָן HADRAN

Hadran is a formula recited at the completion of the study of a masekhet *of the Talmud. The word likely comes from the Hebrew root* H-D-R *meaning "glory" or "adornment" and may be an exclamation of praise: "We adorn you,* masekhet *of Talmud; may you adorn us!" Or it may come from the Aramaic root* H-D-R *signifying "return" and is thus a promise: "We shall return to study you again,* masekhet *of Talmud!"* •

We shall return to you, Talmud;
May you return to us!
Our thoughts are with you, Talmud;
May your thoughts be with us!
We shall not forget you, Talmud;
May you not forget us—
Not in this world, nor in the world that will be!

May it be Your will, Adonai our God, that just as You enabled me to complete this book, so may You help me to begin other books and to complete them, to study, teach, follow, heed and fulfill all the words of Your Torah in love.

May the merits of all of the Tannaim and the Amoraim and the Sages stand by me, so that the Torah never leave my lips.

And may these verses be fulfilled through me:

"When you walk it will lead you;
When you lie down it will watch over you;
And when you are awake it will talk with you."
(Proverbs 6:22)

"For through me your days will increase,
And years be added to your life."
(Proverbs 9:11)

"In her right hand is length of days,
In her left, riches and honor."
(Proverbs 3:16)

"May the Lord grant strength to His people;
may the Lord bestow on His people wellbeing."
(Psalms 29:11)

The End of One Journey . . .

Early next morning, Joshua and all the Israelites set out from Shittim and marched to the Jordan. . . . And so the people speedily crossed over, just as Moses had assured Joshua in his charge to him. And when all the people finished crossing, the Ark of the Lord and the priests advanced to the head of the people. (Joshua 3:1, 4:10–11)

. . . The Beginning of a New Journey

זִיל גְמוֹר Go and learn!

TEXTS FOR FURTHER STUDY

General Introductions to the Talmud

Abrams, Judith Z. *The Talmud for Beginners.* Volume 1: Prayer; Volume 2: Text. Northvale, NJ: Jason Aronson, 1991.

A popular introduction to the subjects of the Talmud for the modern uninitiated reader.

Goldenberg, Robert. "Talmud." Holtz, Barry W. "Midrash." In *Back to the Sources: Reading the Classic Jewish Texts,* edited by Barry W. Holtz. New York: Summit Books, 1984.

A concise, well-written, and intelligent introduction to the world and texts of the Rabbis for a modern reader.

Neusner, Jacob. *Invitation to the Talmud: A Teaching Book.* San Francisco: Harper and Row, 1973.

A detailed introduction to the ideas and text of the Talmud.

Steinsaltz, Adin. *The Essential Talmud,* trans. Chaya Galai. New York: Basic Books, 1976.

A book-length overview, with sections on the history, structure, content, and the method of the Talmud.

History of the Rabbinic Period

Cohen, Gerson D. "The Talmudic Age." In *Great Ages and Ideas of the Jewish People,* edited by Leo Schwarz. New York: Random House, 1956.

Goldin, Judah. "The Period of the Talmud." In *The Jews,* edited by Louis Finkelstein. New York: Schocken, 1970.

Two classic overviews of the world that produced the Talmud.

Neusner, Jacob. *There We Sat Down: Talmudic Judaism in the Making.* Nashville: Abingdon Press, 1972.

This book places the emphasis on the Rabbis in Babylonia, how and why they created the Talmud.

The Rabbis and Their Teachings

Bialik, H.N. and Ravnitzky, Y.H. ed. *The Book of Legends (Sefer ha-Aggadah): Legends from the Talmud and Midrash,* trans. William G. Braude. New York: Schocken, 1992.

Selections from the teachings of the Rabbis on virtually every topic.

Montefiore, C.G. and Loewe, H. *A Rabbinic Anthology.* New York: Schocken, 1974.

Selected texts from the Talmud and Midrash on thirty major subjects, with commentaries and explanations by the editors.

Urbach, Ephraim E. *The Sages: Their Concepts and Beliefs,* trans. Israel Abrahams, 2 vols., Magnes Pres, Hebrew University, 1979.

A study of the religious and social thought of the *Tannaim* and *Amoraim.*

Talmud Texts

Erhman, Rabbi Dr. A, ed. *El-Am Talmud.* Jerusalem-Tel Aviv: Hotza'a Leor Israel, 1965.

A translation and extensive explanations, along with many notes on personalities and topics mentioned in the text. Available only for *Berakhot* and selected other chapters.

Epstein, Rabbi Dr. I., ed. *The Babylonian Talmud,* 18 vols. London: Soncino Press, 1978.

The entire Babylonian Talmud in English with brief notes.

Steinsaltz, Adin. *The Talmud: The Steinsaltz Edition.* New York: Random House, 1989-92.

A new translation and commentary that explains the Talmud to a modern reader. Only selected tractates currently available.

Goldwurm, Rabbi Hersh, ed. *Talmud Bavli: The Gemara (The Schottenstein Edition).* Brooklyn: Mesorah Publications, 1990.

A translation and explanation of the text that brings a traditional understanding as would be taught in a yeshiva.

Basic Tools of Talmud Study

Carmell, Aryeh. *Aiding Talmud Study.* Jerusalem/New York: Feldheim, 1991.

Explication of key words and abbreviations in the Talmud, as well as historical charts and maps that elucidate the text.

Frank, Yitzḥak. *The Practical Talmud Dictionary.* Jerusalem: Ariel, 1991.

Talmudic words, expressions, and technical terms are defined in simple English with numerous examples cited.

Jastrow, Marcus. *A Dictionary of the Targumim, the Talmud Babli and Yerushalmi and the Midrashic Literature.* New York: Judaica Press, 1992.

The basic source for understanding the Aramaic and Hebrew found in the Talmud.

Steinsaltz, Adin. *The Talmud: The Steinsaltz Edition: A Reference Guide.* New York: Random House, 1989.

An indispensable one-volume encyclopedia and dictionary of the Talmud's history, language, and concepts.

GLOSSARY

Aggadah (lit. "telling"). Rabbinic stories and sermons of a nonlegal nature.

Aḥaronim (lit. "latter ones"). Rabbinic authorities in the centuries following the publication of the *Shulḥan Arukh* (mid-sixteenth century).

Alef bet. The first two letters of the Hebrew alphabet.

Aliyah. The honor of being called to recite the blessing before and after the reading of a section of the Torah (and, in some cases, the honor of reading the Torah itself).

Amah. Cubit; a unit of length, measured from the elbow to the tip of the middle finger, approximately eighteen inches.

Am ha-aretz (lit. "person of the land"). Originally, one who did not observe the laws of tithing and ritual purity. Later, it came to refer to an ignoramus.

Amidah (lit. "standing"). A central prayer of the Jewish liturgy, also known as *Shemoneh Esrei* ("eighteen" blessings), or "the *Tefillah.*"

Amoraim (lit. "explainers"). Rabbis from the period of the completion of the Mishnah (c. 200 C.E.) until the editing of the Gemara (sixth or seventh century C.E.).

Asur. Forbidden.

Azazel. The power or place to which one of the he-goats was sent off in the Yom Kippur ritual, as described in Leviticus 16.

Baraita (lit. "outside one"; pl.: *baraitot*). Tannatic teachings not included in the Mishnah of Rabbi Yehudah ha-Nasi; quoted and discussed in the Gemara.

Bar'khu (lit. "Bless!"). The call to prayer in the morning and evening services.

Bat kol (lit. "daughter of a voice"). A voice from heaven that indicates the will of God to humans.

Bavli. The Babylonian Talmud, edited during the sixth or seventh century, C.E..

B.C.E. Before the Common Era. Jews use this designation in place of B.C., which stands for "before Christ."

Bedeken. The custom of placing the veil on the bride just prior to the wedding ceremony.

Bet Hillel, Bet Shammai. Schools of Rabbis in the late first century B.C.E. and early first century C.E. following the teachings, respectively, of Hillel and Shammai.

Bikkur ḥolim. The mitzvah of visiting the sick.

Birkat ha-mazon. The blessings after food, recited at the conclusion of a meal.

B'rit milah (lit. "covenant of circumcision"). The surgical removal of the foreskin as a sign of the covenant between God and the Jewish people.

C.E. Common Era. Jews use this designation in place of A.D. which stands for Anno Domini, "the year of our Lord."

Dinar. A coin.

D'rash (more properly: D'rashah). A sermon usually based on a creative reading of a text.

Edim zommemim. Witnesses who conspire to testify falsely against another person.

Erusin. The betrothal part of a Jewish marriage.

Essenes. One of the Jewish sects in the centuries leading up to the destruction of the Temple in 70 C.E., noted for their communal, pietistic lifestyle.

Etrog. A citron (similar in appearance to a lemon) used with a lulav during various parts of the service on the festival of Sukkot.

Gaon (lit. "excellent one"; pl.: *Geonim*). Head of the Babylonian academy, from the seventh through the eleventh centuries.

Gehinnom. A designation for the place where the wicked are punished after death.

Gemara. Commentaries, explanations and discussions of the Rabbis on the Mishnah, from the third to the sixth or seventh centuries C.E. Originally called "Talmud," the name was changed to "Gemara" in the Middle Ages to fool Christian censors.

Ger (lit. "stranger"). A convert to Judaism.

Get. The document which executes a Jewish divorce.

Hadran. A formula of praise found at the end of a tractate of Talmud.

Haftarah. A selection from the Prophets read in the synagogue following the Torah portion on Shabbat and holidays.

Haggadah (lit. "telling"). The book used as a guide through the Passover Seder.

Ḥakham (lit. "wise one"; pl.: *ḥakhamim*). The sage who taught and explained the laws and traditions of the Torah; a rabbi.

Halakhah. Jewish law.

Ḥalitzah (lit. "loosening"). The ceremony whereby a childless widow is released from the obligation of marrying her dead husband's brother. See Deuteronomy 25:5-10.

Hallel. The psalms of praise recited in the morning service on Jewish festivals, Psalms 114-118.

Hanukkah. The eight-day winter festival that commemorates the victory of the Maccabees over the Syrian-Greeks and the rededication of the Temple in the mid-second century B.C.E..

Ḥaver. A friend or study partner.

Ḥavruta. A group of people who study together.

Ḥerem. A ban of excommunication.

Hidur mitzvah. "Beautifying the commandments." The notion of serving God in an aesthetically pleasing manner.

Ḥuppah. The canopy under which a couple is married.

Ḥusan's tish (Yiddish for "groom's table"). The custom of the friends of the groom meeting just prior to the wedding ceremony to study, sing, and celebrate.

Kaddish. (1) The prayer recited at the conclusion of sections of the service; (2) the prayer recited by a mourner during the year following the death of an immediate relative.

Kaporet. The cover of pure gold which rested on top of the Ark in the Tabernacle and Temple.

Karet. The divine punishment of being "cut off," i.e., dying a premature death.

Kavvanah (pl.: *kavvanot*). Meditation prior to a prayer or mitzvah that serves to focus one's attention on its meaning and significance.

Kedushah (lit. "sanctification"). The third section of the *Amidah,* which imitates the angels in heaven praising and sanctifying God.

Ketubbah. The Jewish marriage document.

Kiddush. The prayer recited over wine to sanctify Shabbat or a festival.

Kiddushin. The betrothal component of the marriage ceremony.

Kilayim. The mixtures of diverse species prohibited by the Torah. See Leviticus 19:19 and Deuteronomy 22:9.

Knesset ha-Gedolah (lit. "the Great Assembly"). The body of leaders and sages of the Jewish people in Israel which supposedly led the Jews from the period of Ezra and Nehemiah until the end of the third century B.C.E..

Kodashim (lit. "Holy Things"). The fifth order of the Mishnah, dealing with sacrifices.

Kohen (pl.: *kohanim*). A descendent of Aaron; one who served as a functionary in the Temple offering sacrifices, often referred to as "priest."

Kohen Gadol. The chief *kohen* (often referred to as the "High Priest") and major officiant in the Temple.

Kol Nidrei (lit. "all vows"). A legal formula prayer recited on Yom Kippur eve that annuls all vows that were made but not kept.

Kosher (lit. "fit"). (1) According to the Jewish dietary laws, food which may be eaten. (2) Ritually fit for use.

Leshon ha-ra (lit. "evil language"). Gossip.

Leshon sagi nahor (lit. "language of great light"). Euphemistic language.

Levi. A descendent of the tribe of Levi, who served as a functionary in the Temple; known in English as "Levite."

Levirate marriage. The biblical obligation of a man to marry the childless widow of his dead brother in order to carry on the name and line of the deceased. See Deuteronomy 25:5-6.

Lulav. A palm branch, with myrtle and willow branches attached, used with an *etrog* during various parts of the service during the festival of Sukkot.

Ma'aser. A tithe of produce, wine, and oil, given to the Levite.

Mamzer. The offspring of an incestuous or adulterous relationship.

Maneh. A coin.

Mara d'atra (lit. "master of the place"). Any local rabbi vested with the authority to make halakhic decisions for the community.

Mar'it ayin (lit. "what the eye sees"). The concept that certain permitted actions should not be done because of how they may be perceived by others.

Masekhet ("tractate"). One of the sixty-three sections of the Mishnah; also refers to any particular book of the Talmud.

Megillah (lit. "scroll"). (1) The book of Esther, especially in scroll form, read on Purim. (2) A tractate of Talmud dealing with the reading of the book of Esther.

Menorah. (1) The seven-branched candelabrum used in the Temple. (2) The eight- (or nine-) branched candelabrum used in celebration of Hanukkah.

Mezuzzah (lit "doorpost"). A case holding parchment with specific portions of the Torah written on it, affixed to the doorposts of Jewish homes.

Midrash. Homiletical or legal interpretations of the Bible.

Mikveh. Either a natural body of water or an artificial pool, used for the ritual of purification.

Min (pl.: *Minim*). A sectarian; a heretic.

Minḥah. (1) A meal-offering brought to the Temple as part of the sacrificial service. (2) The afternoon prayer service.

Minyan. The quorum of ten men (in some communities, ten people) necessary to recite certain prayers.

Mishkan. The portable sanctuary used by the Israelites during the forty years of wandering in the desert; often called the "Tabernacle."

Mishnah. (1) The collection of laws attributed by tradition to the editorship of Rabbi Yehudah ha-Nasi, c. 200 C.E.. (2) Any particular law in this collection.

Mishneh Torah. One of the standard codes of Jewish law, written by the Rambam (Rabbi Moshe ben Maimon, Maimonides) in the twelfth century.

Mitzvah (pl.: Mitzvot). Commandment, usually referring to the 613 laws that the Rabbis derived from the Torah.

Moed (lit. "holiday"). The second order of the Mishnah, dealing with the festivals of the Jewish year.

Mohel. The circumcisor, the person who performs a *b'rit milah,* or *Bris.*

Muad (lit. "warned"). An animal that has previously caused injury or damage.

Nashim (lit. "women"). The third order of the Mishnah, dealing with laws of marriage and divorce.

Navi. A prophet, especially those men and women who, during the period of the Israelite monarchy, brought the word of God to the Israelites.

Netin. A descendent of the Gibeonites. See Joshua 9.

Nezikin (lit. "damages"). The fourth order of the Mishnah, dealing with civil and criminal law.

Nisan. The month of the Jewish year in which Pesaḥ falls.

Oral Law. See *Torah she-b'al peh.*

Pasul. Invalid for use.

Perushim (lit. "those who set themselves apart"). Ascetics who took on self-imposed restrictions in response to the destruction of the Temple.

Pesaḥ. Passover, the spring festival commemorating the exodus of the Israelites from Egypt.

Pharisees. One of the Jewish sects in the centuries prior to the destruction of the Temple in 70 C.E..

Pilpul. Hair-splitting logic.

Pitgam. An epigram or maxim.

P'shat. The simple, contextual meaning of a Biblical text.

Purim. The "Feast of Lots," a religious holiday commemorating the triumph of the Jewish people over their enemies in ancient Persia, as recounted in the Book of Esther.

Rabbenu Tam. A grandson of Rashi and one of the most prominent authors of Tosafot.

Rabbi (lit. "master"). (1) A teacher of Torah. In the Talmud, it signifies a teacher in the land of Israel. (2) The name Yehudah ha-Nasi was known by.

Rashi. Rabbi Shlomo Itzḥaki (1040-1105), the foremost commentator to the Bible and Talmud.

Rav. (1) The title of the rabbis in Babylonia. (2) The name of one specific Babylonian rabbi.

Rebbe. A charismatic hasidic leader.

Rishonim (lit. "the early ones"). Rabbinical authorities in the period following the Geonim and until the publication of the *Shulḥan Arukh* in the mid-sixteenth century.

Rosh Hashanah (lit. "beginning of the year"). (1) The Jewish New Year festival, observed for two days in the fall. (2) A tracate of Talmud dealing with the New Year.

Rosh Ḥodesh. The beginning of the new Hebrew month, observed as a semi-holiday.

Sabbatical year. The seventh year, during which the land is allowed to lie fallow in accordance with biblical injunction. See Leviticus 25.

Sadducees. One of the Jewish sects in the centuries prior to the destruction of the Temple in 70 C.E..

Sanhedrin. (1) The central judicial and legislative institution in Israel during the centuries prior to and just after the destruction of the Temple in 70 C.E.. (2) A tractate of the Talmud.

Satan (lit. "adversary"). The force which seeks to undermine the good; see Job. In rabbinic thought, Satan is subservient to God and does God's will.

Savoraim (lit. "reasoners"). The teachers at the end of the talmudic era who added to the editing of the Talmud which had already started.

Seah. A measure of volume.

Seder (lit. "order"). (1) The service conducted in the home on the first night(s) of Pesaḥ. (2) One of the six major sections ("orders") of the Mishnah.

Sela. A coin.

Sha'atnez. A forbidden mixture of wool and linen. See Leviticus 19:19 and Deuteronomy 22:11.

Shaḥarit. The morning prayer service.

Shavuot. The Feast of Weeks, the holiday that commemorates the giving of the Torah at Sinai.

She-he-ḥeyanu. A *berakhah* recited on holidays and other special occasions, praising God for "granting us life, for sustaining us, and for helping us to reach this day."

Shekel. A coin.

Shemini Atzeret (lit. "the eighth day of assembly"). The one-day festival following Sukkot.

Shemoneh Esrei (lit. "the eighteen"). Another name for the *Amidah,* so-called because it originally contained eighteen sections and blessings. (Now it contains nineteen blessings.)

Sh'muah R'ḥokah. "Delayed news," when the report of the death of a relative is received thirty days or more after the fact.

Shevah Berakhot. The seven blessings recited in celebration of a Jewish wedding.

Shivah (lit. "seven"). The seven-day period of mourning following the death of a close relative.

Sh'ma. A central element of the liturgy, comprised of three biblical sections: Deuteronomy 6:4-9; Deuteronomy 11:13-21; and Numbers 15:37-41.

Shofar. A ram's horn used especially on Rosh Hashanah and Yom Kippur.

Shofet. A judge, used specifically to refer to the Israelite leaders after Moses and before the kings.

Shulḥan Arukh. One of the standard codes of Jewish law, written by Rabbi Joseph Caro in the mid-sixteenth century.

Simḥah. A happy, festive occasion.

Sofer (lit. "scribe"; pl.: *Sofrim*). (1) A craftsman who copied sacred scrolls. (2) A teacher who taught and explained Israelite laws and traditions.

Sotah. A woman suspected of having committed adultery and subjected to a trial by ordeal. See Numbers 5:11-31.

Sugya (pl.: *sugyot*). Any self-contained unit in the Gemara.

Sukkah (pl.: *sukkot*). (1) A temporary hut, similar to those used by the Israelites during the 40 years in the wilderness, built and used by Jews during the Festival of Sukkot. (2) The tractate of Talmud dealing with the festival of Sukkot.

Sukkot. The holiday, often called the Feast of Booths or Tabernacles, celebrated in the fall, which commemorates the Israelites' forty years of wandering in the wilderness by living in a *sukkah.*

Tallit. A prayer shawl with *tzitzit* attached to the four corners, worn during the morning service.

Talmid ḥakham (lit. "a student of the wise"). A student-scholar.

Talmud (lit. "argumentation"). The Jewish legal and nonlegal work by the Rabbis of the first century B.C.E. through the seventh century C.E., composed of the Mishnah and the Gemara. The term originally referred to the teaching that we now called "the Gemara."

Tam (lit. "simple," "innocent"). An animal for which no damages are assessed when causing injury.

Tameh. Ritually impure.

Tannaim (lit. "repeaters," sing.: *tanna*). The Rabbis during the period of the Mishnah.

Tanna Kamma (lit. "The first *tanna*"). The first unnamed teacher or source in a Tannaitic Sugya.

Tefaḥ. A unit of length, measured across a closed fist, approx. 3 inches.

Tefillah (lit. "prayer"). (1) Term used to refer to the prayer par excellence, the *Amidah* or *Shemoneh Esrei.* (2) One of the set of tefillin.

Tefillin. Two boxes containing parchment-written selections of the Torah which are tied to the arm and forehead by leather straps and are worn during the morning weekday service.

Tent of Meeting. See ***Mishkan.***

Terumah. A specific portion of the produce and sacrifices that were given to the *kohanim* during the Temple period.

Teshuvah (lit. "return"). Repentance.

Tisha b'Av. The ninth day of the Hebrew month of Av, the date on which Jews traditionally believe that both the first and second Temples were destroyed.

Tishrei. The month of the Jewish year in which Rosh Hashanah and Yom Kippur fall.

Teharot (lit. "clean things"). The sixth order of the Mishnah, dealing with ritual purity.

Torah (lit. "instruction"). (1) The Five Books of Moses. (2) A scroll of the Five Books. (3) The sum of Jewish knowledge and wisdom.

Torah she-b'al peh (lit. "the Oral Law"). (1) The traditions given by God to Moses as a supplement to the Written Law and which were not committed to writing until some time in the rabbinic period. (2) The compilations of laws and traditions which were originally oral and then became written in the Talmud, as opposed to the "Written Law" of the Bible.

Torah she-bikhtav (lit. "the Written Law"). (1) The law given by God to Moses on Sinai and committed to writing. (2) The laws of the Torah or Bible, as opposed to the "Oral Law" which was not originally committed to writing.

Tosafot. Commentaries on the Talmud by the disciples of Rashi in the twelfth through the fourteenth centuries.

Tosefta. A collection of Tannaitic teachings not included in the Mishnah but arranged according to the same order.

Tractate. See ***Masekhet.***

Treif (lit. "torn"). Nonkosher food.

Tzara'at. A skin disease described in Leviticus 13-15, attributed by the Rabbis as a punishment for gossip.

Tzedakah (lit. "righteousness"). The mitzvah of giving material assistance to those in need.

Tzitzit. The fringes or strings, knotted and tied in a prescribed manner to a tallit or other garment, serving to remind the wearer of God's commandments.

Written Law. See ***Torah she-bikhtav.***

Yerushalmi. The "Jerusalem" Talmud or, more precisely, the Talmud of the land of Israel, edited around the beginning of the fifth century C.E.

Yetzer ha-ra (lit. "the evil inclination"). The selfish side of human motivation.

Yibum. See **Levirate marriage.**

Yiḥus. Lineage; family background.

Yissurin shel ahavah (lit. "afflictions of love"). The afflictions which, according to the Talmud, a good person might suffer not as a punishment for sins but as a token of God's love.

Yom Kippur. The Day of Atonement, a fast day dedicated to seeking forgiveness from sins, observed on the tenth of Tishrei, in the fall.

Zealots. One of the Jewish sects in the centuries leading up to the destruction of the Temple in the year 70 C.E..

Zeraim (lit. "seeds"). The first order of the Mishnah, dealing with agricultural laws.

Zimmun (lit. "invitation"). The introductory formula recited in the presence of a quorum prior to *birkat ha-mazon.*

Zugot (lit. "pairs"). Two teachers in each generation who, according to later tradition, were the main leaders of the Jews in Israel in the third, second, and first centuries B.C.E..

Zuz. A coin.

A Timeline of Jewish History

with special reference to personalities mentioned in this book

	THE BIBLICAL AGE
ca. 19th–16th cent. B.C.E.	*Period of the Patriarchs*
	Abraham, Isaac, Jacob, Joseph
ca. 13th cent. B.C.E.	*Period of the Exodus and the Giving of the Torah*
	Moses, Aaron, Nadav and Avihu; Mishael and Eltzaphan, Eldad and Medad; Building of the Mishkan (Tabernacle), Joshua and Achan
ca. 12th–11th cent. B.C.E.	*Period of the Judges*
	Deborah, Barak, Jael, Sisera, Jepthah, Jerubbaal (Gideon), Bedan (Samson), Samuel
ca. 11th–6th cent. B.C.E.	*Period of the Monarchy*
ca. 1000–960 B.C.E.	David
ca. 960–930 B.C.E.	Solomon; building of the first Temple
ca. 922 B.C.E.	Rehoboam; nation split into two kingdoms; Naaman.
8th–6th cent. B.C.E.	*Period of the Prophets*
722 B.C.E.	Destruction of the Northern Kingdom (the "Ten Lost Tribes") by the Assyrians
587/6 B.C.E.	Destruction of the Southern Kingdom and the Temple by Babylonia
538, 520–515 B.C.E.	Return to Zion; building of the Second Temple
5th cent. B.C.E.	Ezra the Scribe institutes weekly reading of the Torah
163 B.C.E.	Maccabees liberate and rededicate the Temple
	THE TALMUDIC AGE
1st cent. B.C.E.	*Period of the "Zugot" (the "pairs")* Hillel and Shammai

1st–3rd cent. C.E.	*Period of the Tannaim*	
1st generation (40–80 C.E.)	Bet Hillel and Bet Shammai; Rabbi Yoḥanan ben Zakkai	
70 C.E.	Destruction of the Second Temple by the Romans	
2nd generation (80–110 C.E.)	Rabban Gamliel of Yavneh, Rabbi Eliezer ben Hyrkanos, Rabbi Yehoshua ben Ḥananiah	
3rd generation (110–135 C.E.)	Rabbi Akiva, Rabbi Yishmael, Rabbi Tarfon, Ben Zoma, Ben Azzai	
4th generation (135–170 C.E.)	Rabbi Meir, Rabban Shimon ben Gamliel, Rabbi Yehudah (bar Ilai), Rabbi Shimon (bar Yoḥai)	
5th generation (170–200 C.E.)	Rabbi Yehudah ha-Nasi (d. 226 C.E.), editing of the Mishnah	
3rd–6th cent. C.E.	*Period of the Amoraim*	
	Israel	*Babylonia*
1st generation 220–250 C.E.	Rabbi Yehoshua ben Levi	Rav, Shmuel
2nd generation 250–290 C.E.	Rabbi Yoḥanan, Resh Lakish, Rabbi Elazar ben Pedat, Rabbi Yitzḥak	Rav Huna, Rav Yehudah (bar Yeḥezkel), Rav Ḥisda, Rav Sheshet, Rav Naḥman
3rd generation 290–320 C.E.	Rabbi Ammi, Rabbi Assi	Rabbah bar bar Ḥana, Rabbah (bar Naḥmani), Rav Yosef
4th generation 320–350 C.E.		Abaye, Rava, Rav Dimi
5th generation 350–375 C.E.		Rav Papa
6th generation 375–425 C.E.	Yerushalmi (Talmud of the Land of Israel) is completed	Rav Ashi, Ravina
7th generation 425–460 C.E.		Mar, son of Rav Ashi
8th generation 460–500 C.E.		
6th or 7th century		Bavli (Babylonian Talmud) is completed

Generational Chart of Rabbis Cited in This Book

KEY TO GENERATIONS

T = *Tanna* (Rabbi prior to editing of the Mishnah)
A = *Amora* (Rabbi after editing of the Mishnah)
Approximate Dates of Generations

Tannaim		*Amoraim*	
T 1	40–80 C.E.	A 1	220–250 C.E.
T 2	80–110	A 2	250–290
T 3	110–135	A 3	290–320
T 4	135–170	A 4	320–350
T 5	170–200	A 5	350–375
T 6	200–220	A 6	375–425
		A7	425–460
		A 8	460–500

Dates in the chart follow *Encyclopedia of Talmudic and Geonic Literature* (Hebrew), edited by Mordechai Margalioth (Tel Aviv: Yavneh Publishing House, Ltd., 1973).

NAME	WHERE	DATES (C.E.) (GENERATION)	TEACHER	OTHER INFORMATION
Abaye	Bavel (Babylonia)	280–338 (A 3,4)	Rabbah Rav Yosef	Head of study house in Pumbedita
Abba	Born in Bavel, Came to Israel	Late 3rd– early 4th cent. (A 3)		
Abba bar Zavda	Born in Israel, went to Bavel	Mid 3rd, early 4th cent. (A 2–3)	Rav, Rav Huna	Considered the most important sage in Israel in his time
Abba son of Rabbi Ḥiyya bar Abba	Israel	Late 3rd– early 4th cent. (A 3)	Rabbi Ḥiyya bar Abba, his father	

NAME	WHERE	DATES (C.E.) (GENERATION)	TEACHER	OTHER INFORMATION
Abba Yosé bar Dostai	Israel	Mid 2nd cent. (T 4)		
Ada bar Ahava	Bavel	Mid 3rd cent. (A 1–2)	Rav	
Aḥa (Ḥana) bar Bizna	Bavel	Mid 3rd, early 4th cent. (A 2–3)	Rabbi Shimon Ḥasida	
Aḥa son of Rabbi Ḥanina	Israel	Late 3rd, early 4th cent (A 3)	Rabbi Assi	
Akiva	Israel	D. 135 (T 3)	Rabbi Eliezer, Rabbi Yehoshua	
Ammi	Israel	Late 3rd early 4th cent. (A 3)	Rabbi Yoḥanan	Head of study house at Tiberias
Ashi	Bavel	D. 427 (A 6)	Rav Kahana	Head of study house at Sura for 52 years; editor of the Bavli
Assi	Born in Bavel; came to Israel	Late 3rd, early 4th cent. (A 3)	Shmuel, Rabbi Yoḥanan	
Avya	Bavel	Early–mid 4th cent. (A 3–4)		
Ben Azzai (Shimon ben Azzai)	Israel	Early 2nd cent. (T 3)	Rabbi Yehoshua	
Ben Zoma (Shimon ben Zoma)	Israel	Early 2nd cent. (T 3)		
Bivi bar Abaye	Bavel	Mid 4th–5th cent. (A 5)	Abaye (his father), Rav Yosef	Head of study house at Pumbedita after his father, Abaye
Daniel bar Katina	Bavel	Late 3rd, early 4th cent. (A 3)		

NAME	WHERE	DATES (C.E.) (GENERATION)	TEACHER	OTHER INFORMATION
Dimi	Bavel	Early–mid 4th cent. (A 3–4)	Rav Naḥman	One of the Neḥutei: Brought the traditions of Israel to Bavel
Elazar (ben Pedat)	Born in Bavel, came to Israel	D. 279 3rd cent. (A 2)	Rav, Shmuel	
Elazar ben Rabbi Shimon	Israel	End of 2nd cent. (T 5)	Rabbi Shimon bar Yoḥai (his father)	
Eliezer (ben Hyrkanos)	Israel	Late 1st–Early 2nd cent. (T 2)	Rabbi Yoḥanan ben Zakkai	"A plastered cistern that does not lose a drop"
Elisha ben Avuyah	Israel	Early 2nd Cent. (T 3)		"Aḥer"; became an Apostate
Gamliel (II, of Yavneh)	Israel	Late 1st–early 2nd cent. (T 2)		Nasi of the Sanhedrin after Rabbi Yoḥanan ben Zakkai
Ḥama bar Gurya	Bavel	Mid–late 2nd cent. (A 2)	Rav	
Ḥanina bar Ḥama	Born Bavel, came to Israel	180–260 (A 1)	Rabbi Yehudah ha-Nasi	Head of study house at Sepphoris
Ḥanina bar Papa	Israel	Early 4th cent. (A 3)	Rabbi Shmuel bar Naḥman	
Ḥelbo	Born in Babel, came to Israel	Late 3rd–early 4th cent (A 3)	Rav Huna	
Hillel	Born Bavel, Israel	5th generation Zugot	Shemaya, Avtalyon	According to later rabbinic tradition, the Nasi was descended from him
Ḥinena son of Rav Ikka	Bavel	Mid 4th cent. (A 5)		
Ḥisda	Bavel	217–309 (A 2–3)	Rav	Head of study house at Sura

NAME	WHERE	DATES (C.E.) (GENERATION)	TEACHER	OTHER INFORMATION
Ḥiyya (bar Abba)	Born in Bavel, came to Israel	Early to mid 3rd cent. (T 6, A 1)	Rabbi Yehudah ha-Nasi	
Ḥiyya bar Rav	Bavel	Mid-late 3rd cent. (A 2)	Rav Yehudah	
Huna	Bavel	212–297 (A 2)	Rav, Shmuel	Head of Sura study house for 40 years
Huna bar Yehudah	Bavel	Early 4th cent. (A 4)		
Kahana	Bavel			Four different Amoraim known by this name
Mani	Israel	Early–mid 3rd cent. (A 1)		
Mar bar Rav Huna (or Ravina)	Bavel	Early–mid 4th cent. (A 4)		
Matnah	Bavel	Mid–late 3rd cent. (A 2)	Rav, Shmuel	
Meir	Israel	Mid– 2nd cent. (T 4)	R. Akiva, Elisha ben Avuya	
Naḥman (bar Yaakov)	Bavel	d. 320 (A 2–3)	Shmuel	
Naḥman bar Yitzḥak	Bavel	d. 356 (A 4)	Rav Naḥman, Rav Ḥisda	Head of study house at Pumbedita
Oshaya Rabbah	Israel	Early 3rd cent. (T 6, A 1)	Rabbi Ḥiyya	Founded study house at Caesarea
Papa (bar Ḥanan)	Bavel	300–375 (A 5)	Abaye, Rava	Founded study house at Naresh

NAME	WHERE	DATES (C.E.) (GENERATION)	TEACHER	OTHER INFORMATION
Rabbah (bar Naḥmani)	Bavel	270–330 (A 3)	Rav Huna, Rav Yehudah	Head of study house at Pumbedita; called *oker harim,* "uprooter of mountains," because of incisive mind
Rabbah bar bar Ḥana	Born in Bavel, came to Israel	Late 3rd–early 4th cent. (A 3)	Rabbi Yoḥanan	
Rabbah bar Mari	Israel	Early–mid 4th cent. (A 3–4)		
Rabbah bar Rav Huna	Bavel	d. 322 (A 2–3)	Rav, Rav Huna (his father)	Head of study house at Sura after Rav Ḥisda
Rabbah bar Rav Shela	Bavel	Early–mid 4th cent. (A 3–4)	Rav Ḥisda	
Rami bar Ḥama	Bavel	Mid 4th cent. (A 4)	Rav Ḥisda, Rav Sheshet	
Rav (Rav Abba bar Aybo, or "Abba Arikha")	Bavel	175–247 (A 1)	Rabbi Yehudah ha-Nasi	Founded study house at Sura
Rava (Rav Abba bar Yosef)	Bavel	299–352 (A 4)	Rav Naḥman, Rav Ḥisda	Founded study house at Maḥuza
Rava bar Meḥasya	Bavel	Mid–late 3rd cent. (A 2–3)		
Rava bar Rav Ḥanan	Bavel	Early–mid 4th cent. (A 4)	Rabbah, Abaye	
Ravina	Bavel	Late 4th–early 5th cent. (A 6)	Rava	Involved in the final editing of the Talmud
Resh Lakish (Shimon ben Lakish)	Israel	Mid–late 3rd cent. (A 2)	Rabbi Yoḥanan	

NAME	WHERE	DATES (C.E.) (GENERATION)	TEACHER	OTHER INFORMATION
Safra	Born in Bavel, went to Israel and back	Early–mid 4th cent. (A 3–4)		
Sheshet	Bavel	Mid 3rd–early 4th cent. (A 2–3)		Founded study house at Shilhi
Shimon (bar Yoḥai)	Israel	Mid 2nd cent. (T 4)	Rabbi Akiva	
Shimon ben Gamliel	Israel	Mid 2nd cent. (T 4)		Son of Gamliel of Yavneh, father of Yehudah ha-Nasi
Shimon ben Elazar	Israel	Late 2nd cent. (T 5)	Rabbi Meir	
Shimon ben Pazi	Israel	Mid 3rd–early 4th cent. (A 2–3)	Rabbi Yehoshua ben Levi	
Shimon ha-Pakuli	Israel	Late 1st–early 2nd cent. (T 2)		
Shimon Ḥasida	Israel	Mid 3rd cent. (A 1–2)		
Shimon ha-Tzaddik	Israel	3rd cent. B.C.E.		Served as Kohen Gadol
Shmuel	Bavel	180–257 (A 1)	Abba bar Abba (the father of Shmuel)	Head of study house at Nehardea
Shmuel bar Naḥmani	Israel	Mid 3rd–early 4th cent. (A 2–3)	Rabbi Yonatan (ben Elazar)	
Shmuel bar Rav Yitzḥak	Born in Bavel, came to Israel	Late 3rd–early 4th cent. (A 3)		
Tarfon	Israel	Late 1st–early 2nd cent. (T 2)	Rabban Gamliel the Elder	

NAME	WHERE	DATES (C.E.) (GENERATION)	TEACHER	OTHER INFORMATION
Ulla	Born in Israel, to Bavel and back	Mid 3rd–early 4th cent. (A 2–3)		One of the Neḥutei: Brought traditions of Israel to Bavel
Yaakov (ben Korshai)	Israel	Mid 2nd cent. (T 4)	Rabbi Meir	
Yannai	Israel	Early–mid 3rd cent. (A 1)	Rabbi Yehudah ha-Nasi, Rabbi Ḥiyya	
Yehoshua (ben Ḥananiah)	Israel	Late 1st–early 2nd cent. (T 2)	Rabbi Yoḥanan ben Zakkai	
Yehoshua ben Gamla	Israel	c. 70		
Yehoshua ben Levi	Israel	Early–mid 3rd cent. (A 1)	Bar Kapara	
Yehoshua ben Peraḥia	Israel	2nd cent. B.C.E. (Zugot)		
Yehudah (bar Ilai)	Israel	Mid 2nd cent (T 4)	Rabbi Akiva, Rabbi Eliezer	
Yehudah of K'far Giboriya (?K'far Gibor Ḥayil)	Israel	(??)		
Yehudah (bar Yeḥezkel)	Bavel	Mid–late 3rd cent. (A 2)	Rav, Shmuel	Founded the study house at Pumbedita
Yehudah ha-Nasi (called "Rabbi")	Israel	Late 2nd cent. (T 5)	Rabbi Meir	Nasi of the Sanhedrin, editor of the Mishnah
Yehudah Nesiah	Israel	Mid 3rd. cent (A 1–2)	Rabban Gamliel, his father	Grandson of Rabbi Yehudah ha-Nasi
Yishmael (ben Elisha)	Israel	Early 2nd cent. (T 3)	Rabbi Yehoshua, Rabbi Eliezer	

NAME	WHERE	DATES (C.E.) (GENERATION)	TEACHER	OTHER INFORMATION
Yitzḥak (Nappaḥa)	Israel	Mid 3rd–early 4th cent. (A 2–3)		
Yitzḥak bar Shela	Bavel	Late 3rd–early 4th cent. (A 3)		
Yitzḥak son of Rav Yehudah	Bavel	Late 3rd–early 4th cent. (A 3)	Rabbi Yehudah ben Yeḥezkel, his father	
Yoḥanan (bar Nappaḥa)	Israel	199–279 (A 2)	Rabbi Yehudah ha-Nasi	Founded study house at Tiberias
Yoḥanan ben Zakkai	Israel	Mid–late 1st cent. (T 1)	Hillel	Founded study house at Yavneh
Yosé (bar Ḥalafta)	Israel	Mid 2nd cent. (T 4)	Rabbi Akiva	
Yosé bar Avin	Israel	Mid 4th cent. (A 5)	Rav Ashi	
Yosé bar Zavida	Israel	Mid 4th cent. (A 5)		One of the last of the rabbinical authorities in Israel
Yosé ha-G'lili	Israel	Early 2nd cent. (T 3)		
Yosef (bar Ḥiyya)	Bavel	d. 333 (A 3)	Rav Yehudah	Head of study house at Pumbedita; called "Sinai" because of his mastery of tradition
Zeira	Born in Bavel, came to Israel	Late 3rd–early 4th cent. (A 3)	Rav Huna, Rav Yehudah	
Zevid	Bavel	Late 4th–early 5th cent. (A 4–5)	Abaye, Rava	Head of study house at Pumbedita, 377–385

INDEX

Alphabetical List of Rabbis

Index of Biblical References

by books of the Bible
Note: Page numbers are set in *Italics.*

Deuteronomy

Joshua

Judges

Samuel

Kings

Isaiah

Jeremiah

Ezekiel

The Twelve "Minor Prophets"

Psalms

Proverbs

Job

Song of Songs

Lamentations

Esther

Chronicles

General Index

**denotes Rabbi cited in the Talmud*